# Toni Morrison

## AND THE BIBLE

# AFRICAN AMERICAN
# LITERATURE
# AND CULTURE

Expanding and Exploding the Boundaries

Carlyle V. Thompson
*General Editor*

Vol. 12

PETER LANG
New York • Washington, D.C./Baltimore • Bern
Frankfurt am Main • Berlin • Brussels • Vienna • Oxford

# Toni Morrison

## AND THE BIBLE

## Contested Intertextualities

### EDITED BY
### Shirley A. Stave

PETER LANG
New York • Washington, D.C./Baltimore • Bern
Frankfurt am Main • Berlin • Brussels • Vienna • Oxford

Library of Congress Cataloging-in-Publication Data

Toni Morrison and the Bible: contested intertextualities / edited by Shirley A. Stave.
p. cm. — (African-American literature and culture; v. 12)
Includes bibliographical references.
1. Morrison, Toni—Criticism and interpretation. 2. Bible—In literature.
3. Women and literature—United States—History—20th century.
4. African Americans in literature. 5. Spirituality in literature.
I. Stave, Shirley A. II. Title. III. Series.
PS3563.O8749Z8957   813'.54—dc22   2006001206
ISBN 0-8204-6935-1
ISSN 1528-3887


Bibliographic information published by **Die Deutsche Bibliothek**.
**Die Deutsche Bibliothek** lists this publication in the "Deutsche
Nationalbibliografie"; detailed bibliographic data is available
on the Internet at http://dnb.ddb.de/.

Cover design by Lisa Barfield


The paper in this book meets the guidelines for permanence and durability
of the Committee on Production Guidelines for Book Longevity
of the Council of Library Resources.

# CONTENTS

# ACKNOWLEDGMENTS

I am indebted to many people who have been instrumental in my bringing this project to completion. First of all, my thanks to Henry A. Blackwell, who handed the project over to me in its early stages. It is rare that an opportunity to work on a topic as invigorating as this simply falls into one's lap, but that is exactly what happened. I am honored that he believed in my abilities to complete the text, and I hope this work lives up to the expectations he had for it. Second, Phyllis Korper and Bernadette Shade at Peter Lang Publishing have been truly wonderful to work with. They have been beyond patient with me and have always responded to my e-mails promptly and cordially. Third, I could not have completed the project without the help of Monica Gremillon, my technologically savvy student who could translate what I could only perceive as gibberish and thereby create the final copy of the text. It has been a joy working with her; her calm reassurance was so vital in channeling my confused panic into coherent text. Finally, my thanks to my terrific contributors. In the time that we have worked together, we have shared news of graduations, marriages, births, and deaths, we have traveled and moved and survived extraordinary natural disasters and very mundane, if decidedly unpleasant, university politics. I have enjoyed so very much working with them and learned so very much from their piercing analyses and perceptive readings.

I gratefully acknowledge International Creative Managment, Inc., for permission to cite from *Song of Solomon*, *Sula*, *Paradise*, *Beloved*, and *The Bluest Eye*. And most of all, thank you to Toni Morrison for enriching all of lives so very much with her dazzling fiction.

# INTRODUCTION

*Shirley A. Stave*

Densely interwoven and richly textured with literary and cultural allusion, Toni Morrison's novels reveal a dazzling vision and critique of contemporary society, underwritten by narrative authority, wit, and eloquence. Referencing texts as divergent as the film *Imitation of Life* and the heroic epic *The Odyssey*, alluding to personages as various as Roman emperors and postmodern cultural theorists, Morrison's work requires, if one approaches it as seriously as it deserves, knowledge of the multiplicity of literary and cultural confluences that constitute American identity. Among the encyclopedia of source material Morrison engages, one text appears consistently throughout her works: the Bible. We should not assume Morrison uses this source innocently or straightforwardly, however; her strategies are as various as her range of source material overall. The essays in this book interrogate and dissect Morrison's use of the Bible, question her theological positioning, and even contest her ultimate stance. In sometimes mutually contradictory essays, the writers here articulate their understanding of Morrison's use of, argument with, celebration of, antagonism toward, play with, and complication of that Ur-text.

Several of the essayists remain very close to the Bible in their analyses of Morrison's work. Beverley Foulks, in "Trial by Fire: The Theodicy of Toni Morrison in *Sula*," addresses *Sula*'s engagement with the theological concept of evil, using two well-known biblical references as representative of two possible responses to the presence of evil in the human community. Exploring what she refers to as the "trials by fire" encountered by characters such as Shadrack, Plum, Sula, and Nel, Foulks contrasts the response of Shadrach, Meshach, and Abednego to King Nebuchadnezzar's demands with that of John the Baptist to the Messiah's arrival; the former, she suggests, parallels Black theodicy, while the latter reveals a white understanding of oppression and injustice. The community of the Bottom, Foulks argues, does not use theology to justify oppression, as one might argue John the Baptist does when he foretells the reward of the righteous and the punishment of the wicked. Rather, the Black community acknowledges suffering—"trials by fire" like the one posed by King Nebuchadnezzar—through ritual acts, through the body, and affirms life on earth in the present rather than in heaven hereafter. Further, Foulks argues that through the belief of the characters in a fourth face of God—an unnamed brother responsible for evil—*Sula* "criticizes the impulse to expel or annihilate evil." Instead, Shadrack becomes a model for engaging evil, acknowledging its existence but "defend[ing] his freedom to choose his own life or death."

On a very different note, Nancy Bate, in her piece entitled, "Toni Morrison's *Beloved*: A Psalm and a Sacrament," reads Morrison's historical novel of slavery and freedom through the enslavement of another people—the ancient Israelites. Using the often vexing "124" of the novel as a roadmap, Bate reads Morrison's text in relation to Psalm 124, citing historical, linguistic, and theological parallels and arguing that the Passover Haggadah, biblical readings that communicate the exodus story and the origins of the Passover rituals, "provide a structural referent for the novel." She argues that both texts follow the mythic pattern outlined by Joseph Campbell: "imperiled birth, suffering/adventure, sacrifice/death, resurrection, ritualized remembering, and communal redemption." Paralleling the Hebrew Bible's theme of redemption from slavery with the New Testament's focus on redemption from sin, Bate analyzes the Eucharistic moments in *Beloved*, understanding the novel's emphasis on multiple tellings of the horrific history of the characters as the process through which healing—redemption—may be achieved. Both texts, she argues, "suggest that the ghosts of the past can be transcended through communal solidarity."

Some of the essays here argue that Morrison's stance toward the Bible is oppositional, that she employs biblical or theological concepts in such a way as to reveal their limitations. David Z. Wehmer, in "To Live This Life Intensely and Well: The Rebirth of Milkman Dead in Toni Morrison's *Song of Solomon*," argues that the novel can be read as "a conversion narrative outside the Christian paradigm." Using Morrison's claim in an interview that the theme of her works could be "how and why we learn to live this life intensely and well," Wehmer explores the concept of didacticism as it relates to the rise of the novel as a genre. Morrison's novels, he suggests, must be read in the light of how they *work*—how they reveal "what is killing African Americans and what will bring them back to life." Contrasting the characters of Pilate and Milkman, Wehmer suggests that Pilate "embodies the intense life," while Milkman begins the novel, as his name suggests, Dead. To be born again, he must "not only negotiate a relationship to the dominant white culture [… and] to the black community [… but] to the past." Paralleling Milkman's rebirth with that of Christ, Wehmer moves away from the biblical text to assert that Milkman's conversion requires the abandonment of the Western cultural ideal of the economic individual as well as the abandonment of what Wehmer calls "the master's language." Rejecting "the Word" and its signifying system that aligns light with goodness and darkness with its absence, Milkman (and other Morrison characters as well) are reborn to a prior understanding of identity that challenges received notions of race and gender.

Beth Hawkins also discusses *Song of Solomon* in her essay, "Intimate Fatality: *Song of Solomon* and the Journey Home." Reading that work against the biblical Song of Solomon and the Book of Ruth, Hawkins argues that Morrison's novel is a "revaluation" of its sources. Seeing the biblical books as explorations of love, exile, identity, and family, Hawkins probes Morrison's handling of those concepts in a work in which "the ultimate act of self-expression slides into self-destruction; power collides with helplessness, desire with resignation." Hawkins reads the novel's various characters as traversing the complexities and contradictions inherent in the way love, exile, identity and family are understood. Citing Guitar and Circe as examples of characters whose understanding of love have led them to radically different positionalities, Hawkins returns to the Song of Solomon to argue that it, too, warns of "the incompatibility of love with life." Both texts, she claims, reveal a tension "between the anxiety of abandonment and the claustrophobia of being too closely held." Moving on to the Book of Ruth, Hawkins sees Morrison as rewriting its central character through Ruth Foster Dead. However, whereas the biblical Ruth chooses exile and bears a child only to have it claimed by Naomi, Morrison's Ruth stands her ground in her father's home and seizes motherhood in a way that, although pathological, "inscribes Milkman's name upon his body."

Moving in a more purely theoretical direction, Agnes Suranyi, in "The Bible as Intertext in Toni Morrison's Novels," explores Morrison's use of intertextuality through Michael Riffaterre's claim that we must view "text and intertext/s [as] variants of the same structural matrix." Suryani argues that the text (Morrison's novels) can impose demands on the intertext (the Bible), citing Henry Louis Gates, Jr.'s concept of "signifyin(g)" by way of explanation. Hence, Morrison's reworking of the Bible functions as pastiche or parody. Suryani goes on to elaborate on Morrison's various forms of "signifyin(g)"— literal citations, titling, epigraphs, and naming, as well as Riffaterrean "ungrammaticalities" or "traces"—and to explore specific biblical references within Morrison's novels to determine whether her treatment is ironic or whether she may have been using the source text to affirm her own theological position. Suryani argues that Pauline Christianity, particularly insofar as it concerns "generous love… free of the desire to possess," is "the most relevant and closest to Morrison's concept of Christianity," although Morrison extends her understanding of love to include a "fusion of communality and individuality, caring for the other and the self, and cherishing the spirit as well as the body."

Not surprisingly, several of the essays focus on syncretic spirituality, especially exploring the intersection of African religions with contemporary American Christianity to form a new, distinctly African American religion. Sharon Jessee's "The 'Female Revealer' in *Beloved*, *Jazz*, and *Paradise*: Syncretic Spirituality in Toni Morrison's Trilogy" argues that Morrison works "to resurrect an African American historical/cultural consciousness under the signs of multiple theologies and religious practices." Each novel "dramatizes distinct beliefs about a metaphysical dimension, 'here' or 'beyond,' salvific encounters with godlike or extraordinary personages, and prophetic divinations of the future." Morrison employs what Jessee cites as "theocracy"—God-mixing—in her fusion of slave religion, African American Christian traditions, Black and womanist theologies, and Gnosticism. Morrison's articulation of such theological concepts as salvation, transformation, and the afterlife reveals the development of those concepts in African American thought. Jessee especially explores Gnosticism as a parallel to the belief structure of the Black church in that it affirms "visionary sanctuary in *this* life, [and] a transformative experience based on a 'Call' that can change one's relationship to the illusory and gross material environment of life on earth."

Benjamin Burr also addresses syncretism in "Mythopoetic Syncretism in *Paradise* and the Deconstruction of Hospitality in *Love*." He reads *Paradise* as "a deconstruction of Christianity as a dominant mythological discourse" through Morrison's use of mythopoetic syncretism. Burr argues that the two sets of twins appearing in the novel become the device whereby Morrison can link her text to biblical, African American, American, and ancient Roman sources, unraveling all of them to reconstruct an alternative "salvation discourse." Burr reads the narrative of the twin brothers, Deek and Steward, against that of Mavis, whose twins have died, aligning the former with the biblical Jacob and Esau as well as the Roman Romulus and Remus; Mavis, on the other hand, is tied to the Yoruban Orisa, Osun, "the pure essence of joy." However, Burr argues, Morrison does not privilege any one paradigm and allows the possibility of redemption for all the characters. By the time she writes *Love*, however, Morrison "calls into question the relevance of mythological paradigms in general," Burr argues. Using Derrida's analysis of hospitality as a way to enter the text, Burr explores how *Love* functions as a "deconstructive hermeneutic commentary on Paul's Other-oriented model of love." If the syncretism of *Paradise* parallels the Derridean sense of hospitality as welcoming and sheltering, Burr argues, *Love* engages Derrida's second, or deconstructive, sense of hospitality, which acknowledges the possibility of theft and violation. In *Love*, then, Morrison arrives at a "new ontological model" in which "redemption is only possible when one comes to terms with hospitality's deconstruction of itself."

Anissa Janine Wardi's exploration of syncretism, "Jazz Funerals and Mourning Songs: Toni Morrison's Call to the Ancestors in *Sula*," grounds itself in historical and cultural practices. Arguing that "Morrison relies on the discourse of Christianity" and that she employs Christian rituals in her work, Wardi claims that Morrison's treatment of "theologically based sacraments ... [is] steeped in an African American cultural and historical epistemology, which derives in part from West African spiritual practices and their transformation on American soil." In *Sula*, then, we can see the Christianity of the characters "as a palimpsest of an African diasporic history," grown out of both West African belief and the violence encountered by Africans once they set foot on American soil. Wardi argues that the novel's referencing of New Orleans—a city where West Africa meets Europe and Catholicism coexists with Afro-Caribbean religions—has been overlooked, that in fact it "establishes a paradigm for conceptualizing the treatment of death, its attendance practices and communal rituals." To approach *Sula*, a novel "steeped in mourning," Wardi cites practices such as the placing of wreaths on doors, aboveground burials, and jazz parades with their second-line followers; she delves into the history of funerary hymns, the history of burial societies, and the devastating race riots of 1921. Arguing that the novel's beginning and end are both elegiac, Wardi claims that "the entire novel becomes a hymn of comfort, a mourning song that promises healing."

Jennifer Terry, in "New World Religion? Creolisation and Candomblé in Toni Morrison's *Paradise*," moves still further south, to Brazil, where, Terry argues, the African Brazilian practices of Candomble are "invoked to formulate a positive model of New World creolisation." Claiming that, in Morrison's text, "institutionalized religion is allied with patriarchy, conservativism, and colonization," Terry asserts that not only the mean-spirited interpretation of Christianity practiced by Pulliam, but also the Catholicism of the loving Mary Magna and the enlightened theology of Misner are troubling—the former for its implication in the destruction of the indigenous culture of the region, the latter because of its nostalgic desire for a return to Africa in favor of other responses to diasporic dislocation. By contrast, the religious practice Connie instates in the Convent, which Terry shows is linked to the initiation rituals within Candomblé, "challenges the gender ideology, the denial of the bodily *and* the promises of deferred reward in heaven of the established church, allowing Morrison to engage critically with Christianity and its part in repressive diasporic encounters." Thus syncretic models of worship incorporating African beliefs can become new models of resistance to such repression.

The final two essays in the collection look beyond both the Judeo-Christian tradition and African religion as a way of approaching Morrison's texts. My own essay, "The Master's Tools: Morrison's *Paradise* and the Problem of Christianity," explores Morrison's use of magic realism—a literary genre developed as a strategy of resistance to Western cultural epistemology in all its forms—to challenge Christian theology. I argue that Morrison, through her use of biblical myth—specifically the stories of the exodus of the Israelites and the birth of the Messiah—and through her exploration of narrative, contrasts ossified, static religion to vital, life-giving spirituality. By way of Lacan and Kristeva, I maintain that the novel ties biblical language to the Word, the Order of the Father, which does not allow for the inclusion of women; by contrast, the spirituality of the Convent women is developed in terms of the semiotic, which disrupts patriarchy and subverts masculine-imposed codes of femininity, celebrating both body and spirit. The novel's conclusion, I argue, reaches outside of both Western and African religions to invoke the religions of the East in a stunning relocation and redefinition of paradise.

Rebecca Degler, in "Ritual and 'Other' Religions in *The Bluest Eye*," explores Morrison's use of ritual sacrifice in the novel. Degler discusses the concept of sacrifice as it functions in both biblical (specifically Old Testament) and classical Greek contexts. Understanding ritual practices as a mechanism for creating membership in society, the essay explores how Pecola's exclusion from the community works not only to create cohesion among its members, but also to transform those individuals into that which they desire to be. Degler contrasts the biblical requirement that the sacrificial victim be pure with the Attic understanding that the victim is personally culpable on some level, reading the character of Pecola through that dual construction. Pecola's ritual sacrifice, Degler suggests, is tied to the agrarian cycle upon which the novel is structured, aligning the text with the Greek, rather than the biblical, antecedent. Unpacking the novel's multiple scenes showing sympathetic magic, Degler argues that "superstitious beliefs and the accompanying magic influence the behavior of the characters," challenging previous readings th[...] dismiss or are contemptuous of Morrison's use of magic within the text. Th[...] novel's ending, however, problematizes our understanding of Pecola's role by recasting her as the biblical sacrificial victim, insisting on her purity, employing, Degler says, "the validation of 'religion' over 'myth' and 'magic' and [purging] anything that does not conform to authorized belief systems."

By engaging with the Bible in diverse ways, these essays enable a multidimensional exploration of Morrison's deployment of theology. From *The Bluest Eye* through *Love*, Morrison has clearly maintained an ongoing dialogue with religion, understanding its vital role in African American consciousness, but approaching it warily: alternately suspicious, respectful, and antagonistic. She requires her readers to push back the parameters of received knowledge and tread on holy ground not merely with reverence, but also with a fully engaged political and critical consciousness.

# 1

# TRIAL BY FIRE:
# THE THEODICY OF TONI MORRISON IN *SULA*

## *Beverley Foulks*

*The poets in the community, who can capture the rhythm and contour of the community's experience—cannot their work be considered a genuine local theology?*

Robert Schreiter (18)

Toni Morrison has said that in all of her novels, she writes "about love and how to survive—not to make a living—but how to survive *whole* in a world where we are all of us, in some measure, *victims of something*" (Bakerman 40). Acknowledging the prevalence of oppression and victimization in the world, *Sula* explores individual and communal responses to evil and its engendered suffering, setting forth a theodicy that emphasizes the importance of sustaining a whole life in spite of various "trials by fire." Toni Morrison accords a prophetic quality to literature: she describes the writer as a "witness bearer," (Taylor-Guthrie 161) her own style as one of "catharsis and revelation," (LeClair 125) and narrative itself as "the best way to learn anything, whether history or theology" (LeClair 125). Morrison develops in *Sula* a unique, local theology of one community's experience with evil and how that experience informs their views of God. As prophet and pariah, Shadrack and Sula challenge the community of Bottom through their marginal behavior and represent local manifestations of suffering and evil, respectively. How their community comes to terms with suffering and evil lies at the heart of Morrison's theodicy.

The term "theodicy," derived from the Greek words *theos* (God) and *dike* (justice), refers to the attempt to justify divine justice and goodness in light of the existence of evil. Theologians propose various theodicies to explain how God can be omniscient, omnipotent, and benevolent despite the presence of evil in the world; some question the reality of evil, others defend the role that evil can play in moral development. Thus theologians may define evil as the privation of good (Augustine), distinguish between "apparent" evil and "genuine" evil (David Ray Griffin), suggest evil is justified in order to recognize that which is good (Alvin Plantinga), or describe evil as a tool to facilitate moral and spiritual development (John Hick). Other theologians admit the reality of evil but deny the benevolence of God (John Roth and Richard Rubenstein), or they cite evil as evidence against the omnipotence of God (Alfred North Whitehead and Harold Kushner).

Morrison's allusions to biblical passages from Daniel (2:8–30) and Matthew (3:11–12) illustrate the complexity of her theological position. (All Biblical citations in this essay refer to the New Revised Standard Version.) Whereas the first passage, from the Old Testament, offers an uncompromising assessment of Shadrach's trial by fire under an oppressive king, the second passage, from the New Testament, predicts impending punishment of the unrighteous when Christ judges humankind through what John the Baptist describes as a baptism of fire. The first passage suggests that divine justice is erratic—God does not always intervene to prevent suffering—while the latter promises eventual divine judgment to deliver the righteous and punish the wicked. In *Sula*, Morrison eschews the latter position in favor of the former. Those at the Bottom know that God does not always deliver people from suffering; they challenge the notion of a wholly benevolent God. Instead, the community attributes a degree of maliciousness to God, to what they call a "fourth head" of the Trinity or a brother of God who did not spare God's son (*Sula* 118).

Scholars like Michael Eric Dyson have proposed the term "black theodicy" to describe how the black community seeks both to understand and survive the existence of suffering and evil (Freedman). Morrison similarly identifies her approach as distinct from that of white thinkers: while the latter tend to focus on abstract arguments about heaven, she engages in theology from within a particular community on earth. She distinguishes between white speculation about heavenly matters and black focus on earthly concerns; instead of anticipating a future "baptism by fire" that will rectify past injustice, Morrison focuses on the present struggle to survive various "trials by fire" that have both natural and human causes. For the community at the Bottom, "the presence of evil was something to be first recognized, then dealt with, survived, outwitted, triumphed over" (118). Morrison criticizes the impulse to expel or annihilate evil; instead, she points out the important role evil can play in mobilizing a community. The community at the Bottom unites in defense against Sula, but after Sula dies, their communal cohesion soon disintegrates.

As noted earlier, Morrison draws from the Old Testament narrative of Shadrach's deliverance from the fiery furnace (Daniel 3:8–30) and John the Baptist's proclamation that Christ will baptize with fire instead of water (Matthew 3:11–12) to illustrate her theodicy. Morrison's character Shadrack recalls the biblical figure of Shadrach. The Book of Daniel recounts how Nebuchadnezzar, the king of Babylon, besieged Jerusalem and brought several Israelites into the court, including Daniel and Shadrach. After Daniel's successful interpretation of the king's dream, the king appoints the Israelites to posts within the kingdom. But when King Nebuchadnezzar demands that everyone worship a golden image that he establishes, the Israelites Shadrach, Meshach, and Abednego refuse to comply. In response to the king's threat to throw them into a fiery furnace because of their disobedience, they retort, "If your God whom we serve is able to deliver us from the furnace of blazing fire and out of your hand, O king, let him deliver us. But if not, be it known to you, O king, that we will not serve your gods, or worship the golden statue that you have set up" (Daniel 3:15–18). Although they are ultimately delivered from the fiery furnace, their response suggests a unique stance towards evil and suffering. They believe in God's capacity to deliver them from the fire, yet they similarly recognize that God does not always intervene in such cases of evil and suffering. Their act of defiance does not depend on God's deliverance—instead, the act itself serves as recognition of the evil in King Nebuchadnezzar's political oppression of Jerusalem.

While some might interpret this passage as signaling passive resignation to their fate, I would argue that their willingness to defend their convictions through a "trial by fire" illustrates their active determination to triumph over evil through their witness. They do not rely on God to intervene on their behalf; they recognize evil and prevail over it through their convictions. Were they to worship the golden image symbolizing the political supremacy of King Nebuchadnezzar, they would be sanctioning his political power. As Frantz Fanon and Albert Memmi have noted, such icons of colonialism—especially those symbols commemorating conquests—seek to keep the colonized in their place (Fanon 51–52; Memmi 104). By refusing to worship the statue, the Israelites challenge the king's political legitimacy, which is predicated on their own suffering, the suffering of the colonized. By submitting to this literal "trial by fire," they show the depth of their conviction and their solidarity with the other oppressed.

As I suggested earlier, this ambivalent recognition of God's capriciousness during a trial by fire contrasts with the expectation of Christ's ultimate judgment through a baptism by fire, a notion derived from Matthew 3:11–12, in which John the Baptist proclaims that although he baptizes with water, Christ will baptize with fire. In Matthew, John the Baptist is a prophetic figure on the margins of society: his clothing of camel's hair and food of locusts and honey set him apart from others (Matthew 3:4); his diet specifically identifies him with the poor of the desert. John the Baptist urges repentance and attacks those who presume that their religious identity might safeguard them against judgment: "Even now the ax is laying at the root of the trees; every tree therefore that does not bear good fruit is cut down and thrown into the fire" (Matthew 3:10). He then makes the following prophetic proclamation: "I baptize you with water for repentance, but one who is more powerful than I is coming after me; I am not worthy to carry his sandals. He will baptize you with the Holy Spirit and with fire" (Matthew 3:11). The fire gathers up the wheat and burns away the chaff, only allowing the righteous and repentant to survive the fire of judgment; thus the notion of "baptism by fire" has eschatological implications. As we will see, Toni Morrison questions its relevance through her depiction of Plum's baptism by fire.

In *Sula*, Morrison's Shadrack survives his trial by fire—World War I—to become a prophetic figure reminiscent of John the Baptist. Shadrack finds himself dehumanized by the war and confined to a straitjacket in a hospital. Having seen the internal organs of fellow soldiers bursting out of their bodies, he finds solace in the hospital food with its clearly restricted zones of "lumpy whiteness of rice, the quivering blood tomatoes, the grayish-brown meat" (8). He trusts that the food, once ingested, will become part of his body without bursting outside of the boundaries of fat, blood, and flesh. Nevertheless, Shadrack cannot control his own body, and his hands grotesquely override their bounds when they become endlessly expanding beanstalks. Two things allow Shadrack to survive his trial by fire: first, he acknowledges his own black presence as both "definite" and "unequivocal"; second, he creates National Suicide Day that calls upon others to similarly embrace their presence or else take their own lives. By recognizing himself and accepting a role in his community, Shadrack survives his trial by fire, the trauma of war.

Whereas Morrison emphasizes the resilience of Shadrack following his trial by fire, she shows the infantile regression of Plum that prompts Eva to instigate his baptism by fire. Plum also returns from World War I dehumanized and broken, yet he finds no strength in his blackness and no space for himself in his community. Instead, he steals from his family and takes trips to Cincinnati. His mother, pained at seeing him so incapacitated, unwittingly drinks from a cup of his blood and immediately resolves to end his torment. Here we see parallels of Christ's narrative: the cup of blood signals the Last Supper, his mother killing him echoes God's sacrifice of his own son. As Eva lights him on fire, Morrison writes, "He opened his eyes and saw what he imagined was the great wing of an eagle pouring a wet lightness over him. Some kind of baptism, some kind of blessing, he thought" (47). While one might be tempted to interpret the apocalyptic images of an eagle through Revelations (4:7; 8:13; 12:14) and baptism of fire through Matthew (3:11–12) as an acceptance of a final judgment, Morrison upsets such expectations with her depiction of the consequences of Eva's action. Eva's act prompts Hannah to question Eva's love for her, influencing Hannah's interaction with Sula, which in turn occasions Sula's wayward tendencies. In a sense, one can point to this baptism by fire as the origin of evil in *Sula*. Morrison makes the point that each individual must accept and survive his or her particular trial by fire. When Eva seeks to deliver her son from such suffering, Morrison portrays her evasion as unnatural and misguided.

Thus we see a juxtaposition of two responses to suffering: whereas Shadrack embraces his freedom following a trial by fire, Eva seeks to deliver Plum from further regression through a baptism by fire. Instead of viewing suffering itself as problematic, Morrison portrays the *response* to suffering as crucial for her theodicy. Whereas most discussions about theodicy explore *why* God might allow for the existence of evil, Toni Morrison instead focuses on *how* people respond to evil and suffering. Her position certainly has implications for how she views God, but Morrison shows more concern for the human response to such challenges. By abnegating Plum's responsibility to survive in the face of suffering, Eva precipitates a series of aberrances. Eva's fault lies in her assumption that she can somehow stop suffering. Instead, Morrison shows that one cannot stop suffering itself—one can only determine how one responds to such suffering. Theologian and philosopher Diogenes Allen echoes this concern as he writes: "Our position in the physical and social world is that of but one reality among many in a system of interconnected events, most of which are utterly beyond our control.... In such circumstances an individual's only real freedom is the manner in which he responds to untoward events beyond his control" (190). Shadrack acknowledges all that lies beyond his control, but he defends his freedom to choose his own life or death. His decision to survive in the face of suffering represents an act of defiance, for he could equally choose to commit suicide. Like the biblical Shadrach, who does not give in to his oppressor's command to worship an idol—the consequences of

the evil of colonialism—Morrison's Shadrack does not succumb to the consequences of the evil of war. Plum, on the other hand, does not embrace his
freedom, instead relinquishing his power in a spiral of self-destructive habits.
His mother sees this process as a slow suicide, and she mistakenly assumes that
her maternal power to give Plum life should also extend to determine his
death. By illustrating the evil consequences of this act, Morrison underscores
the responsibility of each individual to survive his or her respective trial by fire.

What enables Shadrack to survive his trial by fire while Plum perishes in
a baptism by fire? We have seen that Shadrack's response is physical, based on
the recognition of his own body and his power over his own life. Diogenes
Allen suggests that freedom can derive from the recognition of one's materiality: "We are material, and as a piece of matter we are vulnerable to injury, illness, and decay. To realize this is to realize our status, our place—to realize
what we are. It is to come to terms with a hard fact" (193). Just as Shadrach in
Daniel recognizes his own vulnerability in the face of King Nebuchadnezzar,
Shadrack in *Sula* recognizes his own fragility as he sees his fellow soldiers killed
in war. Both figures assume a stoic stance in the face of hard facts: while their
status does not allow them to overthrow despotic kings or prevent war or racial
injustice, their determined opposition challenges such evil. Morrison emphasizes the importance of recognizing the material feature of experience. Instead
of viewing corporality as pessimistic or base, Morrison instead esteems such
materiality as a powerful vehicle for memory and survival. Suffering and one's
response to suffering (theodicy) are thus not matters of intellectual speculation
but lived, bodily acts. In the Bottom, memory is a bodily incorporation of past
experience, a re-member-ing.

Describing the "shucking, knee-slapping, wet-eyed laughter that could
even describe and explain how they came to be where they were" (*Sula* 4),
Morrison suggests that folks at the Bottom literally embody painful experiences: only song (which reveals the core of one's being) and the touch of their
hand (which still bears marks of wood-working despite years of unemploy-
ment) really allow the "valley men" (white people) to appreciate the pain experienced by people at the Bottom. The valley men do not hear pain behind the
laughter, because they assume a simplistic understanding of laughter as happiness. Morrison illuminates the tragicomic aspect of laughter, which another
novelist, the postcolonial African novelist Henri Lopez, calls a *pleurer-rire* (cry-
ing-laugh; laughing-cry). This laughter tells its own narrative. Morrison characterizes it as both descriptive and explanatory, suggesting that a kind of revelation can occur in laughter, that laughter can form part of the script that

explains life. The people at the Bottom reveal their experiences in ways that differ from—or rather, escape the notice of—the valley men. Such memories, inscribed on the body, tell their own stories. Thus, when Shadrack finds his face in the reflection of water in a toilet bowl, it reveals to him an entire script of his life. His face allows him to re-member himself such that his hands no longer escape their bounds. In order to survive in the face of suffering, then, one must fully embrace one's own history, itself inscribed in the body.

Morrison's theodicy stresses how this acceptance of one's corporal nature can enable one to better incorporate fear and other obstacles to human flourishing in the face of suffering and evil. Describing how white people used religious rhetoric to relegate black people to a land of infertile stony hills by calling it "the bottom of heaven," Morrison notes that the black community at the Bottom had no time to think about such past injustices; they were preoccupied with "earthly things and each other" (6). They could not afford the luxury of ruminating on injustice; in order to survive, they had to make their living and focus on the present. Their social location prompts a different kind of theodicy. Shadrack returns from the war, finds strength in his blackness, and tries to make a place for his fear. Morrison describes his response as "a struggle to order and focus experience. It had to do with making a place for fear as a way of controlling it" (14). Instead of seeking to expel or annihilate fear, Shadrack recognizes fear as part of human experience. He makes a place for it in his own life by initiating a ritual of National Suicide Day. Similarly, the Bottom makes a place for Shadrack in their community. Although they recognize that he is insane, they do not seek to institutionalize him or further marginalize him. He becomes a powerful prophetic figure: "His eyes were so wild, his hair so long and matted, his voice was so full of authority and thunder that he caused panic on the first, or Charter, National Suicide Day" (15). Morrison's description of Shadrack alludes to John the Baptist, as Shadrack shares such features of marginality. John the Baptist calls the Israelites to repent or be thrown in the fire; Shadrack the Fisherman gives the Bottom one day in which they can kill themselves or each other. Although he can be drunk, loud, obscene, and outrageous, Shadrack nevertheless becomes incorporated into the community: "Once the people understood the boundaries and nature of his madness, they could fit him, so to speak, into the scheme of things" (15). Just as Shadrack makes a place in his life for fear, the community makes a place for Shadrack in spite of his madness. Absorbed into their thoughts, languages, and lives, Shadrack becomes part of the fabric of the communal life in the Bottom.

As we will see, this emphasis on the body and incorporation will become particularly important for Toni Morrison's discussion of Christ's incarnation. Yet we should first note how Morrison builds her theology from the material experience of particular characters like Shadrack and a specific community like the Bottom. This kind of theologizing stands in marked contrast with that of the white characters, who use theology to justify experience—that is, to justify their oppression and injustice. Toni Morrison describes the bargeman who finds Chicken Little: "Still bemused by God's curse and the terrible burden his own kind had of elevating Ham's sons, he suddenly became alarmed by the thought that the corpse in this heat would have a terrible odor, which might get into the fabric of his woolen cloth" (63). In this portrayal, the white person uses religion as a justification for exploiting black people; moreover, he refuses to remember such injustices or incorporate blackness within his experience. Instead, he wants to expel it, literally dropping it from his boat; he fears the odor of the corpse becoming infused into his own clothes. Whereas the people at the Bottom allow such physicality to pervade every element of their life, the bargeman seeks to escape it.

This is similarly reflected in an episode from a later novel by Toni Morrison, *Tar Baby*, when the powerful white man wants to expel the thought that God would allow for his wife to abuse their son. Instead of questioning the benevolence of God, Valerian concludes that life itself must be unreal. He imagines how his son must have tried to make sense of his mother's violence against him:

> The not knowing when, the never knowing why, and never being able to shape the tongue to speak, let alone the mind to cogitate how the one person in the world upon whom he was totally, completely dependent—the one person he could not even choose not to love—could do that to him. Believing at last as a little boy would that he deserved it, must deserve it, otherwise it would not be happening to him. That no one in the world would be imagined, thought up, or even accidentally formed not to say say say say *created that* would permit such a thing to happen. And he is right. No world in the world would allow it. So this is not the world at all. It must be something else. I have lived in it and I will die out of it but it is not the world. This is not life. This is some other thing. (*Tar Baby* 234)

Valerian stutters at the thought of a baby betrayed by his mother, a child forced to believe he deserved abuse as the only way to make sense out of chaos; he stutters at the idea of God creating a world that permits the abuse of children. When he cannot make sense of such behavior, he rejects the world and its evil as completely absurd, as unreal. Morrison has criticized those who seek to eliminate the problem of evil—"That may be very cleansing, but it's also highly intolerant" (Ruas 101)—and depicts such intolerance through characters like the bargeman in *Sula* and Valerian in *Tar Baby*. By contrast, the community at the Bottom assumes the presence of evil—they accept it as part of human existence.

These different stances prompt diverse theological responses to suffering and evil. Whereas Valerian safeguards the benevolence and omnipotence of God and deems such evil unreal in *Tar Baby*, the community at the Bottom engages in a different kind of theologizing in *Sula*. Instead of using experiences such as the suffering or death of children as a springboard for fairly abstract theological musing, the people at the Bottom use those experiences to understand the human side of suffering. At Chicken Little's funeral, Morrison describes this process:

> And they saw the Lamb's eye and the truly innocent victim: themselves. They acknowledged the innocent child hiding in the corner of their hearts, holding a sugar-and-butter sandwich.[....] Or they thought of their son newly killed and remembered his legs in short pants and wondered where the bullet went in. Or they remembered how dirty the room looked when their father left home and wondered if that is the way the slim, young Jew felt, he who for them was both son and lover and in whose downy face they could see the sugar-and-butter sandwiches and feel the oldest and most devastating pain there is: not the pain of childhood, but the remembrance of it. (65)

In the kind of theology happening at the Bottom, people see themselves as the body of Christ, both individually and communally. Yet they note that this identification also renders them innocent victims. They recognize themselves corporally, locally, intricately wrapped up with Christ. Thus they empathize with the suffering of Christ on a very intimate level, down to the sugar-and-butter sandwich they ate as an innocent child, the short pants of a killed son, and the disheveled room of an abandoned father. Christ figures deeply into their lived experience, not in empty theologies. As Diogenes Allen speculates, the recognition of human vulnerability can draw one closer to Christ; in response to the world, "one must face one's vulnerability to its workings, and not think that this essential vulnerability can be avoided by prayer, any more than Jesus could escape destruction by his prayers in the garden of Gethsemane" (197). Christ calls to the people at the Bottom because they, too, have been forsaken and abandoned by fathers; yet they, too, have lost sons.

The pain comes from the remembering, the actual incorporation of such pain into their bodies. Unlike the bargeman, they allow the smell of the corpse to penetrate not only their clothes, but also their entire beings. Thus, the black community in *Sula* theologically makes sense of death not by justifying it or explaining it, but by incorporating it and remembering it. Instead of railing against God for allowing the death of an innocent, they remember that God allowed the death of his own son, and that they also share this experience as part of Christ. They accept the Christian call to be the body and blood of Christ.

As a result, when Eva refuses to accept her son's suffering, to incorporate his blood, thereby rejecting the Eucharistic moment, this deeply affects Hannah, who believes that Eva must never have loved her children. Hannah's actions, in turn, influence Sula's development, and thus we see the genesis and development of Sula's aberrant behavior. Instead of speculating about God in the face of her behavior, Morrison shows the local causes and their effects: Sula's relationship with her mother has a formative impact, not abstract theology. Hannah's sexual encounters with men frustrate other women (prostitutes and wives) at the Bottom, for they are neither mercenary nor passionate; while conventional attitudes toward sex would dictate a coy or modest approach to such intimate affairs, Sula eschews such norms after observing the happiness on her mother's face following such sexual exchanges (44). When she overhears her mother mention that she may love Sula, but not like her, Sula remains caught in "dark thoughts" that only Nel can deliver her from (57). These childhood experiences mold Sula. Because of her unconventional family history, Sula has little respect for social decorum. Reflecting on her impulse to sleep with Jude, Sula insists that she had no evil intentions towards Nel, but instead lacked any real understanding of marriage (119). Nel later notes that Sula has no sense of morality—she cannot distinguish right from wrong (145). Instead, Sula lets her emotions dictate her behavior (141). Although Sula perceives her actions to be the product of her curiosity and vivid imagination (121; 136), the community condemns her because of her indifference towards her mother's death, her callousness towards her grandmother, and her adulterous behavior that purportedly extends to white men (112).

Morrison also suggests that the black community acknowledges suffering through ritual acts that involve bodily movement and gestures. At Chicken Little's funeral at the Church of Greater Saint Matthews, Morrison writes, "Then they left their pews. For with some emotions one has to stand. They spoke, for they were full and needed to say. They swayed, for the rivulets of grief or of ecstasy must be rocked. And when they thought of all that life and death locked into that little closed coffin they danced and screamed, not to protest God's will but to acknowledge it and confirm once more their conviction that the only way to avoid the Hand of God is to get in it" (65–66). Just as their laughter accesses the deepest pain, their speech and movement serve to incorporate such pain, to express faith bodily, through dancing, speaking, swaying, and screaming. They recognize suffering and evil as God's will, but we should not assume that this lack of protest signals a passive succumbing to evil; instead, the act of survival becomes an act of defiance. Nel also recognizes the importance of bodily protest in the face of her suffering. After her experience of adultery and abandonment, she reflects on those women screaming in the face of death: "They could not let that heart-smashing event pass unrecorded, unidentified. It was poisonous, unnatural to let the dead go with a mere whimpering, a slight murmur, a rose bouquet of good taste" (107). In response to the senselessness of death, Morrison writes, "There must be much rage and saliva in its presence. The body must move and throw itself about, the eyes must roll, the hands should have no peace, and the throat should release all the yearning, despair and outrage that accompany the stupidity of loss" (107). As with memory, the whole body participates in the recognition of loss. The body records the passage of life: it is the vehicle through which one registers suffering. Although they do not expel Sula from their community, people at the Bottom record and identify the suffering that they experience because of her acts.

Morrison emphasizes the importance of surviving whole in the face of such evil. She envisions a different type of love: remembering how she spent her last bit of lard in order to ease Plum's suffering from constipation, Eva states that her love was different from the way Hannah thought—her *survival* was her love (69). Yet when she saw that Plum could not survive after his trial by fire, Eva describes how she could not "deliver" him again: "I had room enough in my heart, but not in my womb, not no more. I birthed him once. I couldn't do it again. He was growed, a big ole thing" (71). So she executes a baptism by fire; but she cannot, Morrison suggests, save him or other people from their respective trials by fire. When Hannah later becomes set on fire, Eva is powerless to deliver her from suffering, and, moreover, witnesses her granddaughter watching her mother burn to death out of interest. While Eva would like to deny this vision (expelling it), she instead remembers and thereby accepts it.

Just as Morrison emphasizes the importance of each individual surviving his or her trial by fire, she also stresses the need for communities to recognize and absorb evil in their midst. *Sula* depicts two events that cause members of the community to suffer, both of which Sula is responsible for: the death of Chicken Little and the adultery of Nel's husband, Jude. When Sula returns to the Bottom, Morrison writes: "In spite of their fear, they reacted to an oppressive oddity, or what they called evil days, with an acceptance that bordered on welcome. Such evil must be avoided, they felt, and precautions must naturally be taken to protect themselves from it. But they let it run its course, fulfill itself, and never invented ways either to alter it, to annihilate it or to prevent its happening again. So also were they with people" (90). Again, Morrison focuses on the importance of how communities respond to what they perceive to be evil: *in spite of* their fear, they welcome Sula back into their midst. Just as Shadrack sought to control his fear, the community does not expel Sula out of fear, but instead accepts her presence—with caution. In this theodicy, Morrison recognizes the reality of evil and suffering, a reality that must be accepted. This would strike the "valley men," the bargeman, and *Tar Baby*'s Valerian as odd, for they seek to reject evil instead of recognizing its legitimacy. Toni Morrison admits that the theology at the Bottom differs from that of "outsiders": "What was taken by outsiders to be slackness, slovenliness, or even generosity was in fact a full recognition of the legitimacy of forces other than good ones. They did not believe doctors could heal—for them, none ever had done so[....] The purpose of evil was to survive it and they determined (without ever knowing they had made up their minds to do it) to survive floods, white people, tuberculosis, famine and ignorance. They knew anger well but not despair" (90).

Theologizing from their experience, the community at the Bottom concludes that evil exists in the world, regardless of their natural or human causes, and vows to survive it. Here "survival" does not mean sanctioning evil, for Morrison writes, "they knew anger well." Instead, survival entails recognizing and weathering natural disasters and human prejudice. Like Shadrach in Daniel, their survival represents defiance in the face of oppression. As the later interchange between Eva and Sula attests, Morrison does not fully accept the notion of a final judgment or "baptism by fire." When Eva vows that God will strike Sula down, Sula points out that God allowed Eva to burn Plum. Morrison's stance recalls that of the Israelites facing King Nebuchadnezzar: although they have faith in God's power to deliver, they simultaneously recognize that he does not always intervene, that suffering is not always rewarded with deliverance. Similarly, after her husband's adultery, Nel waits for the typ-

ical response to suffering, "the oldest cry," a "Why me?" Morrison writes that
"the mud shifted, the leaves stirred, the smell of overripe green things
enveloped her and announced the beginnings of her very own howl. But it did
not come" (108). Morrison does not engage in a theodicy that questions evil or
deems it unnatural or provides automatic deliverance or comfort. Instead, she
focuses on nature itself: shifting mud, stirring leaves, and ripening fruit.
Because evil is as natural as good, the cry of "Why me?" does not come.
Instead, Nel must accept her own suffering: a life of solitude. She does register the weight of her burden, asking Jesus, "What kind of cross is that?" (221).
Nel does not question why it should be her, or why it happens; she accepts the
reality of evil, and she recognizes the suffering that occurs because of it. Thus,
instead of viewing Sula's behavior as anomalous, the community at the
Bottom accepts it as part of nature. Morrison explains the acceptance of Sula
as consistent within a worldview in which "aberrations were as much a part of
nature as grace" (117).

For the community at the Bottom, while God is omnipotent, the reality of
evil means that God cannot be wholly benevolent. In the face of *that* reality,
survival becomes an act of faith and of protest. The Bottom's theology springs
from the black experience of such aberrations: "In their secret awareness of
Him, He was not the God of three faces they sang about. They knew quite
well that He had four, and that the fourth explained Sula. They had lived with
various forms of evil all their days, and it wasn't that they believed God would
take care of them. It was rather that they knew God had a brother and that
brother hadn't spared God's son, so why should he spare them?" (117–118)
Here we must first note the phrase "they had lived with various forms of evil."
Evil and its concomitant suffering remain integral to their life experience.
They have been abandoned, they have lost children, and they have lived with
other forms of evil. These experiences lead them to identify with Jesus as the
abandoned Son and innocent child, and it also prompts them to expand their
version of the Trinity in order to make sense of such suffering. In addition to
the Father, Son, and Holy Spirit, they add the figure of an evil brother. Thus
they make evil co-existent with God. This renders the notion of the godhead
even more complex. They recognize the godhead in all creatures, but this godhead contains suffering.

While evil certainly causes suffering, it can also foster communal cohesion.
When the folks at the Bottom finally identify the cause for their misfortune,
they start loving their spouses, protecting their children, and tending to their
homes. The community finds its voice, rage, and saliva in the presence of Sula.

Nel offers the following character sketch of her friend: "Sula never competed; she simply helped others define themselves. Other people seemed to turn their volume on and up when Sula was in the room" (95). Morrison thereby suggests that Sula prompts a social cohesion because she provides them something to define themselves against. They do not try to harm her or run her out. Instead, Morrison writes, "As always the black people looked at evil stony-eyed and let it run" (113). In fact, the community falls into bickering and divisive habits following the death of Sula: "Without her mockery, affection for others sank into flaccid disrepair" (153). Thus Morrison suggests that evil can also play a formative role in building community; just as communities can mobilize in response to natural disasters, they can also come together when facing evil caused by humans.

Morrison's theodicy does not simplistically assume that Sula is wholly evil or Shadrack wholly crazy. Morrison's moral complexity is best exemplified in the relationship between Shadrack and Sula. Morrison describes a pastoral moment when Shadrack, in the face of Sula's anxiety and suffering, seeks to console her. After throwing Chicken Little into the river, Sula runs into the house of Shadrack, who "nodded his head as though answering a question, and said, in a pleasant conversational tone, a tone of cooled butter, 'Always'"(62). While Sula comes intending to find out whether Shadrack witnessed her act, Shadrack sees how death has struck fear in her heart. He recognizes the fear that plagued him before he found consolation in his own blackness. Thus he tries to rid her of any fear in the face of death. Shadrack later reflects back on the event and notes, "He had said 'always,' so she would not have to be afraid of the change—the falling away of the skin, the drip and slide of blood, and the exposure of the bone underneath. He had said 'always' to convince her, assure her, of permanency" (157). Seeing his own post-traumatic terror reflected in her face, Shadrack seeks to quell such fear with the prospect of permanency and eternity. But just as Eva cannot deliver her son from his suffering through a baptism by fire, Shadrack cannot enable Sula to control her fear with the promise of eternity. Only on her deathbed does she remember his words, and at this point she is burning with fever, which suggests a possible baptism by fire, through which Sula would become burnt like chaff. Indeed, Shadrack addresses a need that she had not even recognized. At the time, Sula remarks: "Always. He had answered a question she had not asked, and its promise licked at her feet" (63). Yet Shadrack cannot enable her to gain a similar sense of self and community that would enable her to survive in the face of suffering. As Sula later admits, she does not have that sense of self that would center or buoy her.

While Shadrack makes a space for his fear in order to control it, Sula often succumbs to her fear, which leads her to do self-destructive and evil acts. Nel reflects on how Sula's self-destructive behavior was prompted more often than not by fear: "And when fear struck her, she did unbelievable things. Like that time with her finger. Whatever those hunkies did, it wouldn't have been as bad as what she did to herself. But Sula was so scared she had mutilated herself, to protect herself" (101). Her childhood experiences mold her into a solitary being without a sense of center. Feeling estranged from her mother and know-ing her mother's capacity to kill another human being, Sula concludes that she cannot rely on others or herself. Thus her experiences engender a hostility and indifference in Sula, and she later admits that she never "meant anything" (147), regardless of their consequences for others. Nel experiences Sula's adul-tery as a loss similar to death—Sula steals the vitality of her thighs, and Jude breaks her heart (111). In order to understand the severity of Nel's reaction, we might recall how Nel views her relationship with Jude as a means of sepa-rating herself from Sula: "Greater than her friendship was this new feeling of being needed by someone who saw her singly" (84). Sula, on the other hand, does not register this distinction, but instead assumes that she can share Jude's affection. Only after she causes Nel pain does Sula realize that they are differ-ent: Nel aspires for a conventional married life, while Sula insists upon follow-ing her own whims (121). Their dissimilarity becomes more apparent when Sula admits that she did not love Jude, but instead slept with him to fill up space (144). Nel interprets Sula's action as a betrayal, whereas Sula challenges conventional morality altogether when she asks Nel, "How you know [...] About who was good. How you know it was you?" (146)

Morrison thus complicates superficial notions of good and evil in her depiction of Sula and Nel. At the end of the book, Morrison draws into ques-tion any assumption of the latter character being good and the former being bad. Reflecting on the drowning of Chicken Little, Nel discovers that she had felt contentment as he disappeared into the water. Morrison writes, "All these years she had been secretly proud of her calm, controlled behavior when Sula was uncontrollable, her compassion for Sula's frightened and shamed eyes. Now it seemed that what she had thought was maturity, serenity and compas-sion was only the tranquility that follows a joyful stimulation" (170). Nel's remarks recall Sula's description of the thrill she felt when she saw her moth-er dance on fire. Morrison thereby suggests that one cannot easily distinguish between the socially acceptable Nel and the social pariah Sula. Just as Morrison admits a greater degree of complexity in describing the godhead, she reveals a complexity to humankind that sees evil in relationship with good, that sees both as elements of existence, and that admits that suffering can bring a community together. Her description of Sula's death precludes any firm conclusion that she will face retribution for her acts. Instead, Morrison allows for the possibility that Sula *might* experience a sort of rebirth, a reversion to her state of innocence as an infant, missing those "dark walls" that recall her painful childhood experiences, and find solace in a baptism of water. Could this image signal repentance and rebirth? Morrison seems to allow for the possibility of Sula's transformation, as she describes the water that might envelop, carry, and wash her body (149). Ultimately, Nel issues a cry simply recognizing her sense of loss after Sula's death: "It was a fine cry—loud and long—but it had no bottom and it had no top, just circles and circles of sorrow" (174). Instead of drawing clear (and artificial) distinctions between top and bottom, or good and evil, Morrison emphasizes the universality of suffering. Being present to the suffering, recognizing it, and registering it with her voice, Nel joins her call with other calls issued throughout the course of the book. Together they form the circles of sorrow that have no pat resolution, but instead must be survived.

Thus we have seen how the people at the Bottom respond to evil and suffering. By accepting Sula and Shadrack as part of their community, they expose themselves to death and suffering. Sula swings Chicken Little into the river, she watches her mother burn to death, and she cheats with Nel's husband; Shadrack's summons ends up in a catastrophic tunnel collapse. The people at the Bottom alter their theological understanding of God in light of such suffering. By rendering evil present and visible, Morrison shows an alternative way of theologizing that begins with what is earthly rather than heavenly. Earthly experiences are not discounted because of heavenly propositions; instead, the former informs the latter. In an interview, Morrison relates that in *Sula* she wanted to depict "how they see [evil]. What they do with it. Black people in general don't annihilate evil…. We try to avoid it or defend ourselves against it but we are not surprised at its existence or horrified or outraged. We may, in fact, live right next door to it, not only in the form of something metaphysical, but also in terms of people" (Parker 62).

In that light, I would disagree slightly with Helen C. Benet-Goodman's characterization of Sula as "a personification or embodiment of the apocalyptic post-modern" (82). Indeed, we have noted the many allusions to the apocalyptic in *Sula*, but we cannot assume that such allusions signal acceptance of a final judgment or eschatology. Speaking about the final scene in *Sula*, Benet-Goodman argues, "Morrison builds to a revelation, but fails to provide it.... In the apocalyptic moment, Morrison's list of who dies is immediately followed by a list of who survives, thus 'downgrading' the event from the apocalyptic to the 'merely' cataclysmic" (81). I would argue that such lists underscore the importance of her underlying theodicy. We have seen how the notion of "trial by fire" distinguishes Plum from Shadrack: the former succumbs to the dehumanization of war, while the latter survived its effects. By providing a list of survivors that remain, Morrison does not belittle or downgrade the horror of death. Instead, we can imagine that those survivors will issue calls similar to that of Nel after Sula's death. They will recognize suffering in the face of death—they will remember such suffering not only in their hearts, but also in their bodies. Moreover, Morrison's theodicy suggests that community can develop in response to such suffering. While the communal places of congregation have been destroyed, there remain the laughter, the songs, and the hands of those woodcarvers now unemployed. Their act of survival enables them to summon the rage and saliva in the face of senseless death and suffering.

## Works Cited

Allen, Diogenes. "Natural Evil and the Love of God." In *The Problem of Evil*, edited by Marilyn McCord Adams and Robert Merrihew Adams. Oxford: Oxford University Press, 1990. 189–208.

Bakerman, Jane. "The Seams Can't Show: An Interview with Toni Morrison." In Taylor-Guthrie, *Conversations*, 30–42.

Benet-Goodman, Helen C. "*Sula* and the Destabilizations of Apocalypse." *Literature and Theology* 13.1 (1999): 76–97.

Fanon, Frantz. *The Wretched of the Earth*. New York: Grove Press, 1963.

Freedman, Samuel G. "Mr. Freeman, You Look Divine." *New York Times* June 11 2003.

Griffin, David Ray. *God, Power, and Evil: A Process Theodicy*. Philadelphia: Westminster Press, 1976.

Hick, John. *Evil and the God of Love*. New York: Harper and Row, 1978.

Kushner, Harold. *When Bad Things Happen to Good People*. New York: Schocken Books, 1981.

LeClair, Thomas. "The Language Must Not Sweat." In Taylor-Guthrie, *Conversations*, 119–128.

Memmi, Albert. *The Colonizer and the Colonized*. Boston: Beacon Press, 1965.

Morrison, Toni. *Tar Baby*. New York: Alfred A. Knopf, 1981.

———. *Sula*. New York: Plume, 1973.

Parker, Betty Jean. "Complexity: Toni Morrison's Women." In Taylor-Guthrie, *Conversations*, 60–66.

Plantinga, Alvin. *God, Freedom, and Evil.* Grand Rapids, MI: William B. Eerdmans Publishing Company, 1977.

Roth, John K. "A Theodicy of Protest." In *Encountering Evil: Live Options in Theodicy*, edited by Stephen T. Davis. Atlanta: John Knox Press, 1981. 7–38.

Ruas, Charles. "Toni Morrison." In Taylor-Guthrie, *Conversations*, 93–118.

Rubenstein, Richard L. *After Auschwitz: Radical Theology and Contemporary Judaism.* Indianapolis: Bobbs-Merrill, 1966.

Schreiter, Robert J. *Constructing Local Theologies.* Maryknoll, NY: Orbis Books, 1985.

Taylor-Guthrie, Danielle, ed. *Conversations with Toni Morrison.* Jackson: University Press of Mississippi, 1994.

Whitehead, Alfred North. *Religion in the Making.* New York: World Publishing Company, 1960.

# 2

# TONI MORRISON'S *BELOVED:*
## PSALM AND SACRAMENT

*Nancy Berkowitz Bate*

*If [it] had not [been] the LORD who was on our side, now may Israel say;*
*If [it had] not [been] the LORD who was on our side, when men rose up*
*    against us:*
*Then they had swallowed us up quick, when their wrath was kindled against us:*
*Then the waters had overwhelmed us, the stream had gone over our soul:*
*Then the proud waters had gone over our soul.*
*Blessed [be] the LORD, who hath not given us [as] a prey to their teeth.*
*Our soul is escaped as a bird out of the snare of the fowlers: the snare is broken,*
*    and we are escaped.*
*Our help [is] in the name of the LORD, who made heaven and earth.*

Psalms 124, A Song of Degrees of David

Like Toni Morrison, I am a descendent of slaves, but my people's anguish was
never fully reified for me until I read *Beloved.* My ancestors' slave narrative, as
it has been handed down in Exodus and in the Passover Haggadah, lacks the
passion, the realism, the immediacy of Morrison's novel. The Haggadah presents a formalized view of slavery in comparison with Toni Morrison's intensely visceral portrayal. Nevertheless, a comparison of the two documents is illu-
minating. Morrison has structured her book like contemporary Passover
Haggadot (plural of Haggadah). *Beloved* is a matrix of tellings; the
"Haggadah," derived from the Talmudic Hebrew "to tell,"[1] consists of various readings that tell the Exodus story and explain Passover rituals. To tell its
story and to appeal to a broad range of celebrants, the Haggadah draws upon
diverse sources. Portions of Exodus may be recited as well as twentieth-century Holocaust narratives (Bronstein 40, 41). Similarly, Morrison's *Beloved* draws
upon varied sources. Her referents include the Gospels (another series of
tellings), other narratives and songs from the Bible, the dances of Africa, and
other works of literature as well.[2] I do not mean to imply here that Morrison

wrote *Beloved* with the intention of revising the Haggadah or even that the Haggadah is a source for *Beloved*, though that is a possibility, but rather, that since both African Americans and Jews have been traumatized by the past and by the humiliations of enslavement, the documents composed to assist each of these communities in remembering and transcending that trauma have some features in common.[3] *Beloved* and the Haggadah each seek, through multiple *tellings*, to awaken their respective communities of readers to a horrific past and to acts of divine grace which afforded redemption; they seek to heal and unify the community through a process of dialogic storytelling. They suggest that the ghosts of the past can be transcended through communal solidarity.

Before Haggadot were used to guide Passover observance, before the destruction of the Jerusalem Temple, psalms were integral to Passover celebration.[4] In accordance with that tradition, most Haggadot include Psalms 113–18. But Psalm 124, a psalm usually omitted from the Haggadah, powerfully conveys the desperation and triumph of escaping slaves, and it is my view that Morrison, like the authors of the Haggadah, has found in David's poetry a source of truth and inspiration. If the Passover Haggadah provides a structural referent for the novel, Psalm 124 is a theological and rhetorical source: the tellings in *Beloved* follow a typical mythic pattern: imperiled birth, suffering/adventure, sacrifice/death, resurrection, ritualized remembering, and communal redemption.[5] At each stage of her characters' monomythic journey, Morrison's prose is laced with rhetoric that finds its correlates in the Haggadah, this psalm, and other sources.

Psalm 124 suffuses the novel's mythic framework. Each of the three parts of *Beloved* opens with "124," providing a backdrop of freedom and a memory of slavery for each section. The house number itself possibly refers to the 124th "psalm"—or song—of David, whose name means "beloved"[6]; the timbre of the household at 124 is also determined by someone called Beloved—the ghost of a baby girl whose mother, Sethe, killed her rather than return her to slavery.

Morrison's use of the psalm's exodus narrative—the progression from slavery to freedom—is seamlessly interwoven with the pathos evoked by its "beloved" composer, with what Robert Graves deemed "'the *single* poetic theme of Life and Death… the question of what survives of the beloved'" (Graves, *White* 21). Morrison's blending of these themes mirrors an analogous synthesis ritualized at the inception of the Christian community, at the first Eucharist. At the Last Supper—a Passover seder that presumably bore some similarity to the seder described in the Haggadah—the concept of redemption from slavery was linked to the redemption from sin afforded by the sacrifice of Jesus, "beloved Son" (Matthew 3:17). The act of communion recalls the sacrifice of the "beloved Son" and the redemption from sin, but in the millennia since that first Eucharist, has lost, for some Christians, the connection with redemption from slavery.[7] Morrison's *Beloved* contains three Eucharists that fuse and allegorize the concepts conveyed at the Last Supper: redemption from slavery, redemption from sin/the past,[8] and the survival/remembrance of the beloved/Beloved. Morrison's book is itself a kind of Eucharist for her readers; by reading it, we consume, assimilate, and remember the anguish of slavery, the elation of freedom, and the sacrifice of Beloved.

Morrison's revision of the Eucharist also emphasizes love of the earth and of the body. Through her characters, she reminds the reader that dance, like prayer, is a potent avenue for the expression of religious ecstasy, thus presenting a characteristically African American conception of Christian practice. In African religion, dance, the body, and communion with nature have not been marginalized but remain central to religious experience and expression. Such may have been the case in early Judaism and Christianity as well, when Passover celebrations and Christian Eucharists may have included these features; in some chapters of the Bible, dance, appreciation of the flesh, and a delight in nature are readily apparent, but these aspects of faith were ultimately marginalized or discouraged by both Jewish and Christian religious authorities. The lyrics of Psalm 124, using visceral imagery and metaphors from the world of nature, express the ecstatic joy of the Israelites in their redemption from slavery and the triumphal crossing of the Red Sea. Slaves made this imagery and the exodus narrative their own: Albert Raboteau has observed that African American slaves identified themselves "with the children of Israel" (250–251), and Lawrence Levine states, "The most persistent single image the slave songs contain is that of the chosen people. The vast majority of the spirituals identify the singers as 'de people dat is born of God,' 'We are the people of God,' 'we are de people of de Lord'" (33).

The people at 124 Bluestone Road are living within the psalm; its music envelops them.[9] Poised at the center of a web of associations that reveal the novel's numerous and diverse sources, "124" provides a referent that renders *Beloved* a unified and cohesive text. The themes and imagery extant in the psalm are repeated throughout the book in endless permutations, and the love integral to David's name—"beloved"—instigates the book's transcendent episodes: Amy, a white runaway teenager, helps Sethe give birth to her youngest daughter, Denver, an act of love; Sethe kills Beloved out of love.

Sethe and Denver have the power to resurrect Beloved because they have loved her, exemplifying the statement in Song of Solomon that "love is stronger than death" (8:6). These developments are each linked, through themes or word play, to the psalm whose number opens *Beloved*.

In "Unspeakable Things Unspoken," Morrison herself has given highly detailed intensive readings of her novels' first sentences. Referring to *Beloved*, she states:

> Beginning *Beloved* with numerals rather than spelled out numbers, it was my intention to give the house an identity... the way plantations were named, but not with nouns or "proper" names—with numbers instead because numbers have... no posture of coziness or grandeur... laying claim to instant history and legend. Numbers here constitute an address, a thrilling enough prospect for slaves who had owned nothing....
>
> Also there is something about numerals that makes them spoken, heard, in this context, because one expects words to read ... not numbers to say, or hear. And the sound of the novel, sometimes cacophonous, sometimes harmonious, must be an inner ear sound or a sound just beyond hearing, infusing the text with a musical emphasis that words can do sometimes even better than music can....
>
> Whatever the risks of confronting the reader with what must be immediately incomprehensible... the risk of unsettling him or her, I determined to take.... The reader is snatched, yanked... just as the slaves were from one place to another.... A few words have to be read before it is clear that 124 refers to a house. ("Unspeakable" 228–229)

Morrison's references to the numbers 1–2–4 as "heard," "harmonious," and "musical" point to their association with song or psalm. She has stated that her prose is an "effort... to be *like* something that has probably only been fully expressed perhaps in music, or in some other culture-gen" (McKay 152). Her analysis conflicts with my own in some instances, but her exposition clearly applies to a first reading. In re-readings, the reader is well aware that "124 refers to a house." Upon subsequent readings, the reader is not "snatched," but plunges knowingly into 124.

Throughout the first five years of Baby Suggs's sojourn, 124 is "a cheerful, buzzing house where Baby Suggs, holy, loved, cautioned, fed, chastised and soothed. Where not one but two pots simmered on the stove; where the lamp burned all night long. Strangers rested there while children tried on their shoes. Messages were left there, for whoever needed them was sure to stop in one day soon" (86–87). Five years after Baby Suggs moved to 124, Sethe arrives, having escaped from Sweet Home plantation and its cruel manager, schoolteacher. She has

twenty-eight days—the travel of one whole moon—of unslaved life. [...] Days of
healing, ease and real-talk. Days of company: knowing the names of forty, fifty other
Negroes[....] One taught her the alphabet; another a stitch. All taught her how it felt
to wake up at dawn and *decide* what to do with the day. [...] Bit by bit, at 124 [...]
along with the others, she had claimed herself. (95)

The house undergoes a radical transformation twenty-eight days after
Sethe's arrival. When Sethe kills her daughter to save her from enslavement,
"124 and everybody in it [...] closed down[.... It] had become the plaything
of spirits and the home of the chafed" (86). The house is haunted by the ghost
of Beloved; 124 holds Sethe in thrall. But when her friend, Paul D, suggests
that Sethe leave her haunted house, she is adamantly opposed to relinquishing
the "house he told her to leave as though a house was a little thing—a shirt-
waist or a sewing basket you could walk off from or give away[....] She who
had never had one but this one" (22). Her reluctance to leave 124 indicates
that the house must represent, like the psalm, faith in the possibility of genuine
freedom. Sethe remembers the days when the house, as a community center
for the African American population of Cincinnati (173), realized the redemption celebrated in the psalm. Denver, Sethe's daughter, is equally attached to
the house. Dimly aware of the house's history, of its transformation after
Beloved's death into a haunted house, Denver sees the house as mystical and
alive. Thus she approaches "the house, regarding it, as she always did, as a person rather than a structure. A person that wept, sighed, trembled and fell into
fits" (29). For Denver, "124 and the field behind it were all the world she knew
or wanted" (101). Denver perceives the outside world as threatening, and 124
provides her with a sanctuary of sorts. She identifies the house with its ghost,
who is "her company" (205).

After the murder, the psalm and the house itself assume the irony associated with blues music, blues tones, punning on "Bluestone Road."[10] When the
novel opens, eighteen years after the death of Beloved, Sethe and the other
inhabitants of 124 are in a sense enslaved by the "spite" (3) of the baby ghost:
no one would visit "while the baby ghost filled the house, and [Sethe] returned
their disapproval with the potent pride of the mistreated" (96). She is occupied
each day with "the serious work of beating back the past" (73), and in the years
since Beloved's death has given little thought to the future, has "never dared"
to make plans. She has been afraid to "go ahead and feel" (38). In 124, a house
named for a song of freedom, Sethe has neither the freedom to plan for the
future nor the freedom to feel in the present.

Not only Sethe's residence but the structure of her narrative can be described as having a "blues tone." Like the blues—and the Haggadah—the novel employs a call-response pattern.[11] Sethe's children ask her to "tell" them about her life in slavery and her escape: "'Tell me,' said Beloved, smiling a wide happy smile, 'Tell me your diamonds'" (58), thus prompting Sethe to recite her story. When Denver complains, "You never told me all what happened. Just that they whipped you and you run off, pregnant. With me," Sethe answers, "Nothing to tell except schoolteacher" and then tells about her cruel overseer (36). The word "tell" is repeated throughout the novel. Sethe wanted her friend, Paul D, to remain with her "[n]o matter what he told[....] Her story was bearable because it was his as well—to tell, to refine and tell again" (99). The Haggadah, too, has a call-and-response pattern, a script in which a leader or a child asks questions that prompt other participants to respond with explanatory songs, stories, or homilies. "Why is this night different from all other nights?" asks the child at the Passover table (Bronstein 29). Then, the "Haggadah"—the "telling" of the story of enslavement and the flight to freedom—begins.

The exodus story narrated in the Haggadah, as well as the storytelling performed by Morrison's characters, represents efforts to remember and to cope with the past. As Bruno Bettelheim explains, one must acknowledge trauma in order to transcend it: "A precondition for a new integration [of a fragmented personality, a dismembered/disremembered self,] is acceptance of how severely one has been traumatized" (34–35). *Beloved* and the stories within it perform this function by acknowledging the trauma of the past. Herbert Bronstein describes the Haggadah in similar terms: "If one should desire to compress time and space so as to distill and preserve the accumulated Jewish experience of centuries and relive it... he would do well to turn to the Haggadah" (Bronstein 9). The Haggadah states, "In every generation, each of us should feel as though we ourselves had gone forth from Egypt, as it is written: 'And you shall explain to your child'" (Bronstein 56; see also Exodus 12:26, 13:8, 13:14, and Deuteronomy 6:20). When Sethe warns her youngest daughter, Denver, about the dangers of the past, the atrocity of enslavement, her phrasing seems to resonate with the Haggadah but has intensified urgency and vividness: "Where I was before I came here, that place is real. It's never going away[.... I]f you go there—you who never was there—if you go there and stand in the place where it was, it will happen again; it will be there for you [...] it's going to always be there waiting for you. That's how come I had to get all my children out" (*Beloved* 36). Though she warns Denver about the

dangers of the past, Sethe exposes her daughter to the past by telling her stories about it, enabling Denver to integrate those stories with her own interpo-
lations, to make the past her own, to move into the future. Denver's favorite
story, told by Sethe and retold by Denver, is the description of her birth.

## Birth

Denver's birth story is tinged with the miraculous, like the story of Moses's
birth in Exodus or Jesus's birth in the Gospels, and seems to draw on African
conceptions of life and death. Denver is called "charmed" (41, 209), because
her birth was "magic" (29). During Sethe's escape, "when it got clear that [she
…] wasn't going to make it—which meant [… Denver] wasn't going to make
it either—she pulled a whitegirl out of the hill" (42) to save the lives of both
mother and child. Though Sethe was physically lying on a hill (30) in
Kentucky to give birth, the word "hill," in the symbol system of Morrison's
novel, suggests a "hill of dead people" (211) remembered by Beloved after her
resurrection. That the "whitegirl," Amy, is pulled from a hill implies that she
is a spirit or ghost, summoned into being. In Africa, the ghosts of the dead
were not always thought of as dangerous aberrations, but rather considered
natural phenomena, a stage of existence. Spirits of beloved friends or relatives
could offer help, protection, or advice (Levine 79). Denver, evidently, has the
power to conjure the spirit of "whitegirl" Amy Denver.

Amy is cast as a spirit, a ghost, or a product of the collective imagination
very much in the way Beloved is. Amy Denver is connected to Beloved, and
thus to Psalm 124, onomastically. "Amy," from the Old French "Amée," trans-
lates as "beloved."[12] Amy also shares many "other-worldly" characteristics
with Beloved. Amy and Beloved both have low voices: Sethe thinks Amy's
voice is "like a sixteen-year-old boy's" (34) and Beloved's "raspy voice" is "low
and rough" (54, 52). Amy has "slow-moving eyes" (32, 80), and Beloved has
"sleepy eyes" (51). Amy, like Beloved, has fallen asleep with the sun in her face
(51, 80, 192). Amy speaks in a "dreamwalker's voice" (79), and Denver considers Beloved "a dream-come-true" (123). Taking quotes out of context, the
reader learns Amy is "like nobody in this world" (32) and "wouldn't be caught
dead" (85).

Amy is also other-worldly in her surname; "Denver" puns on the French
*d'envers*, "from the other side."[13] Positing a French pun here may seem a bit far-
fetched,[14] but Morrison frequently associates Amy's presence with puns, word-

play, and fiction. Amy's given name is French for "friend" as well as "beloved." Morrison herself alludes to the etymology of Amy's given name stating that the "magic of [Denver's …] birth, its miracle […], testified to that *friend*liness as did her [Denver's] own name" (29, emphasis added). Just before Amy appears, Denver dances the antelope in her mother's womb (30), and Sethe remembers that dancing the antelope transformed dancers into something "other" (31).

"The other side" refers to that state rationalists designate as death; however, in African religion, the dead can return in spirit form. Sethe killed Beloved because her "plan was to take us all to the *other side* where my own ma'am is." In Sethe's plan, "they would all be together on the *other side*" (emphasis added, 203, 241). Sethe assumes Baby Suggs "on the *other side*, helped" bring Beloved back (emphasis added, 200). When Beloved haunts 124, Sethe lives "for eighteen years […] in a house full of touches from the other side" (98). Like Beloved and Amy, the newborn Denver is from the other side, from the death before life. In African religions, it is "commonly held that ancestors are born again in their descendants. A resemblance between a grandchild and his deceased grandfather, for example, is proof that the latter has been reincarnated" (Raboteau 12). Dancing the antelope, Denver may well be an incarnation of her grandmother, who danced the antelope as well (*Beloved* 31). In Africa, a person's spirit could wander while the body slept (Raboteau 83); thus, Amy might be presumed to incarnate the wandering spirit of Denver's older sister, Beloved, come to rescue her sibling.[15] Whether Amy is the ghost of Denver's grandmother, the spirit of Denver's sister, or a fictional name, a mere shell, Morrison has made Amy "other-worldly," a created "object" woven into the novel's fabric by characters who are storytellers—that is, subjects—in the "real" world.

Amy—"beloved of the other side"—can be viewed as the reverse, the white side, of Beloved. When Morrison was in the midst of writing her novel, she described Beloved as "the mirror, so to speak… a *twin*" (Naylor 208–209) of other women in the book. Mirror images are reversals, and Amy Denver is the mirror image of Beloved. In both her infant state and her adult reincarnation, Beloved is, like all babies, selfish, wanting to nurse, to devour Sethe, to love Sethe to death; Sethe is "licked, tasted, eaten by Beloved's eyes" (57). Amy, the mirror image of Beloved, is able to ignore her own gnawing hunger (32) and to unselfishly act as nurse to Sethe. Amy's altruism is evidenced in the fact that, though she is starving, she fails to notice the bed of wild onions (30, 31) surrounding Sethe—she is concerned only with healing Sethe.

Amy and Beloved are incarnations of fictional stereotypes extant in the imaginations of black and white Americans. Morrison, speaking of the duality in Hemingway's black male characters, states this contrast succinctly: "There are nurse figures… dedicated, thoughtful, and ministering… tender helpers" (*Playing* 82) "The *other side* of nursing… is the figure of destruction—the devouring predator… always hungry[;] these figures are nevertheless seductive, elusive, and theatrical in their combination of power and deceit, love and death" (emphasis added, *Playing* 84). With Amy and Beloved, Morrison has divided and feminized the dualistic black nurse figure in Hemingway's fiction. Only an imaginary, fictive white woman, it appears, can be as altruistic as Amy Denver and regard a black woman as human, not animal; only an imaginary, fictive black woman, by contrast, can be as demonic, dangerous, beautiful, and voracious as Beloved. With Amy and Beloved, Morrison personifies love taken to its extremes of altruism and voracity.

Love, in the form of Amy Denver, is rendered incarnate through the magic, the transcendent power, of the dance. As aforementioned, Sethe compares Denver's kicking in the womb to an antelope (30, 31, 34). In the "antelope" dance performed by Sethe's mother, slaves "shifted shapes and became something *other*. Some unchained, demanding *other*" (emphasis added, 31). By the phrase, "danced the antelope" (31), I assume that Morrison is referring to the dance performed by a specific brotherhood group, the tyiwara (chiwara), within the Bambara (Baumana or Banmana) tribe of Mali. The tyiwara dancers often wear headdresses decorated with carved wooden antelopes (Huet 50–52) as they scuff up earth with their dancing feet symbolically preparing it for penetration, that is, planting. Referring to the symbolism of the tyiwara, Morrison states that Denver "pawed the ground of her womb with impatient hooves" (30). Denver, performing this fertility dance in her mother's womb, has shaped or called Amy Denver to bring Sethe's incipient fertility to fruition.

In contrast to Africa, where dance and the body were considered integral to spiritual expression, mainstream Western religions have frequently, though not consistently, embraced a dualism that conceives of the body and spirit as separate and distinct, of the spirit or the soul as a pure immaterial entity trapped within a corrupt material body. Morrison's use of dance as a vehicle for spiritual transcendence seems to represent a subtle opposition to that dualism. Her position is consistent not only with the African world view but with that expressed in Psalms, the literary context of Psalm 124. In Psalms, the worshipper is exhorted to "praise his name in the dance […] sing praises unto him with the timbrel and harp"(149:3); "Praise him with the timbrel and dance: praise him with stringed instruments and organs" (150:4). The Haggadah, too, alludes (though indirectly) to dance as an expression or instigator of fertility. *Pesah*, the Hebrew word usually translated as "Passover," may be derived "from the root 'dance' or 'leap,' connecting it with an ancient spring-festival... probably... the barley harvest."[16] Additionally, some Passover Haggadot (Bronstein 25) include portions of Song of Solomon, parts of which were traditionally recited by Ashkenazim[17] on Sabbath during Passover. This harks back to the time when *Pesah* celebrated the fertility of the earth. Solomon's love poem also furnished the titles of two earlier books by Toni Morrison, *Sula*, named for the "Shulamite" (Song of Solomon 6:13), and *Song of Solomon*.

The Song of Solomon serves as a subtext for *Beloved* as well. The Song celebrates spring and the delight of young lovers:

> [M]y beloved!
> Behold, he cometh
> leaping upon the mountains,
> skipping upon the hills.
> My beloved is like a roe
> or a young hart
> [...] the winter is past
> [...] flowers appear on the earth (Song of Solomon 2:8–12).

The biblical beloved, who dances like a young hart in praise of the fertility of the earth and of love, bears a striking similarity to Denver, who dances the antelope to precipitate the materialization of Amy, "beloved." Further, both Denver and the biblical beloved, dancing respectively the antelope and the hart, are similar to the tyiwara dancing the antelope to promote fertility. This kind of cross-cultural comparison is not alien to Morrison. She states, "I was a Classics minor.... There was something about the Greek chorus... that reminds me of what goes on in Black churches" (Jones and Vinson 176). Thus, Morrison's deployment of the phrase, "danced the antelope," has characteristically African and biblical precedents.

The language of Denver's birth narrative parallels the language of Psalm 124. "Beloved" and "Amy" are each connected etymologically to David's name and to his poetry. His 124th psalm's references to teeth, the sea, swallowing, and help also have their counterparts in the imagery Morrison has used to narrate the events leading to Denver's birth and the birth process itself. Sethe's flight from slavery is itself an exodus parallel to that described in the psalm: when Sethe runs away from Sweet Home, she is fleeing the "mossy teeth" (31) of white boys who held her down and nursed her by force. The correlate in Psalm 124 states, "Blessed [be] the LORD, who hath not given us [as] prey to their teeth." When Sethe hides from patrollers in the woods and hears the low voice of Amy Denver, she assumes Amy is another predatory teenage white boy. In defense, Sethe imagines herself to be an all-devouring snake: "'Look like I was just cold jaws grinding' [...] eager [...] to bite [...] to gnaw [...] 'hungry' [...] Like a snake. All jaws and hungry" (31). Amy reverses the metaphor and tells Sethe, "Thank your Maker I come along[....] Snake come along he bite you. Bear eat you up" (79).[18] When Sethe reaches the Ohio, she finds "a whole boat to steal. It had one oar," the relevance of which becomes clear later: "Sethe was looking at one mile of dark water, which would have to be *split* with one oar" (emphasis added, 83). Like the Red Sea, the "proud waters" of the psalm, the Ohio needs splitting by the Deity, whom Amy invokes saying, "Jesus looking at you" (83). When Sethe goes into labor, her baby is described as "drowning in its mother's [red] blood" (84), just as the waters of the Red Sea "had" almost "overwhelmed" and "gone over" the "soul" of the Israelites in Psalm 124. After Denver is delivered, the women wrapped the infant in "the rags they wore" as the water of the Ohio "sucked and swallowed itself beneath them" (85). Finally, when Sethe tells the story of Denver's birth, Amy is always associated with "help" or "helping" (8, 29, 92), and Psalm 124 states that "Our help [is] the name of the Lord."

That Denver nearly drowned in her mother's birth canal and was rescued by Amy is reminiscent of several incidents in Exodus and the Haggadah. Egyptian midwives were instructed by Pharoah to "kill" the sons of Hebrew women but refused to comply (Exodus 1:15–20). Like the Hebrew sons, Denver is saved by a midwife, Amy, who ignores the edicts of her government, which forbid aiding an escaping slave. When the biblical midwives refused to kill the Hebrew children, Pharoah ordered: "Every son that is born ye shall cast into the river, and every daughter ye shall save alive" (Exodus 1:22). This verse is quoted in the Haggadah (Wiesel 49). In response to this edict, Moses was set afloat in an ark on the Nile and saved. His name puns on the Hebrew "taken out of water" (Cruden 799). Similarly, Denver is taken from the waters of the Ohio as well as from the amniotic waters of her mother's womb.

Denver's watery birth anticipates her destiny as a savior of sorts. This imagery is extant in the psalm's reference to "waters" which "overwhelm" and from which the "soul is escaped." Emergence from water suggests baptism, the ritual which anoints the recipient as a reborn individual or as a savior.[19] Thus

Denver's immersion marks her as savior. As the novel approaches its climax, Morrison specifically refers to Denver's function as rescuer: "[Denver] would have to [...] go ask somebody for help"; "Somebody had to be saved, but unless Denver got work, there would be no one to save, no one to come home to, and no Denver either" (243, 252). When Denver asks her community for help and alerts them to the presence of Beloved, her actions trigger a chain of events which ultimately save her mother, save Denver, and heal her community.

## Suffering

While Denver's birth story serves to illustrate clearly and simply how *Beloved* conforms to the birth stage of Joseph Cambell's monomythic pattern (*Hero* 297–314), subsequent stages of the monomyth are enacted by multiple characters rather than a single hero. The next stage of the pattern, adventure (*Hero* 30, 36), is not glamorized in *Beloved*. In Morrison's book as in classical myths and biblical stories, adventure is pervaded with challenge as well as with suffering. Morrison explores the legal and religious roots of various characters' suffering, compares their suffering to that of biblical and mythical characters, and in so doing, implies a nuanced analysis of the etiology of American racism. She also demonstrates the devastating psychological effects of her characters' suffering.

In the Haggadah and in the Bible, the Israelites suffer from the indignities of slavery: "[T]he Egyptians ... set over them taskmasters to afflict them with their burdens" (Glatzer 43, Exodus 1:11); "God [heeded] ... our plight, our misery, and our oppression" (Bronstein 41, Wiesel 46, Deuteronomy 26:7). Various Haggadot furnish differing interpretations of the word "misery," but the word is usually emphasized through a discussion of its meaning. Bronstein's Haggadah links "misery" to the separation of husbands and wives under slavery (41). The Wiesel Haggadah states that "misery" refers to the drowning of Hebrew male children (49). Morrison's novel seems to echo the Haggadah when she capitalizes "misery" and labels the slaying of Beloved "the Misery" (171, 177). Morrison's characters, like the Israelites, suffer in slavery and during its aftermath, but the novel provides a broader range of narrative detail to reveal the interior lives of slaves.

Morrison's descriptions of the natural world furnish a setting that complements the subjective states of her characters; imagery from nature reflects or amplifies suffering. In particular, her depictions of freed and captured birds illustrate the devastating effects of slavery upon the psyche. The bird has been a symbol of slavery and freedom since David composed his psalms. Psalm 124 figures a snared bird to evoke the suffering of the enslaved Israelites, and Morrison extends the trope to endow birds with an instinctive apprehension of the nuances of slavery and freedom. Sethe "heard wings" when she recognized schoolteacher's hat outside 124. "Little hummingbirds stuck their needle beaks right through her headcloth into her hair and beat their wings" (163), reminding her that at Sweet Home, her "scalp was "prickly" and her "head itched like the devil. Like somebody was sticking fine needles in" (193) when she heard schoolteacher instructing his pupils to compartmentalize her human and animal characteristics. When Sethe took her children to the shed to slaughter them, "she flew, snatching up her children like a hawk on the wing; how her face beaked, how her hands worked like claws" (157). Her actions proclaim that her children belong to her, not a "master," that she is "escaped as a bird out of the snare of the fowlers." Sethe is free, like the freed Israelites, to determine what is best for her children. Paul D remembers that the rooster, Mister, seemed to mock Paul D's enslavement: Mister "sat right there on the tub looking at me. I swear he smiled. [...] Mister, he looked so... free. Better than me" (72). When Paul D worked in a chain gang, he "could hear doves" (107); the grunts of the guards were "like the doves'" sounds (108). Later, when Paul D's underground prison began to flood, threatening to drown him and his fellow prisoners, "the doves were nowhere in sight" (109). Like Noah's dove, they had flown to dry land. Paul D, as well, escapes.[20]

Like Paul D, Baby Suggs suffers under slavery and its aftermath. The death of Beloved transforms her from an inspiring preacher to a woman utterly bereft of faith and hope. As a lay preacher she had exhorted her followers to love their bodies: "Love [...] your flesh" (88). Her vision of God had been commensurate with that found in African religion, in Song of Solomon, and in some of the psalms identifying God's mercy with the body and flesh: "[T]hou [art] he that took me out of the womb: thou didst make me hope [when I was] upon my mother's breasts. I was cast upon thee from the womb: thou [art] my God from my mother's belly" (Psalms 22); Thou preparest a table before me in the presence of mine enemies: thou anointest my head with oil; my cup runneth over" (Psalms 23). After Beloved's death, Baby Suggs stops her services in the Clearing and states, "'He punish me'" (179). She thought that "she [had] made a mistake. That what she thought about what the heart and the body could do was wrong. The whitepeople came anyway. In her yard" (209)—thus defying the putative talismanic power of the psalm for which that property was named. She contends, "She had done everything right, and they came in her yard anyway. And she didn't know what to think" (209); "God puzzled her and she was too ashamed of Him to say so" (177).

In her spiritual anguish, she is like the Israelite Jacob, one who wrestles with God (Genesis 32). Jacob's name was changed to Israel ("God-wrestler") after he wrestled with God and was left with an injured hip: "the hollow of Jacob's thigh was out of joint, as he wrestled with him" (Genesis 32:25) Jacob's descendants, the nation of "God-wrestlers" called Israel, are redeemed in Psalm 124. Like Jacob, Baby Suggs had a "twisted hip" (89), and as an "Israelite"—as one who wrestles or struggles with God—Baby Suggs merits redemption. But whereas Jacob "prevailed" (Genesis 32:28) with God, Baby Suggs, after years of praying and working, chooses to relinquish faith in God's power to overcome whitefolks who "came anyway." She finally tires of wrestling the angel: "Her marrow was tired" (177). A latter-day Job, she can see no cause for her affliction. Her faith in God's redemptive power, like her granddaughter and her eight children (5, 8), is a casualty of slavery, of school-teacher, of unjust law. The apostle Paul states, "[T]he law was our schoolmas-ter[....] But after that faith is come, we are no longer under a schoolmaster" (Galatians 3:24–25). Morrison has reversed this sequence: Baby Suggs had faith, but afterwards, the law and schoolteacher shake her faith.[21] Ultimately, she does, like Job, cling fast to her integrity (Job 27:5) as far as her veneration of the body is concerned. Though God, in her view, seems to punish her for putting Christmas to shame, she never relinquishes faith in her gospel of the body. Baby Suggs tells Denver that she should "always listen to [her] body and love it" (209).

Her friend, Stamp Paid, realizes that God's seeming abandonment was not the sole cause of Baby Suggs's "fatigue" (177). He thinks that "to have [the] community step back and hold itself at a distance—well, it could wear out even a Baby Suggs, holy" (177). He gives voice to Toni Morrison's own concern with community. Speaking of the black community in *Beloved*, Morrison states, "They took the sense of community for granted. It never occurred to them they could live outside of it. There was no life out there, and they wouldn't have chosen it anyway. Those were the days of Black people who really loved the company of other Black people" (Washington 235–236). Baby's "feast" included ninety people, "who ate so well, and laughed so much, it made them angry" (136). Her generosity has caused some in her communi-ty to envy her: "Loaves and fishes were His powers—they did not belong to an ex-slave"; "The scent of their disapproval lay heavy in the air" (137). Baby Suggs's suffering is caused by her community's envy and lassitude—their consequent failure to warn her of the slave catchers' approach—as well as her interior spiritual conflicts.

Other characters suffer from the anxiety precipitated by interior conflicts. Morrison tropes Song of Solomon to illustrate her characters' suffering. "I am Beloved and she is mine," (210 and 214) chants Beloved: "I see her take flowers away from leaves she puts them in a round basket the leaves are not for her" (210). The rhythm indicated by the spacing of these words is similar to that in the Bible's Song of Solomon:

> My beloved is gone down to his garden,
> To the beds of spices,
> To feed in the gardens,
> And to gather lilies.
> I am my beloved's, and my beloved is mine,
> That feedeth among the lilies. (Song of Solomon 6:2–3).

"I am Beloved and she is mine" implies that Beloved, although she has taken the shape of a twenty-year-old woman, has the mental age of an infant and does not see her self as differentiated from her mother's. When she imagines her mother's face, she exclaims, "'Over there. Her face.' Denver looks where Beloved's eyes go; there is nothing but darkness there. 'Whose face? Who is it?' [Denver asks.] 'Me. It's me'" (124). Beloved is incapable of viewing herself as autonomous; she sees herself as diffuse and ephemeral as darkness, akin to the Shulamite in Song of Solomon, who, Barbara Walker argues, "seems to have been no more than an ancient Canaanite title of the Goddess, Zulumat, 'Darkness'" (949). Beloved's love is infantile, that of a child who is not individuated: "I am not separate from her […] her face is my own" (210). The biblical poem, similarly, describes a boundless love that is ecstatic, transcendent, and fuses the identities—the *ownership*—of the two selves.

The biblical poem is a fitting referent for an African American novel. The woman of the biblical poem is described as "black, but comely" (Song of Solomon 1:5), or, in more recent translations, "black *and* radiant" (Falk, poem 2). The Song has been interpreted as an allegory of the love between God and the children of Israel or between Jesus and the church, but Morrison's interpretation is more nuanced. Jane Bakerman points out, "With fresh insight, Morrison echoes the Song's conflation of love and ownership to highlight an analogous distortion in the institution of slavery, a conundrum which

Morrison explores in-depth throughout the novel. As Morrison has stated, 'Too frequently love has to do with owning that other person'" (Bakerman 42). The word "mine," used frequently in most translations of the biblical Song and repeated in the novel as a kind of litany to introduce several chapters (200, 210, 214), indicates possession. Sethe's friend Stamp Paid comes to her house and hears "a conflagration of hasty voices[....] All he could make out was the word *mine*" (172). The possessive love shared by Sethe and Beloved is ultimately fatal.

Morrison's novel thereby brings to the fore perhaps the most tragic result of slavery—that it inculcates in the slave an inability to conceive of love dissociated from the paradigm of ownership and a reluctance to love wholeheartedly. There is an emotional risk when *any* lovers dissolve the boundaries of their autonomous selves and "own" one another. For slaves, who literally do not own themselves, intermingling of identities is particularly threatening to the sense of self. For the slave, tragically, indifference is often preferable to love. Sethe's mother-in-law, Baby Suggs, after having three children sold, "would not" (23) love the rest of her children. After Sethe has given birth to Denver, her rescuer, a former slave named Ella, looks at the newborn and advises Sethe, "If anybody was to ask me I'd say, 'Don't love nothing'" (92). When Sethe tells her friend, Paul D that she "can't hear a word against" (45) Denver, Paul D labels Sethe's love "very risky." He explains, "For a used-to-be-slave woman to love anything that much was dangerous, especially if it was her children she had settled on to love. The best thing, he knew, was to love just a little bit; everything, just a little bit, so when they broke its back, or shoved it in a croaker sack, well, maybe you'd have a little love left over for the next one" (45).

After Sethe escapes slavery, she is able to love her children more than a little. She informs Paul D, "I loved em more after I got here. Or maybe I couldn't love em proper in Kentucky because they wasn't mine to love. But when I got here, when I jumped down off that wagon—there wasn't nobody in the world I couldn't love if I wanted to" (162). With freedom comes the freedom to love without reservation. The mother-child bond provides the model for all our subsequent loves, but motherlove is not as uncomplicated as it appears from the vantage point of the child. Sethe reminds us that being a mother means "Needing to be good enough, alert enough, strong enough, *that* caring—again. Having to stay alive just that much longer. [...] Unless carefree, motherlove was a killer" (132). The most visceral expression of maternal love is nursing, thus by stealing her milk, Sethe's masters metaphorically steal the love Sethe wants to lavish on her own child.

The ownership of one human being by another is heinous in slavery and, as Morrison demonstrates, destructive in love. Sethe prefers to own Beloved in death rather than allowing her to be owned in slavery, a fate she believes to be worse than death. Out of love, she slaughters her child. Morrison does not criminalize Sethe, but sympathizes with her. The book invites the reader to question the notion of ownership, not solely in the context of slavery, but in the realm of love as well.[22] Even under the most dire of circumstances, or the most idyllic, does anyone, even a parent, have the right to *own* another person? The evil of slavery is that its central notion, the idea of ownership, can pervert even the most sublime ideal: love.

That ownership in love is infantile and destructive is emphasized in the book's closing chapters. Beloved, reincarnated, wants to possess Sethe totally, selfishly, as most infants do their mothers. Sethe, in turn, becomes so obsessed with her reincarnated daughter that she stops working and nearly starves herself to keep Beloved fed. Significantly, Denver's monologue does not state that Beloved is "mine," but rather that "Beloved is my sister" (205). Denver, who has been cruelly excluded from this intense dyad, asks the community to help save her mother. Because Denver has been excluded from the neurotic version of love her mother and sister have developed, she is capable of saving her mother by sending her sister, once again, to the other side.

Sethe, tired of her life's hardships and disappointments, racked with remorse for her child's death and bereaved of her Beloved, goes to bed to die. When Paul D visits her, she tells him that Beloved was "my best thing" (272). Sethe conceives of herself as the owner of her child, but has not achieved a sense of self-ownership. As Morrison explains it, "Freeing yourself was one thing; claiming ownership of that freed self was another" (95). Paul D, in the spirit of St. Paul's[23] epistle to the "not beloved," brings Sethe a redemptive message. He reminds Sethe that freedom means self-ownership: "You your best thing, Sethe. You are" (273). With characteristic courage, Sethe and Paul D are once more willing to attempt love—not the possessive love of the verse, "My beloved is mine and I am his" (Song of Solomon 2:16), but the more mature love of their friend Sixo: "She is a friend of my mind. [...] The pieces I am, she gather them and give them *back to me* in all the right order" (emphasis added, 272–273). In Sixo's version of love, the lover encourages self-ownership, as Paul does with Sethe and as the Song of Solomon declares: "This [is] my beloved and this [is] my friend" (5:16).

Until the end of the novel, Sethe suffers as both god and scapegoat. Like God the Father, Sethe is goddess/creator and sacrificer of Beloved. Morrison's symbolism has linked Sethe, Denver, and Beloved to Demeter and other goddesses.[24] One of Demeter's titles is "Corn Goddess" (Grimal 131); Sethe and Halle consummated their marriage in the corn (26–27). "Greek *meter* is 'mother'" (Walker 218), and Demeter served for a time as a "wet-nurse" (Grimal 133); Sethe, similarly, has "milk enough for all" (100). Since Demeter's "Mysteries" were brought to Greece from Egypt (Graves, *Myths* 201), she was "identified in ancient times with the Egyptian Isis" (Grant and Hazel 106), who swallowed Osiris, brought him back to life under another name, dismembered him, and reassembled him (Walker 455). Demeter, too, is a flesh-eating goddess, having eaten the flesh of Pelops (Graves, *Myths* 387). Similarly, Beloved imagines her mother swallowing her (213). Sethe had nearly dismembered Beloved, had "to hold her face so her head would stay on" (251), and Denver, too, imagines Sethe cutting off her head (206). Beloved's monologue pictures Sethe with a basket (210), one of Demeter's attributes (Eliade section 5.84). Like Demeter with Persephone, Sethe retrieves her daughter, temporarily, from the land of the dead. Demeter is often "portrayed ... with ... a serpent" (Grimal 133), and appropriately, Sethe imagines herself as a snake (31). Robert Graves mentions an Ethiopian mythology, *Legends of Our Lady Mary*, which posits the biblical Seth as an earlier incarnation of Jesus to whom the Virgin comes (*White* 162–163). Sethe is clearly a goddess figure, and in myths that reflect the transition from matriarchal to patriarchal systems, goddesses or their priestesses can play the role of scapegoats.

Morrison alludes several times to the scapegoat ethos. Sethe was nursed by schoolteacher's nephews "like the cow, no, the goat, back behind the stable because it was too nasty to stay in with the horses" (200). Schoolteacher beats Sethe after she tells Mrs. Garner how he abused her (202), displacing the punishment for his own sin to her innocent back. Like a scapegoat, she suffers for schoolteacher's sins, a metaphor Morrison intensifies with the tree-shaped scar—a figure for the cross—on Sethe's back. She both sacrifices her child and bears a cross on her back as does Jesus.[25] In another reference to the scapegoat dynamic, Sethe's employer, Sawyer, exploits her as his namesake Tom Sawyer exploited Jim. Morrison has discussed the "fatal ending" of Huckleberry Finn at length in *Playing in the Dark* (55–57). Her characters also refer pejoratively to Tom Sawyer in *Song of Solomon* (81). In *Beloved*, Sawyer uses Sethe, her racial identity in particular, to fulfill the role of scapegoat in his life story: "He used to be a sweet man. Patient, tender in his dealings with his help. But each year, following the death of his son in the War, he grew more and more crotchety. As though Sethe's dark face was to blame" (191). In Sawyer's skewed view, Sethe carries the sin of his son's killer upon her back.

Sethe functions as a scapegoat for members of the black community of Cincinnati as well. They had envied Baby Suggs's good fortune and had failed to warn Sethe and Baby Suggs that schoolteacher was on his way:

> [N]obody ran on ahead; [...] nobody sent a fleet-footed son to cut 'cross a field soon as they saw the four horses in town[....] Nobody warned them[....] [M]eanness [...] let them stand aside, or not pay attention, or tell themselves somebody else was probably bearing the news already to the house on Bluestone[....] Maybe they just wanted to know if Baby really was special, blessed in some way they were not. (157)

The community thus bears some, albeit slight, responsibility for Beloved's death, as well as for the travesty of Baby Suggs's funeral, when Sethe's neighbors refused to enter her house. Though Sethe is directly responsible for Beloved's death, and America, which should never have legalized slavery, bears the greatest burden of responsibility, Sethe's neighbors must feel some guilt for their failure to sound the alarm and save her from "the wrath [...] the teeth [...] the snare" (Psalm 124) of her enslavers. The ethos in the African American community was one of mutual protection from the ravages of racism. They were a cohesive Christian community that presumably was aware of God's biblical injunctions to the Israelites, freed slaves like themselves in passages such as "Thou shalt not avenge, nor bear any grudge against the children of thy people, but thou shalt love thy neighbour as thyself" (Leviticus 19:17–8; Also see Matthew 22:39, Mark 12:31, Luke 10:27 and "Thou shalt not [...] stand against the blood of thy neighbor" (Leviticus 19:16). Guilty of their sins of omission, they draw away from Sethe, ostensibly for her pride: "Was her head a bit too high? Her back a little too straight? Probably. Otherwise the singing would have begun [...] Some cape of sound [...] to hold and steady her on the way" (152) to jail after the death of her Beloved. Her neighbors fail to sing her to jail, not only because they resent her pride, but because they are focused on transferring their own sin of omission to her proud back—focused on making her their scapegoat.[26]

Paul D rejects this notion of substitutional atonement. When Denver is rude to him, he and Sethe quarrel, and he whispers, "Jesus," then exclaims, "Jesus! I said Jesus!" Sethe apologizes for Denver, but Paul D rejects the apology: "You can't apologize for nobody. She [Denver] got to do that" (44). The proximity of Paul D's "Jesus" to his rejection of the concept of substitutional atonement implies that either Jesus or no one is entitled to atone for others' sins. Paul is censuring Sethe's presumptuousness in casting herself in Jesus's role. Though she attempts to act the role of the Great Mother to her children, Paul D's comment foresees that she cannot be their deity or their scapegoat, and certainly, she cannot function as scapegoat for her entire community.

The novel takes a complex, seemingly contradictory, view towards Sethe's affiliation with deities. Morrison's rhetoric connects Sethe to Demeter, Isis, and Jesus, but Paul D sees her as a vulnerable mortal woman. This apparent discrepancy dissolves when *Beloved* is read as collective memory frozen at the moment of crossing the (always nebulous) border into myth. The novel represents historical persons, the ex-slave Margaret Garner and her family, in the process of transition from history to myth.[27] Garner had escaped from Kentucky and killed her daughter to prevent her return to slavery. Morrison read the story in old newspapers, and it inspired *Beloved*. The novel's narrative technique, especially its apparent contradictions, is a fictive rendering of the process by which history develops into myth. Some people and their stories are larger than life, and as these narratives are retold and revised, such historical events and charismatic personalities are extraordinary enough to transcend death and time, becoming timeless myths of immortal gods and heroes.

## Sacrifice

In traditional myths, sacrifice, death, or a journey to the "other side" is the culmination of a hero's temporal suffering. The sacrifice frequently confers some benefit to those left behind in the phenomenal world. Sethe's sacrifice of Beloved is thus comparable to God's sacrifice of Jesus in Gospels and the sacrifice of the Israelites' pascal lamb. The Haggadah paraphrases Exodus 12: "[The sacrifice of the lamb] is the Passover sacrifice for God who passed over the houses of the Children of Israel in Egypt, when He killed the Egyptians and spared our houses" (Wiesel 66). The sacrifices of Jesus, Lamb of God, and of the pascal lambs were prerequisites, respectively, for freedom from past sin and redemption from slavery; and as Jacqueline Trace has noted, the sacrifice of Beloved buys freedom of a sort for Sethe and her remaining children (20). Though one might argue that Sethe's remorse is as cruel and domineering as any "master"—that it enslaves her, that the freedom she gains is illusory—in Sethe's own view, slavery is so horrific that her sacrifice is justified. Sethe conceives of Beloved's murder as an act of love: "I took and put my babies where they'd be safe" (164). Sethe believed the sacrifice of Beloved afforded the child genuine freedom. God's sacrifice of Jesus, his "Beloved Son," like Sethe's sacrifice of her daughter Beloved, conflates love and death—is regarded, simultaneously, as a painful death and as an act of divine love that frees Jesus (and the world) from pain and death. Slave religion embraced an analogous rationale: the distinction between freedom in this world and the glory of life after death was vague, to say the least. "Death was the passage to freedom where," in the words of a spiritual, "Dere's no whips a-crackin', / O, yes I want to go home," where "dere's no stormy weather, / O, yes, I want to go home" (quoted in Raboteau 261). As Raboteau explains, "Important though it is to recognize that the spirituals sometimes expressed the slaves' desire for freedom in this world as well as in the next, it is at least as important to understand the profound connection between the other world and this world in the religious consciousness of the slaves" (250). When Sethe killed Beloved, in her own mind she was giving her daughter the freedom that the spirituals praised again and again.

The dual interpretation of spirituals might pertain to Psalm 124 as well. The psalm may praise the freedom found on "the other side" of temporal life as well as the freedom from chattel slavery. The psalm may be interpreted as what Campbell calls a "night-sea journey," in which mythic heroes are immersed in a sea or in darkness, or are consumed by whales or other beasts. Night-sea journeys represent the hero's excursion to what Campbell calls "the World Womb" (*Hero* 92). Jesus's entombment, Moses's sojourn in the bulrushes, and Jonah's days in the belly of the whale, Campbell suggests, are all night-sea journeys in prelude to rebirth (*Hero* 90–95).

In Morrison's myth, Beloved, though she is unwilling and unprepared for the journey, functions as a hero who, as Campbell phrases it, "ventures forth from the world of common day into a region of supernatural wonder" (*Hero* 30). Thus, when Beloved is slain, she does not find the freedom from strife afforded by "Sweet Canaan" of the slave spiritual. Instead, she undertakes a night-sea journey and ultimately, though inadvertently, brings "back from [her]. . . adventure the means for the regeneration of. . . [her] society" (Campbell, *Hero* 38). "I am not dead," Beloved complains (211). She seems to be "overwhelmed" by the "waters," "swallowed," "prey to [the] teeth" that Psalm 124 describe: see her comments, "I was there in the water" (215) and "she chews and swallows me" (213). As Morrison explains in an interview, Beloved is both Sethe's "child returned to her from the dead. . . [and] a survivor from the true, factual slave ship" (Darling 247). The "other side" as described by

Beloved is both womb and tomb, a slave ship where she crouches in the fetal position. She experiences an indeterminate time/space wherein she lacks a single autonomous ego. Instead, she perceives a mutual collective memory of slave ships—"I am always crouching. . . and watching others who are crouching" (210); "I cannot fall because there is no room to" (211). Her lack of "self " is a prelude to rebirth. As Campbell explains, "The passage of the threshold is a form of self-annihilation... a transit into a sphere of rebirth" (*Hero* 90).[28] Beloved wants to die on the slave ship—"we are all trying to leave our bodies behind" (210)—and melds the desire to escape the restrictive bounds of her own flesh with a paradoxical desire to return to the womb her mother. Beloved states, "She [...] chewed me" (214): "She chews and swallows" (216). Whether through death and a consequent merging with the dead or through a merging with her mother, Beloved seeks to discard her individuality. Her vision of consumption by her mother is analogous to the protoypical hero's "night-sea journey" to the "World Womb," a "life-renewing, life-centering act" (Campbell, *Hero* 92).

Although Beloved does not die on the "other side," others on the slave ship do die, and Morrison uses imagery from the psalm to describe their dying. A man "fighting hard to leave his body which is a small bird trembling" (210–211) is similar to the psalm's "soul escaped as a bird out of a 'snare.'" The implication is that Beloved and those on the slave ships who do not die remain—"the black and angry dead" (198)—poised for rebirth, ready to haunt us, to bestir us from our complacency.

Slain, banished to the other world, Beloved and the dead on the slave ship function as scapegoats for both the black and white communities. They bear the sins of others upon their heads. Beloved embodies the idea of the black jungle predator (Bowers 67) and carries upon her head the sin of the white community's senseless cruelty. David Lawrence refers to Beloved as a "scapegoat for evils of the past" (198). She also bears the black community's sin of omission, the sin of forgetting. As Morrison explains, "Afro-Americans in rushing away from slavery... also rushed away from slaves because it was painful to dwell there, and they may have abandoned some responsibilities in so doing. It was a double-edged sword, if you understand me" (Darling 247). Morrison continues, "The purpose of making... [Beloved] real is making history possible, making memory real" (Darling 249). Morrison brings that sin of omission, the sin of forgetting, back to haunt her fictional community in Cincinnati as well as her community of readers. Though both black and white communities want to forget Beloved and get on with their day-to-day lives, resurrected, she reminds white readers of their sins and black readers of a heritage of unspeakable suffering. She brings the guilt that survivors of trauma frequently repress to the surface (Bettelheim 33).

## Resurrection

Beloved's emergence from the waters of the creek concludes her night-sea journey in a baptismal immersion-rebirth sequence. As Joseph Campbell states:

> To enter into [the baptismal] ... font is to plunge into the mythological realm; to break the surface is to cross the threshold into the night-sea. Symbolically, the infant makes the journey when the water is poured on its head.... Few of us have any inkling of the sense of the rite of baptism.... [I]t clearly appears in the words of Jesus: "Verily, verily, I say unto thee, Except a man be born again, he cannot see the kingdom of God ... Except a man be born of water and the spirit, he cannot enter into the kingdom of God." (*Hero* 251, see also John 3:3–5)

The sacrament of baptism symbolizes a night-sea journey and gives the baptized person new life. Several other allusions to baptism or night-sea journey linked to the attainment of freedom, new life as a free person, occur in *Beloved*. Denver's birth, as has been mentioned, is similar to baptism. Sethe is bathed by Baby Suggs when she is freed (93), embraces Paul D in the bath (100), and anticipates being bathed by Paul D when he encourages her to initiate a new life with him at her side. Paul D's prison is flooded (110), immersing him and enabling his escape, his rebirth, as a free man. The novel culminates in a baptism of sound— "a wave of sound wide enough to sound deep water and [...] Sethe [...] trembled like the baptized in its wash" (261).

Beloved's resurrection is instigated by the power of imagination, that of Morrison, Sethe, and Denver. As is typical of survivors described by Bettelheim, Sethe is traumatized.[29] She loves Beloved with enough power (4) to generate a sense of remorse that resurrects the past. As Andrew Levy has pointed out, "*Beloved*... is... a novel where the past literally returns in corporeal form" (119). In my view, the power of Sethe's love and remorse contributes to the revival of the slain Beloved, first as an invisible baby ghost and later as a corporeal nineteen- or twenty-year-old ghost. Sethe's remorse is not so much for killing Beloved as over her failure to kill herself and her other children, inadvertently leaving Beloved alone on the "other side" (203).

Rationalizing her actions to Beloved, "Sethe cried, saying she never did, or meant to—[…] That her plan was always that they would all be together on the other side" (241).

Morrison has apparently modeled Beloved as an incarnation of Emily Dickinson's description of remorse:

> REMORSE—is Memory—awake—
> Her Parties all astir—A Presence of Departed Acts—
> At window—and at Door—
> Its Past—set down before the Soul
> And lighted with a Match—
> Perusal—to facilitate—
> And help Belief to stretch—
>
> Remorse is cureless—the Disease
> Not even God—can heal—
> For 'tis His institution—and
> The Adequate of Hell— (Number 744, page 365)

Dickinson, like Morrison, provides discerning insight regarding the nature of remorse—its intimacy with the memory and the past.[30] Beloved reifies Dickinson's metaphors. After Beloved died, Sethe "couldn't lay down nowhere in peace" (204). She "worked hard to *remember* as close to nothing as was safe. Unfortunately her brain was devious" (emphasis added, 6). Beloved, as a baby ghost, makes "a pool of red and undulating light" inside the "door" (8). Later, Beloved "was in the window at two when Sethe returned, or the doorway" (57). Sethe wants to beat "back the past" (73) that causes her remorse. Beloved is compared repeatedly to a devil or a witch, "adequates of hell." Paul D calls Beloved a "lowdown something that looked like a sweet young girl" (127), "a room-and-board witch" (164). The "coloredwomen" say Sethe is "bedeviled" by her resurrected daughter; Ella imagines Beloved is "the devil himself" (255, 256), and the neighborhood women see her as a "devil-child" (261).

Beloved's ghost is a powerful manifestation of Sethe's love and its con-comitant remorse, but remorse is not the sole impetus for Beloved's haunting presence. Beloved's younger sister, Denver, seemingly has the magical ability to bring the dead back to life and to maintain life. Sethe called Denver "charmed" not only because, dancing the antelope, she pulled Amy out of a hill, but also because the rats in Sethe's jail cell "bit everything in there" (42) except Denver, a month-old baby. As a little girl, Denver conjures her dead sister Beloved into existence, almost as a child's imaginary friend. Denver calls her "my secret company" and relates, "Ever since I was little she was my company and she helped me wait for my daddy" (205). Denver later asks the resurrected Beloved, "Don't you remember we played together by the stream?" (75). Denver "knew the downright pleasure of enchantment, of not suspecting but *knowing* the things behind things. [...] None could appreciate the safety of ghost company" (37) except Denver. Beloved seems to be a projection of Denver, a projection that expresses the forbidden emotions Denver represses. When Denver begins to fear and resent her mother, the ghost's personality reflects the change in Denver: "[T]he monstrous and unmanageable dreams about Sethe found release in the concentration Denver began to fix on the baby ghost [...] it held for her all the anger, love and fear she didn't know what to do with[....] From then on the presence was full of spite. Instead of sighs and accidents there was pointed and deliberate abuse" (103–104).

When Paul D comes to visit, he chases away the baby ghost, and Denver, bereft, resents "the man who had gotten rid of the only other company she had" besides her mother. At this juncture, the narrator turns to other characters, and when Denver's storyline is taken up again, she is enclosed by the circular boxwood temple she calls her "emerald closet" (37), a structure reminiscent of Demeter's earliest cult centers, known as *tholi*—tombs that "represented the womb of the Goddess from which rebirth might come" (Walker 218). The *tholos* is "a beehive-shaped ghost-house... [probably] of African origin, and introduced into Greece by way of Palestine" (Graves, *Myths* 181). Denver's "secret house" (209) is also beehive-shaped: "five boxwood bushes, planted in a ring, had started stretching toward each other four feet off the ground to form a round, empty room seven high, its walls fifty inches of murmuring leaves" (28). The *tholos* tomb of Greece and Africa was entered through a "short vaginal passage" (Walker 218). Similarly, Denver can only enter her emerald closet "[b]ent low" to "crawl into this room" (28). Morrison makes the parallel to matriarchal spirituality explicit here, thus associating Denver, as in the instance of the antelope dance, with Africa and with the power to extract life from the jaws of death, for the power to resurrect the dead was held by the priestesses of Demeter.

Denver's *tholos* demonstrates a continuity of cultural and religious practice from Africa to Greece to African America. Greek, Judeo-Christian, and African myth and religion have enriched Morrison's work. She states, "In *Song of Solomon*, ... I used... biblical names to show the impact of the Bible on the lives of black people.... I also used some pre-Christian names to give the sense of mixture of cosmologies" (LeClair 126). Morrison not only practices a kind of cultural syncretism in her fiction, but excoriates the marginalization of Africa's role in the historiography of Western civilization: "The satisfaction I have always received from reading Greek tragedy... is in its similarity to Afro-American communal structures (the function of song and chorus, the heroic struggle between the claims of community and individual hubris) and African religion and philosophy" ("Unspeakable" 202).

African American Denver, in her womb-like "temple of boxwood" (50), magically arranges Beloved's rebirth. Denver's world is "flat, mostly, with the exception of an emerald closet[....] Her mother had secrets [...] Denver had them too. And hers were sweet—sweet as lily-of-the-valley cologne" (37–38). Denver's "lily-of-the-valley" is Beloved, named after the "Beloved" woman in the Song of Solomon (2:1–4), who was "a lily-of-the-valley."[31] With the disappearance of the baby ghost, Denver had sought comfort in her emerald closet: "During the first days after Paul D moved in, Denver stayed in her emerald closet as long as she could, lonely as a mountain[....] So when she saw the black dress with two unlaced shoes beneath it she trembled with secret thanks. Whatever her *power* and however she used it, Beloved was *hers*" (emphasis added, 104).

The resurrection of Beloved loosely parallels the resurrection of Jesus in Gospels, the saving of the Israelites in Psalm 124 and the Haggadah, and the visitation of Elijah during the Passover meal. As the Haggadah states, "Legend has it that Elijah returns to earth, from time to time.... This man of mystery became associated with the End of Days, with the Messianic hopes of our people.... Hence, he has a place in every Seder. We open the door that he may enter, and set a cup of wine to represent the final Messianic promise" (Bronstein 68). When Sethe, Denver, and Paul D open the door of 124 to Beloved, a visitor, like Elijah, from the "other side," they trigger a series of events that culminate in the (transitory) redemption of their community from the shackles of its past.

Resurrected, Beloved displays little curiosity about her own rebirth, but she is fascinated with the story of Denver's birth, and to amuse her sister, Denver tells her birth story. During the narration, Denver realizes, "This was the part of the story she loved [...] but she hated it too because it made her feel like a bill was owing somewhere and she, Denver, had to pay it. But whom she owed or what to pay it with eluded her" (77). The part of the story Denver loves is Amy, who saved Denver from "drowning" in her "mother's blood" (84), snatched her from the other side, and brought her into this world. Though she is unaware of it, Denver has repaid Amy Denver (onomastically "the other side of Beloved") "the bill that was owing." Denver has coaxed Amy's black side—Beloved—into this world from the other side where she, like Denver in the womb, may have been drowning. Beloved comes to 124 after she "walked out of [...] water"; "Everything hurt but her lungs most of all [.... She was] breathing shallow [... and] had what sounded like asthma" (50). As Trudier Harris points out, Beloved's resurrection follows the "African belief that the demise of the body is not the end of being" (154). In Chinua Achebe's "Things Fall Apart," a medicine man tells of "wicked children who, when they died, entered their mother's wombs to be born again" (81). That Beloved's return is accompanied by Sethe's water breaking (51) seems to link her with this African belief.

Morrison's narrator compares Denver to an author/creator who gives "blood to the scraps" (78) of Sethe's and Baby Suggs's briefer versions of her birth story. The metaphor is a double entendre since Denver's conjurings, the resurrections she catalyzes, have endowed Beloved and Amy with blood and flesh. Morrison here seems to say that fiction and fictional characters, like ghosts, impinge as powerfully and effectively as history upon the "real" world of flesh-and-blood people. Beloved is well aware that her physical integrity is dependent upon the imaginations of Denver and Sethe; when they are not thinking of her, she begins to disintegrate. While Sethe is occupied making love to Paul D, Beloved loses a tooth (133). She thinks, "Next would be her arm, her hand, a toe. Pieces of her would drop maybe one at a time, maybe all at once. Or on one of those mornings before Denver woke and after Sethe left she would fly apart. It is difficult keeping her head on her neck, her legs attached [...] when she is *by herself*" (emphasis added, 133). And ultimately, Beloved disappears when she is psychologically by herself for the first time— when both Sethe and Denver are cognitively oblivious of her. As the novel draws to an end, Sethe holds Beloved's hand but drops it to attempt to slay Edward Bodwin, whom Sethe mistakenly identifies with schoolteacher. While her neighbors and Denver prevent Sethe's crazed murder attempt, Beloved is left "[s]tanding alone [... H]er hand is empty. Sethe is running away from her [...] and she feels the emptiness in the hand Sethe has been holding. Now she is running into the faces of the people [...] leaving Beloved behind. Alone. Again. Then Denver, running too. Away from her" (262). Left alone, Beloved disintegrates. Her existence has been dependent upon Sethe's and Denver's imaginations, just as the existence of the novel relies upon the reader's suspension of disbelief.

## Eucharist

Beloved's disappearance is not final. People in the community project her image onto the pictures of their loved ones and find her footprints in the mud, footprints that change to fit the size and shape of anyone who steps into them. Beloved—a symbol of the forgotten American slave—is within each person, each reader, who has heard of her or perceived the most ephemeral evidence of her passing. But the memory of her has been repressed: "They forgot her like a bad dream [...] all trace is gone" (274–5).

Until *Beloved*, a Eucharist of sorts, no sacrificial blood was given "to the scraps." No blood or body was consumed to remember—to internalize the memory of—Beloved. Morrison's book is Eucharistic in its comparisons of eating to reading, in its frequent juxtapositions of episodes of storytelling and images of eating or food preparation, and finally, in its inclusion of three symbolic Eucharists in the novel. In conversation, she states that a novel's purpose is to re-member the past and to give nourishment: "Novels ought to identify those things in the past that are useful ... and they ought to give nourishment" (LeClair 121). Novels, then, are similar to communion, in which the Christian remembers the life and crucifixion of Jesus, "beloved Son." The communicant internalizes—eats—that memory, thus integrating Jesus with the self. In kind, Morrison desires that readers consume or internalize her ideas and her *Beloved*/Beloved: "I do want to penetrate the readerly subconsciousness so that the response is ... very somatic, visceral, a physical response so that you really think you see it or you can smell it" (Moyers 274). She, in her own words, "like[s] to dust off... clichés, dust off the language, make them mean whatever they may have meant originally.... [T]he books that mean something—treat old ideas.... [N]arrative remains the best way to learn anything, whether history or theology" (LeClair 122–3). *Beloved* dusts off the cliché of the Eucharist and revitalizes it.

Morrison's narrative deliberately associates food and food preparation with storytelling and memory. When Sethe and Denver tell Beloved stories of the past, "It bec[omes] a way to feed her" (58). When Sethe learns from Paul D that Halle witnessed her humiliation and succumbed to insanity, she "[shakes] her head from side to side, resigned to her rebellious brain. [...] Like a greedy child it snatched up everything. Just once, could it say, No thank you? I just ate and can't hold another bite? I am full God damn it [...] I am still full [...] I don't want to [...] remember that. [...] But her brain was [...l]oaded with the past and hungry for more" (70). Similarly, Denver tells Beloved stories "like a lover whose pleasure was to overfeed the loved" (78).

The storytelling and auditing within Morrison's novels provide a model for the relationship between Morrison and her readers, enabling the reader/consumer to internalize the story of Beloved (symbol of the forgotten slave) or to elevate a repressed memory of Beloved, of slavery, to the level of consciousness. This is what the first Eucharist was intended to do: renew or instill within the communicant the memory of the "*beloved* Son." The stories in *Beloved* are comparable to the Passover *matzoth*, labeled in the Bible and Haggadah as the bread of affliction (Deuteronomy 16:3, Wiesel 23, Bronstein 26), and subsequently sacralized in the Gospels as communion wafers, the *body* of Jesus, "beloved Son."

During Passover, and presumably, at the Last Supper, the baking and eating of bread was associated with memory and storytelling: "Why do we eat unleavened bread? ... As the Bible says: '... they baked the dough... into unleavened cakes; it did not rise, because they were driven out of Egypt and could not delay' [Exodus 12:39]" (Wiesel 66). Morrison, too, associates bread preparation with storytelling and memory: "Sethe [...] opened the oven door and slid the pan of biscuits in. [...s]he felt Paul D behind her[....] There was something blessed in his manner Women saw him and wanted [...] to tell him [...] things they only told each other" (17). Sethe compares kneading "dough" with "the day's serious work of beating back the past," but paradoxically, "working dough" (73) is associated by the narrator with memory and storytelling: "[Sethe] scooped half a handful of lard. Deftly she squeezed the flour through it, then with her left hand sprinkling water, she formed the dough. 'I had milk.' she said. 'I was pregnant with Denver [...]' Now she rolled the dough out with a wooden pin. 'Anybody could smell me long before he saw me'" (16). The story she tells, like that told at Passover and at the Last Supper, is a story of slavery and of exodus, a story associated with the first Eucharist. The Haggadah connects episodes of storytelling to the consumption of foods intended to reinforce the process of memory. Morrison's association of food with story is thus reminiscent of the Passover celebration at which the Eucharist was instituted.

Reifying Eucharistic symbolism, the *blood* of the "beloved" is consumed by characters in the novel. After Sethe kills Beloved, Denver drinks her sister's blood: "Sethe was aiming a bloody nipple into the baby's mouth[....] Denver took her mother's milk right along with the blood of her sister" (152). Denver's power to maintain or resurrect life seems to derive, in part, from this Eucharist:

"Grandma Baby [...] told me [...] I shouldn't be afraid of the ghost. It wouldn't harm me because I tasted its blood" (209). Denver's redemption from chattel slavery is purchased with her sister's blood.

Denver's suckling is one of three "suppers" that advance the eucharistic themes Morrison explores throughout the novel: the survival/remembrance of the beloved, redemption from sin/the past, and redemption from enslavement. Having partaken of her sister's blood, Denver seemingly *wished* and remembered the ephemeral ghostly Beloved into flesh and blood, specifically the Eucharistic blood Denver drank. The consumption of redemptive, sacrificial blood abets memory, which is, to use Robert Graves's phrase, "what survives of the beloved." Morrison's narrator, focalized through Denver, labels Beloved's return to flesh a "miraculous resurrection" (105), an allusion to Jesus: "Denver's imagination had produced its own hunger and its own food [...] salvation was as easy as a wish" (28–29). With the resurrection of Beloved, Denver—like Christians partaking of Jesus's sacrifice in the form of the Eucharist—attains "salvation."

Salvation is described in the Gospel of John as Eucharistic: "Whoso [...] drinketh my blood [...] I will raise him up at the last day[....] He [...] dwelleth in me, and I in him" (John 6:54–56). The mutual indwelling described in John is experienced by Denver, Sethe, and the resurrected Beloved as a merging of identities, with all its attendant risks and ecstasies. Beloved and Sethe merge their identities in the book's second section. Sethe imagines herself telling Beloved, "[W]hen I tell you you mine, I also mean I'm yours. I wouldn't draw breath without my children" (203). Beloved attempts to become one with Sethe. She "imitate[s] Sethe [...] it was difficult for Denver to tell who was who" (241). Denver merges, temporarily, with Beloved as well: "Luckily for Denver, looking [at Beloved] was food enough to last. But to be looked at in turn was beyond appetite[....] It was lovely[....] Denver's skin dissolved under that gaze[....] She floated near but outside her own body" (118). But Denver feels that she does not live when Beloved leaves her alone. Alone in the cider house, Denver cries "because she does not know where her body stops, which part of her is an arm, a foot or a knee [...] she has no self. Death is a skipped meal compared to this" (123).

By drinking her sister's blood and resurrecting her, Denver imitated not only Christian communion, but the rites of Demeter celebrated at Eleusis, which means "advent." The ceremonies there "brought about the advent of the Divine Child or Savior ... the Liberator.... His flesh was eaten by communicants in the form of bread.... His blood was drunk in the form of wine. Like

Jesus he entered the Earth and rose again. Communicants were supposed to partake of his immortality" (Walker 219).

Denver's Eucharist is comparable to the first Eucharist in other respects. At the Last Supper, the freedom—redemption—of the Israelites was associated with bloodshed and sacrifice. The Passover ritual reminded the participant of the deaths of the first-born children of the Egyptians (Bronstein 51, Wiesel 51, Glatzer 45) that preceded the Exodus. The Haggadah recalls the sacrifice of the lamb whose blood was painted on Jewish doorposts and thus, "God [...] passed over the houses of our ancestors.... 'He killed the Egyptians and spared our houses'" (Wiesel 66).[32] John the Baptist compared Jesus to the pascal lamb: "Behold the Lamb of God, which taketh away the sin of the world" (John 1:29). Communion is partaken by Christians to "remember" (Luke 22:19) that "Christ our passover is sacrificed for us" (1 Corinthians 5:7). Denver was similarly passed over. Her freedom, her *salvation*, was purchased with the blood of Beloved.

With Denver's Eucharist, Morrison unites two of the ideas inherent in the first Eucharist, remembrance of the beloved and freedom from slavery. A third element of the Eucharist, remission from sin/freedom from the past, is dependent, paradoxically, upon *remembering* that past. The past must be remembered to be transcended. Beloved resurrected is an incarnation of memory and as such has the power to redeem or destroy the traumatized characters living at 124. After her night-sea journey, Beloved brings back the past—past sin and past shame—that must be remembered in order that the community can move forward. Thus Denver's Eucharist and the consequent resurrection of Beloved is potentially redemptive for her community.

Paul D also partakes of a Eucharist. When he is escaping from slavery, running north toward freedom, he is starving and eats "raw meat barely dead [...] crunch[es] through a dove's breast before its heart stop[s] beating" (126). Doves have often been identified with Jesus and more particularly with the Holy Spirit (Matthew 3:16). During Jesus's ministry and for centuries before it, doves had been sacrificed at the temple as "sin offerings" (Leviticus 12:6).[33] Paul D's dove is such a sacrifice. His Eucharist incorporates Morrison's three eucharistic themes: eating the dove, Paul D asserts that he can be as free as a bird. Having taken communion, he is eventually liberated from his past, from slavery, and tells Sethe he wants to spend his future with her. Finally, Christians ritually partake of Jesus's body in an attempt to remember, as well as to realize within themselves, the qualities of love and altruism identified with Jesus's ministry. Paul D, having partaken of the sacrifice, has "something blessed in his manner." (17). Sethe "looks at him [...] his ready, waiting eyes and sees it [...] the blessedness, that has made him the kind of man who can [...] make the women cry. Because with him, [...] they could. Cry and tell him things" (272). He internalizes, physically and emotionally, both the freedom and the gentleness in the heart of the dove.

The novel's third Eucharist is Baby Suggs's feast—the banquet she held as a way of "thanking God" (135) for the deliverance of Sethe and her grand-children.[34] This celebration contradicts later Judeo-Christian theology that marginalizes the role of the body in worship; instead, her feast recalls the early Christian love feasts called "agape." During the first few centuries after the Crucifixion, Christians came together for such feasts,[35] but the "historical rela-tionship between the agape, the Lord's Supper, and the Eucharist is still uncer-tain. Some scholars believe the agape was a form of the Lord's Supper and the Eucharist the sacramental aspect of that celebration" (*New Encyclopaedia Britannica*, 15th ed., *s.v.* "Agape").The agape, a "meal of fellowship to which the poor were invited," was linked with the Eucharist, but later became separate from it until the agape "gradually passed out of existence or was preserved only as a feast of charity for the poor" (*International Standard Bible Encyclopedia*, "Agape" 1.66). Morrison, with Baby Suggs's agape, envisions a return to a less formalized, more joyous Eucharist or "thanksgiving." The narrator compares the feast to spiritual ecstasy, stating that eating the blackberries plucked for Baby Suggs's "feast [...] was like being in church" (136). Her feast and her services in the Clearing are designed to strengthen the African American com-munity in order to give the attendees a sense of belonging to a vital, joyous, cohesive Christian community. The people who attend Baby Suggs's "love feast," reminiscent of Jesus's "loaves and fishes" (137) miracle, are a loving community giving thanks for their community's redemption from slavery, for God's saving grace. The first Eucharist took place during a similar celebration, the Jewish Passover, instituted to give thanks and to remember the Israelites' redemption from Egypt.

### Redemption

The three Eucharists within *Beloved* and the novel as a Eucharist itself can rep-resent and/or instigate redemption for readers and characters. The process of remembering, putting past sins away, freeing the bodies and souls of charac-ters or of readers, opens the possibility of redemption in the form of "a new

and transformed life" (Williamson 259). When Paul D, Denver, or the participants in Baby Suggs's feast participate in the Eucharist, they mark their tran-
sitions to new lives as freed persons. When Sethe, newly freed, reaches 124,
Baby Suggs advises her, "'Lay em down, Sethe. Sword and shield. Down.
Down. Both of em down. Down by the riverside" (86). She is quoting a spiritual, "Study War No More" (Lovell 215–216). The spiritual is commonly
thought to refer to Isaiah 2:4: "they shall beat their swords into plowshares:
and their spears into pruninghooks: nation shall not lift up sword against
nation, neither shall they learn war any more." But the spiritual also resonates
with the biblical account of David's triumph over Goliath. David had laid his
"armor [...] and [...] sword" by a "brook" (1 Samuels 17:38–40) and man-
aged to slay Goliath with only a sling and stones. In concert with David, composer of Psalm 124, Baby Suggs counsels her community to "lay down" the
defenses that engender hostility and tension in order that they may triumph
over the Goliath of hatred, particularly self-hatred.

In Baby Suggs's theology, the transition to freedom enjoins one to learn to
love the self despised under slavery. Love of the body is a redeeming step
toward compensating the injured self for psychological and physical abuse.
Just as her agape celebrates the flesh through food, song, and fellowship, Baby
Suggs's worship services preach a gospel of flesh that encourages her congre-
gation to love themselves and to love their bodies. She preaches, "[W]e flesh
[...] Love it. Love it hard" (88). She is "calling" her people, the "not beloved"
of America and the novel's epigraph, and telling them they are "beloved."
Like a prophet or apostle, she actuates God's work of love as described in
Morrison's epigraph.

The worship service is not a conventional Christian service. The gatherings in the Clearing are similar to slaves' "ring shouts." The ring shout or
dance, "a strong example of African-influenced dance style in the United
States" (Raboteau 68), was performed as part of Christian services (Raboteau
66–69).[36] Quoting W. F. Allen, Raboteau's *Slave Religion* states that "'the
monotonous thud, thud, thud of the feet prevents sleep within half a mile'"
(71) of a ring shout. *Beloved* evokes the rhetoric of the ring shout: Baby Suggs
"shouted" for the people to come toward the center of the Clearing to dance,
and the freed people of Cincinnati "stepped out [...] from among the ringing
trees [...] and groundlife shuddered under their feet" (87).

Worshipping with the body as well as the spirit is integral to African culture. Alphonse Tiérou explains, "African tradition… never makes an abstraction of nature and cosmic laws…. [I]t gives the primary importance to the

body, the necessary intermediary without which spiritual life would be an abstraction… in rediscovering the body, one rediscovers one's own identity in the midst of humanity and returns it to its rightful place in the macrocosm…. To dance in the African manner is to recognize that man is inseparable from the universe" (12). Tiérou's notion of rediscovered identity is precisely what Morrison wished to convey with Baby Suggs's ring shout; the narrator states that "in the Clearing, along with the others, [Sethe] had claimed herself. Freeing yourself was one thing; claiming ownership of that freed self was another" (95).

Dancing on the north side of the Ohio River to celebrate their freedom, the African American community of Cincinnati reminds us that the Israelites, too, danced in celebration of their freedom after crossing the Red Sea: "Miriam the prophetess […] took a timbrel in her hand; and all the women went out after her with timbrels and with dances" (Exodus 15:20). Baby Suggs's preaching, in its frank corporeality, is similar not only to African dance, but also to messages of love and freedom found in the Bible. Baby Suggs tells her people to love their "flesh […] eyes […] hands[….] Raise them up and kiss them. Touch others with them, pat them together[….] Flesh […] needs to be loved […] love your neck […] your […] womb and your life-giving private parts" (88–89). The biblical correlate is equally corporeal: "Thou hast ravished my heart[….] How much better is thy love than wine! and the smell of thine ointments than all spices!" (Song of Solomon 4: 9–10); "This is thy stature like to a palm tree and thy breasts to clusters […] I will go up to the palm tree, I will take hold of the boughs […] now also thy breasts shall be as clusters of the vine, and the smell of thy nose like apples" (Song of Solomon 7:7–8). In spite of Baby Suggs's efforts, her community is not wholly loving. As the Bible states in the verse that gave Toni Morrison/Chloe Wofford her name, it is "declared by them *which are of the house* of Chloe, that there [were] contentions among" them (1 Corinthians 1:11). They are envious of Baby Suggs, and, after the death of Beloved, they shun Sethe, sharing some guilt for the death of Beloved, a guilt which poisons their relations with one another. To transcend a trauma, it must be remembered, but if that traumatic memory dominates the present and future, or if that memory is suffused with remorse, it can devastate the individual and the community. Both Sethe and her community associate some guilt or remorse with their survival. They wonder, in Bettelheim's words, "'Why was I spared?'" (26), and "behind this in a whisper might be heard an even more severe, critical accusation: 'Some of them died because you… did not give them some help, such as food…. You rejoiced that it was some other who had died rather than you'" (27). These kinds of memories, tinged with remorse, are evident in Morrison's characters: Ella remembers refusing to nurse her biracial child, the product of a brutal rape; Stamp Paid remembers wanting to strangle his wife after she slept with their master; both Sethe and Paul D are devastated by the deaths of Halle, Sixo, and Paul A. Paul D is called "last of the Sweet Home men" (6) in reference to those he survived. When Ella rescues Sethe, she listens "for the unnamed, unmentioned people left behind" (92). Baby Suggs, in an attempt to help her community bring repressed memories and guilt into consciousness, instructs her followers to "Cry [...] For the living and the dead. Just cry" (88).

But after Beloved's death, Baby Suggs stops holding her services. The community likely felt some remorse over Beloved's death, but they no longer had an outlet for their anguish. The sense of remorse that Beloved later incarnates threatens Sethe and the community as a whole. Memory, as Bettelheim has stated, is a prelude to recovery for the victim of trauma, but remorse can dominate the present and preclude or pollute the future:

> Being one of the very few who were saved when millions [according to Morrison's epigraph, "sixty million"] like oneself perished seems to entail a special obligation to justify one's luck and very existence, since it was permitted to continue when that of so many others exactly like oneself was not.... Feelings of guilt and of owing a special obligation are irrational, but this does not reduce their power to dominate a life ... to be a survivor does not entail a special obligation, it is nevertheless an extremely unusual and heavy burden. (Bettelheim 26–27)

As an incarnation of remorse, Beloved's continuing intrusive presence is a "heavy burden" for her community. Just as Beloved threatens to devour Sethe, her continuing demonic presence may destroy the community.

Ella correctly regards Beloved as "the devil himself" (256), but paradoxically, her advent, the return of Beloved from the "other side," unites the community and ultimately redeems it. Beloved's arrival from "a region of supernatural wonder" triggers a series of events culminating in the redemption of Cincinnati's African American community from its state of internal strife and communal guilt. But Beloved is not a monomythic hero/redeemer by her own intent. She is utterly egocentric, having died in infancy. She is "an outside thing that embraces while it accuses" (271). The redemption her return brings about is seemingly coincidental. In Morrison's novel, the process of redemption is incremental, its accomplishment owed to numerous characters:

Beloved, Amy, Paul D, Denver, Ella, Stamp Paid, the Bodwins, and Janey, among others.

Morrison thus revises our conception of miracle's reliance on a *single* hero to provide redemption. The miracle of redemption or salvation in her novel is clearly a *communal* affair, instigated by diverse heroes. Denver decides to save her mother thinking, "Somebody had to be saved, but unless Denver got work, there would be no one to save." She goes to the Bodwins, because she knows "The Bodwins were most likely to help" (252). When Denver tells Janey, the Bodwins' black servant, about "the girl in her house who plagued her mother" (254), Janey tells the other black women about the ghost: "The news that Janey got hold of she spread among the other colored women. Sethe's dead daughter [...] had come back" (255). Ella, the de facto leader of the black women, is up in arms, eager to help Sethe and put an end to the devilish Beloved: "When Ella heard 124 was occupied by something-or-other beating up on Sethe, it [...] gave her another opportunity to measure [...] the devil himself" (256).

The banishment of Beloved parallels the Crucifixion. It provides remission from past sin, as the narrator states: "Ella didn't like the idea of past errors taking possession of the present [...] she could not countenance the possibility of sin moving on [...] the past [was] something to leave behind. And if it didn't stay behind, well, you might have to stomp it out" (256). Like the crucifixion of Jesus, Beloved's dissolution takes place on a Friday, a day of unusual weather, "so wet and hot Cincinnati's stench had traveled to the country [...] trust the devil to make his presence known" (257–258). The weather on the day of the Crucifixion was also unusual: the "sun was darkened" (Luke 23:45), and there was an "earthquake" (Matthew 27:54).

Beloved's banishment is preceded by the sound of "singing" (261) women, a sound that dates, as Morrison's narrator tells it, back "to the beginning. In the beginning there were no words. In the beginning was the sound, and they all knew what that sound sounded like" (259). Morrison's description resonates with the wording of Genesis: "In the beginning" (Genesis 1:1), before God spoke the *words*, "Let there be light" (Genesis 1:3), the "Spirit of God moved upon the face of the waters" (Genesis 1:2). The singing women are presumably imbued with "the spirit" as their song washes over the faces of Sethe, Denver, and Beloved.[37] Sethe and Beloved have been faces in water: she wanted Sethe "to watch the layer of brown leaves waving at them from the bottom of the creek[....] Beloved gazed at her gazing face, rippling, folding, spreading, disappearing into the leaves below. She [...] touched the rocking faces with her own" (240–241). Denver and Beloved as well have seen their faces "in the water" (101). Beloved is compared to water: "Coupling with her wasn't even fun […] afterward [Paul D was] beached and gobbling air having been escorted to some ocean-deep place" (264). After she is banished, she has "fish for hair" (267). Beloved, as well as Sethe and Denver, are the "faces of the waters" over which the "spirit" moves.

Filled with the spirit of God, the singers, psalmists of a sort, will give Sethe and her community a new beginning. They have come to 124, named for a psalm, to save Sethe and their community from "a grown-up evil […] ghost" (257). Similarly, David, the beloved psalmist, played his harp to banish "an evil spirit from God" that was plaguing King Saul (1 Samuel 16:16): "And it came to pass, when the [evil] spirit from God was upon Saul, that David took a harp, and played with his hand: so Saul was refreshed, and was well, and the evil spirit departed from him" (1 Samuel 16:23). When the women arrive at 124, they remember Baby Suggs's agape, where they had "moved their shoulders to mouth harps" (258), reminiscent of the psalmist's harp.[38]

Beloved's departure is accompanied or instigated by the singing voices of thirty women (257, 258, 261). Edwin Bodwin, who rides up to 124 just before Beloved vanishes, has not seen the house in thirty (259) years. Thirty is the number of redemption in the Bible; slaves were worth (redeemed at) thirty shekels. In Exodus, God informs Israel, "If the ox shall push a manservant or a maidservant; he shall give unto their master thirty shekels of silver" (Exodus 21:32). People, in biblical times, were "valued" at thirty shekels, or in Jesus's case, "thirty pieces of silver" (Matthew 27:3). The voices of the thirty women—thirty pieces of silver—condemn Beloved to the watery afterlife from which she came and eternal life in literature, just as Judas's thirty pieces of silver sent Jesus to the cross and an eternal afterlife in Paradise as well as in the Gospels.[39] Jesus's sacrifice was made to redeem Christians, and similarly, Beloved's second sacrifice redeems Sethe and her community.

The singing women who banish Beloved, redeem Sethe, and free their community of evil are not only routing out the demonic Beloved, but are also atoning for their own sins of envy, self-righteousness, and communal divisiveness. The scapegoat sacrifice was an atonement sacrifice. Their singing at 124—their thirty pieces of silver—atones for their failure to sing Sethe to jail eighteen years earlier. Sethe identifies their presence with those moments when her community was most unified: "it was as though the Clearing had come to her with all its heat and simmering leaves […] a wave of sound […] broke over Sethe and she trembled like the baptized in its wash" (261). With her neighbors' baptism of sound, Sethe, like a newly baptized Christian, is "born again" (John 3:3) into a loving Christian community. The African American community saves Sethe. Morrison seems to instruct us that communal solidarity is essential to survival; redemption is accessible to Sethe only through community. The community, free of its divisiveness, has some hope of realizing the freedom praised in David's psalm.

With Beloved's disappearance, they are free of her—for a while, at least. But Beloved can never be entirely forgotten; her footprints continue to come and go. Perhaps the safest place to preserve her is upon the pages of a book, a book read, re-read and passed on from generation to generation. In fiction-as-Eucharist she is safely remembered, enabling contemporary American readers, survivors of a sort, to internalize her, to give "full cognizance to the most tragic experience of their lives [and] become able to accept and to live constructively with the feelings of guilt, without any need to justify [them]selve[s] and [their] surviving" (Bettelheim 35). The survivor, to live in the present, cycles between moments of remembering and repressing the past. Such is the case with reading, forgetting, and rereading a novel. *Beloved* is "disremembered" (274) until Morrison and her readers "giv[e] blood to the scraps" (78) and, through reading resurrect her once again, Beloved.

### Notes

[1] *Webster's New World Dictionary*, 3rd college ed., s. v. "Haggada" or "Haggadah."

[2] The events in *Beloved* have referents in African, Greek, and Judeo-Christian mythology. This synthesis figures the development of what Albert Raboteau has called "slave religion" in the United States. As Lawrence Levine explains it, "African and West European [religion]... had enough in common to facilitate syncretism (59); in the ways in which the slaves expressed their new religion, important elements of their shared African heritage remained alive... as vitally creative elements of slave culture" (53). The synthesis of African religion and Christianity has enabled the black community to develop a unique culture and to endure.

Danille Taylor-Guthrie has also noted that Morrison's *Beloved* is in dialogue with the Bible and that the text "recreates the ... complexity of African-American song" ("Who" 119). Mae Henderson's article, like my own, notes that Morrison produces a "rewriting of Scripture" (64). These critics are not concerned, as I am, with the connection of Morrison's book with Psalms, the monomyth, and sacraments.

[3] My choice of the Haggadah as a referent for the study of *Beloved* is, of course, subjective, but I think Morrison would approve. She has stated, "Part of the satisfaction I have always received from reading Greek tragedy ... is in its similarity to Afro-American communal structures ... and African religion and philosophy ... that is part of the reason it has *quality for me*— I feel intellectually at home there" (emphasis added, *Unspeakable* 202). Similarly, I feel intellectu-

ally at home with Morrison's *Beloved* because of its similarity to the Haggadah. This way of appreciating Morrison's work will, I hope, make the "quality" of the novel more apparent to others as well.

4 "The Mishnah, a work compiled at the turn of the third century, describes a Seder much like ours ... Psalms 113–118 ... sung originally by the Levites at the Temple, were chanted" (Bronstein 9–10).

5 The pattern I describe is inspired by, but not identical to, Joseph Campbell's "monomyth," a term Campbell borrowed from *Finnegans Wake*. Campbell defines the monomyth as follows: "A hero ventures forth from the world of common day into a region of supernatural wonder: fabulous forces are there encountered and a decisive victory is won: the hero comes back from this mysterious adventure with the power to bestow boons on his fellow man" (Campbell, *Hero* 30). Campbell describes how Jesus, Buddha, and Moses each follow this pattern (*Hero* 36).

Though ritual is not part of Campbell's concise definition, it is integral to faiths centered on monomythic heroes. In Christianity, for example, the memory of the monomythic pattern is catalyzed by the ritual of the Eucharist: "this do in *remembrance* of me" (emphasis added, Luke 22:21).Wilfred Samuels and Clenora Hudson-Weems have also noted that *Beloved* has a mythological structure (96).

6 *Webster's New World Dictionary*, 3rd college ed., s.v. "David."

7 Clark Williamson traces the history of this divergence: "The early controversy over the date of Easter, whether Easter was to be dated in relation to Passover in the Jewish calendar was settled at Nicaea by severing Easter from the Jewish liturgical year and dating it in relation to the spring equinox.... Nicaea's decision helped remove Easter from a Jewish and biblical context ... thus de-Judaizing Easter" (Williamson 27–28). Williamson proceeds to explain the link between Passover's bread of freedom and the Eucharist. He laments the interpretation of Eucharist as solely a reminder of "forgiveness of sin" and reminds the reader that Eucharist "represents" God's grace as the gift of life—freedom or "liberation"—given at Exodus (258–29).

8 In Matthew, Jesus states, "This is my blood of the new testament, which is shed for many for the remission of sins" (Matthew 26:28). Paul interprets this notion as follows: "*redemption* ... is in Christ Jesus: Whom God hath set forth [to be] a propitiation through faith in his blood, to declare his righteousness for the remission of sins that are *past*" (emphasis added, Romans 3:24–25).

9 Critics have recognized that Sethe's house, usually referred to as "124," has almost mystical significance in the novel. David Cunningham, noting that "black worship is highly Trinitarian," suggests, "The harmony of the inhabitants of 124 Bluestone Road is always being disrupted—always threatening to dissolve into undifferentiated chaos, or to merge into a destructive dualism or monism. Given the pain and conflict that takes place within its walls, the house is very aptly numbered: 1–2–4. The 'three' is missing" (198–199). Wilfred Samuels and Clenora Hudson-Weems remind the reader that the digits of the house number "total seven, the number of creation" (136).

10 Mae Henderson has also noted the pun on "Blues tone Road" (73), though she develops it differently than I do here.

11 Kristin Boudreau also compares *Beloved* with blues music and quotes Sherley A. Williams's reference to "the statement/response pattern" characteristic of blues songs (Williams 127, quoted in Boudreau 449). Boudreau points out that "blues articulation ... expands into a

public realm what had hitherto been a private experience of suffering" (Boudreau 449). Marilyn Mobley, too, has pointed out that the text of *Beloved* "illustrates the call and response pattern of the African-American oral tradition" (193).

12 *Webster's New World Dictionary*, 3rd college ed., s.v. "Amy." Wilfred Samuels and Clenora Hudson-Weems have also noted that Amy's name means "beloved" (116), but they do not propose, as I do, that she is ghostly or imaginary.

13 *Oxford Paperback French Dictionary*, 2nd ed., s.v. "envers."

14 In Morrison's *Tar Baby*, the pseudo-sophisticated Jadine attempts to make a similar pun on "Phil" and the French *fils*: "'What is [your name]?[... ]Phil? [... ]That's Anglicized French for son'" (173–174).

15 Amy's reference to "Wilson" (32), a store in Boston, supports the notion that Amy is Beloved's spirit. "Wilson" calls to mind Poe's story "William Wilson," wherein the narrator claims to be tormented by a double (whom critics usually interpret as a spirit or psychological projection) who bears his name. Like the two William Wilsons, Amy and Beloved have the same name (though only in translation) and are mirror images of one another. Beloved, like the narrator of "William Wilson," is self-centered, immature, and amoral; Amy, like the double in Poe's story, is generous, kind, and ethical. Wilson sees his double in a mirror; Morrison refers to Beloved as a twin or mirror (Naylor 208–209) of her other characters.

16 *Standard Jewish Encyclopedia*, rev. ed., s. v. "Passover."

17 "Ashkenazim" denotes Jews of German or eastern European, rather than Spanish or Portuguese, descent.

18 Aside from its association with Eden, the serpent has been associated with Demeter (Grimal 133) and the tyiwara of the Bambara people (Goldwater 16).

19 John's Gospel seems to connect water to birth and rebirth: "Except a man be born of water and [of] the Spirit, he cannot enter into the kingdom of God[....] Ye must be born again" (John 3:3–7). Moses and Jesus were spiritually reborn after contact with water. Moses's name may mean "drawn from water" as stated above, or "Moses" may be related to the Egyptian word that means "unfathered son of a princess," as in "Thutmose, Ahmoses, etc" (Walker 676). Moses was taken from the Nile and reared—reborn—as a prince rather than a slave (Exodus 2:5–10). Jesus was baptized by John the Baptist, and God announces, "This is my beloved Son" (Matthew 3:16–7). Both Moses and Jesus are believed to have saved their followers.

Barbara Walker informs us that the "The fatherless hero born of 'waters'... was a universal image of the sacred king, repeated in the myths of Perseus, Horus, Jason.... The Goddess Cunti ... gave birth to the sun god and placed him in a basket of rushes" (676). Denver's birth conforms to this mythical context.

20 The flooding of Paul D's prison seems to be connected with a psalm. Morrison states six times (107–113) that Paul D was one of forty-six prisoners. The forty-sixth psalm refers to flooding: "the earth [...] removed," "the mountains [...] carried into the midst of the sea," "the waters [...] troubled," and the "earth melted." Morrison "riffs on" Psalm 46 as jazz musicians do with one another's melodies. She speaks of "unreliable earth" (109) and "all Georgia [...] melting away" (111).

21 Mae Henderson also associates "the law was our schoolmaster" with schoolteacher, stating that it "is this white/male construction of the law according to authority of the master discourse that Sethe must first dismantle in order to construct her own story" (72).

22 Samuels and Hudson-Weems have also noted that "Morrison seems ... interested in exploring ... further the whole issue of ownership" (109). Mutual gratification is an "aspect of maternal love" and the child an object of gratification to its mother, they suggest, but they do not differentiate this concept from the heinous notion of placing a numerical value, a price, on the head of that child. When Morrison uses the word "mine," I believe she intends to imply a corruption of love—of the mutual gratification associated with love—by the notion of owner-ship.

23 Danille Taylor-Guthrie has compared Paul D to his "new Testament counterpart... author of the epistle to the Romans" ("Who" 128).

24 Several critics have noted Sethe's role as a goddess figure. Shirley Stave has explored Sethe's affiliation with Lilith and the Great Mother (51). Jacqueline Trace has pointed out that Sethe, as well as the other black women in *Beloved*, are goddess figures, that Sethe "carries the tree of crucifixion on her back" (20). Wilfred Samuels and Clenora Hudson-Weems have assert-ed that Sethe is a "great mother... [an] embodiment of the feminine principle.... The Demeter-like image of the nursing figure is not new for Morrison" (102).

25 Carolyn Mitchell compares the tree on Sethe's back to the cross (28). Lorraine Liscio notes that "Sethe's Calvary is the murder of Beloved" (36). Trudier Harris points out that "Morrison's female characters ... are superficially considered to be witches and scapegoats" (189). These writers have not seen her specifically as a scapegoat for schoolteacher and Sawyer.

26 David Lawrence states, "The narrator observes that, had Sethe not been ... convinced of her rectitude ... songs would have bodied forth" (197). I am not entirely convinced of this. The narrator's voice in *Beloved* is usually filtered through one character or another and is not consistently reliable. Sethe's neighbors, in my view, withhold their songs not just because they resent Sethe's rectitude, but because they are partly at fault for Beloved's death. They are stunned into silence that their sin of omission spawned such catastrophic results.

27 In *Modern Medea*, Steven Weisenburger relates how Margaret Garner was compared to the mythic Medea in contemporary newspapers.

28 Danille Taylor-Guthrie has pointed out that the circled cross, a symbol that had been branded on Sethe's mother, is a "cosmogram" in the Bakongo cultural area. It signifies the world of the dead and the world of the living divided by a horizontal line representing water. A watery crossing, it seems, is a prelude to entering the world of the living or the world of the dead. For the Bakongo people, the Middles Passage might have been "perceived as leaving the world of the living and entering that of the dead" (Taylor-Guthrie, "Who" 125–126).

29 Bettelheim speaks of survivors' "feelings of guilt and of owning obligation." These feel-ings can have the "power to dominate a life.... To be a survivor is ... an extremely unusual and heavy burden." It is typical for the conscience to plague the survivor, to suggest, "The reason you had the chance to survive was that some other prisoner died in your stead" (Bettelheim 27). Hence the survivor is "persecuted by guilt, tortured by obviously unanswerable questions" (Bettelheim 30).

30 Morrison has mentioned Dickinson in "Unspeakable Things Unspoken" (204) and has referred to Dickinson and quoted her extemporaneously in interviews: "I feel perfectly qualified to discuss Emily Dickinson" (Tate 160); "I don't... need certain slants of light in order to write" (Le Clair 120).

[31] This quote comes from the New International Version of the Bible. In most other versions, the term "beloved" is applied to the young man in the love song. "Beloved" was a term used throughout the ancient near East to designate god-kings, who were frequently destined for sacrifice (Walker 3). Giving the sacrificed Beloved this name, Morrison conforms to the practice of designating the sacrificial victim as "beloved."

[32] Some Haggadot omit the phrase that depicts God as a killer (Bronstein 55), reflecting a more contemporary notion that God is not vengeful.

[33] "Jesus went into the temple of God and [...] overthrew the [...] seats of them that sold doves" (Matthew 21:12). The doves were sold for purposes of sacrifice.

[34] "Eucharist" means "thanksgiving" (*New Encyclopaedia Britannica*, 15th ed., s.v. "Rites and Ceremonies").

[35] Joseph Campbell, quoting Saint Epiphanius, assumes that agape or "Christian Love Feasts" were orgiastic (*Masks* 159–161). Among contemporary historians there does not seem to be a consensus regarding the nature of agape. In Morrison's book, the agape, presumably based upon 1 Corinthians 11:17–24, does not seem to involve sexual license.

[36] Danille Taylor-Guthrie has noted the similarity of Sethe's circling of Paul D (*Beloved* 162–163) to the ring shout but does not link the ring shout to Baby Suggs's worship service in the Clearing ("Who" 126).

[37] Mae Henderson asserts that Morrison is revising John 1:1, which states, "In the beginning was the Word," but Henderson makes no mention of Genesis 1:2. It is my position that Morrison is returning to Genesis, the source John revised. Henderson further states, and I agree, that Sethe achieves redemption through "*possession* by the spirit.... Significantly, for Morrison it is not through Law, but the spirit that the individual achieves 'deliverance' from the 'sins' of the past. *Beloved*, then, (re)inscribes the conditions of the promise in the New Testament" (82).

[38] The word "psalm" is derived from a Greek word that refers to the plucking of harp strings.

[39] Taylor-Guthrie considers the thirty women to be an "amplified trinity" ("Who" 128). The number "thirty," which Morrison repeats four times, may refer to Psalm 30 as well as to the thirty pieces of silver. Psalm 30 is termed a thanksgiving for deliverance from death, "A psalm [and] song [at] the dedication of the house of David." The speaker is assumed to be David, whose name, as has been mentioned, means "beloved." The psalm's salient lines follow:

> O Lord, thou hast brought up my soul from the grave:
> thou hast kept me alive that I should not go down to the pit / ... /
> Lord, by thy favor
> thou hast made my mountain to stand strong:
> thou didst hide thy face
> [and] I was troubled. /... /
> Thou hast turned for me my mourning into dancing:

## Works Cited

Achebe, Chinua. *Things Fall Apart*. New York: Astor-Honor, 1959.

Bakerman, Jane. "The Seams Can't Show: An Interview with Toni Morrison." In Taylor-Guthrie, *Conversations*, 30–42.

Bettelheim, Bruno. "Trauma and Reintegration." *Surviving and Other Essays.* New York: Alfred A. Knopf, 1979, 19–37.

Boudreau, Kristin. "Pain and the Unmaking of Self in Toni Morrison's *Beloved*." *Contemporary Literature* 36 (1995): 447–465.

Bowers, Susan. "*Beloved* and the New Apocalypse." *Journal of Ethnic Studies* 18.1 (1990): 59–77.

Bronstein, Herbert, ed. *A Passover Haggadah: The New Union Haggadah*. Rev. ed. New York: Central Conference of American Rabbis, 1974.

Campbell, Joseph. *The Hero with a Thousand Faces*. 2nd ed. Bollingen Series 17. Princeton: Princeton University Press, 1968.

———. *The Masks of God: Creative Mythology*. New York: Arkana-Penguin, 1991.

Cruden, Alexander. *Cruden's Complete Concordance to the Old and New Testaments*. Edited by A. D. Adams, C. H. Irwin, and S. A. Waters. Grand Rapids, MI: Zondervan Publishing House, 1968.

Darling, Marsha. "In the Realm of Responsibility: A Conversation with Toni Morrison." In Taylor-Guthrie, *Conversations*, 246–254.

Dickinson, Emily. *The Complete Poems of Emily Dickinson*. Edited by Thomas H. Johnson. Boston: Little, Brown, 1960.

Eliade, Mircea, ed. *The Encyclopedia of Religion*. New York: Macmillan, 1987.

Falk, Marcia. *The Song of Songs: A New Translation and Interpretation*. San Francisco: Harper, 1990. Rev. ed. of *Love Lyrics from the Bible*. 1982.

Glatzer, Nahum N., ed. *The Schocken Passover Haggadah*. Exp. ed. New York: Schocken Books, 1996.

Goldwater, Robert. Introduction to *Bambara Sculpture from the Western Sudan*. New York: Museum of Primitive Art, 1960.

Grant, Michael, and John Hazel. *Who's Who in Classical Mythology*. New York: Oxford University Press, 1993.

Graves, Robert. *The Greek Myths*. Comb. ed. London: Penguin Books, 1992.

———. *The White Goddess: A Historical Grammar of Poetic Myth*. Rev. ed. New York: Farrar, Straus, and Giroux, 1948.

Grimal, Pierre. *The Dictionary of Classical Mythology*. Translated by A. R. Maxwell-Hyslop. Cambridge, MA: Blackwell, 1996.

Harris, Trudier. *Fiction and Folklore: The Novels of Toni Morrison*. Knoxville: University of Tennessee Press, 1991.

Henderson, Mae G. "Toni Morrison's *Beloved*: Re-Membering the Body as Historical Text." In *Comparative American Identities: Race, Sex, and Nationality in the Modern Text*, edited by Hortense J. Spillers. New York: Routledge, 1991, 62–86.

Huet, Michel. *The Dances of Africa*. New York: Harry N. Abrams, 1996.

Jones, Bessie W., and Audrey Vinson. "An Interview with Toni Morrison." In Taylor-Guthrie, *Conversations*, 171–187.

Lawrence, David. "Fleshly Ghosts and Ghostly Flesh: The Word and the Body in *Beloved*." *Studies in American Fiction* 19.2 (1991): 189–202.

LeClair, Thomas. "The Language Must Not Sweat: A Conversation with Toni Morrison." In Taylor-Guthrie, *Conversations*, 119–128.

Levine, Lawrence W. *Black Culture and Black Consciousness: Afro-American Folk Thought from Slavery to Freedom*. New York: Oxford University Press, 1977.

Levy, Andrew. "Telling *Beloved*." *Texas Studies in Literature and Language* 33.1 (Spring 1991): 114–123.

Liscio, Lorraine. "*Beloved*'s Narrative: Writing Mother's Milk." *Tulsa Studies in Women's Literature* 11.1 (Spring 1992): 31–46.

Lovell, John Jr. *Black Song: The Forge and the Flame: The Story of How the Afro-American Spiritual Was Hammered Out*. New York: Macmillan, 1972.

McConnell, Frank D. *Four Postwar American Novelists: Bellow, Mailer, Barth, and Pynchon*. Chicago: University of Chicago Press, 1977.

McKay, Nellie. "An Interview with Toni Morrison." In Taylor-Guthrie, *Conversations*, 138–155.

Mitchell, Carolyn. "'I Love to Tell the Story': Biblical Revisions in *Beloved*." *Religion and Literature* 23.3 (Autumn 1991): 27–42.

Mobley, Marilyn Sanders. "A Different Remembering: Memory, History and Meaning in Toni Morrison's *Beloved*." In *Modern Critical Views: Toni Morrison*, edited by Harold Bloom. New York: Chelsea House, 1990, 189–99.

Morrison, Toni. *Beloved*. New York: Plume-Penguin Books, 1988.

———. *Playing in the Dark: Whiteness and the Literary Imagination*. New York: Vintage-Random House, 1992.

———. *Song of Solomon*. New York: Plume-Penguin Books, 1977.

———. *Tar Baby*. New York: Alfred A. Knopf, 1981.

———. "Unspeakable Things Unspoken: The Afro-American Presence in American Literature." In *Modern Critical Views: Toni Morrison*, edited by Harold Bloom. New York: Chelsea House, 1990. 201–30.

Moyers, Bill. "A Conversation with Toni Morrison." In Taylor-Guthrie, *Conversations*, 262–274.

Naylor, Gloria. "A Conversation: Gloria Naylor and Toni Morrison." In Taylor-Guthrie, *Conversations*, 188–217.

Raboteau, Albert J. *Slave Religion: The "Invisible Institution" in the Antebellum South*. Oxford: Oxford University Press, 1978.

Samuels, Wilfred D., and Clenora Hudson-Weems. *Toni Morrison*. New York: Twayne Publishers–Simon & Schuster Macmillan, 1990.

Stave, Shirley. "Toni Morrison's *Beloved* and the Vindication of Lilith." *South Atlantic Review* 58.1 (1993): 49–66.

Tate, Claudia. "Toni Morrison." In Taylor-Guthrie, *Conversations*, 156-170.

Taylor-Guthrie, Danille, ed. *Conversations with Toni Morrison*. Jackson: University Press of Mississippi, 1994.

———. "Who are the Beloved? Old and New Testments, Old and New Communities of Faith." *Religion and Literature* 27.1 (Spring 1995): 119–129.

Tiérou, Alphonse. *Dooplé, The Eternal Law of African Dance*. Translated by Deirdre McMahon. Choreography and Dance Studies 2. Switzerland: Harwood, 1992.

Trace, Jacqueline. "Dark Goddesses: Black Feminist Theology in Morrison's *Beloved*." *Obsidian II* 6.3 (1991): 14–30.

Walker, Barbara G. *The Woman's Encyclopedia of Myths and Secrets*. San Francisco: HarperCollins, HarperSanFrancisco, 1983.

Washington, Elsie. "Talk with Toni Morrison." In Taylor-Guthrie, *Conversations*, 234–238.

Weisenburger, Steven. *Modern Medea: A Family Story of Slavery and Child-murder from the Old South*. New York: Hill and Wang, 1998.

Wiesel, Elie, commentator. *A Passover Haggadah as Commented upon by Elie Wiesel*. New York: Touchstone–Simon & Schuster, 1993.

Williamson, Clark M. *A Guest in the House of Israel: Post-Holocaust Church Theology*. Louisville, KY: Westminster/John Knox Press, 1993.

# 3

# TO LIVE THIS LIFE INTENSELY AND WELL: THE REBIRTH OF MILKMAN DEAD IN TONI MORRISON'S *SONG OF SOLOMON*

*David Z. Wehner*

*"I have come that they may have life, and that they may have it more abundantly."*
Jesus Christ, John 10:10[1]

*"You listen! You got a life? Live it! Live the motherfuckin life! Live it!"*
Guitar Baines, *Song of Solomon* 183

While Saul travels the road to Damascus, a bright light strikes him, knocking him off his horse to the ground. "Saul, why are you persecuting me?" the light asks him. "Who are you, Lord?" Saul returns. "I am Jesus, whom you are persecuting." Jesus then sends Saul, now Paul, to the Gentiles "to turn them from darkness to light" (Acts 26:18). Caravaggio's painting *The Conversion of St. Paul* (1601) depicts this scene, the moment Paul "sees the light." Paul lies flat on his back, having already been knocked off his horse, and his arms reach out toward the light, seemingly at once embracing it and holding it at bay. Because of the painter's stark use of light and dark, his dramatic use of foreshortening, and because of Paul's outstretched arms, the viewer of the painting cannot help but feel the power of this light—powerful enough to knock Paul to the ground and blind him for three days. "Conversion" comes from the Latin *convertere*, "to turn round." Caravaggio captures the moment Paul turns round from darkness to light, from death to life—the moment he is, to use a well-worn expression, born again.

We tend to associate the story of someone being "born again" with religion in general, with Christianity specifically, and, in the current American context, with the religious right, but Pierre Hadot in his work on classical Greek philosophy outlines a paradigm of conversion that predates the Christian paradigm by half a millennium. He argues that each of the major schools of Greek thought—the Platonists, the Aristotelians, the Epicureans, and the Stoics—had what he calls "spiritual exercises" designed to "make possible the indispensable metamorphosis of our inner self…. This constitutes a conversion (*metastrophe*)" (83, 96). Using Hadot, one, then, can look at Plato's allegory of the cave as an Ur–conversion narrative in Western letters. In the allegory, the cave dwellers are chained facing a wall. At one point, Plato likens them to the dead; when the chains are cut, the inhabitants turn and walk out of the darkness into the light, out of death into life, in what the philosopher calls, "the upward journey of the soul" (189). Drawing on Toni Morrison's entire body of work, this essay examines Morrison's *Song of Solomon* as a conversion narrative outside the Christian paradigm. Indeed, in *Circles of Sorrow, Lines of Struggle: The Novels of Toni Morrison*, Gurleen Grewal argues that the author appropriates biblical stories, Greek culture, Anglo-Saxon fairy tales, and the canonical writing of high modernism "and places them in the matrix of black culture" (65).

What would it mean to place this specific story—the story of someone being reborn—in the matrix of black culture in post–civil rights America? Might it look like the moment early in *Sula* when Shadrack returns ravaged from the trenches of World War I and confronts his reflection?

> There in the toilet water he saw a grave black face. A black so definite, so unequivocal, it astonished him. He had been harboring skittish apprehension that he was not real—that he didn't exist at all. But when the blackness greeted him with its indisputable presence, he wanted nothing more[….] Shadrack rose and returned to the cot, where he fell into the first sleep of his new life. (11)

Like Paul, Shadrack is astonished, which means "to be filled with sudden wonder and amazement, confounded"; unlike Paul, a blackness "so definite, so unequivocal" affords Shadrack his rebirth. It is no accident that Morrison has Shadrack find his reflection "in the toilet." Her first novel, *The Bluest Eye*, ends with Pecola Breedlove gone insane, rummaging through a garbage heap; society has discarded her. Her second novel begins with Shadrack finding his reflection in a toilet bowl, a space that normally harbors that which is to be discarded, but a space from which Shadrack salvages that which is to give him new life. In "Memory, Creation, and Writing," Morrison writes, "If my work is to confront a reality unlike that received reality of the West, it must centralize and animate information discredited by the West" (388). If Morrison is to visualize and outline what it would mean for an African American to be reborn—as this essay will argue—she must sift through her received reality of the West to retrieve discredited and discarded cultural information.

Stories handed down from early Christianity and ancient Greece constitute part of that received reality, but the Enlightenment's discourse around a
new self and its new life constitute another not-so-distant part. Morrison continually refers to the Age of Reason in essays such as "Rootedness: The
Ancestor as Foundation," in which she writes, "When the industrial revolution
began, there emerged a new class of people who were neither peasants nor
aristocrats.... So they produced an art form: we call it the novel of manners,
an art form designed to tell people something they didn't know ... what a good
living was" (340). Morrison's comments here could be seen as, in a nutshell,
Ian Watt's argument in *The Rise of the Novel*, that the novel can be seen as a
manifestation

> of a larger change—that vast transformation of Western civilisation since the
> Renaissance which has replaced the unified world picture of the Middle Ages with
> another very different one—one which presents us, essentially, with a developing but
> unplanned aggregate of particular individuals having particular experiences at par-
> ticular times and at particular places. (31)

Watt sees the character Robinson Crusoe as embodying "the processes associated with the rise of economic individualism" and that novel as "the first fictional narrative in which an ordinary person's daily activities are the center of
continuous literary attention" (64, 74). The birth of the bildungsroman comes
on the heels of Watt's rise of the novel, in that most critics locate the Ur-bil-
dungsroman in Goethe's 1795 *Wilhelm Meister's Apprenticeship*, and just as
Morrison sees the African American novel as a new art form showing a new
class of post–civil rights blacks how to live, Randolph Shaffer argues that "the
idea that living is an art which the apprentice may learn" stands as one of the
corollaries to the novel of education (quoted in Poey 207). Both the novel and
the bildungsroman, then, outline the life of this "ordinary person."

Like Morrison, like Watt, Michel Foucault often stands as a late-twentieth-
century writer looking back to the eighteenth century, with an eye toward this
new "self" and its new "life." Early in his career, in *The Order of Things*,
Foucault states this baldly: "Before the end of the eighteenth century, man did
not exist.... He is a quite recent creature, which the demiurge of knowledge
fabricated with its own hands less than two hundred years ago" (308).[2] Late in
his career, in 1982, in a lecture "Technologies of the Self" given at the
University of Vermont, Foucault tells his audience that to sketch out the existence of this "fabricated creature" has been his objective for more than twenty-five years, and he ends his lecture saying, "From the eighteenth century to

the present, the techniques of verbalization have been reinserted in a different context by the so-called human sciences in order ... to constitute, positively, a new self" (248). The birth of knowledges in this period interests the philosopher/historian because they still form "the immediate space of our reflection. We think in that area" (*Order* 384).

Concurrent with the rise of this new "self," Foucault argues, a new discourse around its rights and its life arises; he writes, "The 'right' to life, to one's body, to health, to happiness, to the satisfaction of needs, and beyond all the oppressions or 'alienation,' the 'right' to rediscover what one is and all that one can be, this 'right'... was the political response to all these new procedures of power" (*Sexuality* 145). These rights and this life are emphasized in Thomas Jefferson's words from the same period: "We hold these truths to be self evident: that all men are created equal; that they are endowed by their Creator with certain inalienable rights; that among these are life, liberty, and the pursuit of happiness" (715). In Watt, Shaffer, Foucault, and Jefferson, therefore, we have four men writing about or in this same moment, interested in this "new self" and its "life"—its daily activities described in the novel, its growth depicted in the bildungsroman, its discursive existence limned in the human sciences, and its political existence asserted in the Declaration of Independence.

Like these writers, Morrison returns to this moment with an eye toward the creation of a new individual; unlike these writers, Morrison considers how race and gender factor into this creation. Whereas Watt focuses on how *Robinson Crusoe* signals the emergence of a new economic individual, Morrison, in "Friday on the Potomac," focuses on how Defoe's novel constructs that new individual in relation to his subjugated black counterpart, Friday. Whereas Jefferson links the emergence of a new nation with a new discourse around "the rights of man," Morrison links the emergence of a "new" African American with the new discourse around the civil rights of African Americans. Whereas Jefferson wants to declare the rights of this new American, Morrison, in *Playing in the Dark: Whiteness and the Literary Imagination*, wants to connect those rights to "the historical connection between the Enlightenment and the institution of slavery—the rights of man and his enslavement" (42). Regarding American literature of the early nineteenth century, Morrison notes, "What seemed to be on the 'mind' of the literature of the United States was the self-conscious but highly problematic construction of the American as a new white man" (39). This newness recurs as one of the perennial themes in the literature of this period: "The flight from the Old

World to the New is generally seen to be a flight from oppression and limitation to freedom and possibility…. The attraction was of the 'clean-slate' variety, a once-in-a-lifetime opportunity not only to be born again but to be born again in new clothes" (34). But, of course, this flight applies only to this new white man; for blacks, the trip from the Old World to the New, the Middle Passage, represented the antithesis: a trip from freedom and possibility to oppression and bondage. If for the new white male, the trip to the New World was an opportunity "to be born again in new clothes," Morrison captures this irony in the character Beloved: in the course of that novel, Beloved is literally born again in new clothes after crossing over from "the other side," which the text depicts as the Middle Passage. The European's rebirth in the New World appears positive, even spiritual, the African's "rebirth" horrific. If one of the inalienable rights, then, of this new American is freedom, in *Playing in the Dark* Morrison asks, "How free can I be as an African-American woman writer in my genderized, sexualized, wholly racialized world?" (4). If one of the inalienable rights is life, Morrison's body of work—this essay will argue—attempts to imagine what that "life" looks like for an African American, seeing as her received tradition does not imagine it for her.

Thus in a 1977 interview, when Morrison says, "If there is one consistent theme in my fiction, I guess that's it—how and why we learn to live this life intensely and well," clearly her "we" is not the "we" of her received reality (Taylor-Guthrie 47). African Americans constitute this "we," and Morrison's oeuvre wants to answer how and why blacks learn to live this life intensely and well; part of her answer comes in imagining those who are *not* living this life intensely and well.[3] Early in *The Bluest Eye*, the narrator tells us, "The only living thing in the Breedloves' house was the coal stove" (37). Late in *Sula*, the title character tells her best friend Nel, "I know what every colored woman in this country is doing […] dying. Just like me. But the difference is they dying like a stump. Me, I'm going down like one of those redwoods. I sure did live in this world" (123). In *Song of Solomon*, we discover that Ruth Foster "was dying of lovelessness then and seemed to be dying of it now," while the men in Danville, Pennsylvania, when the Butlers murder Jake Dead, "began to die and were dying still" (151, 235). Like the Breedloves' home, *Beloved*'s 124 Bluestone Road is dead in that the narrator refers to a different time, "when 124 was alive" (95). Similarly, the narrator of *Jazz* tells us that Dorcas Manfred's photo "seems like the only living presence in the house" (11). That is, four of Morrison's seven novels present African American homes in which the text tells us directly that the inhabitants are not living; seven of her seven novels, on some level, meditate on how these non-living come back to life.[4]

For Morrison, her characters carve out this life, in part, by carving out a new, whole self. Sula tells her grandmother, Eva Peace, "I don't want to make somebody else. I want to make myself" (80), and when Milkman Dead is down South in search of the gold and, later, in search of his heritage, "self—that cocoon that was 'personality'—gave way," allowing for a new self to emerge (277). The defining characteristic of this new self, for Morrison, appears to be a certain completeness, wholeness. Early in *Solomon*, Milkman looks at his reflection: "Taken apart, it looked all right [...] but it lacked coherence, a coming together of the features into a total self" (69). Again and again in her interviews, Morrison says *Solomon* concerns Milkman's becoming a complete person; in the year of its publication, 1977, the author told Robert Stepto, "The book I'm working on now is about a man [who] will learn to be a complete person, or at least have a notion of it" (Taylor-Guthrie 20). Morrison says one of her basic themes is "how to survive—not to make a living—but how to survive *whole* in a world where we are all of us, in some measure, *victims of something*" (Taylor-Guthrie 40).[5] The narrative of someone coming back to life, then, serves as a site on which to meditate upon this new, whole self—what is it that is killing off the protagonist in the first place, and what is it that will bring him or her back to life?[6]

Morrison, however, wants her readers to do more than meditate upon how "to live this life intensely and well"; she wants them to act upon it. She writes, "I want my fiction to urge the reader into active participation in the non-narrative, nonliterary experience of the text, which makes it difficult for the reader to confine himself to a cool and distant acceptance of data" ("Memory" 387). In "Rootedness," she echoes this idea: her fiction "should try deliberately to make you stand up and make you feel something profoundly in the same way that a Black preacher requires his congregation to speak, to join him in the sermon, to behave in a certain way, to standup and to weep and to cry and to accede or to change and to modify" (341). The last line of *Paradise* reads, "Now they will rest before shouldering the endless work they were created to do down here in Paradise" (318). Here, "they" refers, immediately, to the ship passengers, but the sentiment opens out into Morrison's work as a whole: to bring about paradise—to modify, to change—requires endless work one must be willing to shoulder.

One can think of Morrison's emphasis on "the endless work" required "to change and to modify" in relation, again, to Pierre Hadot's *Philosophy as a Way of Life.* He argues that ancient philosophy appears

> not as a theoretical construct, but as a method for training people to live and to look at the world in a new way. It is an attempt to transform mankind. Contemporary historians of philosophy are today scarcely inclined to pay attention to this aspect, although it is an essential one. The reason for this is that, in conformity with a tradition inherited from the Middle Ages and from the modern era, they consider philosophy to be a purely abstract-theoretical activity. (107)

The title of Hadot's work encapsulates his thesis: the ancient Greeks thought of philosophy as a way of life—not as something one thought about in the abstract, but as something one *did* in order to transform oneself. Late in his life, Foucault was reading Hadot, whose influence one can see in what Foucault terms "technologies of the self," "which permit individuals to effect by their own means, or with the help of others, a certain number of operations on their own bodies and souls, thoughts, conduct, and way of being, so as to transform themselves in order to attain a certain state of happiness, purity, wisdom, perfection, or immortality" ("Technologies" 225). I argue that we can look at Morrison's body of work in general, and *Song of Solomon* specifically, as a "technology of conversion," as a body of writing that outlines "a method for training people to live and to look at the world in a new way," or, in Morrison's words, "to live this life intensely and well."

Critics both praise and malign this impetus in Morrison to train and to teach. Grewal comments on it early in *Circles of Sorrow*: "This impulse to reveal/educate/change is consistently present in Toni Morrison's work and accounts for much of its emotive force" (xi). Yet this very impulse draws Michiko Kakutani's ire in her review of *Paradise* in *The New York Times*: "The novel's language feels closer to the hectoring, didactic voice that warped her 1992 essay *Playing in the Dark*" (E8). Morrison uses this very word—"didactic"—when talking about the eighteenth-century novel; as stated above, she sees the novel as a new art form, for a new class of people, designed to tell people what a good living was: "They were didactic in that sense" ("Rootedness" 340). The OED defines "didactic" firstly as "intended to instruct" and secondly as "inclined to teach or moralize too much." Clearly, Kakutani sees *Paradise* as the latter, while Morrison sees her work and the work of the eighteenth-century novel as the former. Indeed, the author sees her work doing for twentieth-century African Americans what the eighteenth-century novel did for the British:

For a long time, the art form that was healing for Black people was music. That music is no longer *exclusively* ours ... so another form has to take that place, and it seems to me that the novel is needed by African-Americans now in a way that it was not needed before—and it is following along the lines of the function of novels everywhere.... But new information has got to get out, and there are several ways to do it. One is the novel. ("Rootedness" 340)

In this same essay, Morrison argues that the African American novel "should be beautiful, and powerful, but it should also *work*. It should have something in it that enlightens; something in it that opens the door and points the way" (341). In *Circles of Sorrow*, Grewal echoes Morrison's metaphor, writing that novels like *The Bluest Eye* show "the saving power of narrative, its capacity to open a door, to point out the fire *and* the fire escape" (x). Whether or not one sees Morrison's novels as didactic in a negative sense, she clearly sees them as performing a certain kind of *work* (her emphasis), a work that then outlines the reader's work. Morrison's texts forcefully point out the fire and the fire escape, what is killing African Americans and what will bring them back to life, what will allow this turning round, this *metastrophe*, this rebirth.

When critics consider the narrative structure of *Song of Solomon*, they tend to talk about the bildungsroman or the quest of the hero as outlined by Joseph Campbell. Similarly, if they consider controlling metaphors, they focus on the novel's central metaphor of flight and its relation to the folktale of the flying African. Oddly, criticism on this novel says very little about the work as a conversion narrative or about the metaphor of rebirth, though both feature prominently.[7] Morrison is a subtle writer, but her naming of this novel's protagonist represents one of the few times in her body of work that she hits the reader over the head: his name is Milkman Dead, he comes from the Dead family, they drive a black, hearse-like car. Figuratively, Milkman is dead; I would argue that in the course of the text, he comes back to life—he learns to live this life intensely and well. To live this intense life, *Song of Solomon* suggests, Milkman must rethink his position in relation to the African American community, must rethink his relationship to his past, and, in doing so, interrogate received notions of blackness. Hence, to "turn around," an African American must question the ideology of whiteness, must question the dominant culture's economic philosophy, language, and notions of gender.

More than any of Morrison's characters, Pilate Dead in *Song of Solomon* embodies the intense life. We see her vitality early in the novel, when Milkman Dead first meets her; the narrator tells us, "It was the first time in his life that he remembered being completely happy [...] no wonder his father was afraid of [her]" (47). Though the father, Macon Dead, fears Pilate and is ashamed of her, he, too, cannot help but be attracted to her as well. After a day that leaves Macon tired, irritable, and lonely, he uses a shortcut home that takes him by Pilate's house. He stands outside in the dark simply to hear Pilate, Reba, and Hagar sing: "Surrendering to the sound, Macon moved closer. He wanted no conversation, no witness, only to listen and perhaps to see the three of them, the source of that music that made him think of fields and wild turkey and calico." As Macon stands in the darkness, his irritability drains from him as he watches the beauty of the women in the candlelight. After a while, the women stop singing, "yet Macon could not leave" (29–30). The reader notes the power and energy radiating from Pilate's house, and Morrison, too, sees this power; she describes Pilate as "the oldest Black woman in the world, the mother of mothers" ("Memory" 387). In a 1983 interview with Nellie McKay, Morrison says of her character, "Pilate is larger than life and never really dies in that sense. She was not born, anyway—she gave birth to herself. So the question of her birth and death is irrelevant." She goes on to say that Pilate exists as "someone who already 'is'" (Taylor-Guthrie 146–147). Unlike many of Morrison's characters, Pilate does not need rebirth; she already "is."

Pilate's position in her community and in her world, in part, allows this "being" in that Pilate's house is "off the grid"—her house has no electricity, no telephone, no number (27, 131). A quick survey of twentieth-century African American literature reveals an ongoing metaphor associating electricity with the power and ubiquity of white hegemonic culture. Zora Neale Hurston's 1937 *Their Eyes Were Watching God* tells us that one of the main characters, Joe Starks, "acted like Mr. Washington"; that is, he acted like a white man. When he establishes the all-black town of Eatonville, Florida, "the rest of the town looked like servants' quarters surrounding the 'big house'" (26, 44). Starks adopts the hierarchical structure of the dominant culture and places himself in the position of master. No sooner does he create this new town, than "the very next day with money out of his own pocket he sent off to Sears, Roebuck and Company for the street lamp" (41). Joe Starks's first action, then, as mayor of Eatonville is to put the town "on the grid." Three years later, towards the end of Richard Wright's 1940 *Native Son*, Bigger Thomas "lay down again on the cot, on his back, and stared at the tiny bright-yellow electric bulb glowing on the ceiling above his head. It contained the fire of death," the very "fire" that will electrocute him shortly (384). A decade later in *Invisible Man*, the title character sits in the basement of an all-white apartment building amid 1,369 lights and surreptitiously sucks "a hell of a lot of free current" away from the Monopolated Light and Power Company (5). This is to say, Joe Starks gets on the grid, Bigger Thomas gets killed by the grid, the "invisible man" clandestinely uses the grid, and Pilate gets off the grid. To have life as an African American, Morrison suggests, is partly a question of where one positions oneself in relation to the grid of white hegemonic culture.

*Song of Solomon*, however, does not attempt to position Pilate as the rugged individualist, the lone wolf who defies all authority and custom to live life her own way. It does not attempt to position her as a protagonist in the tradition of the novel as outlined by Watt, who argues that "from the Renaissance onwards, there was a growing tendency for individual experience to replace collective tradition as the ultimate arbiter of reality," and that the novel "tends towards the assertion of individual freedom from family ties" (14, 141). Indeed, much contemporary multicultural literature wants to critique this very individualism; Friedman notes, "Isolate individualism is an illusion. It is also the privilege of power. A white man has the luxury of forgetting his skin color and sex. He can think of himself as an 'individual.' Women and minorities, reminded at every turn in the great cultural hall of mirrors of their sex or color, have no such luxury" (quoted in Poey 213). Indeed, Grewal suggests that Morrison writes in general about the collective which subverts bourgeois individualism, and that *Song of Solomon* "is about the interdependence of individuals and the insurance of mutual life; redemption cannot be individual" (73). Morrison, herself, adamantly stresses in her interviews and essays that the artist, her art, and black art in general must not be about the individual, but the community: "If anything I do, in the way of writing novels (or whatever I write) isn't about the village or the community or about you, then it is not about anything. I am not interested in indulging myself in some private, closed exercise of my imagination that fulfills only the obligation of my personal dreams" ("Rootedness" 345).

Because of this lack of a sense of community, Sula draws Morrison's condemnation: "Critics devoted to the Western heroic tradition—the individual alone and triumphant—see Sula as a survivor. In the Black community she is lost." The author does not critique Sula for sleeping with Nel's husband, but for putting her grandmother in a nursing home, because Morrison believes blacks "must take care of each other" (Taylor-Guthrie 68). The community needs Sula because it defines itself against her "evil"; Sula needs the community because it permits her to be. Morrison writes, "Whether or not Sula is nourished by that village depends on your view of it…. My own special view is that there was no other place where she could live. She would have been destroyed by any other place; she was permitted to 'be' only in that context, and no one stoned her or killed her or threw her out" ("Rootedness" 343). One might maintain, then, that Morrison's work privileges a communal space in contradistinction to the Western heroic individual.

Yet Morrison's work contains a third space between these two traditions, a space occupied by the character Sula. The author writes that "the critical voice which upholds tradition and communal values and which also provides occasion for an individual to transcend and/or defy group restrictions" serves as one of the aesthetic traditions of Afro-American culture ("Memory" 389). Sula represents the nascent outline of such an individual. Yes, she puts Eva in a nursing home; yes, she seemingly has no regard for the community; but the fact that she willingly defies the community clearly holds a certain fascination for the author. At the end of the novel, as Sula lies on her deathbed, she tells Nel, "You think I don't know what your life is like just because I ain't living it? I know what every colored woman in this country is doing […] dying. Just like me. But the difference is they dying like a stump. Me, I'm going down like one of those redwoods. I sure did live in this world" (123). Sula's "life" contrasts Nel's and the community's lack of it: "Alive was what they, and now Nel, did not want to be. Too dangerous" (104). That is, this third space lies between the rugged individualist of the Western heroic tradition and the individual, like Nel, who surrenders completely to the community and ends up dying because s/he is afraid to "live in this world."

If one sees the inchoate beginnings of this third space in the character Sula, one sees its fruition in characters like Pilate in *Solomon* and Sixo in *Beloved*. Just as Pilate represents "the mother of mothers," Paul D says of Sixo, "Now *there* was a man" (*Beloved* 21). Just as Pilate exists off the grid electrically, Sixo exists off the grid linguistically: he first declines Garner's offer to teach him to read and later stops speaking English all together. Both Pilate and Sixo represent characters who already "are"; both have negotiated a relationship to the hegemonic culture, yet both also preserve a relationship to their communities. Morrison represents Sixo as part of the men of Sweet Home, yet separate from them: his experimentation with night-cooked potatoes, his maintaining a relationship with the Thirty-Mile Woman, and his willingness to stand up to schoolteacher set him apart from the other Sweet Home men. So, too, Pilate exists as part of her community, but not in the way Macon Dead does. Her lack of a navel always somewhat marginalizes Pilate, even within the African American community; the narrator tells us:

> When she realized what her situation in the world was and would probably always be
> she threw away every assumption she had learned and began at zero [...] then she
> tackled the problem of trying to decide how she wanted to live and what was valuable
> to her. When am I happy and when am I sad and what is the difference? What do I
> need to know to stay alive? What is true in the world? (*Solomon* 149)

At one point in the novel, Reverend Cooper asks Milkman if Pilate is still living. "Oh, yes," Milkman replies, "Very much living" (230). Pilate's willingness,
the narrative suggests, to "throw away every assumption," even those assumptions held by her community, allows Pilate to be "very much living."

To be "very much living," Morrison's work shows, one must not only
negotiate a relationship to the dominant white culture and a relationship to the
black community, one must also negotiate a certain relationship to the past,
which, for African Americans, is embodied in the South. One must not only
rethink Western traditions, but African American traditions as well. Richard
Wright ends his memoir *Black Boy: A Record of Childhood and Youth* heading north
to Chicago, leaving Mississippi and the South: "I had somehow gotten the idea
that life could be different, could be lived in a fuller and richer manner"; "I
headed North, full of a hazy notion that life could be lived with dignity" (281,
285). Wright's sentences capture the impetus behind much of the Great
Migration, but Morrison asks blacks to interrogate that impetus. In
"Unspeakable Things Unspoken: The Afro-American Presence in American
Literature," the author closely reads the opening sentence of *Solomon*: "The
North Carolina Mutual Life Insurance agent promised to fly from Mercy to
the other side of Lake Superior at three o'clock" (3). Morrison states, "The
sentence also moves from North Carolina to Lake Superior—geographical
locations, but with a sly implication that the move from North Carolina (the
south) to Lake Superior (the north) might not actually involve progress to some
'superior state'—which of course it does not" (27). Similarly, Violet Trace in
*Jazz* says, "Before I came North I made sense" (207). Grewal argues that one
of the results of the Great Migration was "the specific cultural discontinuity
created by migration from the South to the urban North and by the black middle-class's repudiation of a stigmatized past" (66). We see this discontinuity in
the difference between Macon's and Pilate's reactions to Milkman's trip down
South. The men who remember him in Danville, Pennsylvania interest
Macon, but regarding the story of his grandfather, Solomon, who could fly,
"he wasn't a bit interested in the flying part." Macon suggests he should make
a trip down there. Milkman asks, "Virginia?" To which his father replies,
"Danville. I ought to go by and see some of those boys before these legs stop

moving" (*Solomon* 334). That is, going to Virginia to see about his ancestry does not interest Macon; going to Pennsylvania, where the "boys" remember him, does. Pilate, on the other hand, immediately makes a trip back to Shalimar with Milkman, and she "blended into the population like a stick of butter in a churn" (335). Going down South forces Milkman to rethink his family's flight from the South.

Milkman also reverses the movement of the Great Migration: he travels from Michigan to Pennsylvania to Virginia. Milkman's rebirth comes from his reconnecting with the "ancient properties" Morrison mentions in the epigraph to *Tar Baby*. Soon after the publication of *Solomon*, Morrison told Colette Dowling, "Once you leave home, the things that feed you are not available to you anymore, the *life* is not available to you anymore. And the American life, the *white* life, that's certainly not available to you" (Taylor-Guthrie 58). When Milkman returns "home," he finds that *life*; when he returns to the South, he rejects the values of *white* life—his father's values. Morrison writes, "If my work is to be functional to the group (to the village, as it were) then it must bear witness and identify that which is useful from the past and that which ought to be discarded" ("Memory" 389). In Shalimar, Milkman discovers, in part, what is useful from his past—that his past *is* useful, that it holds *life*.

Interrogating received notions of blackness also holds life. In Shalimar and Danville, Milkman learns not only about his great grandfather, Solomon, but also about his grandfather, Jake Dead, who was vibrant, vital, and "black as coal" (*Solomon* 321).[8] The narrator tells us that Pilate "look just like Papa and he looked like all them pictures you ever see of Africans"—that is, Pilate is also black as coal (54). These are the first of many Morrison characters described as dark. In Morrison's next novel, *Tar Baby*, we meet the woman in the yellow dress, "that woman's woman—that mother/sister/she" with "skin like tar" (46). In *Beloved*, Sixo is "indigo," and in *Jazz*, Wild has "coal-black skin" (21, 171). Morrison links this deep skin color with life and vitality and thereby asks her readers to reconceptualize their received notions of blackness. In the Christian rebirth, the believer goes from darkness to light; in Milkman's rebirth, he goes from light to darkness. He leaves the ways of his father—who Guitar says "behaves like a white man, thinks like a white man"—to adopt the ways of his aunt and his grandfather, both of whom are black as coal (*Solomon* 223). When Milkman first arrives in Virginia, the men of Shalimar "looked at his skin and saw it was as black as theirs, but they knew he had the heart of the white men who came to pick them up in the trucks"; Milkman's "white heart," this part of "the cocoon of personality," gives way down South (266).

Just as Morrison associates blackness with life, by contrast she associates whiteness with death. When the white family, the Butlers, murder Jake Dead, the men in Danville begin dying. Jake's death has a similar effect on his son; the narrator tells us that the fact that Macon "distorted life, bent it, for the sake of gain, was a measure of his loss at his father's death" (300). This "distorted life," then, affects all who associate with Macon; Pilate sees that his wife, Ruth, "was dying of lovelessness then, and seemed to be dying of it now" (151). That is, metaphoric death seems to radiate out from Jake's literal death, a crime perpetrated by a white family. Even the family's name, Dead, is given to them by a drunk Yankee (54). Just as this white man gives this family death in name, white culture gives blacks death in spirit.

The Butlers, perhaps, get their comeuppance in that "the last one, the girl Elizabeth, died a couple years back. Barren as a rock" (232). Morrison uses this very word in the afterword to *The Bluest Eye* to describe the Dick-and-Jane reader that envelops the narrative; she calls it the "barren white-family primer" (215). Morrison's work continually represents whiteness as lifeless, even lethal. In *Tar Baby*, when Jadine Childs visits the all-black town of Eloe, Florida, she "looked out into the blackest nothing she had ever seen. Blacker and bleaker than Isle des Chevaliers, and loud. Loud with the presence of plants and field life" (251). The narrative contrasts this with the Isle des Chevaliers, Valerian Street's house, where "no crickets, no mosquitoes, no frogs," exist, and where "the bees have no sting […] nor honey" (*Tar* 78, 81). Gideon says of this house, "Not much life going on over there," just as Claudia MacTeer says the lakefront houses, the white houses, show "no sign of life" (*Tar* 154, *Bluest* 105). Perhaps Son puts it most baldly when he thinks of "*them*, the aliens, the people who in a mere three hundred years had killed a world millions of years old. From Micronesia to Liverpool, from Kentucky to Dresden, they killed everything they touched including their own coastlines, their own hills and forests" (*Tar* 269).

Is this image of whiteness, then, just a form of essentialism? Does this suggest that blacks are, in their essence, nurturing and life-sustaining, while whites, by nature, are murderous and life-destroying? Does this suggest that Morrison shares the views of her character Guitar Bains, who tells Milkman, "Hitler was the most natural white man in the world. He killed Jews and Gypsies because he didn't have us [….] White people are unnatural. As a race they are unnatural." When Milkman tries to argue with him, Guitar returns, "What I'm saying is, under certain conditions they would *all* do it. And under the same circumstances we would not […] the disease they have is in their blood, in the structure of their chromosomes" (*Solomon* 157). The answer to these questions comes, in part, in "Unspeakable Things Unspoken" when Morrison gives her reading of *Moby-Dick*. Critics have discussed ad infinitum what the whale's whiteness signifies, but for Morrison, it signifies a question of race. She points out that Melville's father-in-law, Judge Shaw, handed down the decision that enacted the Fugitive Slave Law in April 1851, at the very time Melville was writing his massive tome. She argues, then, "Melville is not exploring white *people*, but whiteness idealized," and the work is not about "satanizing white people," but about "whiteness as ideology" ("Unspeakable" 16–17).

In *Playing in the Dark*, Morrison gives an image that could embody her idea of the ideology of whiteness. While setting up her argument, she explains how she gradually became aware of how blacks and images of blackness are used in American literature. When she finally realizes that "the subject of the dream is the dreamer," that the use of black characters is reflexive, she writes, "It is as if I had been looking at a fishbowl … and suddenly I saw the bowl, the structure that transparently (and invisibly) permits the ordered life it contains to exist in the larger world" (*Playing* 17). Morrison sees the ideology of whiteness as this bowl, a bowl that invisibly permits and shapes the "ordered life" of African Americans, and with her work, she wants to point out, to make visible, this bowl. She wants to suggest that there are other "lives" outside this bowl.

She also wants to suggest that just as the bowl shapes the life within, it also constricts and can even choke off the life within. Schur writes, "It is precisely the 'infection' of racialized thinking, among people of all racial identifications, that is the subject of Morrison's work" (13). For an African American to come into contact with the ideology of whiteness is to risk "infection," and infection risks death. From her first novel to her last, Morrison continually warns about the dangers of adopting this belief system. Many literary texts contain moments when the character and the plot seem to drop away, and the reader gets a glimpse into the author's thoughts, unmediated by the storyline or the character's personality. One such moment comes at the end of *The Bluest Eye* when Soaphead Church writes a letter to God:

> We in this colony took as our own the most dramatic, and the most obvious, of our white masters' characteristics, which were, of course, their worst [...] consequently we were not royal but snobbish, not aristocratic but class-conscious; we believed authority was cruelty to our inferiors, and education was being at school [...] we

raised our children and reared our crops; we let infants grow, and property develop. Our manhood was defined by acquisitions. Our womanhood by acquiescence. (177)

One hears a similar critique of African Americans at the end of *Paradise* when Reverend Misner says of the black men of Ruby, "They think they have out-foxed the whiteman when in fact they imitate him. They think they are pro-tecting their wives and children, when in fact they are maiming them" (306). Morrison's work, then, asks, what does it mean to imitate the white man and take on the worst characteristics of the white master? What does it look like to behave as if one has internalized the ideology of whiteness?

Firstly, it means one behaves like Macon Dead, who, as stated above, "behaves like a white man, thinks like a white man"; it means one adopts the master's economic system. Macon tells Milkman, "Money is freedom, Macon. The only real freedom there is" (*Solomon* 163). Early in the novel, he gives this fatherly advice to his son: "Let me tell you right now the one important thing you'll ever need to know: Own things. And let the things you own own other things. Then you'll own yourself and other people too" (55). The irony and horror of this advice—a fact lost on Macon, but not on Morrison—is that Macon is the son of a slave. The advice he passes on to his son, therefore, embodies an ideology reminiscent of the ideology undergirding slavery: a sys-tem that privileges ownership and property, even to the point of owning and seeing people as property. Pilate and her house stand in contradistinction to Macon and his; the narrator describes Ruth and Pilate as "one wholly depend-ent on money for life, the other indifferent to it" (139). Pilate's house looks much like Gayatri Spivak's "subaltern": "the space out of touch with the logic of capitalism" (quoted in Schur 5). Through the course of the novel, Milkman will travel from his father's capitalist world to a space out of touch with that ethos, namely Pilate's world.

In light of this logic of capitalism and regarding the idea of rebirth, Milkman has two moments in *Solomon* in which a new self emerges, one in each of the two parts of the text. The first occurs as Milkman and Guitar head to Pilate's house to steal, they think, the bag of gold. After much hemming and hawing by Milkman, Guitar yells at him: "You listen! You got a life? Live it! Live the motherfuckin life! Live it!" (183). The text tells us, "all the tentative-ness, doubt, and inauthenticity that plagued him slithered away without a trace, a sound […] he felt a self inside himself emerge, a clean-lined definite self" (183–184). On the next page, the two of them see the bag of gold "and like Easter, it promised everything: the Risen Son and the heart's lone desire"

(185). That is, the text associates the emergence of Milkman's new self with the rebirth of Christ. This could be the moment Milkman turns round from one of the Dead to one who "lives the motherfuckin life," and what would allow this rebirth would be the bag of gold, the embodiment of Macon's economic value system. The second moment, in the latter half of the novel, comes when Milkman goes hunting one night with the men of Shalimar. He becomes separated from the group and, alone, sits on the ground, where "his self—the cocoon that was 'personality'—gave way. He could barely see his own hands and couldn't see his feet. He was only his breath, coming slower now, and his thoughts" (277). The text associates Milkman's first "new self" with the North, with the material values of his father, but that self "gives way" to reveal a second self associated with the South, the values of his aunt, and the immaterial—his body itself fades, and he becomes breath and thought.

For Milkman to rethink his father's economics, he must rethink the dominant culture's economics, and he also must rethink his received tradition. Ian Watt sees Robinson Crusoe as "a symbol of the processes associated with the rise of economic individualism," and one of the recurrent themes in the bildungsroman is the making of a gentleman (62); Jerome Hamilton Buckley tells us, "Money therefore assumes a new and pervasive importance in the bildungsroman" (20). Certainly, Macon Dead embodies the ethos of this economic individualism, but if the bildungsroman depicts the making of a gentleman—if in *Great Expectations* Pip goes from a blacksmith's apprentice to a member of the London bourgeoisie—*Solomon* depicts the un-making of a gentleman as Milkman leaves his middle-class status. Indeed, Grewal argues, "Morrison's novels may be read as anti-Bildung projects that subvert dominant middle-class ideology" (5). Perhaps the harshest critique in Morrison's work of this ethos of economic individualism comes in *Tar Baby*, just after Valerian fires Gideon and Thérèse; Son thinks to himself:

> [Valerian] had been able to dismiss with a flutter of the fingers the people whose sugar and cocoa had allowed him to grow old in regal comfort; although he had taken the sugar and cocoa and paid for it as though it had no value, as though the cutting of cane and picking of beans was child's play and had no value; but he turned it into candy, the invention of which really was child's play, and sold it to other children and made a fortune in order to move near, but not in the midst of, the jungle where the sugar came from and build a palace with more of their labor and then hire them to do more of the work he was not capable of [...] that is why they loved property so, because they had killed it soiled it defecated on it and they loved more than anything the places where they shit. (*Tar* 203)

Macon Dead, constantly fingering the keys in his pockets of the houses he owns, has internalized Valerian's love of property; he has internalized the master's economic ethos, and this, in part, brings to fruition his last name.

In order to effect this *convertere*, one must not only rethink the master's ideas surrounding property, one must also rethink the master's tongue. In *Playing in the Dark*, Morrison writes, "I am a black writer struggling with and through a language that can powerfully evoke and enforce hidden signs of racial superiority, cultural hegemony, and dismissive 'othering' of people" (x). She insists that her work as a writer "requires me to learn how to maneuver ways to free up the language from its sometimes sinister, frequently lazy, almost always predictable employment of racially informed and determined chains" (xi). Just as the writer struggles to negotiate a relationship to this language, so, too, do her characters struggle, but her characters are more aware of the problems inherent in this negotiation than, say, Friday. In "Friday on the Potomac" Morrison writes, "This loss of the mother tongue seems not to disturb Friday, even though he never completely learns the master's" (xxvi). Compare this with Sixo; when his master—literally his slave master—offers to teach him to read, he refuses: "It would change his mind—make him forget things he shouldn't and memorize things he shouldn't and he didn't want his mind messed up" (*Beloved* 208). Eventually, he stops speaking English all together. Paul D, on the other hand, takes up Garner's offer: "If you can't count they can cheat you. If you can't read they can beat you" (*Beloved* 208).

Ella and the thirty women present yet another strategy for negotiating the master's tongue when, at the end of *Beloved*, they go out to exorcise 124 Bluestone Road: "They stopped praying and took a step back to the beginning. In the beginning there were no words. In the beginning was the sound, and they all knew what that sound sounded like" (259). Here, the text alludes to the book of John, which opens, "In the beginning was the Word, and the Word was with God, and the Word was God. He was in the beginning with God[....] In Him was life, and the life was the light of men. And the light shines in the darkness, and the darkness did not comprehend it" (John 1:1–5). But the passage from *Beloved* also has traces of Genesis, which reads:

> In the beginning God created the heavens and the earth. The earth was without form, and void; and darkness was on the face of the deep. And the Spirit of God was hovering over the face of the waters. Then God said, "Let there be light"; and there was light. And God saw the light, that it was good; and God divided the light from the darkness. God called the light Day, and the darkness He called Night. So the evening and the morning were the first day. (Genesis 1:1–5)

But these thirty black women go back to a time before the Word, before the first day; they go back to a sound that predates the Word, and when the women's sound hits Sethe, "she tremble[s] like the baptized in its wash" (*Beloved* 261). Likewise, when Milkman's second self emerges down South, he is sitting in a forest at night and hears the hunters and the dogs communicating with one another. At first he thinks he hears language, but "No, it was not language; it was what there was before language. Before things were written down. Language in the time when men and animals did talk to one another [...] when men ran *with* wolves, not from or after them" (*Solomon* 278). In Christianity, one is reborn through Christ, the Word made flesh; in Morrison, Sethe and Milkman are reborn in the wash of a sound that predates the Word, a sound that predates a whole theology that figures light as good and darkness as unable to comprehend the good. This moment in *Beloved* points to an alternative linguistic fishbowl.

Morrison, in her Nobel Prize speech, may offer yet another method to negotiate the master's tongue. If Sixo rejects it, if Paul D masters it, if Ella and the women predate it, Morrison questions the need for it at all. Again, she returns to the Bible and her received tradition. The character of the storyteller in Morrison's Nobel Prize address questions the conventional wisdom that regards the collapse of the Tower of Babel as a misfortune. She questions the idea

> that one monolithic language would have expedited the building and heaven would have been reached. Whose heaven, she wonders? And what kind? Perhaps the achievement of Paradise was premature, a little hasty if no one could take the time to understand other languages, other views, other narratives. Had they, the heaven they imagined might have been found at their feet. Complicated, demanding yes, but a view of heaven as life; not heaven as postlife. (270)

A master tongue implies a single, hegemonic entity that ignores or erases "other languages, other views, other narratives," what Morrison at another point calls other "centers of the self" ("Unspeakable" 9). In her Nobel Prize speech, Morrison, again, interrogates and rewrites her received—here, biblical—tradition. Life lies, she suggests, not in the afterward and a monolithic language; life lies here at our feet in the complicated, demanding task of engaging other centers of self and their languages.

Finally, one must not only rethink the master's money and the master's language, Morrison's work suggests, one must rethink the master himself, one must rethink where life lies in relation to gender. One sees this most clearly in

*Paradise* where, in Ruby, Oklahoma, one finds not only a house, but a whole town "off the grid." The only white man in the novel comes into Ace's Grocery looking for directions; "Houses round here don't seem to have numbers," he says (*Paradise* 121). When Ruby thinks of paving the roads leading to town, the old town members fight it: "They liked being off the county road, accessible only to the lost and the knowledgeable" (186). In Ruby, one finds a town not only all-black, not only coal-black, but eight-rock black, "a deep deep level in the coal mines. Blue-black people" (193). Based on the author's earlier work, one might think that Ruby, Oklahoma would be, in a matter of speaking, paradise, but, clearly, it is not. The question is why? What went wrong with the experiment?

The answer comes, in part, at the novel's end when Deacon confesses to Richard his long remorse "at having become what the Old Fathers cursed: the kind of man who set himself up to judge, rout and even destroy the needy, the defenseless, the different" (302). In *Paradise* "the different" takes the form of the women in the Convent, and thus this novel, more than any of Morrison's novels, ties race to gender. That is, the same apparatus that allows whites "to other" blacks allows these black men "to other" the Convent women. For the nine men, these women become "bitches," "witches," "sluts," "loose," "hussies," "streetwalkers," "uncontrollable," and "unnatural" (276–280). The same mental apparatus that allows for terms like "nigger" allows for the above terms. Eerily, one of the weapons the men take out to the Convent is rope; this is a kind of lynching. Morrison suggests that a desire to control "the different" undergirds both whites' behavior toward blacks and men's behavior toward women. Lone understands that neither Steward nor Deacon "put up with what he couldn't control," and Billie Delia describes Ruby as a "backward noplace ruled by men whose power to control was out of control" (*Paradise* 278, 308). This desire to control difference precludes Ruby from becoming a paradise. By no accident, then, Milkman's metamorphosis comes not by adopting his father's values, but by adopting his aunt's. As Grewal points out, *Solomon* challenges the individual, self-reliant model of male heroism constantly given by the Western tradition in that Milkman must continually rely on women: Pilate, Ruth, Hagar, Corinthians, Magdalene, Circe, and Sweet (74).

This essay began discussing a picture and it will end discussing a picture, the cover art of the edition of *Song of Solomon* that appeared after Morrison received the Nobel Prize in 1993. In the background of the picture stands a sun that radiates sharp, pronounced rays of light, but whereas Caravaggio's Paul reaches out toward the light, our subject here—a man black as coal—

turns away from the light and faces the viewer. A white sheet envelops him, like a shroud, as in a shroud of death, but he opens up the shroud of white death to reveal a night as black as he. The sheet between his two hands forms a vaginal space, which makes sense if one is talking about birth and rebirth, as I am suggesting this picture, this novel, and Morrison's body of work as a whole are. This picture, this novel, and Morrison's oeuvre suggest there exists a different fishbowl which, too, contains life, a different life, one based not on the model of the rugged economic individual, a monolithic master tongue, and on the master himself. The man on the cover looks directly at the viewer, opens a space in the shroud, and beckons him or her to enter into this alternative "light," with its alternative life, and its alternative mode of rebirth.

## Notes

[1] *Holy Bible: The New King James Version* (New York: Thomas Nelson Publishers, 1984.)

[2] In quoting or talking directly about an author, I will retain his or her gender-specific "man," if that is what s/he uses. In my own writing, I will shift to a more gender-neutral term or use scare quotes to problematize the specificity. Still, the specific "man" will be telling when this essay comes to Morrison's thoughts on this "new self."

[3] On this point, see Richard Schur's "The Subject of Law: Toni Morrison, Critical Race Theory, and the Narration of Cultural Criticism," in which he writes, "A necessary starting point is Morrison's statement that she is not writing for white people, as much African American literature has and does" (3).

[4] Unfortunately, I wrote this essay before the release of Morrison's most recent novel, *Love*, and, therefore, the argument here does not reflect or reference this work.

[5] Here and throughout, the emphasis is the author's, unless otherwise noted.

[6] To talk about this "whole" self is not to ignore debates surrounding "the death of the subject." One could argue that this essay only gives half of Foucault's argument on the construction of this new "man"; no sooner does the philosopher/historian declare the birth of this new subject than he adds, "But he has grown old so quickly" (*Order* 308). In *Loose Canons*, Henry Louis Gates, Jr. addresses this issue by first quoting Jacques Derrida's critique: "This is the risk. The effect of Law is to build a structure of the subject, and as soon as you say, 'well, the woman is a subject and this subject deserves equal rights,' and so on—then you are caught in the logic of phallocentricism and you have rebuilt the empire of Law." Gates responds, "The Western male subject has long been constituted historically for himself and in himself. And, while we readily accept, acknowledge, and partake of the critique of *this* subject as transcendent, to deny us the process of exploring and reclaiming our subjectivity … leaves us nowhere, invisible and voiceless in the republic of Western letters. Consider the irony: precisely when we (and other Third World peoples) obtain the complex wherewithal to define our black subjectivity in the republic of Western letters, our theoretical colleagues declare that there ain't no such thing as a subject, so why should we be bothered with that?" (35). Indeed, the beginning of this essay

attempts to delimit the differences between this Western male subject and the subject Morrison tries to outline.

[7] Regarding this novel as a bildungsroman, see Catherine Carr Lee "The South in Toni Morrison's *Song of Solomon*," in *Toni Morrison's "Song of Solomon": A Casebook*, edited by Jan Furman (Oxford: Oxford University Press, 2003). Regarding the myth of the flying African, see Michael Awkward in the same volume.

[8] Since three men are named Macon Dead, I refer to them as Jake Dead, Macon Dead, and Milkman Dead.

## Works Cited

Buckley, Jerome Hamilton. *Season Youth: The Bildungsroman from Dickens to Golding*. Cambridge, MA: Harvard University Press, 1974.

Ellison, Ralph. *Invisible Man*. 1952. New York: Random House, 1972.

Foucault, Michel. *The History of Sexuality: An Introduction*. Vol. 1. 1976. Translated by Robert Hurley. New York: Random House, 1978.

———. *The Order of Things: An Archaeology of the Human Sciences*. 1965. New York: Random House, 1970.

———. "Technologies of the Self." 1982. *Technologies of the Self: A Seminar with Michel Foucault*. Amherst: University of Massachusetts, 1988.

Gates, Henry Louis. *Loose Canons: Notes on the Culture Wars*. New York: Oxford University Press, 1992.

Grewal, Gurleen. *Circles of Sorrow, Lines of Struggle: The Novels of Toni Morrison*. Baton Rouge: Louisiana State University Press, 1998.

Hadot, Pierre. *Philosophy as a Way of Life*. Oxford: Blackwell Publishers Ltd., 1995.

Hurston, Zora Neale. *Their Eyes Were Watching God*. 1937. Foreword by Mary Helen Washington. New York: Harper & Row, 1990.

Jefferson, Thomas. "The Declaration of Independence." *Norton Anthology of American Literature*. Vol. 1. Edited by Nina Baym. New York: W. W. Norton & Company, 1998.

Kakutani, Michiko. "Books of the Times: *Paradise*: Worthy Women, Unredeemable Men." *New York Times* Jan. 6, 1998.

Lee, Catherine Carr. "The South in Toni Morrison's *Song of Solomon*." In *Toni Morrison's "Song of Solomon": A Casebook*, edited by Jan Furman. Oxford: Oxford University Press, 2003. 43–64

Morrison, Toni. *Beloved*. New York: Penguin, 1987.

———. *The Bluest Eye*. New York: Penguin Books, 1970.

———. "Friday on the Potomac." Introduction to *Race-ing Justice, En-gendering Power: Essays on Anita Hill, Clarence Thomas, and the Construction of Social Reality*, edited by Toni Morrison. New York: Pantheon Books, 1992. vii–xxx.

———. *Jazz*. New York: Penguin Books, 1992.

———. "Memory, Creation, and Writing." *Thought* 59 (1984): 385–390.

———. "Nobel Lecture 1993." In *Toni Morrison: Critical and Theoretical Approaches*, edited by Nancy J. Peterson. Baltimore: Johns Hopkins University Press, 1997. 267–273.

———. *Paradise*. New York: Alfred A. Knopf, 1998.

———. *Playing in the Dark: Whiteness and the Literary Imagination*. New York: Vintage Books, 1992.

———. "Rootedness: The Ancestor as Foundation." In *Black Women Writers (1950–1980): A Critical Evaluation*, edited by Mari Evans. New York: Doubleday, 1984. 339–345.

———. *Song of Solomon*. New York: Penguin Books, 1977.

———. *Sula*. New York: Bantam Books, 1973.

———. *Tar Baby*. New York: Penguin, 1981.

———. "Unspeakable Things Unspoken: The Afro-American Presence in American Literature." *Michigan Quarterly Review* 28. (Winter 1989): 1–34.

Plato. *Republic*. Translated by G. M. A. Grube. Hackett Publishing Company, Inc., 1992.

Poey, Delia. "Coming of Age in the Curriculum: *The House on Mango Street* and *Bless Me, Ultima* as Representative Texts." *Americas Review: A Review of Hispanic Literature and Art of the USA* 24.3–4 (1996): 201–17.

Schur, Richard. "The Subject of Law: Toni Morrison, Critical Race Theory, and the Narration of Cultural Criticism." *49th Parallel: An Interdisciplinary Journal of North American Studies 6.* (Autumn 2000). n. pag.

Taylor-Guthrie, Danille, ed. *Conversations with Toni Morrison*. Jackson: University Press of Mississippi, 1994.

Watt, Ian. *The Rise of the Novel*. Berkeley: University of California Press, 1957.

Wright, Richard. *Black Boy: A Record of Childhood and Youth*. New York: Signet Books, 1945.

———. *Native Son*. New York: Harper & Row, 1966.

# 4

# INTIMATE FATALITY:
## *SONG OF SOLOMON* AND THE JOURNEY HOME

*Beth Benedrix*

Toni Morrison's sprawling *Song of Solomon*—deliberately courting a connection to the most erotic and controversial text of the Hebrew Bible, the Song of Songs—begins with an account of a suicide; a man, pledging to "fly away on [his] own wings," announces his simultaneous intentions to transcend and plummet headlong into the street to a tiny crowd assembled only by happenstance. The street where they are assembled takes its name—"Not Doctor Street"—from a conscious and deliberate awareness of that space to which it has no access. Negation upon negation, the ultimate act of self-expression slides into self-destruction; power collides with helplessness, desire with resignation.

This space of negation serves as the site of Morrison's biblical exploration and, ultimately, revaluation. Together with the Song of Songs, Morrison draws heavily on the book of Ruth as she narrates a story of exile within and from the most intimate boundaries of home. Exile supplants the Beloved of *Shir ha Shirim, becomes* the Beloved, both held at a distance—as unfulfilled wish—and subsumed by longing subject as consummate desire. The erotic tale, already a metaphor for national yearning on one level, now becomes as well a tale of identity withheld and granted by an always-elusive other. The choice offered, then, by the book of Ruth—to stay or to follow, though to follow means precisely to lose the stability of nation—now becomes the choice to remain faceless, nameless, or to claim an identity designated by a violent reckoning with memory. Choice itself is less a signal of autonomy in the world Morrison creates—a world in which the reigning family is named, literally, Dead—than it is a temporary deferral of the inevitable crush of fate. To "follow" one's sense of self, one's symbolic home, away from the confines of nation but, as Ruth does, toward an expanding definition of family is, in the context Morrison provides, necessary, even revelatory, but ultimately fatal for the one who takes the journey "home."

In this essay, I will explore how and why Morrison uses this set of biblical texts—which together form a constellation affirming body, nation, and family—as the backdrop for a tale of perpetual self-defeat. As erotic ties blur indiscriminately with familial ties, we're plunged along with her characters into a world marked by transgression, a world where death is at once punishment and redemption.

## Violent Love

At the center of this novel is the search for love, for belonging, for communion. Sought by virtually everyone, it is achieved by no one, save perhaps Pilate, who comes at the moment of her death to what might very well be the prescriptive "message" of the novel overall: "I wish I'd a knowed more people. I would of loved 'em all. If I'd a knowed more, I would a loved more" (336). The novel is often read as a "hero" narrative, a bildungsroman of sorts, with Milkman's quest for identity as the focus. While this focus is certainly a founding layer of the novel, his quest cannot be divorced from the world around him, a world inhabited by those who are as flawed and broken as he is, by those who are equally attempting to understand this elusive thing called love, this thing that they claim to live and die for.

As she provides a spectrum of the various methods of loving, of enacting "being-in-love," Morrison encourages a normative approach to these methods. Though normative, the lines blur quickly, and the reader may very well find herself convinced by the often devastating, often horrifying, effects of the acts these characters take in the name of what they call "love." In forcing readers to bear witness to these acts, Morrison engages us in a process of revaluation, redefinition. "Love" transforms quickly into self-love, possession, vengeance, forcing us to redefine our terms.

The Song of Songs provides a model for just such a revaluation; thoroughly subversive, it stakes its claim on a kind of love that challenges the assumptions and conventions that dominate the Hebrew Bible. A celebration of reciprocal, mutual, bodily desire (desire not bounded by marriage or for simple purposes of reproduction), it is nevertheless enacted in a space where the threat of convention is both violent and perpetual. So, too, in Morrison's *Song of Solomon*, the possibility for a love that would allow respite from the outside world is tempered always by the danger of this world. "Sweetness" is heightened by the contrast of all that threatens to invade.

In chapter 8 of the Song of Songs, the final chapter of this short but intensely rich book, love is brought into connection with death, and a warning is sounded concerning the incompatibility of love with life. Love, it would seem, forces a choice: to live in the world according to its rules, or to choose alienation: "Set me as a seal upon thy heart, as a seal upon thine arm; for love is strong as death, jealousy is cruel as the grave; the flashes thereof are flashes of fire, a very flame of the Lord. Many waters cannot quench love, neither can the floods drown it; if a man would give all the substance of his house for love, he would utterly be contemned" (8:6–7).[1] This last line announces a hypothetical scenario, then undercuts it, as if to suggest no one would choose the fate of being cast out because of love.

Guitar, it would seem, chooses precisely this fate. His affiliation with the Seven Days, a vigilante group that retaliates against the murders of black people by killing white people, cuts off any possibilities he might have for marriage or children. After hearing Guitar's story concerning his involvement with this group, Milkman sits in disbelief and disgust, and finally discounts his friend's logic with: "I can't buy it [...] there's too much wrong with it. Attempting to convince Guitar just *why* it is wrong, he says definitively, "There's no love in it." Guitar responds in a way that becomes quickly emblematic of the ambiguity of love in this world where violence is deemed necessary: "No love? No love? Didn't you hear me? What I'm doing ain't about hating white people. It's about loving us. About loving you. My whole life is love" (*Song of Solomon* 159).

Intuitively, Milkman senses the danger of Guitar's equation of love with murder. But because Guitar lives according to a passion Milkman doesn't share, a passion that necessitates—at least according to its own rhetoric—a subjugation of self to a collective group, Milkman has no means of entrance into this logic, no legitimate way to shoot it down. Milkman, in other words, has no passion: he has neither an overdeveloped sense of self, nor a sense of himself as part of a larger group. At this point, then, he simply does not have access to the argument that would de-legitimize Guitar's so thoroughly misguided claims. Guitar, naming "love" as his most basic motivation, would seem to own the moral legitimacy in this moment. Add to this the fact that *only* Guitar gives voice to the intensity of Hagar's pain after she has been driven, by rejection, to attempt to murder Milkman. *Only* Guitar understands how intimately love is bound to violence (though he can also see in Hagar's case, unlike his own, that when love dictates violence, it is not truly love). He says to her:

You think because he doesn't love you that you are worthless. You think because he doesn't want you anymore that he is right—that his judgment and opinion of you are correct. If he throws you out, then you are garbage. You think he belongs to you because you want to belong to him. It's a bad word, "belong." Especially when you put it with somebody you love. Love shouldn't be like that. Did you ever see the way the clouds love a mountain? They circle all around it; sometimes you can't even see the mountain for the clouds. But you know what? You go up top and what do you see? His head. The clouds never cover the head. His head pokes through, because the clouds let him; they don't wrap him up. They let him keep his head up high, free, with nothing to hide him or bind him. Hear me, Hagar? [...] You can't own a human being. You can't lose what you don't own. Suppose you did own him. Could you really love somebody who was absolutely nobody without you? You really want somebody like that? Somebody who falls apart when you walk out the door? You don't, do you? And neither does he. You're turning over your whole life to him. Your whole life, girl. And if it means so little to you that you can just give it away, hand it to him, then why should it mean any more to him? He can't value you more than you value yourself. (306)

Guitar has identified and rejected a formulation of love—equally misguided—that competes with his own, namely, that to love means to possess, but at the same time, to lose oneself, to lose one's sense of value. This type of love suggests a swallowing up, a usurpation of self by other. It is a reversal of the eradication of otherness necessitated by Guitar's form of love; but though a reversal, the result of both forms is the same: two entities fight to the death of one or the other. Milkman, too, seems to equate love early on with the power to enact violence; to protect his mother, he strikes his father. Ever circumspect in his motives, ever reluctant to attribute his actions to love, "he would not pretend that it was love for his mother. She was too insubstantial, too shadowy for love" (75). Milkman still operates in this moment, however, swiftly and according to a seemingly accepted code of conduct: if one is or appears to be connected to another through the bonds of love, one is not only expected to commit, but justified in committing, violence in the name of this bond.

In the "Song of Songs," violence is depicted as a natural, uncontested result of being in love. Chapter 5 relates this exchange between the two lovers: during the night, the man comes to the woman's door, begging entrance. She first puts him off, claiming she has just "washed [her] feet," preferring not to "defile them" (5:3). But his persistence wins her over; she runs to the door and opens it. He, scared off into the night by an unnamed threat or by her initial resistance (it remains unclear), has disappeared. In pursuit of him, she runs out into the street, only to be accosted and beaten by the "watchmen that go about the city" (5:7). Undeterred by this attack, she calls upon the "daughters of Jerusalem," asking them to send along this message: "If you find him now you must tell him that I am in the fever of love" (5:8).

As though expecting to be punished for loving outside the context of marriage, and yet not impeded by this expectation of punishment, the female lover here accepts the authoritative voice of the watchmen. This authority is never overturned. Though the lovers persist in their love, we are reminded that this affair is illicit; it unfolds—never consummated—under the watchful eyes of those who would beat into submission rather than accommodate anyone who would pursue an unconventional expression of love. The attribution of the Song of Songs to Solomon in the first line of the book marks from the outset the proprietary nature of this affair: ownership—dominion, in other words— is given over to the one who *watches*, the one who witnesses, and in the same moment, it is taken away from those who experience this affair firsthand. Solomon, ever wistful, ever disconnected from the events his song would seek to capture, still remains the normative voice that these lovers attempt to subvert through a kind of civil disobedience.

The chapter that follows the beating of the female lover is marked by vacillation between the anxiety of abandonment and the claustrophobia of being too closely held. The chapter begins with an appeal: "Whither is thy beloved gone?" (6:1). It would seem that here Solomon takes an active questioning stance, steps out, as it were, from the sidelines; here his question is directed to a space marked by absence, retreat. He can only pose a question, in other words, when the lover has retreated from his beloved—Solomon's question thus aggravates the violence of the chapter before, punctuates it, adds insult to injury. As his proprietary gaze continues to fix this encounter, the lovers respond by banishing this gaze altogether from their love-making: "Turn away thine eyes from me, for they have overcome me" (6:5). They recognize, in other words, the trappings of an encounter steeped in power, steeped in the desire to possess, and choose to adopt another mode of encounter. If to gaze upon is to violate, to impose one's will over another, they will choose a method that privileges connection over subsuming. Interestingly, this alternate method is attached once again to sight in the next chapter, but this time, to *see* is to recognize that the beloved is perpetually in a state of retreat, that the beloved has the autonomy to retreat, that the beloved embodies distinction that cannot be collapsed: "Return, return, O Shulamite; Return, return, that we may look upon thee. What will you see in the Shulamite? As it were, a dance of two companies" (7:1).

So, too, Guitar's response to Hagar's frantic, possessive love for Milkman promotes this stance of recognition. He pleads with her to let go, to unclench her fist, to stop equating love with ownership. His suggestion that the clouds "let [the mountain] keep his head up high, free, with nothing to hide him or bind him" is in effect a celebration of difference, distinction, within the context of relation. The power that the lover holds over the beloved, in his view, is the power to *sustain the freedom* of the beloved.

Given that love is so often associated with possession in the world Hagar inhabits, it is no wonder that she has trouble accepting Guitar's vision of love. Similarly, Milkman, in the process of trying to overturn Guitar's admission that he is driven to murder *by* love, finds himself equating love and ownership again and again, and expecting others to do so. For instance, as though despite himself taking Guitar's paradoxical—and pathological—definition of love to heart, Milkman misreads Circe's motivations for remaining in the house where Pilate and Macon had felt imprisoned as children, taking care of dogs that are not hers but are left behind when the mistress of the house kills herself. In a wish fulfillment of sorts, perhaps because he's heard Guitar's misguided attempts to equate love and vengeance, now Milkman seems to want to attribute to love this behavior that would seem to bespeak loyalty:

> "You loved those white folks that much?" he asks her.
> "Love?" she asked. "Love?"
> "Well, what are you taking care of their dogs for?"
> "Do you know why she killed herself? She couldn't stand to see the place go to ruin. She couldn't live without servants and money and what it could buy [...] the thought of having no help, no money—well, she couldn't take that. She had to let everything go."
> "But she didn't let you go [...]"
> "No, she didn't let me go, she killed herself."
> "And you still loyal."
> "You don't listen to people. Your ear is on your head, but it's not connected to your brain. I said she killed herself rather than do the work I'd been doing all my life! Do you hear me? She saw the work I did all her days and *died*, you hear me, *died* rather than live like me. Now, what do you suppose she thought I was! If the way I lived and the work I did was so hateful to her she killed herself to keep from having to do it, and you think I stayed here because I loved her, then you have about as much sense as a fart! [...] They loved this place. Loved it [...] They loved it. Stole for it, lied for it, killed for it. But I'm the one left. Me and the dogs. And I will never clean it again. Never. Nothing." (247)

Milkman thinks he recognizes love in Circe's behavior here, but, just as he fails to see that "love" motivates Guitar, he assumes that Circe's refusal to leave must be an expression of love. He is again mistaken. Circe's motivations have more to do with a kind of self-assertion, with a reclaiming of identity after so many years of having been effectively erased, than they do with love, as she herself vehemently states. He has heard something like this before, from his father who tells him to "own things, and let the things you own own other things. Then you'll own yourself and other people too" (55). His father equates ownership with propagation, proliferation; but, there is no "love" here. What Circe and Macon teach Milkman is that love need not—in fact, *should not*—be a motivating force, if indeed the goal is self-mastery. For them, love prohibits autonomy, self-mastery; love sustains oppression. Circe goes so far as to suggest that love is a relatively weak force, if, in the final analysis, a life is judged by longevity. Her stance is, in this way, a complete reversal of Guitar's, who privileges a life shortened but intensified by "love" for a cause. Macon's position, which erases love from the equation altogether, in effect combines these two stances; he seems to be operating under the assumption that ownership does away with the messiness of passion, at the same time that it ensures longevity. Circe's method would seem to lead naturally to isolation, Macon's to a relationship necessarily defined within a hierarchical context: owner and owned, oppressor and oppressed. In either case, "owning yourself" has little in common with the type of freedom over which Guitar places the lover as sovereign. Circe has chosen self-assertion at the expense of freedom, Macon has chosen ownership at the expense of reciprocity.

### Dominion, Wholeness, and the Power of Metaphor

In an interview with Jane Bakerman in 1977, the year of *Song of Solomon*'s publication, Morrison says this about her intentions for the book:

> Beauty, love […] actually, I think, all the time that I write, I'm writing about love or its absence. Although I don't start out this way […] In this last book, *Song of Solomon*, about dominion (that book is about men, the leading characters are men). And I thought I was writing about the way in which men do things or see things and relate to one another. But I think that I still write about the same thing, which is how people relate to one another and miss it or hang on to it […] or are tenacious about love. About love and how to survive—not to make a living—but how to survive whole in a world where we are all of us, in some measure, *victims* of something. Each one of us

is in some way at some moment a victim and in no position to do a thing about it. Some child is always left unpicked up at some moment. In a world like that, how does one remain whole—is it just impossible to do that? (*Conversations* 40)

"Wholeness," a condition that would seem to combine apparently incompatible impulses—love and dominion—is both courted and deferred in this novel. The gesture toward wholeness is always caught mid-air, and yet, this gesture occupies a protected space between (between self and other, presence and absence, plenitude and loss), a space that refuses merger, and therefore, completion. Victimhood, powerlessness, abandonment, the constellation of this world with which Morrison presents us, do not preclude wholeness; in Morrison's formulation, it is possible to "survive whole," to "remain whole" in this world. Wholeness, then, embodies the wound of brokenness. It is not a matter of *becoming again* whole, but of sustaining a wholeness that embraces vulnerability. To be tenacious about love is to choose the relation over separation, to choose an inexorably fractured community over solitude. To choose this does not necessitate death, Morrison suggests, at least not in the case of her two leading men, Guitar and Milkman. She explains:

> In *Song of Solomon*, I really did not mean to suggest that they kill each other, but out of a commitment and love and selflessness they are willing to risk the one thing that we have, life, and that's the positive nature of the action. I never really believed that those two men would kill each other. I thought they would, like antelopes, lock horns, but it is important that Guitar put his gun down and does not blow Milkman out of the air, as he could. It's important that he look at everything with his new eyes and say "my man, my main man." It's important that the metaphor be in the killing of this brother, that the two men who love each other nevertheless have no area in which they can talk, so they exercise some dominion over and demolition of the other. I wanted the language to be placid enough to suggest he was suspended in the air in the leap towards this thing, both loved and despised, and that he was willing to die for that idea, but not necessarily to die. (Taylor-Guthrie 111)

Describing this ending as essentially metaphorical—that is, approaching this last moment in terms of its *linguistic* capacities—Morrison makes use of one of the dominant modes of the Song of Songs. This meeting that brings together but does not collapse—a meeting that is dynamic and potentially violent, but organically so (like "antelope," these two "lock horns" but reject the artificial tools of violence)—captures the way in which metaphor works to *relate* two disparate, but equally powerful, entities without forcing them into shared identity. The perpetual dance of Lover and Beloved—a "dance of two companies"—is a dynamic, fluid movement of pursuit and retreat. This "dance," which brings contact only momentarily and without consummation, *is* the dance of metaphor. Similarly, Morrison suggests that the moment of contact for Guitar and Milkman eludes linguistic capture; their love has no language to describe or capture it. In this sense, the moment of contact is "suspended" perpetually, hovers without resolution between the poles of "dominion and demolition." In this space between, the dynamic gesture—the leap—is itself suspended, sounding a vibrant, and violent refusal to collapse division.[2]

Metaphor, or perhaps more precisely, the metaphor that acts as simile in the Song of Songs, serves the function of sustaining this "space between." This necessarily unconsummated love is sustained and bolstered by a discourse that is mindful of the distance between the lovers at the same time that it expresses the wish to close that distance; a wish fulfillment that acknowledges its own impossibility, as it were. The lover pleads with the beloved, for instance: "O my dove, that art in the clefts of the rock, in the covert of the cliff, let me see thy countenance, let me hear thy voice; for sweet is thy voice, and thy countenance is comely" (2:14). The space of absence here, the non-viability of seeing or hearing the one whom the lover so desperately craves to see and hear, fuels the exchange, the wished-for encounter. Should the implied "as" or "like" in this description of the beloved (i.e., "like a dove") collapse into a statement of identity, should lover find a descriptive language that fixes the identity of the beloved, should the beloved *show* himself, the relation between lover and beloved would be destroyed.

In her introduction to *Conversations with Toni Morrison*, Danille Taylor-Guthrie suggests that, among "certain characteristics that Morrison has identified as authenticating a piece as 'black'" is "an acceptance of and keen ability to detect differences versus a thrust toward homogenization" (x). The metaphoric strategy Morrison implements throughout *Song of Solomon*, most powerfully depicted in the metaphor "of the killing of this brother, that the two men who love each other nevertheless have no area in which they can talk," a metaphor that remains open, ambiguous (and significantly *silent*), allows for—*encourages*—this difference, enables disparate parts to come into relation without subsuming one another. In her essay "Home," Morrison describes the landscape that would reflect a natural consequence of metaphor-made-practice, a space she longs to call home: "I want to inhabit, walk around, a site clear of racist detritus; a place where race both matters and is rendered impotent [...] I want to imagine not the threat of freedom, or its tentative panting fragility, but the concrete thrill of borderlessness" (9). *A place where race both matters and is rendered impotent*, a place reconfigured such that power and privilege have no dominion over particularity, where *dominion* now implies a dynamic expansion of possibility, a pushing outwards against boundaries, as opposed to consolidation, crystallization, paralysis.

In this last moment of the novel, Milkman identifies and locates himself—shows himself—to Guitar: "'Over here, brother man! Can you see me?' Milkman cupped his mouth with one hand and waved the other over his head. 'Here I am!'" (337). Significantly, the metaphoric quality of this moment is initiated by this self-identification, by this *showing*. In the Song of Songs, the physicality of the love affair is always impeded (but also protected) by the lovers' *not* showing themselves to one another; here Milkman makes himself vulnerable to, and thus more intimate with, Guitar by revealing himself. As though to answer the imploring "Return, that we may look upon thee" (7:1), Milkman makes himself visible to Guitar. They become "brothers" only in this moment of visibility. The completion of this gesture to sight has surprising implications for the dynamics of the relationship that emerges. We will return to these implications in a moment.

In her article, "Call and Response: Voice, Community, and Dialogic Structures," Marilyn Mobley suggests that, in this last section of the novel, "drawing on the black vernacular tradition of call and response that informs African American music, storytelling and verbal communication, Morrison enacts how the process of call and response operates to connect speaker and listener" (60). Similarly, Joyce Middleton writes, "The acoustic effect of this passage structures the call and response pattern. This oral language style underscores the harmony that Milkman has achieved: he is no longer separate from, no longer isolated from, the life-sustaining knowledge of his past" (36). And yet, at the same time that Milkman enacts this traditional call and response, he subverts this tradition; the *call*, rather than response, is the statement of location—"Here I am!" "Here I am" (*hinenni*) is Abraham's response to God in Genesis 22:1, the chapter known as the *Akedah*, or the binding of Isaac. Likewise, Moses responds, "Here I am" when God calls to him from the burning bush (Exodus 3:4). These two moments, taken together, present at once a challenge to and reinscription of the covenant in the Hebrew Bible. In both of these cases, the response—the locating of oneself—indicates an acceptance of the terms that are about to be placed upon these two men, an acceptance, in other words, of the conditional relationship between themselves and God.

Milkman preempts Guitar's call with his response; he demonstrates a desire not to dissolve connection, but to reestablish it on his own terms. Are we to read in this preemption the fear that he has been abandoned? That he reestablishes a connection with Guitar in this potentially fatal moment *because* Guitar has grown silent? In this final moment, Milkman speaks to, poses questions to, Guitar, who continues to remain silent, save for the inaudible and self-directed murmur, "My man, my main man." As readers, *we* see Guitar's acknowledgment of Milkman's speech, his expression of intimacy, but *for Milkman*, the call remains unanswered. His final realization—"If you surrendered to the air, you could ride it"—is thoroughly bound to Guitar's lack of audible response, driven by the unconsummated, unclosed circuit of call and response. Surrender, subjugation, the giving up of self to other—*this* is the prescriptive message of the leap that propels him toward Guitar, the leap that solidifies for him that death is negligible in the context of this newly understood relation. In this leap, Milkman joins Solomon and the agent who pledges to "fly away" in the first moments of the novel. Morrison explains of this flight, that at first glance resembles a death wish:

> So the agent's flight, like that of Solomon in the title, although toward asylum […] and although it carries the possibility of failure and certainty of danger, is toward change, an alternative way, a cessation of things-as-they-are. It should not be understood as a simple desperate act, the end of a fruitless life, a life without gesture, without examination, but as obedience to a deeper contract with his people. It is his commitment to them, regardless of whether, in all its details, they understand it. (Quoted in Smith's introduction 14)

This act of pledging connection, this privileging of the collective, finally, over the self, this surrender of self to other, is tied firmly to its incommunicability. The gesture to the other, this "obedience to a deeper contract," though internalized as command, originates in a space of silence, of miscomprehension; the probability of being misheard or not heard at all is great, but in no way renders the gesture irrelevant. Milkman's leap becomes authentically collective when he embraces this space of silence, when he acknowledges the fragility and paucity of his own ego.

In a connected way, the movement of the Song of Songs is generated by a call—lyrical, dramatic, dynamic—that wishes for response, but most often is left unanswered. The anxious "Whither art thou?" punctuates the condition of abandonment revealed by the lover's plea, "Return, return, O Shulamite." In the Jewish tradition, the prayer service enacts this wished-for response of the persistent call, is in fact conducted on the model of this method. Rabbi "calls" and congregation "responds," reinforcing in this exchange the communal aspect of worship, the communal possibilities of a marginalized group, but also the clearly defined roles and divisions operating within the synagogue. The deferred and unanswered call of lover to beloved suggests the potentially fearful moment of silence that the call and response, enacted in worship, over- comes. Worship, then, reflects faith in a covenantal relationship; the Song of Songs invokes this relationship only to undercut it, challenge it, complicate it. The circuit between call and response is left uncompleted, disconnected, as though deliberately refusing a closed system such as this, a system that can only recycle, can only perpetuate and reinforce, the vagaries of power.

It is significant, then, in the final moments of Morrison's novel, that the gaze fractures, splits, shatters; we see differently from how Milkman does and are prompted to witness the events that culminate in Milkman's "surrender." The gesture to call and response, in other words, is mirrored in our relation- ship as readers to the text. The anxiety produced when we see Milkman sur- render himself to a force that has silently, but decisively, surrendered to him ("he put the rifle on the ground and stood up") reenacts something of the ten- sion that Solomon must experience when he looks upon those lovers who have rejected him and his kingdom. His gaze is rendered peculiarly, and simultane- ously, omnipotent and powerless; to enforce his power here would be a matter of deliberate choice, an act of resentment for his having been excluded. Similarly, to "allow" this affair to continue is to disavow everything he stands for. The continuation of this affair is, in effect, an admission to his own limit- ed sphere of power; but power can only be relinquished by those who first pos- sess it.

## Power and the Male Gaze

By naming this novel *Song of Solomon*, Morrison effectively returns power back to the male gaze. She chooses the subsidiary title of the Song of Songs for an account of love that knows no bounds. She reminds us, in so doing, that *Solomon* owns this tale; she reinscribes, redefines, the boundaries that are always already there, even (and perhaps especially) when Solomon should choose to ignore them.[3] Curiously, biblical scholars have suggested that the "attribution to Solomon in the title was a factor for [the Song of Song's] admission to the canon" (Bloch and Bloch 28). Solomon's gaze in this sense lends legitimacy to a tale that would otherwise threaten the normative function of the Bible. Under his gaze, subversion of the norm is contained; acknowledged, witnessed, *seen*, the threat of this subversion is thus minimized.

Morrison's Solomon looms over, quite literally flies above, the "song" that chronicles his rebellion against, rejection of, and eventual escape from an oppressive and hostile system. The biblical Solomon looks on an affair that threatens to disrupt his own system of values; in looking, he reifies this affair *as* illicit, as perpetually in contrast to his own position. His gaze reenacts division and reaffirms the possibility for transgression when lines of distinction have been drawn. He presides above, but never *belongs* to, the space his gaze falls upon. Morrison's Solomon experiences rupture of a different sort. He, too, has become detached from the space of his song. But he has *chosen*, though perhaps reluctantly, to detach himself from this space. He has chosen flight, transcendence, as his means of escape. His flight, in opposition to the biblical Solomon's, expands the boundaries of subversion. Where the biblical Solomon fixes with his gaze, Morrison's Solomon introduces and occupies wholly new realms in which movement is possible. His dominion over the space from which he has chosen to escape is bound to his having once occupied this space, having once belonged to it and participated in it. His flight from this space is punctuated by his intimate connection to and knowledge of it. His positioning is far different from that of the biblical Solomon who gazes wistfully upon a world to which he will never have access, from which his role as empowered sovereign always bars his entrance.

Morrison identifies flying as the "central metaphor" of *Song of Solomon*:

> I used it not only in the African sense of whirling dervishes and getting out of one's skin, but also in the majestic sense of a man who goes too far, whose adventures take him away [...] It's a part of black life, a positive, majestic thing, but there is a price to pay—the price is the children. The fathers may soar, they may triumph, they may leave, but the children know who they are; they remember, half in glory, half in accusation. That is one of the points of Song: all the men have left someone, and it is the children who remember it, sing about it, mythologize it, make it a part of their family history. (*Conversations* 46)

The lovers in the Song of Songs take flight as well. They reject Solomon's court, defy the gaze that he fixes on them, take refuge in their love as a solace against the "terrors of night" (3:8) that threaten always to intervene. Their stance vis-à-vis Solomon proclaims a clear "despite"; *despite* the gaze trained on them, *despite* the many forces that threaten them, they continue to search for

one another. At the same time, however, the threat of night is a more pervasive one, affecting not only the lovers, but the community at large, and is coun-
tered by a warning of sorts: not to "stir up love, until it please" (3:5). Into the
space of this warning, Solomon's court returns, a protector of sorts: "Who is
this that cometh up out of the wilderness like pillars of smoke, perfumed with
myrrh and frankincense, with all the powders of the merchant? Behold, it is
the litter of Solomon; Threescore mighty men are about it, of the mighty men
of Israel. They all handle the sword, and are expert in war; every man hath
his sword upon his thigh, because of the dread of night" (3:6–8). Whereas
Morrison's Solomon can and does transcend the oppressive forces that had
once contained him, the biblical lovers move horizontally, as it were, along a
trajectory that always already contains at once the source of oppression and
defense mechanism against their own potentially destructive desire. The Song
of Songs, marked by the absence of the divine, introduces the possibility for a
radical immanence, at the same time that it would seem to reject the possibility for transcendence. Morrison reintroduces transcendence, but aligns this
possibility just as definitively with male power as the Song of Songs does—the
ambivalent power, that is, to both harm and protect.

## Grounded Love: The Book of Ruth and the (Unexercised) Power of Maternal Abandonment

As Morrison acknowledges, male flight is bound inextricably to those left
behind. Memory is linked to abandonment, presence to absence; the children's
compulsion to remember, to bear witness, to incorporate into their own sense
of history, is heightened by the father's compulsion to leave behind (Krumholz
205). As we see again and again in *Song of Solomon*, women, as well as children,
are also left behind, left to pine away in grief or to oversee and nurture these
children who "mythologize" their father. We might read the epigraph to this
novel—"The fathers may soar / And the children may know their names"—
as the gesture to a condition that would allow simultaneously for both of these
possibilities. In other words, we might read the epigraph *prescriptively*, in the
efforts of locating the condition that would allow for this simultaneity: women,
in their interactions with one another, should cultivate the space necessary *so
that* fathers may soar and children may know their names.

This "prescription" is fairly troubling, in that it would seem to promote the
quite literal sacrifice of women for the sake of the men and children (Awkward

89). Morrison writes, "Although in sociological terms that is described as a major failing of black men—they do not stay at home and take care of their children, they are not there—that has always been to me one of the most attractive features about black male life. The fact that they would split in a minute just delights me. It's part of that whole business of breaking ground, doing the other thing" (quoted in Krumholz 205). In this context, it would be easy enough to read Pilate's death as an act that renders her own voice secondary to the men's; it is her death, after all, that inspires Milkman to show himself to Guitar once and for all, her death that reinforces the "brotherhood" of these two men. It would be easy enough to read her final moments, accompanied by Milkman's song, as a reinforcement of paternal abandonment. And yet, if we look more closely at the song she hears as she dies, any such clear delineation is complicated. Milkman, in fact, sings a song that is an amalgamation of Solomon's song and the song Pilate sings at Hagar's funeral, "softly, privately [...] the very same reassurance she had promised her when she was a little girl" (318). To Pilate's request, "Sing a little somethin for me," Milkman responds with: "Sugargirl don't leave me here / Cotton balls to choke me / Sugargirl don't leave me here / Buckra's arms to yoke me" (336). Substituting "sugargirl" for "Solomon," Milkman takes on the voice of one abandoned, but abandoned by a maternal figure as opposed to a paternal one. At the same time, he admits guilt, acknowledges accountability, for his part in "botherin' my sweet sugar lumpkin" (the refrain of Pilate's song to Hagar).

It is only here, in this space of the feminine power to abandon (a power Milkman grants as a possibility, though it is a power never exercised), that Milkman becomes capable of male intimacy, capable of calling Guitar his "brother" (Hirsch 89). Here, too, abandonment is finally overcome by or fully reattached to love. The song with which Milkman soothes Pilate resonates in that space already vibrating with her wish for a more expansive, inclusive love. He realizes, finally, "why he loved her so. Without ever leaving the ground, she could fly" (336). Just prior to Pilate's death, Milkman has come to understand the full implications of Solomon's flight: "He left Ryna behind and twenty children. Twenty-one, since he dropped the one he tried to take with him. And Ryna had thrown herself all over the ground, lost her mind, and was still crying in a ditch. Who looked after those twenty children? Jesus Christ, he left twenty-one children!" (332). Alongside of this, he comes to understand Pilate's lesson for him, comes to understand that, in fact, Pilate has been serving an instructive role for him throughout his journey: "She would abide by this commandment from her father herself, and make him do it too. 'You just can't fly on off and leave a body'" (332). That such a lesson should require a thorough melding of the paternal and maternal for Milkman is crucial (Awkward 77).

This "lesson" announces a messy combination of obligation, submission and subversion, a thread of impulses that come together only in a father's commandment to his daughter to choose *not* to take a path that has, previously, been open only to men. He commands her not to take flight, as if to acknowledge that she has the power to do so. Something of this ambivalent commandment—this commandment that empowers as it curbs power—is reflected in the process by which Macon names Pilate. His choice to name her Pilate is tied to family tradition (a tradition, that is, of choosing children's names at random from the Bible) at the same time that it undercuts the authority of the text out of which this tradition grows. In her essay "From Orality to Literacy," Middleton explains:

> It is not due to his illiteracy or ignorance that the father insists upon Pilate's name. The midwife, obviously a reader, voices the authority of the text not only by explaining what the selected word means but also by attempting to persuade the father that he made a wrong choice. But the father resists that authority: he does not automatically submit to the authorized version of the biblical text. Rather, he dares to question the significance of that textual authority for his present purposes. (26)

Macon chooses a name steeped in the weight of its own history, but he frees it from this history, detaches it from its traditional connotations. This act of naming serves as a model for the lesson Pilate goes on both to embody and pass on: "and the children may know their names." Female children, as epitomized by the case of Pilate, are by no means excluded from this authenticating experience. Macon chooses this name arbitrarily, and the very arbitrariness of this choice turns it into an act of subversion. She compounds this act by piercing her own flesh with the "evidence" of this subversive arbitrariness. As Mobley suggests, this act of piercing her name, her father's word, into her body in effect "repairs the absence of relation that has failed to mark her body" (81). Completing this relation in her own flesh, she both internalizes her father's act of subversion and creates herself in his image, an image decidedly opposed to blind acceptance of tradition. Owning this space of absence, this mark that would suggest an immaculate conception, she owns her name, and in this owning, empties it of any vestiges of betrayal; she inscribes into her body what she will refuse to become. She overthrows the burden of her namesake in the fierce loyalty and protectiveness she shows toward her family, in her refusal to compromise her principles for public opinion.

When Hagar dies of her unreciprocated love for Milkman, Pilate commemorates her, though to an audience that remains largely unaware of the extent of Hagar's pain. It is something of a curiosity to them that Hagar should have died for love. Not so for Pilate, who vehemently, and viscerally, confirms how vital an understanding that she loved and was loved is to Hagar's memory: "'My baby girl.' Words tossed like stones into a silent canyon. Suddenly, like an elephant who has just found his anger and lifts his trunk over the heads of the little men who want his teeth or his hide or his flesh or his amazing strength, Pilate trumpeted for the sky itself to hear, 'And she was *loved*!'" (319). In this fierce confirmation, in this admission of love so thoroughly tied to the frustration and anger of *not being heard*, Pilate takes back dominion of this love, refuses to let it dissolve before those who are indifferent to it. At the same time, the tenacious force of this love is tied to *staying*, rather than leaving; this is a love that looks to the sky for affirmation ("trumpeted for the sky to hear"), but remains altogether grounded.

This grounded tenacity finds a model in the book of Ruth. Ruth, remaining loyal to her mother-in-law, Naomi, after the death of Naomi's husband and then her own, follows her into exile, quite literally displaces herself in the service of this loyalty. The catalyst for Ruth's chosen exile is, effectively, male abandonment (Awkard 89). Only in the space of male absence can these women begin to relate to each another as women. Morrison's gestures to the book of Ruth are complicated and often ambivalent. Her choice of the name "Ruth" for Milkman's mother is perhaps the most ambivalent. Ruth Foster Dead is thoroughly committed to her dead father (to the point verging at once on the dual transgression of necrophilia and incest). At the same time, she remains dependent upon Pilate to conceive a son, Milkman. Pilate's plan to trick Macon into making love to Ruth mirrors the seduction plot (of Boaz) orchestrated by Naomi. But Morrison takes this plot further, makes it far more violent; Macon is forced against his will to father a son, whom he attempts again and again to murder. Boaz succumbs quite gladly to Ruth, and the result is the continuation of the Davidic line, the line that will eventually produce the messiah, according to tradition.

## Rewriting Ruth

Morrison's ambivalent reworking of the book of Ruth, like Macon Sr.'s subversive choice of the name Pilate, makes use of tradition precisely where it rejects this tradition. Ruth is the only book in the Hebrew Bible that focuses extensively on female relationships (Caspi and Havrelock 68). At the same time, however, these relationships are still thoroughly tied to power, to divisions of inside and outside. Ruth is, after all, an outsider, a Moabite in the midst of Israelites. Her choice to follow Naomi is bound to her renouncing her own culture, her own god: "And Ruth said: 'Entreat me not to leave thee, and to return from following after thee; for whither thou goest, I will go; and where thou lodgest, I will lodge; thy people shall be my people, and thy God my God'" (1:16). Her encounters with Boaz mark her consistently as "other." Though he protects her from those who would abuse her because she is an outsider, she is nevertheless encouraged to assimilate, to "take refuge" (2:12) by claiming obedience to a belief system that is not her own. And, in the end:

> Ruth is eclipsed by a silent Naomi claiming a son and heir [...] She disappears into the household of Boaz and a genealogy of her husband and son and the future king David closes the covers of her story [...] She has striven with the patriarchy and wrought security out of insecurity; yet her action has been all along conditioned by the system which set her story going and which remains firmly in place as it ends. (Fewell and Gunn 105)

An imperial triumph, the triumph not only of patriarchy but of nation, is enacted on Ruth's body. Her womb, quite literally, reinforces lines of division, reinscribes the boundaries of power and privilege from which she remains excluded even now. We are left to witness this troubling scene: "Naomi took the child, and laid it on her bosom, and became nurse to it" (4:16). We can only speculate that Ruth, too, witnesses this most intimate act between *her* son and mother-in-law; that she watches in anguish as her own connection to this child is eradicated by those for whom she chose exile over home.

In his article "Rejecting Rank's Monomyth and Feminism," Gerry Brenner makes this claim: "Ruth Foster Dead seems little more than a weak replica of her biblical namesake, exemplar of dutiful, self-abnegating obedience, certainly no candidate for praise" (103). Certainly, Morrison's Ruth is an often pathetic and pitiable creature, a woman entirely cut off from her own desire, her body thoroughly abandoned and rejected by her husband. But where the biblical Ruth leaves her family—her father—behind, Morrison's Ruth stands her ground, literally. She and Macon live in her father's house; her father's legacy renders Macon powerless, even in his violent attempts to usurp power. The watermark at the center of the dinner table, the site of contemptuous battle for Macon and Ruth, is the tangible mark of the father who will not "fly away," if only because his daughter will not let him:

> Like a lighthouse keeper drawn to his window to gaze once again at the sea, or a pris-
> oner automatically searching out the sun as he steps into the yard for his hour of exer-
> cise, Ruth looked for the water mark several times during the day. She knew it was
> there, would always be there, but she needed to confirm its presence. Like the keeper
> of the lighthouse and the prisoner, she regarded it as a mooring, a checkpoint, some
> stable visual object that assured her that the world was still there; that this was life and
> not a dream. That she was alive somewhere, inside, which she acknowledged to be
> true only because a thing she knew intimately was out there, outside herself. (11)

Here, in this moment, rendered in simile (in the metaphor that refuses to collapse), Ruth claims a "mooring"; though perhaps a "prisoner" to this legacy,
unlike her biblical namesake, Morrison's Ruth refuses exile, refuses to be cast
out of her home. And, in this claim, which is also a refusal, Morrison's Ruth
seizes her motherhood in a way the biblical Ruth never can:

> But there was nothing you could do with a mooring except acknowledge it, use it for
> the verification of some idea you wanted to keep alive. Something else is needed to
> get from sunup to sundown: a balm, a gentle touch or nuzzling of some sort. So Ruth
> rose up and out of her guileless inefficiency to claim her bit of balm right after the
> preparation of dinner and just before the return of her husband from his office. It was
> one of her two secret indulgences—the one that involved her son—and part of the
> pleasure it gave her came from the room in which she did it. A damp greenness lived
> there, made by the evergreen that pressed against the window and filtered the light.
> It was just a little room the Doctor had called a study, and aside from a sewing
> machine that stood in the corner along with a dress form, there was only a rocker and
> tiny footstool. She sat in this room holding her son on her lap, staring at his closed eye-
> lids and listening to the sound of his sucking. Staring not so much from maternal joy
> as from a wish to avoid seeing his legs dangling almost to the floor. (13)

Though pathological—and reminiscent of the type of love Guitar warns
Hagar against, the type of love that strangles its object—this act, born perhaps
of a mother's love, perhaps of a mother's desperation, marks Milkman, *names*
him. In her refusal to give up her father's legacy, her refusal to *follow*, as the
biblical Ruth does, Ruth inscribes Milkman's name upon his body, just as
Pilate inscribes the name her father chooses for her upon herself.

## Toward a Non-Messianism

This bodily mark of name, this name that marks the insistent maternal presence on the son, suggests the implications of Morrison's radical revision of the book of Ruth. The biblical Ruth becomes "mother of the Messiah" only contingently, only, that is, once she has abandoned her own beliefs, her home, herself. In Fewell and Gunn's retelling of the story, Ruth acknowledges that she follows Naomi because she has "nowhere else to go" (31). Her choice to follow her mother-in-law into an unknown future, to leave behind the burden of past death and dead men, is, in this sense, a choice born out of negation; she reacts against death but also actively abandons her own subjectivity. A messiah born under these conditions is a messiah that promotes an erasure of difference, who asserts a subtle but insidious power. A messiah who commands, albeit quietly: Assimilate into the "host" culture, or be excluded. The messianic wish is, at base, a homogeneous one. In subverting the tale that would silence the mother-as-perpetual-outsider, in granting Ruth not only the power to nurse her son, but to *name* her son by means of this nursing, Morrison effectively identifies and vehemently rejects the potentially violent layer of the messianic wish, this will-towards-sameness. She writes:

> The overweening, defining event of the modern world is the mass movement of raced populations, beginning with the largest forced transfer of people in the history of the world: slavery. The consequences of which transfer have determined all the wars following it as well as the current ones being waged on every continent [...] Nationhood—the very definition of citizenship—is constantly being demarcated and redemarcated in response to exiles, refugees, *Gastarbeiter*, immigrants, migrations, the displaced, the fleeing, the besieged. The anxiety of belonging is entombed within the central metaphors on the discourse of globalism, transnationalism, nationalism, the break-up of federations, the rescheduling of alliances, and the fictions of sovereignty. Yet these figurations of nationhood and identity are frequently as raced themselves as the originating racial house that defined them. When they are not raced, they are [...] imaginary landscape, never inscape; Utopia, never home [...] It is therefore more urgent than ever to develop a nonmessianic language to refigure the raced community, to decipher the deracing of the world. ("Home" 11)

In this context, we might return to the Song of Songs. To justify its place in "the canon," all manner of allegorical readings were imposed upon the text; a text which includes no mention of God, and originally wildly popular for its secular eroticism, was systematically "sanctified." Once recited in taverns and by women seeking husbands, the Song of Songs became the subject of prohibition. The rabbis attached to it a normative reading, and anyone who would insist on reading it otherwise was warned "[will have] no portion in the World to Come" (Bloch and Bloch 30). And so the allegorical readings, explicitly driven by the messianic wish, supplanted the popular interpretation of a song about love, about desire. In this process of canonization, love becomes conditional, exclusive, representative of God's love for his nation, Israel, and later, of Christ's love for his "bride," the Church (Bloch and Bloch 30). In the process of canonization, the local power and currency of this text was erased, written over by the sterile, oppressive, and potentially imperialistic readings promoted and promulgated by the theologians.

The final stage of Milkman's journey is driven by nostalgia, by that yearned-for, never-felt connection to his own family, his own culture, to a family that—until the devastating loss of one father (Macon senior) and the oppressive weight of another (Doctor Foster) come to serve as the monolithic voice of inheritance—luxuriated in the richness of its legends. The nostalgia that drives this journey home is also the nostalgia for the sublimated—the repressed—text, the text that is covered over by the politics of power, ownership, and hierarchy. This text is recovered, finally, when unselfish love wins out over possessive love, when Milkman, singing a rewritten Song of Solomon into a space reverberating with *life, life, life, life* (337) surrenders to—finds—home, by embracing who he is.

## Notes

[1] All biblical quotes taken from *The Holy Scriptures according to the Masoretic Text* (Philadelphia: The Jewish Publication Society of America, 1955).

[2] For a discussion of this leap, see Mobley 61, Hirsch 87.

[3] For a discussion of the dynamic of this gaze in Macon and Pilate's relationship, see Mobley 59.

## Works Cited

Awkward, Michael. "'Unruly and Let Loose': Myth, Ideology, and Gender in *Song of Solomon*." In Furman, *A Casebook*, 67-94.

Bakerman, Jane. "The Seams Can't Show: An Interview with Toni Morrison." In Taylor-Guthrie, *Conversations*, 30-42.

Bloch, Ariel, and Chana Bloch, eds. *The Song of Songs: A New Translation*. Berkeley: University of California Press, 1995.

Brenner, Gerry. "*Song of Solomon*: Rejecting Rank's Monomyth and Feminism." In Furman, *A*

*Casebook*, 95–112.

Caspi, Mishael, and Rachel Havrelock. *Women on the Biblical Road: Ruth, Naomi, and the Female Journey*. Lanham: University Press of America, 1996.

Fewell, Danna Nolan, and David Miller Gunn. *Compromising Redemption: Relating Characters in the Book of Ruth*. Westminster: John Knox Press, 1990.

Furman, Jan, ed. *Toni Morrison's "Song of Solomon": A Casebook*. Oxford: Oxford University Press, 2003.

Hirsch, Marianne. "Knowing Their Names: Toni Morrison's *Song of Solomon*." In Smith, *New Essays*, 69–92.

Krumholz, Linda. "Dead Teachers: Rituals of Manhood and Rituals of Reading in *Song of Solomon*." In Furman, *A Casebook*, 201–232.

Middleton, Joyce Irene. "From Orality to Literacy: Oral Memory in Toni Morrison's *Song of Solomon*." In Smith, *New Essays*, 19–40.

Mobley, Marilyn Sanders. "Call and Response: Voice, Community, and Dialogic Structures in Toni Morrison's *Song of Solomon*." In Smith, *New Essays*, 41–68.

Morrison, Toni. "Home." In *The House that Race Built*, edited by Wahneema Lubiano. New York: Pantheon Books, 1997. 3–12.

———. "Rootedness: The Ancestor as Foundation." In *The Woman that I Am: The Literature and Culture of Contemporary Women of Color*, edited by D. Soyini Madison. New York: St. Martin's Press, 1994. 492–497.

———. *Song of Solomon*. 1977. New York: Plume Books, 1987.

Smith, Valerie, ed. *New Essays on "Song of Solomon."* Cambridge: Cambridge University Press, 1995.

Taylor-Guthrie, Danille, ed. *Conversations with Toni Morrison*. Jackson: University Press of Mississippi, 1994.

# 5

# THE BIBLE AS INTERTEXT
# IN TONI MORRISON'S NOVELS

## *Ágnes Surányi*

Toni Morrison's fascination with and critical stance towards the Bible has been long acknowledged; her attempts to appropriate and resist the Bible through allegory, the use of reversal, literalization, signifying, or covert citation are a trademark of her novels. As Alexander Allen has noted, references to her own black religious culture "both from Western and African sources, abound in Toni Morrison's fiction (293), which addresses spirituality, religious experience, and the concept of love in the face of a materialist (racist, sexist) world. Scholars of literature as well as historical theologians have focused on this aspect of Morrison's fiction, foregrounding intertextuality and biblical allusions in their analyses. Our awareness of intertextuality, according to Worton and Still, "makes us, readers [and critics], keen to re-read our source texts in that [new] light" (2). Conversely, the critical discourse of interpreting Morrison's fiction frequently uses exegesis and hermeneutic reading traditionally reserved for scripture.

In spite of the fact that Morrison declared her desire to weave "a seamless textual fabric" (Bakerman 31), she often resorts to intertextuality as a narrative device, which may result in textual fragmentation that requires a "centrifugality of reading" (Worton and Still 11). In Michael Riffaterre's view, however, the presupposition of intertextuality points toward the structural and semantic unity of the text (57). In this essay, I wish to emphasize that our readings of Morrison's novels, which rely on a deliberate use of the Bible as an intertext, must use a different strategy from that for novels without that intertext. Her novels are characterized by a demand for what Roland Barthes calls the "circular memory" (quoted in Worton and Still 10), as opposed to that of linear reading.

In the interpretation of Morrison's works, Riffaterre's admonition has to be kept in mind. He argues, "Intertextuality is not a free association of the given narrative with whatever previously read texts the individual can recall at the moment"; rather, "the text and the intertext/s are variants of the same structural matrix" (67). The relevance of Riffaterre's theory is proven by Barbara Hill Rigney's book *Lilith's Daughters*. Her book is a valuable study of religions and women in contemporary fiction, but her claim, that Sula is "a composite of archetypal scapegoats: Christ, Cain, even Lilith" (17), is somewhat forced and far-fetched. It is important to see "the constraints that the structure of the text imposes on its own intertexts" (Riffaterre 68). The literary text carries out a dialogue "with other texts that it notices [. . .], *never fully assimilating or controlling their language or their ideology*" (Morgan 271, emphasis added). The inclination to assimilate other texts is enhanced when the author revises the intertext from a rather different social and cultural perspective.

An overview of critical discourse on Morrison's dialogue with the Bible will show that, with the exception of Nicole Wilkinson, none of the critics question that her novels have religious or biblical overtones. On the contrary, Louis Menand complains that in his opinion, Morrison's penultimate novel is "obsessed with a subject that many readers may not feel particularly engaged with—which is Christianity," while Michiko Kakutani objects to Morrison's use of "gratuitous biblical allusions " in the same text (quoted in Tally, *Paradise Reconsidered* 68). As to the intention of the author, Margaret Atwood states that Morrison deliberately uses the Bible as an intertext. She contends that "the author is too smart, and too much of a writer not to have intended" that context (147). The complex and layered nature of Morrison's fiction, the commitment of various scholars to different theories of intertextuality, and the ambiguity of biblical intertextuality in her works have resulted in a variety of critical responses, as this essay will explore in relation to some of Morrison's major works.

First we must note that intertextuality in Morrison's fiction is layered, as Gurleen Grewal has observed: "Morrison appropriates classical and biblical myths and the canonical writings of high modernism and places them in the matrix of black culture. In this she is supported by the long vernacular tradition of work songs, spirituals, and blues that had already appropriated the Bible and renamed the Israelites as the people chosen from Africa" (10). The intertextuality in Morrison's work, then, is extremely complex, since it is double-edged. The combination of explicit and implicit intertextuality forms a great challenge to the explicator of Morrison's texts. Morrison rarely makes explicit references to printed literature or deploys literal citations from literary and non-literary work; when she does, in a convoluted way, she usually refers to the Bible, or the works of a few (overwhelmingly male modernist) writers to whom she feels it is necessary to respond.

I find Henry Louis Gates's term "signifyin(g)" more apt than intertextuality, for it conflates dialogue and intertextuality usefully. In *Black Literature and Literary Theory*, Gates states, Black people have always been masters of the figurative: saying one thing to mean something quite other has been basic to black survival in oppressive Western cultures (6). He emphasizes that Afro-American authors seem to *revise at least two antecedent texts*, often taken from different generations or periods within the tradition (290, emphasis added). This is what he calls tertiary formal revision" (290). In Afro-American literary history, signifying is often characterized by pastiche. Gates attributes this parody of forms, which turns on repetition of formal structures and their difference (285, 286), to African American literature, identifying it as the trope of tropes, or master trope because it encompasses all others…in the ritual of signifying" (286). Signifying may be defined as a "rhetorical game characteristic of the black vernacular tradition, the dominant satiric form of the Afro-American verbal expression, the tone of which may range "from harmless teasing to bitter and caustic diatribe" (Brogan 271). In Gates's definition, it is repetition with a difference" (3). It has also been called marking," "rapping," "loud-talking," "testifying," "calling out," "sounding," "playing the dozens, giving a reading, or specifying (19).

Numerous examples of signifying upon religion and the Bible appear in Morrison's writing. That her use of intertextuality is often encoded by a textual scar or disruption in the Riffaterrean sense is illustrated by the following quotation from a character's letter to (or rather, imaginary conversation with) God, from *The Bluest Eye*:

> But I am called Soaphead Church. I cannot remember how or why I got the name. What makes one name more a person than another? Is the name the real thing, then? And the person only what his name says? Is that why to the simplest and friendliest of questions: "What is your name?" put to you by Moses, You would not say, and said instead "*I am who I am.*" Like Popeye? *I Yam What I Yam?* (180, emphasis added)

*The Bluest Eye*, in Michael Awkward's reading, is a reinterpretation and rewriting of the central plot situation of the Jim Trueblood episode in Ellison's *Invisible Man*, through a feminist lens (81). In the passage quoted above, "I yam what I yam" is cited from a scene in *Invisible Man* (260), in which the hero is reflecting about issues of name and identity while buying a yam from the street vendor (266). After reference is made to Moses (the Old Testament), it seems an unmotivated or even clumsy pun to twist God's reply into "I yam what I yam," but John N. Duvall remarks that "Awkard's reading helps prepare the ground for understanding Soaphead Church's letter to God as Morrison's letter to Ellison" ("Naming Invisible Authority" 246). He suggests that at the time of writing her first two novels, Morrison was still struggling with the process of forming her authorial identity through engaging other texts. Duvall's parallel between Soaphead Church and Toni Morrison is supported by the fact that this segment of the novel is one of the few places in Morrison's fiction where she highlights (her character's) views on written literature at length; elsewhere she makes only brief literary allusions. The omniscient narrator tells us that Church went to America to study, finally settling down in Lorrain, Ohio. He took over Western values in a rather selective way: he read *Hamlet, Othello*, Gibbon's history, and the Bible, admired Dante's and despised Dostoyevsky's works, but chose to remember only Hamlet's abuse of Ophelia and his frivolous politics, and preferred Gibbon's acidity to his tolerance. "For all his exposure to the best minds of the Western world, he allowed only the narrowest interpretation to touch him," the narrator remarks (*The Bluest Eye* 169). This dense passage verifies Gates's theory of signifying, namely, that in African-American writing, the author signifies upon two anterior texts at least (290)—in this case, upon the Bible and *The Invisible Man*, but another intertext emerges as well.

Jane Caputi has discovered that *The Bluest Eye* is "specifying" on another novel, Fannie Hurst's *Imitation of Life*; Langston Hughes's *Limitations of Life* and Zora Neale Hurston's *Their Eyes Were Watching God* also signify upon Hurst's stereotypical depiction of racial relations. On the African American art of name-calling, Susan Willis comments that specifying is frequently circumscribed, held in check, by the larger system of domination (quoted in Caputi 714); consequently, Morrison's technique of indirection may be indebted to this practice. In Caputi's interpretation, Morrison offers the heroine Pecola as an "unimpeachable witness against the very system that caused *peola* [a very white black girl] to become a household word" (710). Pauline may have named her daughter after Peola, for "Pecola's name is an inversion of Peola, the mulatta who hates her black mother in the movie *Imitation of Life*" (Christian quoted in Caputi 711). In *The Bluest Eye*, the black mother hates her own child and adores the baby of the white family she works for, inverting the narrative of *Imitation of Life*, in which the light-complexioned daughter rejects her own black mother.

In the afterword to the 1997 reprint of *The Bluest Eye*, Morrison condemns the racist culture for its worship of white standards of beauty and reacts against the damaging internalization of assumptions of immutable inferiority originating in the outside gaze (210). As Trudier Harris has pointed out, this narrative is also "an inversion of fairy tales—the ugly duckling does not become the beautiful swan" (Harris 11).

In addition to literal citations, the act of titling also often calls attention to intertextuality, such as the names of central characters in titles, or titles borrowed from other literary works: *Sula, Song of Solomon, Tar Baby, Beloved, Paradise*, and *Love*. In titling her two last novels, Morrison's dialogic imagination is manifested by her application of the technique of reversal. True, she entitled the last volume of her trilogy *Paradise* upon her publisher's request; the original title she had in mind was *War*. Similarly, her recent novel *Love*, against all expectations, is concerned with contention and hatred among the central women characters, with bonding and love coming too late in the book. *Love* uses reversal to undermine dualities; Morrison's main concern is not what is, but rather the process of becoming. The title of the novel depends on the First Epistle to the Corinthians as its intertext. The author/narrator makes an explicit demand on the reader to open the Bible and read the chapter that she designates in the novel. In the soliloquy of the mysterious character L—the L probably standing for Love—we read: "If your name is the subject of First Corinthians, chapter 13, it's natural to make it your business" (199).

The use of the epigraph (a case of Genette's paratextuality), the plainest possible form of allusion (Wilkinson 242), signals intertextuality in a direct way. Epigraphs summarize the main concerns of the novels in the fewest possible words and introduce Morrison's *The Bluest Eye* (from the American primer), *Sula* (Tennessee Williams's *The Rose Tattoo*), *Tar Baby* (1 Corinthians 1:11), *Jazz* (*The Nag Hammadi*), *Beloved* (Romans 9:25), and *Paradise* (*The Nag Hammadi*).

Naming is another form of intertextuality that Morrison utilizes. Various protagonists' names are borrowed from the Bible: Sula/Shulamite, Shadrack; Pilate, First Corinthians, Magdalene, Hagar, Ruth; Dorcas; Seth/e and Beloved. In most of her works, Morrison gives her characters double names, one determined by the white oppressor and one chosen and favored by the black community. The use of multiple intertextuality by Morrison is possibly connected to the partially overlapping Du Boisean "double consciousness," the Gatesean "two-voiced" or "two-toned Afro-American heritage," the Afro-

American trope of antiphony call and response, and Bakhtin's "double-voiced discourse."

In Morrison's reference to the Bible, as Wilkinson argues, it often turns out that Riffaterrean ungrammaticalities or traces" hidden in the interstices or sutures of the text are merely red herrings, for in spite of the fact that it [the Bible] pops up continually, the sound of its contents never resounds in the story (240). With reference to the Bible as an intertext, Wilkinson stresses that even though intertextuality may be regarded as a necessary element of all literature, not all literature celebrates its literary past" (235). Morrison's persistent reference to the Bible results in anti-intertextuality, Wilkinson argues, in fact not exploiting the possibilities inherent in that intertext, for in a society in which writing is the primary currency for knowledge, "the biblical text is suspect," just like reading and writing … ; alien to African American culture and tainted by their use in the hands of the white oppressor (235). Examining *Song of Solomon* and *Beloved* from this perspective, Wilkinson makes the point that in Morrison's novels the Biblical text is silent, unresponsive and at other times notably irrelevant (235). She highlights the tension between the presence of the Bible and the absence of the Bible's written content (235) in Morrison's oeuvre, offering the following explanation:

> Writing is one of the weapons belonging to whites, and to read is to invite white voices into the reader's head. Intertextuality, in the sense of an *echoing between written texts*, is in these novels not perceived as a strengthening resource, but as *an inextricable relationship with the self-perpetuating past*. Representing not only the white man's religion, but in its cold writtenness his very thought processes, and the forcible imposition of both, the Bible in these novels is handed on unread. (236, emphasis added)

The citation above seems to contradict, or even question what Morrison said in an interview—that the Bible was not merely part of her reading, it was her life (Ruas 97). If this is so, why should the Bible be silent and handed on unread by her characters?

As Wilkinson argues, the illiterate slaves (who were forbidden to learn reading or writing) listened to the Bible being read by the preacher on church-organized occasions and were discouraged at the same time from exercising African religious practices. Since the divine promises of this holy book were rarely fulfilled, the black people's attitude to it was ambiguous and skeptical. They started signifying upon it, sometimes even using it to exclude whites from their communication. Mention of Jerusalem, for example, could be a signal for escape to freedom. Wilkinson mentions various examples of what she calls anti-intertextuality. She is right to point out that the getting of black children's names at random from the Bible—those of Pilate, First Corinthians, or Magdalene—is never fully explained in *Song of Solomon*; the biblical names used in the novel rarely fit the person named. Morrison comments, "I used the Biblical names to show the impact of the Bible on the lives of black people, their *awe and respect for it coupled with their ability to distort it for their own purposes*" (LeClair 126, emphasis added). Pilate's name acquires its biblical meaning despite its randomness: causing her mother's death at birth makes Pilate similar to the Roman Christ-killer in a sense, and her father takes revenge on God for not listening to his prayers by insisting on naming his newborn female child Pilate even after the midwife tells him it that it is inappropriate. Morrison's comment on her use of biblical names does not support Wilkinson's claim of anti-intertextuality at all, but in Morrison's attitude and her use of reversal, the reader might yet discover a covert resistance to the Bible. This reversal, which she also applies in her appropriation of folklore materials, is a form of under-cutting, where "outcomes consistently fall short of [readers'] expectations (Harris 11).

In *Song of Solomon*, however, Wilkinson has spotted a totally misleading trace, which she calls a red herring (239), in the scene of Pilate's metamorpho-sis at the police station from a tall, imposing figure to a diminutive shuffling old woman (Rosier Smith 110). Pilate acts as a humble mammy in order to get Milkman out of jail, pleading to the jail-keepers and impressing them by appearing to meet their stereotype of the very religious uneducated black woman—in line with one of the stereotypes that Michele Wallace mentions in her *Black Macho and the Myth of the Superwoman* (106). This mammy figure allegedly knows the Bible from the spoken words of the preacher, as she cites the New Testament, designating the precise—but incorrect—source of the citation: Bible say what so e'er the Lord hath brought together, let no man put asunder—Matthew Twenty-one: Two. We was bony fide and legal wed, shu" (*Song of Solomon* 207). Possibly neither the white authorities in the book, nor most readers will realize Pilate's mistake. The quotation is not from Matthew 21:2 ("Saying unto them, Go into the village over against you, and straightway ye shall find an ass tied, and a colt with her: loose them, and bring them unto me"), but from Matthew 19:6, which reads as follows: "Wherefore they are no more twain, but one flesh. What therefore God has joined together, let not man put asunder" (all references cite the King James version of the Bible). While pretending to refer to legal wedlock with the man whose bones are in the sack, Pilate wants her nephew and Guitar to be released, just like Jesus ordered the ass and colt to be let loose in Matthew 21:2. That is to say, the deliberate misquotation suggests that intertextuality appears here "deviously."

Peggy Ochoa, who claims that the allegorical revision of the Old Testament in *Song of Solomon* was resumed in *Beloved*, points out that in reading ambiguous passages in Morrison, "'the customary route' corresponds to the obvious meaning of a text when read from the perspective of the dominant discourse," while "'the devious route' creates meanings that are [. . .] carefully concealed from those who read monologically [. . .]" (108, 109). Wilkinson, then, has fallen into the trap of reading from the former perspective. In my reading, the intertextual trace in the passage cited above is indelibly there: letting loose, release, is implied—the reference is not unmotivated. At the same time, I do not claim that Morrison's reference to the Bible in this passage should be interpreted literally; however, a literal reading may be applied if one surmises that irony is suggested in this scene. Instead of "anti-intertextuality" or a "red herring," *dual intertextuality* would be a more appropriate description of the two-way reference in this particular case.

In addition to the use of misleading and ambiguous narrative strategies that require the active participation of the reader, Morrison fully utilizes the intertextual reserves offered by the Bible, signifying upon them through her characters. Signifying, I argue, is certainly a form of echoing and not of unresponsiveness. The appearance of a figure named Hagar in Morrison's *Song of Solomon* demonstrates that Morrison's application of literary intertextuality is much more complex than is customary; it is what Jean Wyatt calls a "double take" (478). Clues help the reader decode the text and determine how to reconstruct the significance of the biblical allusions from bits and pieces in the narrative. Hagar's name recalls the story of Sarah's Egyptian slave, who becomes a concubine of Abraham, a name which stands for a complexly racialized yet empowering icon of female imagination and endurance in the face of male brutality and abandonment" (Chaney 311). Similarly, the dialogue between the biblical lovers in the Song of Songs (the Song of Solomon) speaks to Milkman's relationship with Hagar. When Milkman abandons Hagar, the line Look not upon me, because I am black" (Song of Solomon 1:6) describes her situation and sexual suffering, for she believes that she has lost her lover because of her dark complexion. Looking at Hagar, Guitar muses: "Pretty. Pretty little black girl. Pretty black-skinned girl" (*Song of Solomon* 306). The relevance of the lines, I am black but comely, O ye daughters of Jerusalem, as the tents of Kedar, as the curtains of Solomon (Song of Solomon 1:5), is never made explicit, yet it is implied in Guitar's words. He is trying to convince the forlorn Hagar thus: "He [Milkman] can't value you more than you value yourself" (*Song of Solomon* 306). This key sentence in the book suggests that "black but comely" should be replaced by "black *and* comely." Morrison further signifies upon the biblical Song of Solomon when Pilate and Reba make desperate attempts to shower gifts upon the inconsolable Hagar, in the same way as the biblical lovers desire to give their best to their sweetheart. As compared to the significance of the biblical text, however, interest in African-American history and the myth of the flying African gain precedence; this creates tension but not anti-intertextuality.

That the biblical Song of Solomon has occupied Morrison beyond writing her third novel is shown by "the reverberation of phrases and images throughout *Beloved*" (Byatt and Sodre 205). Susan Bowers points out that in *Beloved*, "Morrison fuses Christian notions of the apocalypse with West African beliefs to create a revised apocalyptic vision that principally looks backward, not forward in time [. . .]" (210). She explains:

> Most white apocalyptic literature has been based on optimistic expectation of historical, material change. The reverse experience is, of course, true for African Americans. They did not leave an Old World of death and decadence for a New World of hope and rebirth but were torn from the world of their families, communities, their own spiritual traditions, and languages, to be taken to a world of suffering, death, alienation. The good life lay not before them but behind them, yet every attempt was made to crush their memories of the past. (210, 211)

From the point of view of West African philosophy, apocalypse is repeatable and survivable, given that the notion of time is cyclical. Bowers concludes, The constant circling of the narrative in *Beloved* from present to past and back again enacts the West African perspective (212). Though the four horsemen of the apocalypse are agents of divine justice, Morrison's four horsemen— schoolteacher, the sheriff, the nephew, and slave catcher—embody evil. According to Bowers, Morrison's revision of the classic apocalyptic image suggests that she does not share with many apocalyptic writers a belief in moral force at work in history, the invisible presence of God who will come again to judge sinners and rescue and reward the oppressed. Instead, *Beloved* insists that if change is possible, it will happen only when individuals are integrated with the natural world and each other (221).

Concerning biblical intertextuality in *Beloved*, R. Clifton Spargo has demonstrated that the parody of Pauline language is suggested in Baby Suggs's sermon in *Beloved* through literalization. He points out that through Baby

Suggs, Morrison revises upon a famous conceit: "For as the body is one, and hath many members and all the members of that one body, being many, are one body: so also is Christ. For by one spirit we are all baptized into one body, whether we be Jews or Gentiles, whether we be bond or free; and have all been made to drink one spirit" (1 Corinthians 12:12–13). As Spargo notes, The Pauline allegory erases individual distinctions under the rubric of communal faith, denying the affliction and individualism [. . .] of any particular part (119). Paul posits the question: If the foot shall say, Because I am not the hand, I am not the body; is it therefore not of the body? (12:15). The analogy of the whole body and body parts is then parodied and secularized when Baby Suggs converts the transcendental touch of grace into physical caress no longer divinely abstract and no longer dependent upon the hands of another (Spargo 119). In defiance, Baby Suggs preaches: And O my people, out yonder, hear me, they do not love your neck unnoosed and straight. So love your neck; put a hand on it, grace it, stroke it, hold it up (*Beloved* 88). In Baby Suggs's sermon, the excess of spirit is transformed into an ethic of self-love. Her Call revises the corporate body, which stood for the community of faith in Paul, into a collection of unassembled corporeal parts, loved in their separateness and pain (Spargo 119). In the same passage, another reference to the Bible occurs when, after praying silently, Baby Suggs repeats the words of Jesus Christ: "'Let the children come!' and they ran from the trees toward her" (88). In *Beloved*, Baby Suggs is the incarnation of Christian love, free of the possessiveness of all the other characters' love.

In *Tar Baby*, the African American folk tale in which the white farmer uses the tar baby to catch Br'er Rabbit is signaled as an explicit intertext. This novel is an attempt to rethink blackness and its relation to class (Duvall 98), but in my reading, the implied presence of the Bible again creates tension. The novel contains an ironic overwriting and revision of Genesis; Isle des Chevaliers is reminiscent not only of the biblical paradise, but also of the landscape that unfolded itself before the pilgrims landing in America. This Eden, in which apples are a luxury, may be welcoming to Son, but not to Jadine. In this empire, Valerian rules as a self-appointed God, apples belong to Valerian's household, and Thérèse has to steal when she craves them. Geese replace the Pilgrims' wild turkeys, and Valerian gains knowledge of good and evil—that is, his wife's abuse of his son. This instance of dual intertextuality may serve again as "a representation of the doubleness of African American racial identity" (Duvall 100). *Jazz* is also encoded with several motifs of Eden.

As for *Paradise*, Justine Tally points out that "by far the most obvious overtones … are those references to the Bible: the major mythologies of Ruby are patterned on both the Old and the New Testament" (*Paradise Reconsidered* 68). In her detailed analysis of *Paradise*, Tally explores the many ways in which the Bible is present in the last part of Morrison's trilogy. The Bible is read and interpreted—rarely by the characters—but often by the author. Morrison engages in questioning the adequacy of Western theological models for those who have been marginalized by the dominant white culture (Allen 293). It is a grand vision of what true Christian love should be like, a critique of the distortions of the original tenets of Christianity in the Western world. False Christianity, its relentlessness in judging the other, is transferred onto the black community of Ruby, causing its decay. The ambiguous inscription on the oven allows for various interpretations. Beware the Furrow of His Brow, invokes an angry and relentless God, in opposition to Reverend Misner's concept of true Christianity. Alternatively, the new generation of blacks in the community, who increasingly ignore faith and God, have translated the inscription as Be the Furrow of His Brow. Both inscriptions are phrased in the style of the Old Testament and subject to criticism. In *Paradise*, the characters often think about the Ten Commandments and also read the Bible (the psalms and prayer books). The central symbol of the cross is interpreted by a number of characters, too. The history of African Americans is foregrounded in this novel, and the dominant discourse on Western history and myths justifying oppression are questioned. The ideal Paradise for Morrison is emphatically a non-exclusive (although preferably female) space.

With the appearance of the mysterious Piedade, the ending of *Paradise* makes us aware of another basic concept of Christianity: mercy. In Portuguese, *piedade* means mercy and grace. On the one hand, this name refers to the origin of Connie, the orphan stolen and saved by the nuns in Brazil; on the other, to the possibility of redemption for these "sinful" women. Though this religious reference may not be obvious to the monoglottal reader, it is necessary for the full understanding of the ending of the text: "In ocean hush a woman black as firewood is singing [. . .]. There is nothing to beat this solace which is what Piedade's song is about, although the words evoke memories neither one has ever had: [. . .] the unambivalent bliss of going home to be at home—the ease of coming back to love begun" (318).

Although the novel *Love* is outside the scope of this essay, after my first reading I am convinced that a devious course will be required in the interpretation process again. My investigation of Morrison's use of the Bible as an intertext has led me to the conclusion, however, that the ideology of St. Paul's letters is the most relevant and closest to Morrison's concept of Christianity; paralleling St. Paul's faith, the generous love that Morrison advocates is free of the desire to possess. Her kind of love is a fusion of communality and individuality, caring for the other and the self, a love which cherishes the spirit as well as the body.

## Works Cited

Allen, Alexander. The Fourth Face: The Image of God in Toni Morrison's *The Bluest Eye*. *African American Review* 32.2 (1998): 293–303.

Atwood, Margaret. "Haunted by Nightmares." In *Toni Morrison*, Modern Critical Series, edited by Harold Bloom. New York: Chelsea House, 1999. 143–147.

Awkward, Michael. *Inspiriting Influences: Tradition, Revision, and Afro-American Women's Novels*. New York: Columbia University Press, 1989.

Bakerman, Jane. The Seams Can't Show': An Interview with Toni Morrison." In Taylor-Guthrie, *Conversations*, 30–42.

Bakhtin, M. M. *The Dialogic Imagination*. Edited by Michael Holquist. Translated by Caryl Emerson and Michael Holquist. Austin: University of Texas Press, 1990.

Bowers, Susan. "Beloved and the New Apocalypse." In Middleton, *Toni Morrison's Fiction*, 209–228.

Brogan, T.V.F., ed. *The New Princeton Handbook of Poetic Terms*. Princeton: Princeton University Press, 1994.

Byatt, A. S., and Ignes Sodré. Toni Morrison's *Beloved*." In *Imagining Characters: Six Conversations about Women Writers*, edited by Rebecca Swift. New York: Vintage, 1997. 92–229.

Calvocoressi, Peter, ed. *Who's Who in the Bible*. London: Penguin, 1987.

Caputi, Jean. Specifying Fannie Hurst: Langston Hughes Limitations of Life, Zora Neale Hurstons *Their Eyes Were Watching God*, and Toni Morrisons *The Bluest Eye* as Answers to Hursts *Imitation of Life*." *Black American Literature Forum* 24.4 (1990): 697–715.

Chaney, Michael A. Review of *Dreaming Black/Writing White: The Hagar Myth in American Cultural History* by Janet Gabler-Hovler. *African American Review* 35.2 (2001): 311–312.

Du Bois, W. E. B. *The Souls of Black Folk*. 1903. New York: Penguin, 1982.

Duvall, John. *The Identifying Fictions of Toni Morrison: Modernist Authenticity and Postmodernist Blackness*. New York and Houndsmills: Palgrave, 2000.

Ellison, Ralph. *Invisible Man*. 1952. New York: Vintage, 1989.

Gates, Henry Louis, Jr. ed. *Black Literature and Literary Theory*. New York: Methuen, 1984.

Genette, Gérard. "*Transztextualitás*" [Transtextuality]. *Helikon* 1–2 (1996): 82–90.

Grewal, Gurleen. *Circles of Sorrow, Lines of Struggle: The Novels of Toni Morrison*. Baton Rouge: Louisiana State University Press, 1998.

Harris, Trudier. *Fiction and Folklore: The Novels of Toni Morrison*. Knoxville: University of Tennessee Press, 1991.

LeClair, Thomas. "The Language Must Not Sweat: A Conversation with Toni Morrison." In Taylor-Guthrie, *Conversations*, 119–128.

Middleton, David L., ed. *Toni Morrison's Fiction: Contemporary Criticism.* New York: Garland, 1997.

Morgan, Thais. The Space of Intertextuality." In O'Donnell and Davis, *Intertextuality*, 239–276.

Morrison, Toni. *Beloved.* 1987. New York: Plume, 1988.

———. *The Bluest Eye.* 1970. New York: Alfred Knopf, 1997.

———. *Love.* London: Chatto and Windus, 2003.

———. *Paradise.* London: Chatto and Windus, 1998.

———. *Song of Solomon.* 1977. London: Picador, 1993.

———. *Sula.* London: Picador, 1973.

———. *Tar Baby.* 1981. London: Picador, 1993.

Ochoa, Peggy. "Morrison's Beloved: Allegorically Othering 'White' Christianity." *MELUS* 24.2 (1999): 107–23.

O'Donnell, Patrick, and Robert Con Davis, eds. *Intertextuality and Contemporary American Fiction.* Baltimore: Johns Hopkins University Press, 1989.

Riffaterre, Michael. *Az intertextus nyoma*" [The trace of intertext]. *Helikon* 1–2 (1996): 67–81.

Rigney, Barbara Hill. *Lilith's Daughters: Women and Religion in Contemporary Fiction.* Madison: University of Wisconsin Press, 1982.

Rosier Smith, Jeanne. *Writing Tricksters: Mythic Gambols in American Literature.* Berkeley: University of California Press, 1984.

Ruas, Charles. Toni Morrison." In Taylor-Guthrie, *Conversations*, 93–119.

Spargo, R. Clifton. Trauma and the Specters of Enslavement in Morrison's *Beloved*." *Mosaic* 35.1 (March 2002): 113–130.

Tally, Justine. *Paradise Reconsidered: Toni Morrison's (Hi)stories and Truths.* FORECAAST 3. Hamburg: LIT Verlag, 1999.

Taylor-Guthrie, Danille, ed. *Conversations with Toni Morrison.* Jackson: University Press of Mississippi, 1994.

Wallace, Michele. *Black Macho and the Myth of the Superwoman.* New York: Dial Press, 1978.

Wilkinson, Nicole. The Getting of Their Names': Anti-Intertextuality and the Unread Bible in Toni Morrison's *Song of Solomon* and *Beloved*. *Intertextuality and the Bible.* Edited by George Aichele and Gary A. Phillips. In spec. issue of *Semeia: An Experimental Journal for Biblical Criticism* 69/70 (1995) : 235–245.

Worton, Michael, and Judith Still, eds. *Intertextuality: Theory and Practices.* Manchester: Manchester University Press, 1990.

Wyatt, Jean. Giving Body to the Word: The Maternal Symbolic in Toni Morrisons *Beloved*." *PMLA* 108.3 (1993): 474–488.

# 6

# THE "FEMALE REVEALER" IN *BELOVED, JAZZ* AND *PARADISE:* SYNCRETIC SPIRITUALITY IN TONI MORRISON'S TRILOGY

*Sharon Jessee*

> *I am the hearing which is attainable to everyone*
> *and the speech which cannot be grasped.*
> *I am a mute who does not speak,*
> *and great is my multitude of words.*
> *Hear me in gentleness, and learn of me in roughness.*
> *I am she who cries out,*
> *and I am cast forth upon the face of the earth.*
> (The Thunder, Perfect Mind, Nag Hammadi Library 276)

In several interviews, Toni Morrison has characterized her trilogy of novels as an exploration of love, in all its forms of recognition and value in African American experience.[1] And a significant part of her developing discourse on love in *Beloved, Jazz* and *Paradise* resurrects an African American historical/cultural consciousness under the signs of multiple theologies and religious practices. Morrison joins Cornell West, bell hooks, and other African American critics who acknowledge, in Cornell West's words, the centrality of the belief in "a kingdom beyond history" in African American religious practices as a form of "resistance and opposition in the here and now against overwhelming odds" (438). Each of the trilogy's novels dramatizes distinct beliefs about a metaphysical dimension, "here" or "beyond," salvific encounters with godlike or extraordinary personages, and prophetic divinations of the future. Actually, the trilogy can be considered in light of these words by Janice Hale: "A key to the African American notion of faith is its importance in facilitating survival" (207), words which in their emphasis on faith as praxis are not so far removed, philosophically, from early Christianity and Gnosticism. *Beloved, Jazz* and

*Paradise* offer numerous images of African American religious practices, from Paul D's sacralization of a tree he calls "brother" in *Beloved*, to the ladies' auxiliary fund dedicated to helping destitute families in 1920s Harlem in *Jazz*, and finally to the dueling ministers presiding over Ruby's most celebrated wedding in *Paradise*. Indeed, throughout her depictions of the diasporic migrations of African Americans from the slavery period through the twentieth century, Toni Morrison has been concerned with what sustains people in a spiritual sense. How can love achieve a balance between being "too thick" or "thin"? What forms of desire and neediness can be mediated or ameliorated through spiritual beliefs and practices? The spiritual dimensions of individual and communal struggles in reaching freedom in Cincinnati, Ohio in *Beloved* are echoed in the next novel's depiction of making it in the Northern City during the era of the "New Negro," and echoed again in the third novel's speculative history of the difficult migration to the West and "the Promised Land."

Actually, all of Morrison's novels, beginning with *The Bluest Eye*, reflect a familiarity with the Bible.[2] "The Bible wasn't part of my reading, it was part of my life," according to Morrison (Ruas 97), and each of her novels to varying degrees incorporates scriptural elements: parables, epigraphs, names and so forth. *Paradise* was not yet published, for example, when Patricia Hunt considered Morrison's canon to be "constituting a theological discourse" in which "scripture has primary, not secondary, consequence" (3). The focus of this study, however, diverges from Hunt's in several ways. Hunt argues that Morrison's novels "are inscribed theological, and therefore political, meditations which insist on liberation, community, and love as central principles for hope and life in this world" (30). My work focuses on Morrison's iconoclastic presentations of such "principles." The scope of theological materials which animate the trilogy of *Beloved*, *Jazz* and *Paradise* is wide: Morrison not only works with slave religion and African American Christian traditions—"hush harbor" spirituality, African American identifications with both Old and New Testament narratives, contestations between African American Protestant churches, "the black church" and black and womanist theologies—but her novels also invoke heretical Gnostic texts from the second and third centuries. The central focus of this essay, in fact, is why Morrison's narratives provide such a profoundly iconoclastic view of several contemporary discourses on African American spirituality and the role of that spirituality in improving African American quality of life.

Morrison's "theocrasy," or God-mixing, problematizes various religious and spiritual discourses and thereby coaxes, out of her narratives' shaped silences[3] as well as dramatizations, a new kind of theological emphasis, if not a new knowledge. In so doing, she has continued with the postmodern critiques she began to develop in *Playing in the Dark: Whiteness and the Literary Imagination* (1992). *Beloved, Jazz* and *Paradise* construct a complex genealogy as they trace the careers, as it were, of such concepts as salvation, transformation, ancestral reincarnation or life-after-death, specifically as these concepts have developed discursively in African American cultural history. There is the "Call" for spiritual assistance in the here-and-now throughout the narrative worlds of the trilogy, for instance, but transformations through faith experiences are only partially or tentatively put forward.

Several months after the Convent shootings, Deacon Morgan finally begins to feel his losses when he cannot put on his shoes: his lost loyalty to, and love for, his twin brother; his responsibility for Connie's murder; and his inability to practice forgiveness. He has come undone in a deeply personal sense, and at such a point as this in *Paradise*, readers of the trilogy can trace an iconographic line backwards. Deke's barefoot walk (*Paradise*) is not so far from Joe Trace's held-out hand remaining empty, Violet's sitting in the middle of the street (*Jazz*), pregnant Beloved's receding footprints, or Halle's face smeared with clabber (*Beloved*): all images of the failure to hold on, or of nowhere else to turn, or of the final violation which cannot be borne.

While the interception of something metaphysical and divine into the earthly realm is dramatized in *Beloved, Jazz* and *Paradise*, there are parallel instances of irresolutions. The girl/ghost Beloved's spite is gone by the end of the story, but Sethe, bed-ridden, shows how "it cost too much." Joe and Violet may have finally receded beneath the peace and safety of their bed-quilt, but *Jazz* ends with unresolved neediness: reaching hands. A "coal-black woman and her pupil" are in a state of repose on the last page of *Paradise*, but a ship full of "disconsolate" crew and passengers has just arrived, to begin again the struggle to succeed where the Rubyites failed, all of the founding families' efforts laid to waste in the Morgan brothers opening gunfire on a band of female outsiders. Significantly, the pattern of irreconcilable loss in the trilogy is initiated by one of its most strong-hearted and spiritually powerful characters. *Beloved*'s Baby Suggs, "holy," was a community healer until "Sethe's rough response to the Fugitive bill" made her give it up and go to bed until she finally passed on; the "Word," her ability to "Call" like none other in the Clearing, was another thing which she had "had taken away from [her]." God not only "puzzled" her, he "punished" her, and so she punished him ("Not like he punish me") by contemplating colors until she died (*Beloved* 177–179). Perhaps

Baby Suggs's emotional range—her strength, her deep capacity to love and help others, and her almost total collapse in the face of the last burden, Sethe's "big love" killing of her child—can serve as the aperture to the trilogy's presentation of African American spirituality. There are no resolutions; however, by the end of each of the three novels, there is knowledge: a knowledge which "transforms" (Jonas 35) the knower.

In one sense, to follow the flow of the trilogy is to follow a genealogy of spiritual and religious discourses on African American life; *Beloved*'s biblical epigraph, along with Baby Sugg's Calling in the Clearing, suggests some familiar parameters of the "black church." Yet the epigraphs to *Jazz* and *Paradise* introduce Morrison's interests in another religious tradition. Those epigraphs, from a third-century poem discovered in 1945 in the *Nag Hammadi* collection of Gnostic texts, begin to suggest that Morrison finds some correspondences in Gnostic traditions to her critical disposition on African American spiritual matters.

First of all, there is in Gnosticism something highly commensurate with what has been described as the constitutive element of the black church; namely, visionary sanctuary in *this* life, a transformative experience based on a "Call" which can change one's relationship to the illusory and gross material environment of life on earth. Another parallel exists between African American religion during slavery and Gnosticism's developments during the earliest centuries of Christianity: both are highly syncretic. In the former, aspects of African and Christian theologies are mixed; in the latter, aspects of Persian radical dualism and Judaism are joined with (revised) Christian tracts.[4] Indeed, the historical context out of which Gnosticism's full significance emerges also provides a useful analogy for the way in which Morrison's trilogy develops African American religion.

Although Gnosticism developed when "Palestine was seething with eschatological movements," one of which was Christianity, the Gnostic attitude or disposition was the most fervently anti-traditional of them all (Jonas 31). In *The Gnostic Religion: The Message of the Alien God and the Beginnings of Christianity*, Hans Jonas states that Gnosticism met "head on" the values of the cosmopolitan, Hellenic culture in which it appeared: it was "the almost intentional antithesis" of "long-established mental and moral attitudes... sustained by an ideological tradition, Greek in origin and venerable by its intellectual achievements" (239). Gnosticism was definitively anti-traditionalist at its point of historical emergence even while drawing on a variety of traditions. The discourses on Gnosticism aptly parallel the discourses on "as-told-to" slave narratives collected under the auspices of the WPA, which emphasized the *rebellious* orientations of African American spiritual practices and their roots in African beliefs, even as they were emerging within *and* against the developing contexts of patriarchal paternalism in white Southern Christianity.

Actually, the religious orientations—toward knowledge, cosmos and the supranatural—that early Christianity shared with Gnosticism through the first three centuries of the common era, until Gnosticism was declared heretical,[5] are pertinent here as well. As I will show, they resonate with Morrison's discursive presentations of African and African American religion in North America in *Beloved, Jazz* and *Paradise. Gnosis* is Greek for "knowledge," but for the Gnostics, it meant "not just theoretical information about certain things but [was] itself, as a modification of the human condition, charged with performing a function in the bringing about of salvation" (35). This is related to the Christian idea of salvation: "*Gnosis* meant pre-eminently knowledge of God" (Jonas 34). The goal of Gnostic striving is similar to the Christian goal: to forswear the bonds, pleasures and material necessities of the world in order to realize the inner connection to the godspirit, or "light" (Jonas 44), which is unknowable in this world.[6] According to the *Gospel of St. Thomas*, one of the classic Gnostic scriptures, "[Jesus said] it will not be a matter of saying 'Here it is' or 'There it is.' Rather, the kingdom of the Father is spread out upon the earth and men do not see it" (*Nag Hammadi* 130). Unless, that is, they are "Called," in the African American, as well as the Gnostic, sense.

\*     \*     \*

I will call them my people,
which were not my people;
and her beloved,
which was not beloved. (Romans 9:25, *King James Bible*)

With her fifth novel, *Beloved*, Morrison begins a sustained inquiry into the religious practices and experiences of North American slaves and their African American descendents. The epigraph from Romans illustrates the salvation bestowed by God on those who are not professed believers; mercy is God's choice. For *Beloved*, it suggests that the "disremembered and unaccounted for," all of the individuals lost in the Middle Passage, have been granted God's mercy. Likewise, people of "fire-cooked blood" and "broken necks," like Sixo and Sethe's mother, as well as the "crawling already?" baby who had her throat cut, are the beloved for whom Toni Morrison writes her book.[7] Furthermore, Sethe's act of naming her dead daughter at the funeral—"Dearly Beloved" was "every word she heard the preacher say" and "all there was to say, surely" (5)—incisively brings together African, Judeo-Christian and Gnostic traditions under the powerful sign of the Call.

Toni Morrison's trilogy is fundamentally concerned with the traces of African belief having to do with the importance of remembering the ancestors, and this is foregrounded throughout *Beloved*. From Baby Suggs's leafy Clearing to the girl on the slave ship who is "always crouching" under the dead and dying in the ship's hull (210–211) is a stretch not just of time and distance but of remembrance, a sacred temporal continuity which the North Atlantic slave trade disrupted by severing and scattering familial ties (Jessee 199), and which Sethe disrupted for her daughter by causing her sudden death. The ancestral spirits and the "pastness" in which they reside are an important part of the cosmos for many African peoples,[8] and all of *Beloved*'s major characters are in need of a restoration, a rebalancing, of their relations with the recent dead. John S. Mbiti states that in a broad African philosophical view, "death is a process which removes a person gradually from the Sasa period to the Zamani," from the near and present time, which includes the recently deceased, to the distant storehouse of time: "After the physical death, the individual continues to exist in the Sasa period and does not immediately disappear from it. He is *remembered* by relatives and friends who knew him [and] recall him by name (25)." Significantly, Mbiti stresses that "if he [the deceased] appears [to those who knew him] he is recognized *by name*.... This recognition by name is extremely important" (25), and it may continue for four or five generations, or until everyone who knew the person is dead. At that time, the deceased passes into Zamani. Mbiti stresses that while a person is "remembered by name, he is not really dead: he is alive, and such a person, [he] would call the *living-dead*" (25).

By the time Paul D finds 124 Bluestone road, Beloved is fully embodied at the age she would have grown to, had she lived; she comes out of the water because Sethe *brings her back with her thoughts*. Paul D may have driven the baby's ghost out of the house, but more than that, he gave Sethe a safe space in which she could "remember things," and "feel the hurt" she had repressed for eighteen years (19). Both as a ghost and as a nineteen-year-old woman, Beloved can be understood within the context of African religious practices, which "are

chiefly focused upon the relationship between human beings and the departed" (27). As Mbiti explains:

> Man tries to penetrate or project himself into the world of what remains of him after
> this physical life. If the living-dead are suddenly forgotten, this means that they are
> cast out of the Sasa period, and are in effect excommunicated, their personal immor-
> tality is destroyed and they are turned into a state of non-existence. And this is the
> worst possible punishment for anyone. The departed resent it. (27)

Morrison's novel has several explicit allusions to the problem of what happens
when people die violently or are forgotten too soon; Stamp, Ella, Baby Suggs,
Paul D and Sethe all make references to this, such as Ella's declaration that
"people who die bad don't stay in the ground" (*Beloved* 188). And there is
another dimension to the novel's concern with putting the dead to rest, coextensive with the characters' dramatic actions, yet philosophically more all-
encompassing.

According to Swailem Sidhom, in an essay on "The Theological Estimate
of Man," there is a moral foundation to remembering and making offerings to
ancestors: their immortality depends upon it. "To be remembered" and "to be
immortal" in Kikuyu is the same word: *mutigairi*. "This aspect of immortality
is almost common to all Africans.... It is usually through stories about him or
through belongings which he left behind that the person keeps alive in the
memory of the community for generations," states Sidhom (106). In many different African traditions, immortality is "the highest good," and one's entire
family, if not community, is responsible for its maintenance (Sidhom 104–105).
There is a "gradation" into immortality which begins with birth and continues after death, and any offense or sin committed by one person affects the
entire family: "The real power of sin is in disrupting the otherwise normal
flow of life and force in the universe" (Sidhom 113). In *Beloved*, disruptions
occur not only when individuals become susceptible to that "something in
man... always ready to move in the wrong direction" (Sidhom 109), but whole
families or communities as well. When the other residents of the Cincinnati
outskirts community do not warn Baby Suggs's household about the
approaching "Four Horsemen" coming to remand Sethe and her children
back into slavery, when they do not sing or hum at Sethe's arrest after the murder, they are "moving in the wrong direction" into resentment, just as much as
Sethe is committing the sin of pride. That Sethe will not "admit" or behave as
if she did anything wrong is such a major factor in the baby-ghost's spite that
when Beloved appears, reincarnate, she perpetuates both her punishment of

Sethe and her bottomless hunger for her company until the two gestures become inseparable emotional recognitions.

Furthermore, the novel's organization and development is an aesthetic performance of the Africanist moral emphasis on ancestral responsibility. Sethe's tangible "rememory" is a re-member-ing of the recent dead, and the narrative unfolds in such an emotionally charged ebb and flow of past and present in order to construct what had been lost: "*Sixty Million / and more.*" Ancestral memory becomes Morrison's imaginative vehicle for "moving that veil aside" from "the interior life" of the slaves that had been excised "from the records that the slaves themselves told" ("Site of Memory" 111). And yet, even though the narrative so fundamentally evokes Africanist beliefs and orientations, it neither totalizes them nor their North American variations in the Afro-Christian mixture of what is usually called "slave religion."

Several critical studies on the development of Afro-Christianity in the United States over the past four hundred years echo the words by Silvia Frey in her *Water from the Rock: Black Resistance in a Revolutionary Age*: the slaves created "a black rendition of Christian theology and morality that was not identical with Christian goals of planters and not anticipated by white missionaries' vision of Christianity" (283). According to Frey, in fact, the "spiritual odyssey of African Americans from traditional religion to Protestant Christianity forms a critical chapter in the history of the emerging black community and indeed in the history of slavery" (36). In their relatively isolated communities under slavery, along with the "systematic repression of the African heritage" (36), Africans converted to Christianity as missionaries, and some planters supported this until the Vesey conspiracy of 1822 (276). Lawrence Levine's *Black Culture and Black Consciousness*, Lincoln and Mamiya's *The Black Church in the African-American Experience* and Cornell West's *Prophetic Fragments* are a few of the sources that explicate what the slaves found, and what many African Americans still find, to be the resonant biblical stories for their experience. Levine suggests that the "essence of slave religion cannot be fully grasped without understanding Old Testament bias. It is important that Daniel and David and Joshua and Jonah and Moses and Noah, all of whom fill the lines of the spirituals, were delivered in *this* world and delivered in ways which struck the imagination of the slaves" (50). Similarly, Cornell West notes, "Profound preoccupation with the Christian gospel is a distinctive feature of Afro-American culture" because "African slaves' search for collective identity could find historical purpose in the exodus of Israel out of slavery and personal meaning in the bold identification of Jesus Christ with the lowly" (162).

Toni Morrison describes in an interview with Charles Ruas how she remembers her grandparents' religion as a mixture of the Judeo-Christian biblical tradition with some traces of African religious beliefs and practices: they "talked a great deal about Jesus—they selected out of Christianity all the things they felt applicable to their situation—but they also kept this other body of knowledge that we call superstitions. They were way stations in their thinking about how to get on with it and a reason to get up the next morning" (115). Morrison further characterizes African American Christianity in a way which aptly characterizes its presentation in her fiction:

> Christianity says something particularly interesting to black people, and I think it's part of why they were so available to it. It was the love things that were psychically very important. Nobody could have endured that life in constant rage.... But with the love thing—love your enemies, turn the other cheek—they could sublimate the other things, they transcended them.... I suppose if they had been untampered with, they could have made out with the vestiges of that African religion that they brought, because it survived in some forms, in ways in which they worked, sang, talked, and carried on (Ruas 116).

Toward the end of *Beloved*, the women who finally come to rescue a debilitated Sethe from "the devil-child" Beloved's insatiable gaze (261) bring their Christian crosses along with "what they believed would work. Stuffed in apron pockets, strung around their necks, lying in the space between their breasts" (257) were their traces of Africanist religion. And the "holler" with which Ella launches the women's powerful sounding, which "broke the back of words" (259) because it preceded language, is not specifically African, Christian or any other codified utterance. This is precisely its impact: it derives from some amalgamation of traditions, or perhaps from some archetypal collective memory. In this way, Ella's holler succinctly evokes the black church.

One contemporary scholar of African American religion defines a key feature of the black church this way: "It has neither hands nor feet nor form, but we know it when we feel it in our communities." It is not exactly Christianity, Islam, Judaism, "nor any human-made religion," but rather "it comes as God-full presence to our struggles" (Williams 206). The black church does, as will be shown here, ultimately "escape precise definition" (Williams 204) in Morrison's work as well, yet *Beloved*, *Jazz* and *Paradise* also evoke a quality to be found throughout the black church's discursive history: what Cornell West has defined as an existential freedom, "a mode of being-in-the-world which resists dread and despair" (162). Lincoln and Mamiya echo other critics when they assert that "the black sacred cosmos" combines African heritage with Christianity. They also write that "the core experience" of "the black sacred cosmos" is a personal conversion experience (6). To help her mother, Denver finds a way to do what she had not been able to do for many years because she heard Baby Suggs's spirit tell her to "go on out the yard," even when there was "no defense" (*Beloved* 244). This evokes a particular salvationist emphasis in African American religious worship: assistance in the here and now—literally in this or these bodies at this instant—and it parallels the key principle of early Christian Gnosticism that *seeing* the kingdom where "men do not see it" is the only way to realize it. *Beloved*, unlike *Jazz* and *Paradise*, makes no explicit references to Gnosticism, but then neither does it make very many specific references to Christianity. The first novel of Morrison's trilogy, rather, evokes the *development* of a syncretic religion, and in this way shows its affinity with Gnostic tradition.

Transformative knowledge, the opening into something unknown, is the basis for experiencing salvation in this life, and as such, it forms the intersection between the black church and Gnosticism. Both are concerned with the idea of true freedom as an internal, not just material, condition. Lincoln and Mamiya note this emphasis in African American religion: "the Black Church was the first theatre in the black community. Like the Greek theater its functional goal was catharsis, but beyond the Greeks, the Black Church was in search of transcendence... the core experience of the black sacred cosmos was the personal conversion of the individual believer" (6). In a similar way, Jonas observes that for Gnostic sects of the early Christian era, the knowledge of truth came not through "natural reason," but through "sacred and secret lore or through inner illumination" (35). Returning briefly to Morrison's commentary on religion in her family can elucidate this point further: "The openness of being saved was one part of it [Christianity]—you were constantly being redeemed and reborn, and you couldn't fall too far, and couldn't ever fall completely and be totally thrown out" (Ruas 117). Being "saved" or "seeing" God or a representative of God helped one "get through." And this transformative knowing, in both Christian and Gnostic senses, comes to humans by way of a Call.

In *Beloved*, when Stamp Paid is trying to talk Baby Suggs into coming back to preach in the Clearing, he says, "Can't nobody Call like you" (*Beloved* 178). What she had done at the Clearing provided that catharsis identified by Lincoln and Mamiya in their "black sacred cosmos." After exhorting the men, women and children to laugh, dance and cry until they are "exhausted and riven" (88), Baby Suggs begins to "Call" to the people to generate the self-love and self-respect for, first of all, their own bodies, so "despised" "out there": "O my people, out yonder, hear me, they do not love your neck unnoosed and straight. So love your neck; put a hand on it, grace it stroke it and hold it up" (88–89). Yvonne Atkinson identifies aspects of the black English oral tradition in Baby Suggs's calling: she notes both the "witness/testify" and "call/response" character of the gatherings at the Clearing, key features of which are collaborative improvisation, collective memory and cultural solidarity (22–23). "The language of the slaves became their canvas and clay" (Atkinson 13), and in that way, they formed a "gathering" to reverse the "dispersal" of "original unity." These last words are Hans Jonas's from his work on Gnosticism (59), yet they make a strikingly similar description to Atkinson's assertions that black oral traditions perform rituals of restoration in an African sense (Atkinson 24). Jonas here identifies patterns of imagery running through many of the Gnostic scriptures: gathering/dispersal; the one and the many; and finally, falling or sinking/being Called (59–77).

The theme of the Call is prevalent in not only Gnostic scriptures, furthermore, but in the Old as well as New Testaments. In fact, as the leader of a new, Eastern religion developing in the Hellenic world, Jesus is a "Caller of the Call." According to Hans Jonas, the Caller is sent by "the Great Life and invested with authority" to "remind" people of their origins (77): "The symbol of the call as the form in which the transmundane makes its appearance within the world is so fundamental to Eastern Gnosticism that we may even designate [these] as religions of the call" (Jonas 74). Salvation will occur only when there is a real "breach" or "tear" in the world (Jonas 78); only then can "the light" of truth and enlightenment shine through. In the trilogy, this theme is initially most fully realized—and problematized—by Beloved herself.

Jonas notes, "In the numerous literary versions of the call, one or the other of these aspects may preponderate… the reminder of origins, the promise of salvation, the moral instruction" (81). Beloved's return, almost two decades after her death, offers all three possibilities for the characters, narrator, and readers, but only partially, for her disappearance also reminds us that there is no permanent restoration, no infallible *gnosis*, to take us out of ourselves:

> Everybody knew what she was called, but nobody anywhere knew her name. Disremembered and unaccounted for, she cannot be lost because no one is looking for her, and even if they were, *how can they call her if they don't know her name?* Although she has claim, she is not claimed. In the place where long grass opens, the girl who wait-

ed to be loved and cry shame erupts into her separate parts, to make it easy for the chewing laughter to swallow her all away. (Emphasis added, *Beloved* 274)

Not knowing on whom to call appears in Romans 10:14 as well: "How, then, shall they call on him in whom they have not believed? And how shall they believe in him of whom they have not heard?" And not being able to call on one who has not been "named"—literally, *known* or identified—appears in the Gnostic *Gospel of Truth* 21:22–25: "Truly, how is one to hear if his name has not been called?" (*Nag Hammadi* 42). In Romans, Paul is speaking of the Israelites and the problem of salvation for unbelievers. In the *Gospel of Truth*, a Christian Gnostic text of the school of Valentinus,[9] not being named will cause one to "vanish" and become "a creature of oblivion" (*Nag Hammadi* 44). Beloved becomes a crossroads in the epilogue of the novel: having no known name, she stands for all those who were lost and "disremembered" because their descendents could not—or would not—remember them, yet she also "has claim," in her "footprints" that "come and go, come and go" (*Beloved* 275). There is the denial of her in the penultimate line of the novel: "Certainly no clamor for a kiss," just "weather." Yet the last line, or rather last word, of the novel is "Beloved": it is an enunciation, an invocation of her name, a Call. The girl Beloved, then, is gathered and dispersed, dispersed and gathered, in the novel. She is a protean figure whom Morrison creates to signify an opening and unfinished set of ideas. "If you come from Africa, your name is gone," notes Morrison in an interview (LeClair 126), and this becomes a rich, multivalent emblem for *Beloved*.

*Beloved* launches the trilogy with a resounding resistance to closure. Patricia Hunt succinctly characterizes this Morrisonian resistance: "[Morrison] writes against the dualistic philosophical tradition that has enabled and fostered racism, slavery, and the superstructure of white patriarchal dominance. The coextensive, overlapping, non-linear themes in these texts represent an endless tension... each demand [*sic*] the reader's continual questioning of discursive authority" (184–185). The novels of the trilogy do at times evoke the kind of heroism which Kelly Brown Douglas describes in *The Black Christ*: "Christianity did not make these slaves docile.... Rather, it made them rebellious. It radicalized them to fight for their freedom" (25). However, spiritual heroism is not a totalizing discourse in Morrison's works. Baby Suggs gave up her Calling not only because "white folks wore her out at last," but also because her own community turned against her. Toni Morrison's evocation of the black church, therefore, is developed within her larger critical framework of spiritual traditions: a syncretic, and at times, "uneasy" union.

In *Beyond Ontological Blackness*, Victor Anderson argues that "black subjectivity itself is... subjugated under the totality of black faith" (99). His view echoes that of bell hooks, who stated in *Yearnings: Race, Gender, and Cultural Politics* that "unfortunately the need among African Americans to promote a positive racial community has too often a dialectical formation against individuality" (16). The syncretic spirituality in Morrison's works presents a similar disposition. "Post-modern blackness," in Anderson's words, "recognizes that black identities are continually being reconstituted as African Americans inhabit widely different social spaces and communities of moral discourse" (11). Morrison's characters are not enclosed within the totality of a theology "always bound by white racism and the culture of survival" in which "oppression is required for the self-disclosure of the oppressed" (87), in Anderson's sense. Rather, while Morrison does in an important way produce a "theological gaze" which emphasizes the amelioration of oppression through a "hermeneutics of return," in Edward Said's sense, to African traditions, she does not reify it. Similarly, Gnosticism per se is treated in a highly iconoclastic manner in the next two novels, *Jazz* and *Paradise*, since Gnosticism's most foundational concept—the radical dualism of the divine and the earthly which repudiates the world and the flesh—gets dramatically undercut in Morrison's narrative, as I will shortly illustrate.

\* \* \*

I am the name of the sound
and the sound of the name.
I am the sign of the letter
and the designation of the division.
(*The Thunder, Perfect Mind*, from the *Nag Hammadi*)

*Jazz*'s epigraph vocalizes its nameless narrator's performative significance: both present paradoxes of narrative presence. *The Thunder, Perfect Mind* is a text of no known origin, written sometime before 350 CE. Like many other of the *Nag Hammadi* texts found in the Nile Valley in 1945, it was written in Coptic (Egyptian) but translated from Greek. Unlike any other text in the *Nag*, however, it is "virtually unique" and not identifiably Gnostic, Jewish or Christian, according to MacRae and Parrott's introduction to this piece (*Nag Hammadi* 296). Bentley Layton, another translator and editor of *The Thunder*, as it appears in *The Gnostic Scriptures*, suggests that its closest resemblances are to Greek identity riddles and "Wisdom Monologues," a genre in which the female knowledge-bearer "describes herself and summons her souls to her" (Layton 78). The thunder goddess somewhat resembles the Jewish figure Dame Wisdom; the Egyptian goddess Isis, whose cults were all over Greece at the time; and a "fleshly... and celestial Eve" (Layton 78). MacRae and Parrot are more cautious about the poem's possible affinities, but they do emphasize that "thunder, in Greek myth, in the Hebrew Bible, and elsewhere, comes forth from the highest god. It is the way in which the god makes his presence known on earth" (*Nag Hammadi* 296). But how can this describe the whimsical, nameless narrator of *Jazz*, who says about her characters, "Good luck and let me know" (5)?

Antithesis and paradox are the thematic as well as formal characteristics of "The Thunder" poem, and in that sense, the narrator of *Jazz* resembles this powerful "female revealer." Speech that is suggestive rather than direct, in spite of the authority of the speaker's voice, allows Morrison's narrator to be taken seriously and playfully at the same time. In this sense, the narrator closely resembles "that music that laughs and cries at the same time," in Langston Hughes's words: namely, jazz. Indeed, traditional religion appears in *Jazz* only at the periphery of the story; instead, we have the sacred/secular forms of modernism. Not only "that race music," but Alice Manfred's "gathering rope," Dorcas's burning "wood chip" in her throat, and Golden Gray's yearning for "the gash, the slit" are also some of the text's objective correlatives to human—and divine—emotions. "History is over, you all" (*Jazz* 7), and because everyone is noticing the "click" to be heard and felt in the "City," God *seems* to have receded from the scene.[10] However, that is so only if one refuses the novel's project of rehabilitating the "divine."

In *Upheavals of Thought: The Intelligence of the Emotions*, Martha Nussbaum considers how St. Augustine in *The Confessions* and Dante in *The Divine Comedy* rework human need and emotions back into the "Christian ascent" tradition: "Don't we have to like human action, even in its imperfection, if we are to figure out how to live in this world?" asks Nussbaum (527). Any vision of love that has shame about the world "has carried the lover too far beyond the realm of worldly need, suffering, and injustice" (556). The novelist James Joyce, Nussbaum demonstrates in her last chapter, places ascendance back into everyday life; so, I would argue, does Morrison. *Jazz*, like *Ulysses* as Nussbaum describes it, "includes the romantic vision of life as a profound human wish," but "informs us as well that life is more fragmentary, less single-minded" than the romantic vision suggests (Nussbaum 707). The creation of the narrator of *Jazz* is perhaps Morrison's most intricate modernist correlative to divine love—a love that is hungry, comical and vulnerable, and through those very imperfections, most capable of rehabilitating the human spirit.

The "City" over which the narrator presides is a major object of her longing. She is a demigod in this sense: "I'm crazy about this City"; "A city like this one makes me dream tall and feel in on things. Hep"; "Alone, yes, but top-notch and indestructible" (*Jazz* 7). She is a goddess who loves what humans have wrought; their City is appealing because it is a place where individuals "feel more like themselves, more like the people they always believed they were [....] City is what they want it to be" (35). Presenting an environment that can support one's desires, the new urban metropolis seemed to hold promise to African Americans like Violet and Joe, who "train-danced" into New York, Chicago, Cleveland and elsewhere, leaving behind the "pebbly creeks" they seemed to be able to forget (35). But, of course, they could not forget, which is where, and how, the troubles began for the main characters of *Jazz*. And the narrator, herself a subject of neediness and involuntary desire, descends into their flawed world initially to gaze at them, then to "meddle" with them, and finally to respect and love them.

Morrison's goddess/narrator loves the world, and it is finally up to her to bear witness for it, giving testimony to her readers. Yvonne Atkinson sees her as a "Witness and Tell" storyteller (24) in black oral tradition, and significantly, *The Thunder, Perfect Mind*, in its ambiguous status concerning different religious traditions, does not contradict this. The poem is not classically Gnostic because, MacRae and Parrot suggest, it emphasizes the "conception of the immanence of the divine into the world," an extension too broad for Gnosticism's radical dualism (*Nag Hammadi* 296). Classic Gnosticism finds "the cosmos" to be nothing more than a web of deception and illusion (Jonas 42–47). Morrison's narrator does, however, retain some of the characteristics of the Gnostic attitude. "The unknown God," in Hans Jonas's words, both "invites and thwarts" the quest for knowledge of him, and that "in the failure of language he becomes revealed" (4). This is highly appropriate for the narrator of *Jazz* because she explicitly performs that failure of language for her readers.

As the narrator is telling about Golden Gray's arrival in Vesper County, Virginia, to confront his father (and thus his own African American identity),

she initially testifies to his anger, his racism and his seeming to show more concern for his fancy clothes than for the pregnant and naked—and suddenly
unconscious—black woman he finds in the woods. Subsequently, though, the
narrator discovers, she is wrong; he "has the courage" to forego being "an
adored bud" and picks her up, bringing her to Lestroy's cabin: "What was I
thinking of? How could I have imagined him so poorly[....] I have been care-
less and stupid and it infuriates me to discover (again) how unreliable I am"
(*Jazz* 160). In dramatizing her own "failure of language," the narrator
"becomes revealed" for a specific purpose. She is reminding readers of her
power, like the Gnostic Caller of the Call, sent to earth as the "Reminder" of
our original connection with God. In *Jazz*, however, the Caller of the Call is
not omnipotent, and her power is unpredictable, even to herself. She makes,
in the Lacanian sense, many "slips of the tongue."[11] And we can forgive her
for it because she forgives herself: "I want to be the language that wishes him
well, speaks his name, wakes him when his eyes need to be open." And so she
will "have to alter things" in spite of the possibility that she "may be doomed
to another misunderstanding" (161). Morrison humanizes the narrator by
making her capable of love. She presents for our reception what Martha
Nussbaum describes as the "adequate conception of love," which "involves
renouncing the desire to control the universe, and accepting one's own human
vulnerability" (557).

The narrator is not the only character in the novel who is subject to involuntary desire; weeks after he killed his young lover Dorcas, Joe Trace still
hangs on to his infatuation with her, "telling" Dorcas in a long internal monologue that he would "strut out the Garden, strut! as long as you held on to my
hand girl, Dorcas girl" (*Jazz* 134–135). Seeing his affair with Dorcas as a re
enactment of Adam and Eve's expulsion from the Garden of Eden, Joe hangs
on to the emotional complex of erotic desire, pain, remorse, pride and defiance because with Dorcas, he "didn't fall in love"; he "*rose* in it" (emphasis
added, 135). Joe was not prepared for what Dorcas stirred in him, and likewise
neither was Violet/Violent prepared for her own foray into the love-hunger for
a baby which "hit her like a hammer" (108). Alice Manfred still imagined herself driving over and over, until she was "pulpy," the woman who took her husband from her (86). And Dorcas needed to be able to recall the feeling—the
pain—of a burning wood-chip from the fire on the day both her parents were
brutally killed in the St. Louis race riot. This "chip," which *seemed* sometimes
to be lodged in her throat, sank further down, thanks to the Drum on Fifth
Avenue, "somewhere around her navel" where "it would be waiting for and

with her whenever she wanted to be touched by it" (61). Everybody in the novel, in fact, seems to feel just like the narrator when she remarks, "Pain, I have an affection, a kind of sweettooth for it" (219).

All of this attentiveness to human desire does not negate or diminish, however, the righteous response of the African American community in Harlem to the East St. Louis race riot of 1917. The march down Fifth Avenue and the sound of the drums gave Alice Manfred her "gathering rope," which thereafter she grasped with her fist whenever she felt the need. Even that "low-down" jazz music had "a complicated anger" (58–59) which Alice could not ignore. Many readers have already attested to the political aesthetics of jazz music as they pertain to Morrison's novel,[12] yet there is another iconographic "mooring," in Holloway's words, which in *Jazz* is more germane to the question of human/divine love pursued here. And her name is Wild.

Actually, the character of Wild, that "berry-black" woman whom Golden Gray rescues and then seems to run off with (we see his clothes in the cave where Wild seemed to live, 183) is like Beloved: she, too, is given a name which describes what she *means*, her origin and identity being a mystery. Wild, who Joe believes is his mother, is the object of both yearning and revulsion in the novel, again much like Beloved. People in Vesper County know she is around and are very cautious of her; Joe, on the other hand, wants her to tell him, to let him know, that he has a mother. The opening image of Wild is strikingly similar to the closing image of Beloved: dark-skinned, naked and very pregnant, running scared (*Jazz* 144). Wild's importance to *Jazz* is underscored by the narration's three renditions of the initial encounter between Golden Gray and Wild (*Jazz* 144–162) and by the witnessing of Joe's three attempts to find her in the woods when he was a young man. In other ways, however, Wild's significance is much broader, for she lies at the very center of the trilogy and of the trilogy's discourse on African American spirituality.

We meet Wild early in the novel through a brief account of Joe's searching for her; our initial image of her, in fact, is the *possibility* of her hand in the hibiscus. Joe hopes the hand might reach out and "confirm, once and for all, that she was indeed his mother" (36). He was "willing to take the chance of being grateful and humiliated at the same time" and wanted "just a sign." Joe does not seem to know whether or not she is there, but he needs to believe it. "Maybe those were her fingers moving like that," because any "combination of shame and pleasure" would be better than "the inside nothing he traveled with from then on" until he had Dorcas "to tell it to" (37). Wild, through Joe's point of view, carries the knowledge of his ancestry. Similar to the legacy

Beloved created for her family, Wild is Joe's "best thing" (*Beloved* 272) for which Dorcas is but a substitute. There are many instances of sublimated love in *Jazz*, to which Violet testifies when she reflects that she and Joe were each other's substitutes "from the very beginning" (97). Violet had grown up enamored of the stories her Aunt Trubell used to tell her of Golden Gray. Golden Gray is thus a compliment to Wild (both objects of desire "substituted" with other loves), underscoring her protean presence in the novel. That such a "golden" child, furthermore, would choose to live with Wild rather than returning to a comfortable life in Baltimore suggests Wild's power of attraction: she is the root, as it were, of human longing, evoking passion in her progeny, forcing them to substitute other pleasures for that early, almost forgotten one. And even *Jazz*'s Thunder-goddess narrator succumbs.

Thinking over the imagery of Wild's cave (which she got from Joe's memory, or "rememory," in Sethe's sense), the narrator realizes that she would like to be in there, that "home in the rock [...] a place already made for me, both snug and wide open" with a "doorway never needing to be closed" (*Jazz* 221). That doorway will reappear in *Paradise,* where it is felt as a window between the seen and unseen worlds by Richard Misner and Anna Flood; here, however, Wild's cave is that space where a demigod might like to linger, where she "could, without fright" look in and take the hand that was offered: "She has seen me and is not afraid of me. She hugs me. Understands me. Has given me her hand. I am touched by her. Released in secret. Now I know" (221). The narrator discovers that she can live in both worlds, the seen and unseen, and ends the novel by making such an offering to the readers.

We are invited to "join" with her, like Sethe, Denver and Beloved do in the threnody section of *Beloved*. In *Jazz*, however, the language is more erotic than maternal, as the narrator echoes Dorcas's speech pattern ("take me [...] take me" 39) when Dorcas asks Joe to take her to a nightclub: "Make me, remake me. You are free to do it and I am free to let you because look, look. Look where your hands are. Now" (229). These last lines of *Jazz* reveal the collaboration between reader, narrator and writer, implicating the reader's presence in the text in a tactile way. We touch the Wild/narrator/author figuration, just as at the end of *Beloved* we hear the enunciation/Calling of Beloved's name.

Certain lines from the Gnostic *Gospel of Eve* underscore the significance of *Jazz*'s closing words: "You collect me from wherever you wish. / But when you collect me, it is your own self that you collect" (*Gnostics According to St. Epiphanius* 26.2.6, quoted in Layton 205). The immanence of the divine *in and of* the world is what *Jazz* adds to the trilogy in a language both playful and needy:

the language of love. In this way, Wild continues the pattern initiated by Beloved, moving from making restoration for those lost (*Beloved*) toward restoring those who are left behind and still yearning for that which is absent. "Flesh, pinioned by misery, hangs on to it with pleasure" (*Jazz* 228), because misery is a reminder of (lost) divine origins. Again, Martha Nussbaum's work on the "intelligence of the emotions" is instructive for *Jazz*: "Ascent must take place *within* the context of our humanity, not by attempting, out of pride, to depart from it" (emphasis added, Nussbaum 543). *Paradise*, however, must still take up another challenge to the effort to keep open that portal between the seen and unseen, the earthly and the divine.

*   *   *

> For many are the pleasant forms which exist in
>> numerous sins,
>> and incontinencies,
>> and disgraceful passions
>> and fleeting pleasures,
>>> which (men) embrace until they become
>>> sober
>>> and go up to their resting place.

Morrison chose the final lines of *The Thunder, Perfect Mind* for her epigraph to *Paradise*[13]; by doing so, she underscores the distinct possibility that God is, if not woman, then at least as androgynous and mysterious as the speaker of *The Thunder*. The last three lines furthermore recall the message of Jesus Christ to the world, but they are, we must recall, spoken by a "female revealer." Morrison's seventh novel reflects and refracts the debates within African American religious discourse in the post–civil rights era: the patriarchal tendencies of the denominational churches, on the one hand, and the emergence of what one scholar terms "Womanist Christology," on the other. According to Jacquelyn Grant, "Christ among the least must also mean Christ in the community of Black women" (217), an argument also made in works by Mark Chapman, Cain Hope Felder, Sally McFague, and Delores Williams. The story of Hagar (Genesis 16:1–16; 21:9–21) becomes of particular importance in the work of Dolores S. Williams's *Sisters in the Wilderness: The Challenge of Womanist God-Talk* (1996). Williams emphasizes Hagar's slave/surrogate mother status and her exile, with her son, Ishmael, into a desert where there were few resources for survival. Hagar has an encounter with God, "which aided Hagar in the survival struggle of herself and her son" because God "gave her new vision to see survival resources where she had seen none before" (5). God's visit to Hagar, Williams emphasizes, gives her the insight to "make a way out of no way." "Liberation in the Hagar stories is not given by God; it finds its source in human initiative" (5–6), and for Williams and other theologians, this marks a radical new direction beyond Black Liberation Theology. Williams borrows Alice Walker's term to identify a "womanist" theology: a "survival, quality of life formation with God's direction and the work of building a peoplehood and a community" (161). Williams's specific emphasis on the Hagar story resonates with many of the trilogy's women, in fact, but it resonates most instructively with the outcast women of the Convent in *Paradise*.

Juxtaposed with the predominance of African American Protestant churches and their regulative functions in the town of Ruby, Oklahoma, is a newly developing discipline, salvific and mystical, among the Convent's "detritus" women. The "Convent," as the Ruby citizens nicknamed it, had been first an embezzler's mansion and then a Catholic school for Indian girls, but that had been closed before Mavis and the others came to join Connie, or "Consolata," as the nuns called their adoptee. Connie stayed on after all the sisters had departed so that she could care for the dying Mother Superior, and stayed on after her death for lack of anywhere else to go. This initiates what becomes the Convent's almost decade-long existence as safe place for women and a temporary harbor from various desperate citizens of Ruby. Most significantly, it becomes the site of liberation for the five wayward women, not only from the repressive patriarchal town of Ruby, but from the prior communities which despised, mocked or confused them. Connie, Mavis, Grace (Gigi), Seneca and Pallas (Divine) are all throwaways, so to speak; they have each been made into wreckage—by themselves or others, or both—in the relationships from which they have fled. At the Convent, the women come under Connie's tutelage, which, significantly, comes about only after she herself has fallen down, after her affair with one of the married leaders of Ruby, Deacon Morgan (Deke), is terminated by his self-remorse, which he directs at Connie as disgust. Together, the Convent women seem to be given the insight and the spiritual sustenance to make something new out of the disasters of their lives *on their own*, with little help, and much deterrence, from the Rubyites. However, unlike Delores Williams's hermeneutic of the biblical Hagar narrative, Morrison's text does not offer a reading which can provide a resolution to "building a peoplehood and a community." The fate of some of the Convent women is ambiguous, like Beloved's, while back in the all-black town of Ruby, irreconcilable differences remain as much a possibility as does healing. As in *Beloved* and *Jazz*, *Paradise*'s work with African American spirituality is methodologically critical, highly syncretic and resistant to closure.

*Paradise*'s central dramatic event—the shooting of the stray women by Ruby's patriarchs—is set in the mid-1970s, but it has all the trappings and overtones of an ancient battle. The conflict in and around this "one all-black town worth the pain" is between men and women, old age and youth, tradition and change, sobriety and passion. At the center of it is the stubborn, yet admirable, pride of Ruby's founding families, who took what was left of the community their grand- and great-grandparents founded in 1895 in Indian Territory and moved it further west into the Oklahoma panhandle, where land was cheap after the tornadoes of 1949. Moreover, much of the drama in *Paradise* is played out, as it were, within a community profoundly inflected with African American Protestantism. Morrison's critical analysis of African American Christianity is found in *Paradise*'s gradual exposure of the utopian community built by Ruby's patriarchs as a false paradise.

For example, Mavis initially is stricken by "how still [... Ruby] was, as though no one lived there," and she sees "enormous lawns cut to dazzle in front of churches and pastel-colored houses." It seems rather like a paradise, since "the air was scented," "the trees young" and the gardens "snowed with butterflies" (45). But beneath Ruby's placid surface, the two most important patriarchs, Deacon and Steward Morgan, are without issue, and at the end of the other founders' bloodlines there are "broken babies," conflicted young women and young men ridden with post–traumatic stress disorder. There are "garden wars" between the women with too much time on their hands, and a dreaminess for photographic poses among men who have made their communal Oven a forbidding "shrine" (103) to the past glory of their forefathers. Additionally, in the most dramatic example in the novel, year after year, the annual school Christmas play features, instead of Joseph and Mary, the founding fathers and their wives and children being turned away from the Inn on the eve of Christ's birth (209–211). Ruby is in trouble, and the trouble is righteousness.

The older male leaders of the town argue with their sons and daughters over the words, one now faded, carved into the iron plate of the Oven: not "Be the Furrow," as in black power and civil rights activism, which the young people prefer, but "Beware the Furrow of His Brow." Once a useful communal center, the Oven has become the site of contestation and strife. One of the town wives, Dovey, sees the wrongness in this, but by the time she and others—Lone and Soane—realize the danger to the women at the Convent, it is too late. Righteousness has taken over Ruby, to the point where some of its patriarchs have gone too far in its direction to turn, or be turned, around. These are some of the "disgraceful passions" that "men embrace," and it only takes the seductiveness of free, unmarried women for their passions to find a convenient scapegoat. Deacon Morgan's glacial pride in his own righteousness leads to his "personal shame" for initiating his love affair with Connie, after which he realized "how important it was to erase both the shame and the kind of woman he believed was its source" (279).

Baptist minister Richard Misner, new to Ruby and its ways and thus able to identify them through a somewhat distanced perspective, thinks to himself how "exquisitely human was the wish for permanent happiness, and how thin human imagination became trying to achieve it" (306). In the spring before the late-summer shootings during the town's most famous wedding, Misner had held up the plain wooden cross, hoping that the Rubyites would "see" its true meaning. He thinks of the significance of the cross even prior to Christianity, as the true "home" of human spirit: love, not righteousness. Martha Nussbaum would put it this way: anyone "who repudiates bondage to human need is ill-placed to assess properly the needs of other humans" (527). The people of Ruby, especially the twins Deacon and Steward Morgan, had tried with enormous diligence ("deacon" and "steward" describe caretakers), but failed to provide a place where individuals could thrive, because they looked with contempt at the emotional neediness of others.

"Dear Lord, I didn't want to eat him; I just wanted to go home," says Consolata in *Paradise* (240), referring to a wrapped-in-love place she felt she reached when she was kissing and biting Deacon Morgan's lips. The affair with Deke, after decades of celibacy, awakened her to her neediness (depravity, in the Christian sense) and sense of connection, even though their relationship was one of the "disgraceful passions" in the novel. Her wanting to "go home" is about finding that place where all need is fulfilled, but her very eagerness—she licked Deke's blood from her lip—broke off the affair. However, while Deke hardened himself in shame, Connie repented, her act of surrender signified by her having to lose sight in one of her eyes. It is at this point in *Paradise*, when she has fallen spiritually, that Consolata first receives, and then becomes, the Call.

Nowhere is Morrison's radical vision of religion more vivid than in the transformation of Consolata. Connie is Called, in the manner of Gnostic narrative, by a mysterious traveling man, after whose visit she radically changes her life and sets the Convent women on a course of spiritual cleansing. Possessing an ability to "step in," as Lone terms the powers of a healer, Consolata herself becomes "the Caller of the Call" to the other women. When Connie is in the worst state of her despair, when she has run out of intoxications—"without wine, her thoughts, she knew, would be unbearable." (250)—a smiling stranger from "far country" knocks on her door. Wearing reflecting sunglasses, and enchanting Connie with "language like honey oozing from a comb," the man is suddenly within "six inches from her face" but, mysteriously, "without having moved—smiling as if he was having (or expecting) such a good time" (252). Interestingly, some of the imagery in this scene makes allusions to a stock element of Gnostic allegory. Unlike the first appearance in *Paradise* of a "traveling man" (the mystical guide who showed Papa Morgan where to found the first all-black town back in 1895), Connie's traveler resembles the serpent, although in a Gnostic rather than biblical sense.

In the *Gospel of Truth*, Jesus is nailed to the tree of knowledge and then becomes the fruit on it, thereby giving Adam and Eve, who eat the fruit, an internal reminder of their divine connection with God (Layton 254). The serpent from the Genesis story is the beginning of *gnosis* on earth in many such Gnostic allegories, as it was a popular symbol of rebellion (Jonas 93). The detail that most strongly suggests Connie's visitor's link with the Gnostic serpent is what Connie sees after he takes off his hat and his "tea-colored hair" cascades down his back: he "winked, a slow seductive movement of a lid. His eyes, she saw, were as round and green as new apples" (*Paradise* 252). Typical of Morrison's narrative manner, what happens after that is left up to the reader's imagination. There is one more reference to this "far country" man who had also asked her, "Don't you know me?" a few pages—and months—later, as Consolata is dancing in the rain with the other Convent women: "Consolata, fully housed *by the god who sought her out in the garden*, was the more furious dancer" (283, emphasis added).

*Paradise*'s radical theocracy, its syncretic "god-mixing" in Jonas's words, can be located in this rather mystical transference of moral authority to Consolata, the former eleven-year-old prostitute/nun's pupil/seductress and finally near-blind healer, to whom true light returns at the moment before she is shot: "You're back" (289), she says to a spot high above the armed Morgan brothers' heads as Steward opens fire. Due not only to the traveling man's appearance, but to her own surrendering of pride, she finds the strength to turn herself, and the other Convent women, around. Consolata opens herself to transforming experiences until she comes into possession of quite a vivid paradise story. To Mavis, Gigi/Grace, Seneca and Pallas/Divine, who have become by this time her disciples, she describes a scene which is one of the novel's most radical revisions of Judeo-Christian paradise:

> She told them of a place where white sidewalks met the sea and fish the color of plums swam alongside children. She spoke of fruit that tasted the way sapphires look and boys using rubies for dice. Of scented cathedrals made of gold where gods and goddesses sat in the pews with the congregation. Of carnations tall as trees. Dwarfs with diamonds for teeth. Snakes aroused by poetry and bells. Then she told them of a woman named Piedade, who sang but never said a word. (263–264)

The synaesthesia Morrison employs here is pleasantly disorienting, mixing elemental treasures (sapphires, gold) with more organic ones (fruit, plums, snake) and revising our senses (sight, taste, smell, hearing) as well as our sensibilities. Male and female deities are to be found *among* their followers in the church pews in Connie's paradise narrative, a stark visual contrast to the image from Ruby's famous wedding of the two pastors standing above and in front of the congregation, in competition with one another, arguing over interpretations of the one God and His Son. With this emergence of Connie's paradise story, Morrison composes an allegory which challenges the authority of Judeo-Christianity in its late Western patriarchal form. Connie's reference to Piedade, "who sang but never said a word" (264), points us toward the last page of the novel, where the female principle, as in Gnostic cosmology, is the primary link between the true God and humanity.

Morrison's placement of the two women in this scene marks her emphasis on a feminine-centered, spiritual leadership. In this way, she accomplishes what Hans Jonas claims Gnostic allegory had achieved by the third century: "It is itself the source of a new mythology" (94). More dramatically than in her previous six novels, Morrison frames *Paradise* with biblical and apocryphal discourses, all of which culminate in the paradoxical and iconoclastic imagery of the novel's last page: a mysterious ship returning to shore, its passengers "disconsolate," while two women, one "black as firewood" cradling the other on the beach, are resting in "memories neither one has ever had [...] the unambivalent bliss of going home to be at home—the ease of coming back to love" before they must return to work, "again, down here in Paradise" (318). The two women cradled on the beach are Morrison's syncretic image of Mary and Eve, spirit and body, which "should never be separated," and it is an appropriate end to three novels which span a historical time frame from the Middle Passage to the late twentieth century; it concludes within "a vast store-house of time" in an African sense (Mbiti 23). The woman being cradled is an afterlife image of the central figure in *Paradise*, Consolata, but the "black as firewood" woman suggests a composite of characters—the nineteen-year-old girl who emerged from the water in *Beloved*, the naked "wild woman" of the woods in *Jazz*, and the Mother Superior/"Piedade" who saved and was saved by Consolata in *Paradise*. Thus the imagery on the last page *of Paradise* serves to loop together the opening image of the trilogy—the broken house, its two disconsolate occupants putting up with its spiteful ghost in *Beloved*—with the closing iconography of a sanctuary of "repose" in song, if not in actual memory.

Finally, *Paradise* brings into confluence several streams in Morrison's two previous novels, producing a "long, high gaze,"[14] in Carolyn Denard's words, at how African American religion, in its diverse syncretic forms, is grounded in *knowing*, in an African American and Gnostic sense, where to find "home."[15] Returning to final lines of *The Thunder, Perfect Mind*—"And they will find me there / and they will live / and they will not die again"—the tone of peaceful reassurance appropriately describes the tone of the novel's final page. A solace comes when reincarnation will not have to be experienced again ("not die again"). The women on the beach have achieved this solace, if only temporarily; the people on the ships are still working towards it. And there is the promise of salvation for those who will "awaken" or "hear" or "see" and thus escape the "forlornness, dread, and homesickness" of life on earth (Jonas 65).

The final page of the trilogy offers only a temporary state of repose, in which the "dispersal" of the world—a "broken sandal," a "dead radio"—is for a moment "gathered," the latter being the Gnostic metaphor for "restoration of the original unity" (Jonas 59). In Victor Anderson's *Beyond Ontological Blackness*, he states that "the new being of black theology remains an alienated being whose mode of existence is determined by crisis, struggle, resistance, and survival—not thriving, flourishing, or fulfillment. Its self-identity is always bound by white racism and the culture of survival. The motive of transcendence from this unresolved matrix of struggle and survival recedes into the background as oppression is required for the self-disclosure of the oppressed" (87). I believe Morrison's trilogy is, in a vastly different way, also attempting to identify those closures which are hurtful, not helpful, in fulfilling quality-of-life goals in African American communities. Morrison's works make hermeneutic "returns" to African, Christian, African American and Gnostic traditions, but she does not reify them. She attempts always to make space for that "something rogue," in the words of *Jazz*'s narrator, which you "have to figure in before you can figure it out" (228).

## Notes

[1] That Morrison conceived of these novels together is suggested in several interviews; she remarked to Gloria Naylor: "What made these stories [*Beloved* and *Jazz*] connect, I can't explain, but I do know that, in both instances something seemed clear to me. A woman loved something other than herself so much" (Naylor 208).

[2] In an interview with Bessie Jones and Audrey Vinson, Morrison states: "I have a family of people who were highly religious. That was part of their language. Their sources were biblical; they expressed themselves in that fashion. But they combined it with another kind of relationship, to something I think which was outside the Bible.... I mean they were quite willing to remember visions, and signs, and premonitions and all of that. But there was something larger and coherent, and benevolence was always a part of what I was taught and certainly a part of what I believe" (Jones and Vinson 179).

[3] An example of what I mean by "shaped silences" in Beloved is the apprehension that neither the characters nor readers know what happens to Halle. He is lost to us in silence, which is precisely Morrison's intention: "I wanted the reader to feel the loss," she remarked in an interview (Darling 6).

[4] For an example of descriptions of slave religion, see Hopkins and Cummings 68–71; the mixture of Eastern religions in Gnosticism was formed against Hellenism, according to Jonas 37.

[5] Jonas describes the early church fathers as "attorneys for the prosecution" of Gnosticism; there were many "heresiologists" of Gnostic sects up until the fourth century, when the last extant indictment of Gnosticism was written by Epiphanius of Salamis. Refutations of Gnosticism are "as old as Gnosticism itself," but from the fourth century on, "the danger was past and the polemical interest no longer alive" (xiv–xv).

[6] Both Gnosticism and Christianity partake of the dualistic philosophies emanating from Iran and Persia, and Gnosticism is especially radical in this regard. It is not so much a mind/body split, however, as a human/divine one. In Gnostic cosmology, even the Hebrew God is a false god, as the entire cosmos is a delusion, a trap. Morrison's work with Gnosticism does not seem to partake of this radical dualism, although there is a sense in *Beloved*, *Jazz* and *Paradise* of characters who do not see, or if they do, do not maintain their vision of the invisible or unknowable for very long.

[7] In her essay "The Site of Memory," Morrison writes that her work is a literary archaeology, working with "what remains were left behind" (112). "All water," she analogizes, "has a perfect memory and is forever trying to get back to where it was. Writers are like that: remembering where we were, what valley we ran through, what the banks were like, the light that was there and the route back to our original place. It is emotional memory—what the nerves and the skin remember as well as how it appeared. And a rush of imagination is our 'flooding'" (119).

[8] See Stephen N. Ezeanya, "God, Spirits and the Spirit World." Also see Parker English and Kibujjo M. Kakswba's African Philosophy: A Classical Approach, in particular Kwasi Wiredu, "African Philosophical Tradition: A Case Study of the Akan" and Kwame Gyekye, "On Mbiti's View of Time for Traditional Africans" for discussions of John Mbiti's foundational but somewhat apologetic view. See Mbiti's African Religions and Philosophy 22–28 on the concepts of Sasa and Zarnani "time" and the importance of honoring and remembering ancestors.

[9] The Valentinian school of Gnosticism came closest to putting together, through various tractates, a coherent Gnostic theology. See the introduction to the Gospel of Truth in Nag Hammadi 38–89.

[10] The line comes from one of Langston Hughes's poems in his 1927 collection *The Weary Blues*. See Langston Hughes, *Collected Poems*.

[11] Lacan's concept of the "full word" is pertinent for Jazz. Speech, Lacan asserts, can reveal in its ambiguities the unintended meanings of the unconscious. A striking dramatization of this in Jazz is Violet's self-consciousness about her own speech; she is afraid of what comes out of her own mouth. See Lalita Pandit, "Dvani and the 'Full Word': Suggestion and Signification from Abhinavagupta to Jacques Lacan."

[12] See Richard Hardack, "A Music Seeking its Own Words. Double-Timing and Double Consciousness in Toni Morrison's Jazz" and Eusebio Rodrigues, "Experiencing Jazz." In another part of my work on the trilogy, I take up the question of jazz music in relation to Morrison's novel. In this essay, however, I focus more on jazz music's diametric reversal in the novel: the figure of Wild.

[13] Significantly, Morrison provides no source citation for Paradise's epigraph. This makes an interesting challenge to the readers of Paradise to make an investigation that ultimately links the two novels together. Omitting the source citation is itself an exhortation of sorts; a call to the reader to work with The Thunder and understand its significance to her work.

[14] The phrase is Carolyn Denard's in her essay, "The Long, High Gaze: The Mythical Consciousness of Toni Morrison and William Faulkner." Following Ernst Cassirer, Denard suggests that mythical consciousness "creates an awareness in these writers of the role that imaginative narratives may serve in providing a cognitive, unbroken connection of the present with the past and with the future" (19). Applying Denard's formulation to the subject of African

American religion in Morrison's trilogy, I am suggesting that Morrison has raised the subject to a high value, giving it what Bronislaw Malinowski sees as the mythical's "prestige by tracing it back to a higher better more supernatural reality of initial events" (quoted in Denard 20).

15 bell hooks noted at the opening forum of the Second Biennial Conference of the Toni Morrison Society, "Toni Morrison and the Meanings of Home," that within "the diasporic experience of African Americans, home is sanctuary, not just shelter." Marita Golden's forum remarks add to that: "Home is both the shelter—and the tornado." Other members of the forum were Michael Dyson and John Edgar Wideman.

## Works Cited

Anderson, Victor. *Beyond Ontological Blackness: An Essay on African American Religious and Cultural Criticism.* New York: Continuum, 1995.

Atkinson, Yvonne. "Language That Bears Witness: The Black English Oral Tradition in the Works of Toni Morrison." In *The Aesthetics of Toni Morrison: Speaking the Unspeakable*, edited by Marc C. Conner. Jackson: University Press of Mississippi, 2000. 12–30.

Chapman, Mark. *Christianity on Trial: African American Religious Thought Before and After Black Power.* Maryknoll, NY: Orbis Books, 1996.

Cone, Cecil. *The Identity Crisis in Black Theology.* Nashville: African Methodist Episcopal Church, 1975.

Darling, Marsha Jean. "In the Realm of Responsibility: A Conversation with Toni Morrison." In Taylor-Guthrie, *Conversations*, 246-254.

Denard, Carolyn. "The Long, High Gaze: The Mythical Consciousness of Toni Morrison and William Faulkner." In *Unflinching Gaze: Morrison and Faulkner Re-envisioned*, edited by Carol A. Kolmerten, Stephen M. Ross, and Judith Bryant Wittenberg. Jackson: University Press of Mississippi, 1997. 17–30.

Dickson, Kwesi, and Paul Ellingworth, eds. *Biblical Revelation and African Beliefs.* Maryknoll, NY: Orbis Books, 1969.

Douglas, Kelly Brown. *The Black Christ.* Maryknoll, NY: Orbis Books, 1994.

English, Parker, and Kibujjo M. Kalumba M., eds. *African Philosophy: A Classical Approach.* Upper Saddle River, N.J.: Prentice Hall, 1996.

Ezeanya, Stephen N. "God, Spirits and the Spirit World." In Dickson and Ellingworth, *Biblical Revelation*, 43–45.

Felder, Cain Hope. *Troubling Biblical Waters: Race, Class and Family.* Bishop Henry McNeal Turner Studies in North American Black Religion, Vol. II. Maryknoll, NY: Orbis Books, 1989.

Frey, Silvia. *Water from the Rock: Black Resistance in a Revolutionary Age.* Princeton: Princeton University Press, 1991.

Grant, Jacquelyn. *White Women's Christ and Black Women's Jesus: Feminist Christology and Womanist Response.* Atlanta: Scholar's Press, 1989.

Gyekye, Kwame. "On Mbiti's View of Time for Traditional Africans." In English and Kalumba, *African Philosophies*, 93–94.

Hale, Janice E. "The Transmission of Faith to Young African American Children." In *The Recovery of Black Presence: An Interdisciplinary Exploration. Essays in Honor of Dr. Charles B. Gopher*, edited by Randall C. Bailey and Jacquelyn Grant. Nashville: Abingdton Press, 1995. 193–207.

Hardack, Richard. "A Music Seeking its Own Words. Double-Timing and Double Consciousness in Toni Morrison's *Jazz*." *Callaloo* 18.2 (1995): 451–483.

Holloway, Karla C. *Moorings and Metaphors: Figures of Culture and Gender in Black Women's Literature.* New Brunswick, NJ: Rutgers University Press, 1992.

hooks, bell. Address. Toni Morrison and the Meanings of Home Conference. Lorain Community College, Lorain, Ohio. 28 September 2000.

———. *Yearnings: Race, Gender, and Cultural Politics.* Boston: South End Press, 1991.

Hopkins, Dwight N. and George Cummings. *Cut Loose Your Stammering Tongue: Black Theology in the Slave Narratives.* Maryknoll, NY: Orbis Books, 1992.

Hunt, Patricia. "The Texture of Transformation: Theology, History and Politics in the Novels of Toni Morrison." PhD diss., City University of New York, 1994. Ann Arbor: University of Michigan Dissertation Services, order no. 9417474.

Jessee, Sharon. "'Tell Me Your Earrings': Time and the Marvelous in Toni Morrison's *Beloved*." In *Memory, Narrative and Identity: New Essays in Ethnic American Literature*, edited by Amrirjit Singh, Joseph T. Skerrett Jr. and Robert E. Hogan. Boston: Northeastern University Press, 1994. 198–211.

Jonas, Hans. *The Gnostic Religion: The Message of the Alien God and the Beginnings of Christianity*. 1958. 2nd ed. Boston: Beacon Press, 1963.

Jones, Bessie W. and Audrey Vinson. "An Interview with Toni Morrison." In Taylor-Guthrie, *Conversations*, 171–187.

Lincoln, Eric C., and Lawrence H. Mamiya. *The Black Church in the African-American Experience.* Durham: Duke University Press, 1990

Layton, Bentley. *The Gnostic Scriptures: A New Translation*. Annotated and introduced by Bentley Layton. New York: Doubleday, 1987.

LeClair, Thomas. "The Language Must Not Sweat: A Conversation with Toni Morrison," in Taylor-Guthrie, 119–128.

Levine, Lawrence. *Black Culture and Black Consciousness: Afro-American Folk Thought from Slavery to Freedom.* New York: Oxford University Press, 1977

Mbiti, John S. *African Religions and Philosophy.* London: Heinemann, 1969.

Morrison, Toni. *Beloved.* New York: Alfred A. Knopf, 1987.

———. *Jazz.* New York: Alfred A. Knopf, 1992.

———. *Paradise.* New York: Alfred A. Knopf, 1998.

———. "The Site of Memory." In *Inventing the Truth: The Art and Craft of Memoir*. Edited by William Zinsser. Boston: Houghton Mifflin, 1987. 103–124.

*Nag Hammadi Library in English*. Translated by the Coptic Gnostic Library Project, James Robinson, dir. New York: Harper & Row, 1977. Copyright E.J. Brill, Netherlands.

Naylor, Gloria. "A Conversation: Gloria Naylor and Toni Morrison." In Taylor-Guthrie, *Conversations*, 188–217.

Nussbaum, Martha. *Upheavals of Thought: The Intelligence of the Emotions.* Cambridge, UK: Cambridge University Press, 2001.

Pandit, Lalita. "*Dvani* and the 'Full Word': Suggestion and Signification from Abhinavagupta to Jacques Lacan." *College English* 22.1 (1990): 142–163.

Rodrigues, Eusebio. "Experiencing *Jazz.*" *Modern Fiction Studies* 39.3–4 (1993): 734–763.

Ruas, Charles. "Toni Morrison," in Taylor-Guthrie, 93–118.

Sidhom, Swailem. "The Theological Estimate of Man." In Dickson and Ellingworth, *Biblical Revelation and African Beliefs*, 83–115.

Taylor-Guthrie, Danille, ed. *Conversations with Toni Morrison.* Jackson: University Press of Mississippi, 1994.

Truth, Sojourner. "Ain't I a Woman?" In *Feminism: The Essential Historical Writings*, edited by Miriam Schneir. New York: Vintage Books, 1972. 220–221.

West, Cornell. *Prophetic Fragments.* Trenton, NJ: Africa World Press, 1988.

Williams, Delores S. *Sisters in the Wilderness: The Challenge of a Womanist God-Talk.* Maryknoll, NY: Orbis Books, 1993.

Wiredu, Kwasi. "African Philosophical Tradition: A Case Study of the Akan." In English and Kalumba, *African Philosophies*, 101–112.

# 7

# MYTHOPOETIC SYNCRETISM IN *PARADISE* AND THE DECONSTRUCTION OF HOSPITALITY IN *LOVE*

*Benjamin Burr*

Toni Morrison's writing is one of the most important sites for examining the complex relationship that exists between fiction, literary theory, and literary influences. Of all the literary theories that have been used to create reading paradigms for Morrison's writing, deconstruction is a productive theory for examining the role of the Bible in Morrison's writing. Like other canonical American authors, the Bible is one of the primary influences on Morrison's work. However, Morrison's writing is too complex to simply suggest that the biblical influence on Morrison's work can be easily accounted for by a literary theory. The first section of this study will examine how in *Paradise* Morrison places the mythological elements of the Bible in deconstructive juxtaposition with mythological elements from other discourses. The second part of this study takes Derrida's discussion of hospitality into account to demonstrate how *Love* is a deconstructive re-writing of 1 Corinthians 13. Where both of these readings of Morrison are informed by deconstruction and the influence of the Bible, it is clear that Morrison's writing is too complex to be read the same way twice. The same reading paradigm that works for *Paradise* doesn't work for reading *Love*. As a result each of Morrison's texts doesn't just suggest new ways for reading the influence of the Bible of literature, her texts suggest new ways for applying theory to literature. It is also clear that in each of her novels Morrison is constantly deconstructing and re-writing her own theoretical agenda. Consequently, some of greatest keys for reading one of Morrison's texts are her other texts. Ultimately, the purpose of this study is to reveal that instead of using the Bible or deconstruction to understand Morrison's texts, Morrison's texts can be used to better understand the Bible and deconstruction.

The Bible is clearly an influence for *Paradise*, but as the novel examines the dynamics of redemption it becomes apparent that Morrison is wary to privilege the Bible as a mythological foundation for redemption. The following passage from the novel examines the exclusive properties of the cross to demonstrate Morrison's aversion to privileging the Bible as a foundational text. "It was this mark, this, that lay underneath every other. This mark, rendered in the placement of facial features. This mark of a standing human figure poised to embrace. Remove it, as Pulliam had done, and Christianity was like any and every religion in the world" (*Paradise* 145–146). In this passage from *Paradise*, Toni Morrison rhetorically uses Reverend Misner to establish the Christian cross as an essential element in the dominant discourse of salvation. However, for the purposes of the text, the cross only represents one epistemological paradigm. Because of its exclusivity, the cross fails as an integral element in the discourse of salvation. Steward Morgan acknowledges the fallibility of the cross when he says, "A cross was no better than the bearer" (154). By removing the cross as a mythological signifier of salvation, *Paradise* reveals a deconstruction of Christianity and the Bible as dominant mythological discourses. This deconstruction of the Bible is accomplished as other mythological discourses are insinuated into Christianity's terms of reference through a process of mythopoetic syncretism. An examination of the complex mythopoetic architecture of Mavis, Deek, and Steward demonstrates how Morrison uses twins to create a complex mythological foundation for a dynamic paradigm of origin and redemption.

As the potent, twin founding fathers of an exclusive, patriarchal paradigm, Deek and Steward rely on Judeo-Christian, African American, American, and Roman influences for the mythopoetic origins of their salvific discourse. However, *Paradise* positions the possibility of redemption outside of the dominant salvific discourse created by Deek and Steward by giving an equally complex mythopoetic architecture to Mavis and positioning the possibility of redemption within her separate paradigm. Where Deek and Steward represent a site of potent mythological twins, Mavis represents the absence of this site. Within the space of this absence, *Paradise* draws on Judeo-Christian, African American, American, and Yoruban influences to create a salvation discourse separate from the exclusive, patriarchal paradigm created through Deek and Steward.

Although Christianity is disallowed to act as a dominant discourse, Morrison still rhetorically draws on Judeo-Christian references to twins as a viable source of mythological origins for Deek and Steward's discourse of salvation. Jacob and Esau are the most important set of twins in Judeo-Christianity that function as a site of origin. When Esau sells his birthright to

Jacob, he forfeits the privileges of lineage and inheritance. This forfeiture is a site of origin for the establishment of Israel as a chosen people (Gen. 25.34; King James version). The story of Jacob and Esau correlates with Deacon's narration of his own ancestral origins: "Tea, quite reasonably, accommodated the whites, [...] Coffee took a bullet in his foot instead. From that moment they weren't brothers anymore. Coffee began to plan a new life elsewhere [...] Not because he was ashamed of his twin, but because the shame was in himself" (*Paradise* 302–303). In the case of Coffee and Tea, the inherited birthright is the violent history of slavery. By dancing for the whites, Tea despises his birthright. Coffee assumes the shameful birthright, and uses it as a motivating force in founding the exclusive community of Haven. Like the Children of Israel, the citizens of Haven see themselves as a chosen people. As Jacob changes his name to Israel to become the father of many nations, Coffee changes his name to Zechariah to become the Big Papa of his own people. The correlation between Tea, Coffee, Jacob, and Esau incorporates a Judeo-Christian dimension into the mythopoetic origins of Deek and Steward, which validates their exclusive, patriarchal projects.

Although *Paradise* uses Judeo-Christian references to twins to create an exclusive, patriarchal salvation discourse, Morrison rhetorically positions redemption in the space created by Mavis's absence of twins. The central metaphor that connects Mavis's absence of twins with redemption is the rose of Sharon plant in Peg's yard (30). The following lines from a Christian hymn depict the redeeming connotations of this plant as the rose is seen as a symbol of Christ:

> Are you lost in your sins ~ tired of living?
> Is your heart filled with bitterness, too?
> Come to Jesus, the Sweet Rose of Sharon,
> He has the power to make you anew.
> Rose of Sharon now bloomin I see,
> Blessed Jesus, who died on the tree;
> With my whole heart I sing 'Hallelujah!'
> Rose of Sharon, so precious to me. (Smith)

The Rose of Sharon has its origins as a biblical signifier in the Song of Solomon. In the Song of Solomon 2:1–2, it is written, "I am the rose of Sharon, and the lily of the valleys." It isn't clear who is the speaker of this passage, and this ambiguity leaves the verse open for interpretation. Indeed the Song of Solomon has been one of the most widely interpreted sacred texts.

For ancient Israel the text was considered an allegory for the love between the Lord and his covenant people. Christians see the book as an allegory of Christ's love for his church (Ernst par. 11–12). While Morrison strips the cross of its redeeming connotations, the rose of Sharon is a loaded symbol that enhances Mavis's salvation discourse with possibilities of a Christian redemption. Coincidentally this Christian symbol of redemption is associated with loss of her twins. After accidentally killing her twins, Mavis flees her home and husband to Peg's house, where a rose of Sharon grows (*Paradise* 28). Mavis finds a safe space in the convent where she maintains spiritual contact with the twins, Merle and Pearl. At one point in the novel, she returns to Maryland to see her other children. On this trip she finds, "The rose of Sharon, so strong and wild and beautiful, had been chopped completely down [...] With swift and brilliant clarity, she understood that she was not safe out there or any place where Merle and Pearl were not" (258). In this passage the redeeming powers of the rose of Sharon are intricately tied to Mavis's twins. Mavis's act of killing her twins was the cause of her expulsion from the dominant salvation discourse. By associating the result of this act with the redeeming aspects of the rose of Sharon/Jesus, Morrison combines Christian grace with the mythopoetic architecture of Mavis's alternate salvation discourse. This discourse fails to function where "Merle and Pearl [are] not."

A connection to African American culture is the next dimension to play an important role in the mythological origins of Deek and Steward's salvation discourse. Where the Bible can be used to trace Judeo-Christian mythological elements, Zora Neale Hurston's *Their Eyes Were Watching God* is a valuable text for pinpointing African American mythological elements. Joe Starks plays an archetypal role in the mythopoetic architecture of the twins' origins. Deek and Steward are influenced by Joe Starks as the archetypal founder of the archetypal black community. He finds a group of willing participants and grows rich off of real estate (Hurston 38). The Morgans also founded the town of Ruby by financing it through the sale of real estate (*Paradise* 115). The Morgans' devotion to the oven as a founding/religious element of their community correlates with Joe's street lamp. Joe describes the lamp's significance to his town in the following passage: "Dis evenin' we'se all assembled heah tuh light uh lamp. Dis occasion is something for us all tuh remember tuh our dyin' day. De first street lamp in uh colored town" (Hurston 45). Although the oven is a founding element for Haven and Ruby, the idea of a central religious idol in a black township comes from Hurston. Another element that unites the twins to the archetypal founder of the black township is the establishment of patriarchy. When Janie is asked to make a speech, Joe says, "She's uh woman and her place is in de home" (43). This passage among others indicates that Joe's black township is founded upon an idealized domestic femininity. Deek and Steward believe in a similar idealized vision of femininity. This idealization is implied after Deek and Steward see the nineteen summertime ladies. "Deek's image of the nineteen summertime ladies was unlike the photographer's. His remembrance was pastel colored and eternal" (*Paradise* 110). Subjugating the feminine through idealization is certainly a part of Deek and Steward's patriarchal project. These multiple references to Hurston give an African American dimension to Deek and Steward's mythopoetic origins. The emphasis on economic empowerment, founding texts, and patriarchy all play an important role in creating the exclusive salvation discourse.

*Paradise* connects Deek and Steward to an African American mythos through their identification with Joe Starks. However, Joe Starks is an unredeemed character, and therefore an impotent model for redemption. Morrison makes several mythological references to Janie to insinuate her into Mavis's mythopoetic matrix. Where the rose of Sharon functions as a potent symbol of redemption within a Judeo-Christian paradigm, Morrison also connects Mavis' experience with the rose of Sharon to Janie's epiphanic moment under the pear tree. In Hurston's description, "[The pear tree] stirred tremendously [...] It was like a flute song forgotten in another existence and remembered again [...] The thousand sister-calyxes arch to meet the love embrace and the ecstatic shiver of the tree" (Hurston 10–11). Morrison profoundly connects this redemptive imagery to Mavis' first encounter with the rose of Sharon: "A rose of Sharon, taller than Peg's roof and older, was shaking. Stirred by the air conditioner's exhaust it danced, roughing blossoms and buds to the grass. Wild, it looked wild, and Mavis's pulse raced with it" (*Paradise* 28). This connection with nature becomes an archetypal source of redemption for women in African American literature. The redemptive powers of the ecotone are enhanced as Janie migrates to the muck. Morrison combines the redemptive powers of the convent with an ecotone in Mavis' salvific discourse. "When she first arrived she was so happy to find someone at home she had not looked closely at the garden" (40). Mavis's first encounter with the Convent places an important emphasis on the garden, which connects her to the archetypal source of redemption pioneered by Janie. Once again, where Mavis's loss of the twins led her to the Convent, this loss ultimately is Morrison's rhetorical strategy for connecting Mavis to her potent mythological ancestors in litera-

ture. As Joe Starks is incorporated into Steward and Deek's mythopoetic architecture, so is Janie incorporated into Mavis's.

American mythology is the next site of origin for enhancing Deek and
Steward's salvation narrative. Morrison positions Deek and Steward within
the mythological Puritan experience. Both of these mythological matrices act
as sites of origin in the American national story. "It says '... the Furrow of His
Brow'" (86). The ellipsis on the Oven's plaque is a space that is filled with
Puritan connotations by Deek and Steward who believe that it should read
"Beware the Furrow of His Brow." In between the arguments over the actual
meaning of the Oven's inscription is an invocation for the divine to give legitimacy to the Utopian project in Ruby. Along with this invocation for divine
legitimacy comes an excuse to exclude those who don't want to abide by the
conservative ideals of the town's founders. This biblical language of the
inscription could also be seen as a mythological invocation to equate the
Utopian project in Ruby with the Puritan commonwealth. There is also a
direct connection to Puritanism when the founders of Ruby consider calling it
New Haven (17). This latent mythological connection to Puritanism is a powerful way for Morrison to connect Deek and Steward with one of America's
important founding myths, which complies nicely as an origin myth for their
exclusive, patriarchal society.

It is understandable that Morrison continues to construct Deek and
Steward's redemptive narrative with mythopoetic sites of origin that originate
from exclusive, patriarchal sources. However, for every site of origin that
Morrison constructs into Deek and Steward's salvation discourse, an impotent
lack of redemption is constructed into the discourse. Once again, Morrison
associates Mavis's salvation discourse with a potent site of redemption within
American mythology. Mavis becomes associated with the Beatniks and the
great American journey. After she steals her husband's car, Mavis begins a
road trip that echoes Jack Kerouac's *On the Road:* "With a crisp new Mobil map
beside her on the seat, she sped out of Newark heading for route 70. As more
and more of the East was behind her, the happier she became. [...] Now in
flight to California, the memory of the Rocket ride and its rush were with her
at will" (33). This archetypal beginning of a cross-continental journey corresponds with Sal Paradise's similar process of planning a road trip. "I'd been
poring over maps of the United States in Paterson for months, [...] and on the
roadmap was on long red line called Route 6 that led from the tip of Cape
Cod clear to Ely, Nevada, and there dipped down to Los Angeles" (Kerouac
10). This connection to the defining beatnik novel associates Mavis with the

redemptive spiritual quests of the beatnik movement. Mavis's road trip connects her with this redemptive American mythos, and it is important to note that Mavis' decision to steal the car is caused by the loss of her twins. Like the rose of Sharon, the road trip functions rhetorically as a source of redemption. This redemptive American mythos becomes another enhancing element of the mythopoetic architecture of Mavis's salvific discourse.

One of the most potent mythological origins for Deek and Steward's salvation discourse is the presence of Roman mythological elements. Deek and Steward's identification with Romulus and Remus creates a ligature between the founding of Ruby and the Founding story of Western civilization. During Deek's confession at the end of the novel, "He spoke of a wall in Ravenna, Italy, white in the late afternoon sun" (*Paradise* 300). This mention of a wall by the twin recalls the conflict that led to the origin of Rome: "During a quarrel where Remus mocked the height of the walls, Romulus slew Remus and became the sole ruler of the new Rome" ("Romulus"). Deek mentions the wall after the power struggle between brothers: "He lifts his hand to halt his brother's and discovers who, between them is the stronger man" (*Paradise* 289). When Deek cannot prevent Steward from killing Consolata, the twin sense of equality is lost. Steward becomes the ruler of Ruby (300). The tension between Morrison's twins also is prefigured in Romulus' abduction of the Sabine women, the violent act underlying Western patriarchy. Although Deek and Morgan don't steal women, they enforce a rigid ideal for female behavior based on experience with outside women. Their idealization of the nineteen women generates the lack of tolerance with the Convent women and leads to violence: "The women in the Convent were for [Steward] a flaunting parody of the nineteen Negro ladies of his and his brother's youthful memory and perfect understanding" (279). By associating Deek and Steward with the founding myth of Western Civilization, Morrison solidifies their salvation discourse as an exclusive, patriarchal, and violent project.

With Mavis, Morrison makes a distinct separation from Roman mythology, which establishes the violent salvation discourse that has excluded her. Instead, Morrison connects Mavis with the Yoruban Orisa, Osun, as a source of redemptive power. Osun is the pure essence of joy. In Yoruban mythology, joy is connected with having children: "Osun energy is the mother of twins. Osun is easily offended, but rather than contradicting her matrix of Joy, this reaction substantiates it. Joy, in its purest form, wants no negative/sad/sarcastic/angry energy to interfere with the flow of essence" ("Osun"). Morrison rhetorically separates Mavis/Osun from her twins to structure a redemptive discourse about connecting Mavis with the Osun essence of Joy. Indeed, the rose of Sharon is one of the ways she negotiates this connection with Joy. Mavis also finds this joy in odd places, such as the fight with Gigi and cooking. While fighting Gigi, "Mavis was a slow but a steady, joyful hitter" (*Paradise* 168). Mavis also admits of the fight, "she had enjoyed it. Pounding, pounding, even biting Gigi was exhilarating, just as cooking was. It was more proof that the old Mavis was dead" (171). The Convent becomes the healing space where she can connect with this Orisa energy. Ultimately her joy is consummated as she is connected with her twins again: "She still heard Merle and Pearl, felt their flutter in every room of the Convent" (171). In this passage, the twins are described like butterflies implying a redemptive metamorphosis that allows Mavis to participate in the joy of her children once again. By connecting Mavis to the Yoruban Orisa, Osun, Morrison solidifies Mavis's discourse as a site of possible redemption. By complicating the connection to Western mythological origins with Yoruban mythology, she creates a separate redemptive paradigm with Mavis.

Ultimately, the rhetorical outcome of the polarization of Deek and Steward's and Mavis's salvation discourses creates a liminal space. Deek and Steward's mythopoetic architecture, which establishes the origins for their exclusive patriarchal community, and Mavis's mythopoetic architecture, which establishes the possibility for redemption outside of twins' patriarchal mythos, bound this liminal space. Through the use of a deconstructive mythopoetic syncretism Morrison succeeds in preventing the formation of a dominant salvation discourse. The garden is the mythological origin site where the dominant dichotomy between the fall and salvation originated. The cross is where the project initiated in the garden becomes exclusive. Through her use of mythopoetic syncretism, Morrison creates a "window in the garden, [beckoning] toward another place—neither life nor death" (307). The garden and the cross are deconstructed out of the discourse, and a number of healthy mythological paradigms are reconstructed into it. Paradise exists in this liminal space, where myth can accommodate the relentless consequences of change.

Morrison's narrative strategy in *Paradise* involves locating mythological paradigms in a healthy state of opposition, where the alterity of the opposition creates the window through which salvation is a possibility. Through the use of opposing paradigms, Morrison does not privilege any single paradigm. Instead, she engages them in an ethical relationship where one mythological paradigm responds to the omissions and failures of another. The resulting state of play between the different paradigms provides a window or space for redemption. This deconstructive strategy of positioning paradigms in opposition to one another is a narrative strategy that Morrison revises and abandons in her subsequent novel, *Love*. The result is that the same paradigmatic alterity that exists on a mythological level within *Paradise* exists on a theoretical level between *Paradise* and *Love*. In other words, Morrison writes *Love* to respond to the omissions and failures of *Paradise*.

Morrison is a writer who recognizes the cracks in her previous works, and writes into these cracks. Positioning the mythological paradigms in opposition to one another creates a window for understanding *Paradise*. However, in *Love*, Morrison calls into question the relevance of mythological paradigms in general. In between *Paradise* and *Love*, Morrison revises the model of deconstruction that is implemented in *Paradise*.

In an interview with Zia Jaffrey in 1998, Toni Morrison discusses the trauma that comes from loving someone in the innocence of childhood, then discovering that because of race, gender, or class, that person is not worthy of association. Morrison says, "And now this person is gone. Then you don't trust your instincts. You mean, I loved something unlovable? I loved something that's not really among us" (Jaffrey 3). It is clear as early as 1998, what becomes the major conflict in *Love* was already preoccupying the author's mind. In the novel the narrator, L, says speaking of the type of conflict that Morrison discusses with Zia Jaffrey:

> Most people have never felt a passion that strong, that early. If so, they remember it with a smile, dismiss it as a crush that shriveled in time and on time. It's hard to think of it any other way when real life shows up with its list of other people, its swarm of other thoughts. If your name is the subject of First Corinthians, chapter 13, it's natural to make it your business. (*Love* 199)

In this passage, , gives a hint of the monumental ontological deconstruction that is Morrison's project in the novel. She locates a space where love can exist, which is the moment of "a child's first chosen love," which is a moment of undiscriminating hospitality (199). The novel then becomes the documentation of what causes this idealized love or hospitality to fail. Where Morrison involves the Bible in her deconstructive method in *Paradise*, she also involves the Bible in her revision of that method in *Love*. Two verses in First Corinthians, chapter 13, provide the basis for Morrison's deconstruction of hospitality that implies the failure of love. "When I was a child, I spake as a child, I understood as a child, I thought as a child: but when I became a man, I put away childish things. For now we see through a glass, darkly; but then face to face; now I know in part; but then shall I know even as I am known" (1 Cor. 13.11–12). The Apostle Paul writes this chapter as a handbook for acquiring the attribute of love. These two verses designate the role of hospitality in this process. Paul refers to one knowing as one is known as a more complete form of knowing. Knowing as one is known is an epistemological process that magnifies the role of the other. In order to "see through the glass" clearly, or, in other words, gain the attribute of love, a surrender to the other is necessary. This surrender to the other is a function of hospitality. The concept of hospitality as the discourse that gives precedent or welcome to real life's "list of other people, its swarm of other thoughts," becomes Morrison's site of deconstruction. An analysis of the discourse of hospitality in the novel demonstrates how Morrison's novel becomes a deconstructive, hermeneutic commentary on Paul's other-oriented model of love.

It is apparent from the first sentence of the novel that Morrison identifies hospitality as a central theme in the novel, preceded only by the theme of the title. *Love* begins with L saying, "The women's legs are spread wide open, so I hum" (3). It isn't coincidental that Morrison would place the theme of hospitality at the forefront of a novel about an owner of a hotel who is surrounded by women who fight for his attention during a time when the concept of hospitality is at the forefront of the discussion of deconstruction. In 2002, Derrida's seminars on hospitality were translated and published in English. Derrida describes how the concept of hospitality is defined by its deconstruction.

> Indeed, *on the one hand*, hospitality must wait, extend itself toward the other, extend to the other the gifts, the site, the shelter [...] it must prepare and adorn itself for the coming of the hÙte; it must even develop itself into a culture of hospitality, multiply the signs of anticipation, construct and institute what one calls the structures of welcoming, a welcoming apparatus [...].

> But, *on the other hand*, the opposite is nevertheless true, simultaneously and irrepressibly true: to be hospitable is to let oneself be overtaken, *to be ready not to be ready*, if such is possible to let oneself be overtaken, to not even *let* oneself be overtaken, to be surprised, in a fashion almost violent, violated and raped, stolen, precisely where one is not ready to receive. (Derrida 361)

The first part of this statement, Derrida's first definition of the word, describes that model of hospitality on which Paul's model of love is predicated. However, the second part of this statement is one of the cracks in Paul's model into which Morrison writes. Toni Morrison's awareness of this deconstruction of hospitality is apparent in *Love* as hospitality appears in the novel as a readiness to welcome the other and a readiness not to be ready for the encounter. An examination of how *Love* uses both of these aspects of hospitality shows where she is filling in the holes left by Paul and complicating the possibility of love. This examination also provides a framework for understanding how, on a larger level, she is testing the boundaries of deconstruction, or in essence revising previous models of deconstruction that she has used.

The site where the deconstruction of hospitality is most apparent is Heed's position as the hÙte, or welcomed one, in Cosey's culture of hospitality. Christine who is the offspring of the culture of hospitality, and therefore embodies it, is the one who invites Heed into the culture. Christine does this with the welcoming apparatus of food. Heed and Christine "ate ice cream with peaches in it until a smiling woman came and said, 'Go away now. This is private.' Later, making footprints in the mud, she heard the ice cream girl call 'Wait! Wait!" (*Love* 78). Christine's lack of discrimination is explained as Heed says that both Christine and May were "spoiled silly by the wealth of an openhanded man" (78). In other words, Christine is the product of a culture of hospitality, and therefore lacks the discriminating apparatuses that would have prevented her from asking Heed to wait. L describes the absence of discriminating apparatus when she describes the encounter between the two girls: "If such children find each other before they know their own sex, or which of them is starving, which well fed; before they know color from no color, kin from stranger, then they have found a mix of surrender and mutiny they can never live without" (199). By lack of discrimination, Heed is ultimately inducted into the Cosey culture of hospitality. She becomes the hÙte to whom the gifts and shelter of hospitality are extended. In Paul's model of charity, this condition of pure hospitality is what facilitates surrender to the other and allows for the ontological conditions that are necessary for love to exist.

However, as Heed becomes the hÙte of Cosey hospitality, she also occupies the position of being the one who is overtaken by or not ready to receive the hospitality offered her. Where Cosey hospitality borders on excess because of its lack of discrimination, ultimately, this lack of discrimination is what causes Cosey's hospitality to fail on all levels of the text. Cosey's hotel is historically located as a haven of hospitality in an era that is dominantly defined by discourses of discrimination and segregation. L even says, "If colored musicians were treated well, paid well, and coddled, they would tell each other about such a place where they could walk in the front door, not the service entrance; eat in the dining room, not the kitchen; sit with the guests, sleep in beds, not their automobiles, buses, or in a whorehouse across town" (102). As a reaction to the discourses of discrimination of its time, Cosey's hotel is predicated on absence of discrimination. Vida contemplates that lack of discrimination is what causes the failure of the hotel when she asks, "How could they let gangster types, dayworkers, cannery scum, and payday migrants in there, dragging police attention with them like a tail" (36)?

L blames the fall of the hotel on lack of discrimination as well, but her blame regards Cosey's marriage to Heed and the moment where the novel addresses Derrida's second definition of hospitality. L claims, "It was marrying Heed that laid the brickwork for ruination" (104). Where Heed is first welcomed into the Cosey culture of hospitality in a way that conforms with Derrida's first definition of hospitality. She is also overtaken violently, violated, raped, and stolen in way that conforms to Derrida's second definition of hospitality. This second kind of hospitality is enabled by a culture of hospitality that lacks discrimination. Throughout the novel, music functions as an apparatus of hospitality. Bill Cosey's molestation of Heed is provoked by music. "Music is coming from the hotel bar... something so sweet and urgent Heed shakes her hips to the beat as she moves down the hallway" (190). After Cosey touches her nipple, Heed is overtaken. As she is immersed in a culture of hospitality and welcoming, she believes that she welcomes the violation. Although the burning in her chest was a surprise she never knew she had, she believes " she had started it... not him" (191–192). Her youth and lack of discrimination locate her in a position where she is not ready to receive the pleasure of sexual stimulation; however, she becomes the vessel of hospitality that welcomes "an old man's solitary pleasure" into the space reserved for her relationship with Christine (192). With the language of hospitality, Morrison describes how he enters this space, "Like a guest with a long-held reservation arriving in your room at last, a guest you knew would stay" (192).

Bill Cosey admits to Sandler that the reason he married Heed at age eleven was to marry "a girl he could educate to his taste" (110). This admission reveals the deconstructive nature of hospitality, which functions as the lure that Cosey uses to entice Heed to marry him, and therefore becomes the tool for his theft. Hospitality is also the reason he marries her; he wants not just a sexual virgin, where virginity is a type of hospitality, but rather he wants a virgin of discourse. He wants a girl whose identity is a vacancy that will be hospitable to the education he wants her to have. Hospitality is therefore not just the tool for theft, but also the reason for it. In this sense, Morrison is drawing on Derrida's deconstructive definition for the word. In Derrida's first definition of hospitality, he recognizes a condition of surrender that facilitates Paul's ontological model that is necessary for love to exist. However, with his second definition of hospitality, Derrida creates a violent connotation for the word that *Love* defines as mutiny and hatred. Paul's model of surrender allows one's being to be created by welcoming others' definitions of one's being, and this is considered the state from which love is possible. *Love*'s model of mutiny allows one's being to be stolen, violated, and inscribed by others' definitions of being. However, because one's being stolen is an act of surprise and being overtaken it is still considered hospitality. Morrison writes into Paul's spaces by creating a world where hospitality enables the possibility of both love and hatred.

*Love*'s application of the deconstructive nature of hospitality reveals how *Love* is using Derrida's deconstruction of hospitality to revise Paul's model of love. For Paul's model of love is predicated on welcoming the other, which action leads to the possibility of violation by the other and subsequent hatred. However, on a larger philosophical level, the deconstruction of hospitality and the revision of Paul's model of love in First Corinthians 13 are only textual interpretations that create a metonymical framework for understanding Morrison's larger aesthetic project. Through her use of the discourse of hospitality, Morrison revises the model of deconstruction that she implements in *Paradise*.

In order to understand how Morrison is revising deconstruction, Derrida's recent thinking on hospitality needs to be applied to what Morrison is doing with hospitality in *Love*. Where Morrison's novel concerns fictional representations of hospitable relationships between people, Derrida is concerned with the hospitality that exists among metaphysical concepts. He says:

> Each concept opens itself to its opposite, reproducing or producing in advance, in the rapport of one concept to the other, the contradictory and deconstructive law of hospitality. Each concept becomes hospitable to its other, to an other than itself that is no longer *its* other. With this apparent nuance we have a formula of the entire contradiction, which is more than a dialectical contradiction, and which constitutes perhaps the very stakes of all consistent deconstructions (Derrida 362) [...] If every concept shelters or lets itself be haunted by another concept, by an other than itself that is no longer even its other, then no concept remains in place any longer. (Derrida 364)

Derrida's expounding of hospitality in 2002 would not have been available to Morrison as she wrote *Paradise* in 1997. Syncretism therefore becomes her deconstructive model for creating a redemptive space in that novel.

Syncretism is fueled by certain signifying systems sheltering or haunting other signifying systems. The ideal of mythopoetic syncretism occurs when mythopoetic systems exist in a state of play or flux where none of the systems is privileged over the other. This model of mythopoetic syncretism is dependent on the first definition of hospitality that Derrida gives. In other words syncretism functions as a process of welcoming and sheltering. However, syncretism ignores the deconstructive law of hospitality by assuming that a viable signifying system can be maintained in a hospitable state of syncretism with another system. Mythopoetic syncretism doesn't acknowledge that the possibility of theft, violation, and being overtaken are also functions of hospitality. As this theoretical myopia is corrected in *Love*, the construct of mythopoetic syncretism loses its productivity for an analysis of *Love*. However, it becomes a useful tool for recognizing the theoretical progression that exists within Morrison's canon of works.

In *Love*, Morrison revises a model of hospitable syncretism by replacing it with a deconstruction of hospitality. By deconstructing hospitality, Morrison is revising deconstruction itself. Derrida says of hospitality that "this is a name or example of deconstruction" (364). *Love* is a novel about the failure of hospitality. Derrida himself claims that hospitality and deconstruction are examples of each other. In *Paradise* Morrison creates through mythopoetic syncretism a space where hospitality seems to function and succeed. *Love* reveals how aware Morrison is of her own theoretical projects as she realizes the shortcomings of her previous theoretical model and uses them to fuel the theoretical underpinnings of her next novel.

Where Morrison uses syncretism to create a redemptive space in *Paradise*, there are two moments in *Love* that can be considered transcendent despite the deconstructive inclinations of the novel. They are considered transcendent in that they preclude deconstruction, or, in other words, they are spaces that indicate an absence of discourse or mythological paradigms. The first moment is hinted at in the interview with Zia Jaffrey. Morrison is apparently interested in the period of childhood where an absence of discourse determines the ontology of the subject. It is in this state that Heed and Christine meet and become friends. It is in this state that the two children are able to create their own system of signification. Theirs is "called 'idagay.' 'Hey Celestial' was their most private code" (*Love* 188). The space where one can create one's own system of signification is one space where deconstruction can be subverted. However, this autonomous space is contained by its dependence on hospitality. A system of signification will only function in rapport with the other. The dependence on hospitality dooms this autonomous space almost as soon as it begins.

The second transcendent space is mentioned in the novel after Heed and Christine have reconciled their hatred. James E. Faulconer, the specialist on deconstruction at Brigham Young University, provides the following statement to clarify the role of hospitality in Heed's and Christine's reconciliation:

> Actual hospitality requires decision, discrimination. That discrimination, always a limit on hospitality, on inclusion, is indispensable. The point is not the end of exclusion and forgetting, but our thought about them. The point is for us to face those omissions and exclusions and, through facing them, to rethink what we are about ("Deconstruction").

Heed's and Christine's reconciliation comes after they have negotiated the hospitality of their relationship with discrimination. It comes after they face the omissions and exclusions of their memory or past. This process allows them to rethink what they are, thus offering a new ontological model that Morrison describes in a paragraph that is offset from the rest of the text. She writes, "In unlit places without streetlamps or yelping neon, night is profound and often comes as ease [...] The main ingredient offered by the night is escape from watchers and watching. Like stars free to make their own history and not care about another one" (*Love* 194). The reference to stars that make their own history without a dependence on the other is the new ontological model that also subverts deconstruction. However, this new ontological model is only available after one has come to terms with the deconstructive law of hospitality, since one cannot exist, like a star, in a vacuum where hospitality to discourse isn't necessary. Whereas, in *Paradise* Morrison implies that discourses can be deconstructively positioned in a state of syncretic play to allow redemption. In *Love*, redemption is only possible when one comes to terms with hospitality's deconstruction of itself.

### Works Cited

Derrida, Jacques "Hostipitality." *Acts of Religion* Ed. Gil Anidjar. New York: Routledge, 2002. 356–420.

Ernst, Carl W. *Web Site of Carl C. Ernst.* "Interpreting the Song of Songs: The Paradox of Spiritual and Sensual Love." January 24, 2003 http://www.unc.edu/~cernst/articles/sos-intro.htm.

Faulconer, James E. "Deconstruction." June 15, 1998. http://jamesfaulconer.byu.edu/deconstr.htm.

Hurston, Zora Neale. *Their Eyes Were Watching God.* New York: Perennial, 1998.

Jaffrey, Zia. "Toni Morrison: The *Salon* Interview" 2 February 1998. http://archive.salon.com/books/int/1998/02/cov_si_02int3.html.

Kerouac, Jack. *On the Road.* New York: Penguin, 1991.

Morrison, Toni. *Love.* New York: Knopf, 2003.

———. *Paradise.* New York: Plume 1997. *Encyclopedia Mythica: Roman Mythology.* Lindemans, M. F. ed. "Romulus and Remus." http://www.pantheon.org/areas/mythology/europe/roman/ articles.html. 15 April 2003.

Smith, Alfred B. & John Peterson. "The Rose of Sharon." 1959. http://www.my. homewithgod.com/heavenlymidis/songbook/sharon.html

"The Truth of Osun's Orisa Energy." *The Ifa Foundation.* April 15, 2003. http://www.ifafoundation.org/library-osun.html.

# 8

## JAZZ FUNERALS AND MOURNING SONGS: TONI MORRISON'S CALL TO THE ANCESTORS IN *SULA*

*Anissa Janine Wardi*

Rites and rituals of death are deeply resonant throughout Toni Morrison's oeuvre. The action of each novel pivots on the axis of a pronounced death and its aftermath, the most obvious case being the murder of the "crawling-already? baby" in *Beloved*, which provides the catalyst for Sethe's and the community's confrontation with devastated pasts. However, beyond this principal embodiment of the dead, in each of Morrison's novels characters find themselves mired in the culture of death through murder, mercy killing, suicide, mourning, funeral rituals, spiritual death or rememories of genocide. Because Morrison relies on the discourse of Christianity in her work (through character naming and retelling of parables, for example), coupled with the fact that characters identified through an organized religion are routinely cast as Christian, Morrison turns to Christian rituals surrounding the dead. While Morrison employs theologically based sacraments to mediate these grave circumstances, they are steeped in an African American cultural and historical epistemology, which derives in part from West African spiritual practices and their transformation on American soil. Moreover, the African American community's intimate relationship with death, through the history of chattel slavery, the routine execution of lynching and burning rituals, and the recurrent performance of capital punishment, lends greater significance to memorial services, funerals and grave markers. As Holloway notes, "The generational circumstance may change, but the violence done to black bodies has had a consistent history" (27).

For Morrison, the Bible is not a master narrative: in her *Nobel Lecture in Literature*, she argues that theistic discourse is a kind of dead language that does not "permit new knowledge or encourage the mutual exchange of ideas" (16–17), and *Paradise* is a treatise in removing paradise "from its pedestal of exclusion" (quoted in Reames 61). Despite these concerns, Morrison does not reduce the import of Christianity in the lives of her characters, recognizing that much of African American culture is significantly imbricated in Christian thought. However, Morrison illustrates how the narratives, iconography and rituals of Christianity are transformed by the historical exigencies of Black culture. In *Sula*, Morrison portrays African American Christianity as a palimpsest of an African diasporic history, with traces of West African spirituality and the indelible stamp of violence on Black life in America.

The ideological landscape of New Orleans, with its fusion of West African and European cultures, its Catholicism juxtaposed with Afro-Caribbean spiritual practices, occupies a central, though easily overlooked place in *Sula*. Following the prologue, *Sula* begins temporally in 1919 and in the very next year, 1920, the reader is taken from the Ohio neighborhood of Bottom and temporarily relocated to New Orleans. While this is the first and last time that New Orleans appears as a material setting in *Sula*—though it is evoked later as one of the seven cities where Sula lived during her respite from the Bottom—Morrison's positioning of New Orleans in the beginning of the novel establishes a paradigm for conceptualizing the treatment of death and its attendant practices and communal rituals. Reading *Sula* through the lens of New Orleans, with its pronounced cities of the dead, is apt, as the novel is steeped in mourning. Beginning with an elegy for a lost community ("there was once a neighborhood" [3]) and concluding with Nel's explicit scene of mourning in the cemetery (a despair that reverberates in "circles and circles of sorrow" [174]), *Sula* is framed with scenes of death, loss and grief. Novak supports this reading, arguing that "death not only structures the narrative but also governs it, determines the elaboration of character and event. Death presides. And *Sula* endlessly presides over death" (185). That *Sula* is a text of memory reveals the shroud of loss permeating the narrative. Despite the fact that readers bear witness to many deaths, the framing of the novel, which establishes the community in memoriam, is a reminder of the accumulated losses in *Sula*. For Morrison, though, the dead are never really dead, and thus she naturally gestures towards a city where above-ground cemeteries compete with homes for urban space, where throngs of people gather on All Saints Day to whitewash tombs and adorn vaults with yellow chrysanthemums, and where funerals are taken to the streets. In this city, death is not hidden; it is a public, shared event, alternately aggrandized, mourned and celebrated.

New Orleans' tribute to the dead is best exemplified in Shadrack's celebration of National Suicide Day, a death parade that has its genesis in war:

Shadrack "turned his head a little to the right and saw the face of a soldier near him fly off. Before he could register shock, the rest of the soldier's head disappeared under the inverted soup bowl of his helmet. But stubbornly, taking no direction from the pain, the body of the headless soldier ran on, with energy and grace, ignoring altogether the drip and slide of brain tissue down its back" (*Sula* 8). A shell-shocked Shadrack, determined to order and contain the irrationality of death, creates a day of death, January 3rd, in which he invites the community of Bottom to kill each other or commit suicide. The construction of the novel lends credence to the relationship between Shadrack's National Suicide Day and New Orleans, as Morrison follows the first description of National Suicide Day with Helene and Nel Wright's visit to New Orleans, a trip which, suitably, is prompted by loss: the impending death of Cecile Sabat, Helene's grandmother.

The mortuary rituals surrounding this brief interlude in New Orleans are suggestive of African American spiritual customs. The black crepe wreath with purple ribbon hanging on Cecile's front door is the first cultural artifact, one that announces the death of the inhabitant. These memorial wreaths are similar to immortelles, wreaths made of durable material such as glass, tin and beads, which New Orleanians place on crypts and tombs, especially on All Saints Day (Christovich 185). The public sign of mourning that meets Helene and Nel at the door inaugurates the reader into an entire lexicon of New Orleans' unique funerary customs, from Catholic iconography (multiple statues of the Virgin Mary and memorial candles) to the "settin-up" of Cecile in her own home. "[D]eath sighed in every corner" (*Sula* 25) of Cecile's "Frenchified shotgun house," which, with its "magnificent garden in the back and a tiny wrought-iron fence in the front," is a virtual synecdoche of New Orleans itself. While Helene and daughter Nel quickly leave this city of death, the culture of New Orleans undergirds the posthumous rituals that punctuate the novel.

It is perhaps not surprising that this city of death commemoration also claims the first Black Benevolent Society, established in 1783. These organizations, which proliferated in postbellum America, provided a range of social services denied to African Americans. For a fee of twenty-five cents a week, African Americans could join benevolent societies, which were also referred to as burial societies because the administration of a funeral was one of their primary functions: "their final obligation was to sponsor a decent, decorous burial for their dues paying members. Part of this burial contract included at the request of the member and his family, music for the funeral cortege" (Shafer

66).[1] Indeed, as these societies became more numerous, the organizations gained visibility by parading for many occasions. While outsiders tend to think of Mardi Gras celebrations as the only street-based parades in the city, they are part of a larger calendar of public performances that work to coalesce the community and give expression to its members' lives. Regis explains that a series of parades takes place throughout New Orleans' poorest neighborhoods, typically on Sunday afternoons: "These massive moving street festivals, commonly drawing from 3,000–5,000 people, are organized and funded by working-class African Americans to celebrate the anniversaries of their distinctive social clubs and benevolent societies"(1). While the conditions of Black life in post-slavery America created circumstances that made benevolent societies particularly necessary, such social organizations also existed in West Africa: Buerkle and Barker claim that "there are burial societies whose members are sworn to attend one another's funerals and mourn long and loud. There are musical groups whose members concern themselves with ceremony" (quoted in Kein 102). Therefore, the import in African American culture of one's last rites, including the presence of mourners and song, arcs back to an African belief system that prizes the precise administration of such customs. Specific performance, including the prescription of funeral goers' histrionics followed by celebratory music, was staged to illustrate not only respect for the deceased, but to provide solace for the mourners. New Orleans funerals with music, more customarily referred to as jazz funerals, epitomize both staged and improvisational aspects of public mourning and commemoration.[2]

Funerals with music, according to Secundy, which "were popular in New Orleans in the late 1800s and early to mid-1900s," have roots in African funerary practices: "The Dahomeans and the Yoruba of Western Africa laid its foundations" (101). Pairing solemnity with joyful celebration as the soul travels to the domain of the spirits reflects an African worldview. Louisiana poet Marie Osbey offers the following:

> Among the Kongolese brought as captives to Louisiana, it was indeed the tradition first to vent the soul's sorrow with the customary weeping and wailing and then to accompany the dead to their resting place with much rejoicing. Decorum required that the mourners sing, beat the dream and tambourine, and dance the soul to its new home. This was necessary to ensure the traveler's happiness and good reception there in that kingdom. (104)

Osbey further explains the transformation of this African tradition on the shores of America: "And we must remember also that the African forebears, who bequeathed to us and us alone this particular tradition, were themselves adjusting in the face of crisis and rupture, catastrophe and huge suffering" (104). While African-inspired funerary traditions were not routinely administered in antebellum society, the trace of these beliefs is resonant in both hymns and rituals. The performance of this tradition in jazz funerals is unmistakable even today, although it may not be explicitly articulated by the performers: "They are . . . people experiencing and acting out a cultural memory that their ancestors were never allowed to express formally. In viewing them [jazz funerals], one can almost hear the melodic strains of old Protestant hymns echoing through neighborhoods of shotgun houses and corner barrooms" (Marsalis 2). Charles Long's assertion that, "even if they had no conscious memory of Africa, the image of Africa played an enormous part in the religion of blacks," provides a larger context in which to place this communal performance of spirituality (quoted in Matthews 25).

The penultimate chapter of the novel contains the climactic moment of community in *Sula*, as Shadrack's "annual solitary parade" transforms into a symbolic New Orleans jazz funeral, thus galvanizing the community through death.[3] Attending to the details of Shadrack's final performance, it is clear that Morrison overlays the rituals of jazz funerals onto National Suicide Day with the intention of endowing this pariah's private act of existential desperation with African American spiritual practices. Like New Orleans jazz funerals, Shadrack's 1941 funeral parade provides communal healing and solace, despite the overwhelming presence of death. Shadrack, who for twenty years walked through the Bottom ringing his cowbell in a dirge-like fashion, embodies in a "childish" way (Morrison's word) the grand marshal of the jazz funeral procession. Wearing the face of solemnity, the grand marshal is in charge of the spectacle, establishing the mood of the occasion by choosing the music, leading the brass band and regulating the intensity of the performance (Jones). In short, the grand marshal is the barometer of emotion (Jones).

Shadrack, from 1920 to 1941, serves as the self-appointed grand marshal of National Suicide Day. For twenty years he performs this procession alone, mourning, as the novel does, for all those who have passed, while anticipating the deaths that are to come. His solitary show is a concrete reminder of the lives lost through war, slavery and economic dispossession. However, with no one to answer his call, Shadrack, the official mourner, remains trapped in the pain of loss; that is, he is stagnant in his travel toward the cemetery but never "cuts the body loose," which in jazz funeral parlance refers to laying the body to rest in the cemetery.

Traditional funerals with music involve two distinct components of the ritual. First, the brass band accompanies the deceased's loved ones to the cemetery in order to inter the body and perform any final graveside ceremonies.[4] During this procession, traditional sacred hymns such as "Amazing Grace" and "Just a Closer Walk with Thee" are played to accompany the "first line" (mourners, relatives, clergy). Returning from the grave, the band abruptly changes tempo, signaled by the trumpeter's two-beat riff and the drummers' second-line beat, ushering in celebratory music, including such favorites as "When the Saints Go Marching In." Beyond the physical act of interment, then, cutting the body loose brings about the joyful mood of the procession, largely attributed to the presence of the "second line."

The second line is the unofficial, spontaneous, street crowd that forms the heart of the performance, the "uninvited guests that everybody expects to show up" (Jones). Osbey contends that kinship is the essence of second-line parades: "Their grief was a thing we knew. If we had not ourselves experienced that selfsame loss already, we knew that soon enough we would each of us have to look at it dead in the face" (100). The import of the second-liners— those who join the bereaved but do not necessarily know the deceased—is revealed by the fact that the very term "second line" is a synonym for the jazz funeral, itself. Therefore, the second-line parade is a necessary part of the ritual, for it affirms not only the life of the deceased, but celebrates both life and death in general.

Indeed, in such performances, death is not feared as the enemy, but is recognized as a reprieve from the trials, pain and sorrows of life, epitomized in the verse, "you cry when you're born, so rejoice when you die." The residents of Bottom finally perform as the second-line parade to Shadrack's memorial march, thereby transforming it into a joyful affirmation. Novak's reading of mourning in *Sula* as "more than just a means a paying homage to the dead," but also encompassing an "orientation toward survival, a celebration of living on" (189) is epitomized in the community's performance of the funeral parade. Shunning Shadrack and his mourning parade for twenty years, on this occasion—an afternoon optimistically bathed in sunlight—they follow him: "Maybe the sun; maybe the clots of green showing in the hills promising so much; maybe the contrast between Shadrack's doomy, gloomy bell glinting in all that sweet sunshine. Maybe just a brief moment, for once, of not feeling fear, of looking at death in the sunshine and being unafraid" (*Sula* 158–159). Second-liners are often drawn from their homes by the power of the music and the merriment reverberating throughout their neighborhoods, an impression recalled in *Sula*: "Upstairs, Ivy heard her [neighbor] and looked to see what caused the thick music that rocked her neighbor's breasts. Then Ivy laughed too ... their laughter infected Carpenter's Road. Soon children were jumping about and giggling and men came to the porches to chuckle. By the time Shadrack reached the first house, he was facing a line of delighted faces," a "parade" that "actually marched along behind him" (*Sula* 159). The dignity of the earlier funerary march is matched by the seemingly irreverent dancing so common to the second-liners, a kind of "dialectic between the steely discipline and respectability of the grand marshal and the playful satire and parody of the clown" (Regis 13). Morrison's characterization of Shadrack's final march unmistakably evokes New Orleans second-line parades: the three deweys "cut into a wild aping of [Shadrack's] walk, his song and his bell-ringing"; "flocks of teen-agers got into the mood and, laughing, dancing and calling to one another, formed a pied piper's band behind Shadrack." The crowd, which had grown "larger and larger," "strutted, skipped, marched and shuffled down the road" (*Sula* 160).

Jazz great Ellis Marsalis, Jr.'s description of memorial parades echoes the above passage: "Those who are willing and able will fall in behind the band, next to the band, between the band members, affecting the body language of the dance, a strut, a 'booty bounce'" (3). The booty bounce indicates the West Indian "banda," an erotic dance of rebirth, whose purpose it is to reinforce life even in the face of death. Further accentuating the transatlantic funerary continuities, "the banda is also found in Trinidad and Tobago, where it is known as the bongo" and is "danced in honor of the dead" (Kein 104). Suggestive, exuberant dancing and good-natured styling, replete with accoutrements of handkerchiefs and umbrellas, are themselves tributes to the dead. These life-affirming celebrations, endemic to New Orleans jazz funerals, coalesce the community while sending the deceased to the spirit world.

Beyond showing reverence for the dead, jazz funerals are sites of power and community for the living, many of whom are working class. Regis argues that participation in New Orleans funerals "is a profound way of strengthening and repairing the social fabric, which is severely weakened by poverty, joblessness, violence, class- and race-based segregation, and racism" (5). Morrison, too, suggests that the community's willingness to participate in National Suicide Day should be understood as a final, audacious performance of hope in a landscape of stunning oppression: "As the initial group of about twenty people passed more houses, they called to the people standing in doors and leaning out of windows to join them; to help them open further this slit in the veil, this respite from anxiety, from dignity, from gravity, from the weight of that very adult pain that had undergirded them all those years before [. . .] as though there really was hope" (*Sula* 159–160).

Not all of the residents who witness this festival participate: "Some, of course, like Helene Wright, would not go. She watched the ruckus with characteristic scorn" (*Sula* 160). It is fitting that Helene Wright, the embodiment of Bottom's middle class, refuses to take part in Shadrack's parade because, as Regis argues, the Black middle class often are embarrassed by what they deem to be a working-class spectacle (1). Rejecting societal conventions, the second-liners reclaim space, including race- and class-segregated neighborhoods. While some are "too embarrassed to enter the white part of town whooping like banshees," the "aggressive and the abandoned," who formed the majority of the parade, "danced down Main Street" (*Sula* 160–161). For New Orleans residents, parading is a time when they claim the streets as their own, which "renews their strength and hope and allows them to face another Monday" (Regis 6). Inscribing the landscape with a countercultural mark is particularly significant in *Sula*, as Shadrack's parade culminates on the tunnel in New River Road, the very street that symbolizes the community's dashed hopes and dreams. The resistance to dominant space and hegemonic power structures, implicit in New Orleans carnivalesque parading, is made literal in *Sula* as the townspeople's march leads to the destruction of the tunnel.

Since Shadrack's 1941 National Suicide Day parade follows Sula's passing, this death parade can be read as a farewell celebration for Sula, "his visitor, his company, his guest, his social-life, his woman, his daughter, his friend" (*Sula* 157), and a harbinger of the collective death of Bottom residents. Although jazz funerals are provided for those who can afford them, often the passing of jazz musicians provides the occasion for these sendoffs. The iconoclastic lifestyle often associated with musicians and other artists is reflected in the choice of music played on the way back from the cemeteries. One familiar tune, "Didn't He Ramble," includes lyrics that celebrate the life of a man who lived by his own rules, rejected societal mores and rambled "in and out of town" until "the butcher cut him down." This kind of unencumbered freedom, or what Morrison in *The Bluest Eye* characterizes as "dangerous freedom," (159) is typically the domain of men; however, in *Sula* this description best characterizes the title character, who is "an artist without a medium" (121), a woman who spends her adult years rambling from town to town, and, upon her return to Bottom, commits the unthinkable act of putting her own grandmother into an old-age home. Further, the fact that the second-liners join Shadrack on Carpenter's Road, the street where Eva's house is located, and where Sula died, is in keeping with jazz funerals, which parade by the homes where the deceased lived. Although very few residents of the Bottom attended to the preparation of Sula's actual funeral, leaving most details to the whites of the town, they do hover at the edges of her graveside to sing "Shall We Gather at the River." They later pay tribute to her in this National Suicide Day celebration-cum-jazz funeral, the symbolic memorial service that speaks to their own impending mortality, aptly occurring "at the river."

After audaciously marching through town, the paraders die en masse in the water, another bridging of the Bottom with the city of the "wet grave," New Orleans (Upton 135):

> New Orleans presented a problem for the burying of its dead not encountered by any other city in the civilized world. The city was surrounded by a cypress swamp, its terrain was low and for a great part of the year was below the level of the river, besides its outskirts were frequently inundated from high tides and from storms on the lake. Water was found from one to three feet below the surface of the ground, and there was not a high spot near the city where ground burials were possible without submerging the corpses. (Fossier 428)

Heavy rains could result in the disruption of coffins; bodies floating to the land's surface were reported in the nineteenth century, and the gruesomeness of these incidents took hold in the cultural imagination. That the dead were not interred in New Orleans, but drowned (Fossier 428), marks an interesting parallel with *Sula*, in which the Bottomites meet their death at the mouth of New River Road tunnel and their bodies are not recovered. Their parade of jubilation and freedom appropriately ends at the river, a concrete site of oppression: "Old and young, women and children, lame and hearty, they killed, as best they could, the tunnel they were forbidden to build" (*Sula* 161). Their bold assertion of agency results in a confrontation with that which denied them livelihood and locked them in a system of poverty.

Rhetorically, water and fire become place markers for death in *Sula*. Morrison associates death with natural elements undergirded by unnatural acts of race hatred and violence. Throughout, Morrison moves among catastrophes plaguing the Bottomites—"floods, white people, tuberculosis, famine and ignorance" (*Sula* 90)—so that individual deaths take on greater cultural significance. In emphasizing the larger narrative of mid-century African American life, it is apt that Morrison would turn to fire, as it carries with it the historical weight of racial terror. Two of Eva's children are killed by fire, evok-

ing the "familiar odor of cooked flesh" (*Sula* 77), unmistakably drawing attention to the lynching and burning rituals routinely executed in the decades following emancipation and continuing throughout the twentieth century.
Indeed, the racial climate of postwar America, the time period of the novel,
was anything but peaceful (a wordplay on Sula's last name). As Franklin and
Moss note,

> White citizens, in and out of the Klan, poured out wrath upon the black population
> shortly after the war that could hardly be viewed as fit punishment even for traitors.
> More than seventy blacks were lynched during the first year of the postwar period.
> Ten black soldiers, several still in their uniforms, were lynched. Mississippi and
> Georgia mobs each murdered three returned soldiers, in Arkansas two were lynched,
> while Florida and Alabama each took the life of a black soldier by mob violence.
> Fourteen Negroes were burned publicly, eleven of whom were burned alive.[5] (349)

Morrison's staging of intraracial violence is played out against a landscape of
institutionalized racial brutality and killings.

Rhetorically, the many deaths in *Sula* are "aestheticized" (Bouson 61);
Morrison's prose effortlessly "drift[s] . . . from lyricisms to violence" (Novak
185). By decorating gruesome scenes of death, Morrison invokes the spiritual
belief of death as a retreat from earthly suffering, one that finds particular
expression in the African American literary tradition. W. E .B. DuBois's reverie on the passing of his son in *Souls of Black Folk*, published nearly forty years
after Emancipation, provides a paradigm for reading death as an escape from
trauma: "All that day and all that night there sat an awful gladness in my
heart,—nay, blame me not if I see the world thus darkly through the Veil,—
and my soul whispers ever to me, saying 'Not dead, not dead, but escaped; not
bound, but free'" (353). Eva's murder of her beloved son, Plum, likewise
evinces abiding faith in an afterworld salvation. Returning from war a drug
addict, Plum, like Shadrack, is merely a shell of a man, and Eva has no way
to mollify his pathetic situation. Out of love and despair, she kills her youngest
child, "who floated in a constant swaddle of love" and "to whom she hoped to
bequeath everything" (*Sula* 45), in a scene that is as beautiful as it is horrible.
Eva's presence soothes Plum; her maternal rocking and the kerosene with
which she douses his body, which he experiences as a comforting "wet light,"
assure him that "everything is going to be all right." Morrison, who christens
Eva's infanticide a "baptism" likewise uses jarring similes in Hannah's death
"dance": Hannah was "gesturing and bobbing like a sprung jack-in-the-box"
(*Sula* 76). Unlike Plum and Sula, Hannah is silenced in the narration of her

death, yet her demise is likewise random, unexpected and violent. From the opening scene of the novel, where the headless solider runs on the battlefield with "energy and grace" (*Sula* 7), Morrison yokes together discrepant imagery to lyricize death, indicating a kind of redemption in the afterlife: "*Sula* does not comment directly on Christian theology, but the promised freedom of the afterlife does seem to undergird the people's refusal to lose faith" (Reddy 40).

Chicken Little's death at the river advances these associations and serves as a harbinger of the communal deaths at the novel's end. Sula, playfully swinging Chicken Little on the riverbank, loses his grip and the girls watch, stunned, as he sails to his death.[6] The girls run from this scene, and Chicken Little's body is found later that afternoon by a white bargeman, whose handling of his corpse recalls the history of disrespect accorded to Black bodies. Chicken Little is first "dumped" into a burlap sack and "tossed" next to egg crates. Concerned about the deteriorating corpse's effect on his goods, the sailor "dragged" Chicken Little to the side of the boat, so that "he was half in and half out of the water" (*Sula* 64). Chicken Little's body in the Ohio River is a historically salient tableau of African American history, as the river represents a geography of freedom and peril.

In emphasizing death and loss, it is fitting that the narrative stages a funeral. Given the bargeman's treatment of Chicken Little as an abject body, Morrison performs an act of narrative resistance by chronicling the respect and dignity of his funeral, where the community, young and old, stands in tribute to his life. Morrison deftly uses the metaphor of butterflies to localize the pain and trauma of Chicken Little's death for Nel and Sula, co-conspirators in the young boy's drowning:

> Butterflies flew in and out of the bunches of field flowers now loosened from the top of the bier and lying in a small heap at the edge of the grave. [. . .] Nel and Sula stood some distance away from the grave, the space that had sat between them in the pews had dissolved. They held hands and knew that only the coffin would lie in the earth; the bubbly laughter and the press of fingers in the palm would stay aboveground forever. At first, as they stood there, their hands were clenched together. They relaxed slowly until during the walk back home their fingers were laced in as gentle a clasp as that of any two young girlfriends trotting up the road on a summer day wondering what happened to butterflies in the winter. (*Sula* 66)

While the adults openly lament this tragedy and their own losses, the girls, new to death, cannot fathom the enormity of this fatality. Pairing butterflies with Chicken Little, who laughs as he soars to his death, emblematizes the innocence of childhood. Pondering the loss of something as fragile and evanescent as butterflies allows the girls to filter Chicken Little's death onto a manageable and tangible loss.[7]

Existentialist psychologists recognize that young children grapple with issues of death and nonbeing and may evidence related anxiety and fear. Confrontation with this content before there is sufficient fortification or readiness may cause trauma. Young children may be able to contemplate and successfully negotiate ideas of death related to flowers, insects and family pets; however, the death of a human being can be overwhelming (Yalom 104). Thus it is reasonable that Nel and Sula contemplate the random death of butterflies during the funeral of their young contemporary. Moreover, the fate of butterflies in the (white) winter evokes an image of loss layered with racial implications. The omnipresence of white terror, literalized through a winter capable of eradicating an entire species, once again reinforces Morrison's presentation of death as a conflation of the natural and the unnatural. In Christian's words, "the natural order is turned upside down as a result of human society" (75).

Just as Nel and Sula give expression to their grief through lost butterflies, African American spirituals, through metaphor and message, help to ameliorate the community's acute pain. Numerous African American hymns—"Shall We Gather at the River," "In that Sweet By-and-By," "Nearer My God to Thee," "Precious Memories," "Amazing Grace" and "Abide with Me"—echo throughout *Sula*, creating an elegiac tone. Spirituals are living memorials; not unlike stones of memory, these hymns mark lives and absent histories, pairing loss with hope, and death with restoration. The lyrics of spirituals are assurances of God's protection, providing comfort even in times of despair. In this book of death, Morrison's invocation of spirituals mediates the cruelty and permanency of death. In this way, the entire novel becomes a hymn of comfort, a mourning song that promises healing.

Matthews sheds light on a transatlantic context for African American Christianity:

> The ability to produce expressions of community in the situation of oppression is stressed as a unique feature of African American religion, just as it is in the Yoruban context. Therefore, it was not necessary for an African American to be dependent on "traditional" Christianity to develop this tragic sense of hope even within tragedy. Once again we see the effect of an African religious survival in the African American community in the New World. (23)

Morrison focuses on the spirituals, "the foundation of African American religion," as they represent the traces of West African spiritual practices: "the intense feeling and improvisation found in the spirituals . . . also characterize the slaves' West African religious heritage. Although the spirituals were created in a situation of oppression and suffering in America, the cultural tools used to guide religious expression were African cultural features" (Matthews 17). The relationship between West African mourning practices and Protestant hymns captures the hybrid religion of African American Christianity expressed in Morrison's work. While Africa is not materially located in *Sula*, an ancestral presence is manifest through death, mourning practices and healing narratives and rituals. In this way, Hunt's assessment that *Sula* encodes an "African worldview which sees a continuum, rather than a strict boundary, between the living and the dead" (444), brings into relief the presence of jazz funerals and spirituals as well as the absence of characters and geographies.[8]

Just as the reader bears witness to a story that occurs in absence, Plum, Hannah, Chicken Little and even Sula are pronounced absences in the narrative.[9] Plum's body seemingly disintegrates in the fire, Hannah and Chicken Little are so disfigured that they have closed coffins, and Sula, without explanation, had a closed-coffin service as well, an absencing of the body that is against protocol in many African American funerals. Indeed, Holloway argues that "it was traditional in African American communities to leave the casket open for viewing sometime during the wake and church services. A laying-on of hands, touching, kissing, and expressing one's grief by viewing the remains have traditionally mattered deeply" (25). These material absences in *Sula* weigh heavily on the narrative, as does the spectral presence of the unnamed, unspecified "beautiful black boys" of 1921. The elusive beautiful boys that the reader never meets, who "dotted the landscape like jewels" (*Sula* 56), are instead a site of narrative memory, a textual refrain that highlights the fleetingness of the past, the beauty and innocence of a generation of boys lost to war, lynching and mob terror. The underlying melancholy for the missing boys lingers in the nation's memory, which is suggested by the geographic fusion of their bodies with the landscape, a national landscape that, in 1921, was burning in Tulsa, Oklahoma, in one of the country's most notorious race riots.[10] This race war owed its origins to an African American male's rumored assault of a white woman and an angry white mob's threat of lynching (Franklin and Moss 352). The National Guard was called in, and Tulsa was placed under martial law. While this event nationalized and thus made visible postwar racial violence, the material evidence of the crime—the bodies—went missing, obliterated through burning or lost to drowning. As Holloway explains: "In a pattern that became morbidly consistent for post–World War I riots, including those in Rosewood and Tulsa, black mortuaries could only bury those they found. Throughout the century, survivors continued to lament the family and folk who just disappeared and could not even be funeralized" (69).

In honoring that history, Morrison frames *Sula* with a similar semiotics of loss. Temporally beginning in 1919 and ending in 1965, Morrison brackets her novel with war, racial terror and death. The summer of 1919, which James Weldon Johnson called "The Red Summer," was, according to Franklin and Moss, "the greatest period of interracial strife the nation had ever witnessed," with race riots occurring throughout the nation (349). Likewise, in 1965 (a year that the narrator ironically claims only "seemed" better), "the U.S. war in Viet Nam intensified, Malcolm X was assassinated, and the Watts riots began" (Ryan 401). The interplay between the foreground narrative of the death of the Bottom and its background history of mob violence, race riots, and wars, suggests that "peace has many tombstones" (Ryan 401).

Bearing witness to such human loss, it is apt that Morrison leaves the reader in a graveyard, where, with Nel, we are permitted to mourn. The headstones of Beechnut Park cemetery bridge domestic tragedies with international suffering: "each flat slab had one word carved on it. Together, they read like a chant: PEACE 1895–1921, PEACE 1890–1923, PEACE 1910–1940, PEACE 1892–1959. They were not dead people. They were words. Not even words. Wishes, longings" (*Sula* 171). The graveyard, like the jazz funeral, is a place of mourning, remembrance and reconciliation. This final chapter, which functions as a "eulogy" (Christian 94), indicates an end and a beginning. Indeed, the unexpected appearance of Shadrack, the grand marshal of Bottom's jazz funeral procession, ushers in Nel's catharsis. Stagnant in pain, Nel has been essentially trapped in the somber journey towards the cemetery. Only when, on the last page of the novel, she openly communicates her grief, a cry of recognition and resistance, does Nel cut the body loose and journeys back from the graveyard.

### Notes

[1] Burial societies are mentioned throughout Morrison's canon; the most obvious example is in *Song of Solomon*, in which Robert Smith is a burial insurance agent. In the novel under consideration here, Sula, all but disowned by her community, still is afforded a proper funeral

because of burial insurance: "It was all done elegantly, for it was discovered that she had a substantial death policy" (*Sula* 173).

[2] It should be noted that the term "jazz funeral" was coined no later than the 1930s, and since the tradition predates this term by over a century, many prefer the term "funerals with music."

[3] A number of critics read National Suicide Day as a reference to the protest marches of the 1960s. See, for example, Maureen Reddy's "The Tripled Plot and Center of *Sula*."

[4] Currently, marching bands do not follow the first-liners all the way to the grave, because most interments now occur outside of city limits; however, even if the band cannot accompany the mourners graveside, they do mirror the journey to "cut the body loose" by marching a respectable distance before beginning the second-line parade.

[5] The war scene opening the novel, in which Morrison reveals Shadrack's cognitive dissonance ("It was his first encounter with the enemy and he didn't know whether he was running toward them or away" [7]), complicates African American soldiers' loyalties, as they were disenfranchised by the country on whose behalf they were risking their lives.

[6] This scene has engendered divergent critical responses. Barbara Christian claims that "this accident is Sula's baptism into her search for some continuity between the natural world and the social world, between the precariousness of life and the inevitability of death" (82), whereas McKee argues that Sula's "killing" of Chicken Little is meaningless to her (47).

[7] Later in the novel, Morrison again employs this motif to convey Ajax's departure from Sula's life, a loss so pronounced that "[e]very now and then she looked around for tangible evidence of his having ever been there. Where were the butterflies?" (*Sula* 134)

[8] While this analysis specifically attends to Morrison's engagement with ancestral deaths and mourning practices in *Sula*, Hunt's "War and Peace: Transfigured Categories and the Politics of *Sula*" extends the discussion of an ancestral presence in the novel through what she labels Morrison's "Africanized Christian Theology" (444).

[9] Morrison's dedication of *Sula* to her sons, Ford and Slade—"whom I miss although they have not left me"—is an anticipation of loss, a similar gesture to that advanced by the novel, as readers of *Sula* are cognizant of the community's absence despite its existence in the narrative present.

[10] Morrison's conflation of the "boys" with the landscape is foreshadowed at the beginning of *Sula*, when the African American community's displacement is concretized through nature imagery: "In the place, where they tore the nightshade and blackberry patches from their roots to make room for the Medallion City Golf Course, there was once a neighborhood" (3). The uprooting of the community is a violent scene of gentrification, a death so absolute that nothing is left but "dust."

## Works Cited

Bouson, J. Brooks. *Quiet as It's Kept: Shame, Trauma, and Race in the Novels of Toni Morrison*. Albany: State University of New York Press, 2000.

Christian, Barbara. "The Contemporary Fables of Toni Morrison." In *Toni Morrison: Critical Perspectives Past and Present*, edited by Henry Louis Gates, Jr. and K. A. Appiah. New York:

Amistad, 1993. 59–99.

Christovich, Mary Louise. "Cemetery Ironwork." In *New Orleans Architecture, Volume III: The Cemeteries*, edited by Mary Louise Christovich. Gretna: Pelican Publishing, 1974. 139–188.

DuBois, W. E. B. *The Souls of Black Folk*. 1903. In *Three Negro Classics*. New York: Avon, 1965. 207–389.

Fossier, Albert A. *New Orleans: The Glamour Period, 1800–1840*. New Orleans: Pelican Publishing, 1957.

Franklin, John Hope, and Alfred A. Moss Jr. *From Slavery to Freedom: A History of Africa Americans*. 7th ed. New York: McGraw Hill, 1994.

Holloway, Karla. F.C. *Passed On: African American Mourning Stories*. Durham, NC: Duke University Press, 2002.

Hunt, Patricia. "War and Peace: Transfigured Categories and the Politics of *Sula*." *African American Review* 27.3 (1993): 443–459.

Jones, David M, dir. *New Orleans Jazz Funerals from the Inside*. DMJ Productions, 1995.

Kein, Sybil. "The Celebration of Life in New Orleans Jazz Funerals." In *Feasts and Celebrations in North American Ethnic Communities*, edited by Ramon A. Gutierrez and Genevieve Fabre. Albuquerque: University of New Mexico Press, 1995. 101–108.

Marsalis, Ellis L., Jr. "Introduction." *Rejoice When You Die: The New Orleans Jazz Funerals*. Baton Rouge: Louisiana State University Press, 1998. 1–3.

Matthews, Donald H. *Honoring the Ancestors: An African Cultural Interpretation of Black Religion and Literature*. New York: Oxford University Press, 1998.

McKee, Patricia. "Spacing and Placing Experience in Toni Morrison's *Sula*." In *Toni Morrison Critical and Theoretical Approaches*, edited by Nancy J. Peterson. Baltimore: Johns Hopkins University Press. 1997. 37–62.

Morrison, Toni. *The Bluest Eye*. 1970. New York: Plume, 1993.

———. *The Nobel Lecture in Literature*, 1993. New York: Knopf, 2000.

———. *Sula*. New York: Knopf, 1973.

Novak, Phillip. "'Circles and Circles of Sorrow': In the Wake of Morrison's *Sula*." *PMLA* 114.2 (March 1999): 184–193.

Osbey, Brenda. "One More Last Chance: Rituals in Jazz Funerals." *Georgia Review* 50.1 (Spring 1996): 97–107.

Reames, Kelly Lynch. *Toni Morrison's "Paradise": A Reader's Guide*. New York: Continuum, 2001.

Reddy, Maureen. "The Tripled Plot and Center of *Sula*." *Black American Literature Forum* 22.1 (Spring 1988): 29–45.

Regis, Helen A. "Second Lines, Minstrelsy, and the Contested Landscape of New Orleans Afro-Creole Festivals." *Cultural Anthropology* 14.4 (1999): 472–504.

Ryan, Katy. "Revolutionary Suicide in Toni Morrison's Fiction." *African American Review* 34.3 (2000): 389–412.

Secundy, Marian Gray. "Coping with Words and Song: The New Orleans Jazz Funeral." *Literature and Medicine* 8 (1989): 100–105.

Shafer, William J. *Brass Bands and New Orleans Jazz*. Baton Rouge: Louisiana State University Press, 1977.

Upton, Dell. "The Urban Cemetery and the Urban Community: The Origin of the New Orleans Cemetery." In *Exploring Everyday Landscapes: Perspectives in Vernacular Architecture, VII*, edited by Annmarie Adams and Sally McMury. Knoxville: University of Tennessee Press, 1997. 131–145.

Yalom, Irvin D. *Existential Psychotherapy.* New York: Basic Books, 1980.

# 9

# A New World Religion?
## Creolisation and Candomblé in Toni Morrison's *Paradise*

*Jennifer Terry*

Through the oppositional communities of the town of Ruby and the so-called Convent, Toni Morrison's novel *Paradise* details the corruption of a black utopian dream. Part of this narrative project is the exploration of various forms of religious worship, concluding with the proposition of an alternative paradise. The author herself has suggested that this novel is concerned with "organised religion and unorganised magic as two systems," and this essay will examine her portrayal of religion, in particular arguing that it facilitates an engagement with the tangled evolution of black diaspora cultures ("Morrison's Slice of Paradise"). In *Paradise*, as Brooks Bouson points out, "Morrison focuses on… the complex religious heritage of blacks in America" (193). Earlier novels such as *Song of Solomon* and *Beloved* raise issues of faith and healing, depicting, for example, Hagar's funeral and Baby Suggs's preaching; these instances of collective mourning, celebration or even exorcism anticipate the author's later, more sustained consideration of church organisations and theologies. Whilst in *Paradise*, institutional religion is allied with patriarchy, conservatism and colonisation, non-institutional forms of worship are celebrated through the depiction of Consolata's mission; the heterogeneous and renegade household of the Convent is set against the insularity, conformism and ethnic absolutism of the all-black town. I contend here that Morrison not only re-envisions patriarchal Christianity, but also invokes the African Brazilian religious practices of Candomblé to formulate a positive model of New World creolisation.[1] My reading will draw on Edouard Glissant's theory of cross-cultural relations within the diaspora engendered by racial slavery and, more broadly, on the work of Paul Gilroy.

   Although this essay will focus on what Morrison terms unorganised magic, I will first briefly examine her exploration of institutional religion through the three different Protestant churches of Ruby and the Catholic Christ the King School for Native Girls.[2] Indeed, the opposing theological and political positions of the authoritarian Methodist, Reverend Pulliam, and the young and progressive Baptist, Reverend Misner, enable *Paradise*'s portrayal of the town's insularity and conservatism. Whilst the newcomer Misner seeks to end Ruby's isolation, affirming links with the civil rights struggle and supporting pan-African causes, Pulliam condemns such activism and views the disruption rocking the rest of American society as apocalyptic.[3] In addition, Pulliam's "boiling breath" approach is associated with the Old Testament as he asserts that God is "interested only in Himself" and that worshippers must realise this before "the moment when all are judged for the disposition of their eternal lives" (*Paradise* 141–143). In contrast, Misner believes in a benevolent God who is profoundly interested in his followers and can move "you to do your own work as well as His" (142). His emphasis on the self-sacrifice of Christ, rather than God's "begrudging authority," is allied with the New Testament (146).[4] Whilst Pulliam upholds the inscription on the town's communal oven as a divine command to obedience, "Beware the Furrow of His Brow," Misner encourages the community's young people to question traditional narratives and reinterpret it as a call to action: "Be the Furrow of His Brow" (86–87). Such efforts throw into relief the intransigence of the majority of all three of Ruby's congregations.

The townspeople, described as "protective, God-loving, thrifty but not miserly," have a sense of moral superiority as the righteous descendants of the Disallowed, those ancestors oppressed by whites but also shunned by another black community, which is connected to their Protestantism (*Paradise* 160). Indeed, the westward journey of their forefathers in search of a promised land is allied with the biblical story of Exodus. This appropriation of the tale of the Israelites' quest for freedom and Canaan echoes a wider tradition within black churches which found in it an empowering model. According to Raboteau, "No single symbol captures more clearly the distinctiveness of Afro-American Christianity than the symbol of Exodus" (Raboteau 9). The Exodus story could be used to refute the claim that Africans were intended by God to be slaves and so had become a discourse enabling resistance. The Protestants of Ruby are hence located within a context of the evolution of specifically African American forms of Christianity. Yet their separatism and conservatism render this a hollow or even debilitating, rather than affirmative, relation.

The alliance of the Morgan brothers with a judgemental sense of Christian morality, in addition, implicates institutional religion in their pride, avarice and oppressive authority. Deacon and Steward practice an expedient and selective form of faith, attending Calvary because "the Baptists [are] the largest congregation in town as well as the most powerful," and sorting "Misner's opinions carefully to judge which were recommendations easily ignored and which were orders they ought to obey" (*Paradise* 56–57). As the narrative develops, their Protestantism is increasingly associated with material greed rather than religious devotion. In Ruby, the spirit of community and cooperation that marked the founding of Haven has dissipated: the bank is no longer owned collectively, struggling businesses are not assisted, only loaned more money, and social inequality has widened, with the Morgan twins in particular accumulating wealth and therefore political clout within the town. Although Deacon and Steward view themselves as upstanding Christians, the problematical character of their position is exposed when Dovey Morgan wonders, "aside from giving up his wealth, can a rich man be a good one?" (93) Instead of humility, the brothers exhibit pride, behaving "as if God were their silent business partner" and viewing their prosperity as a sign of divine approbation (143). Such religious sanctimony, however, is undercut by the narrative's detailing of their censorious banking decisions and personal avarice. For example, when Misner forms a non-profit credit union—"small emergency loans to church members; no penalty payback schemes"—this aid organisation is viewed with suspicion by Steward, who speculates, "A man like that, willing to throw money away, could give customers ideas. Make them think there was a choice about interest rates" (56). Morrison hence demonstrates how the religious can "become arrogant and prideful and ungenerous."[5] As I will go on to explore, the forms of worship that *Paradise* affirms operate quite differently.

The churchmen of Ruby are perhaps most effectively exposed as hypocritical and censorious through their attitude toward and assault upon the female household of the Convent. Their all-black utopia is conceived as a place where women are safe to walk at night, where "[n]othing for ninety miles around [thinks they are] prey" (*Paradise* 8). The definition of the town as an enclave of security, as "free and protected," however, is dependent upon exclusion, obedience and conformity (8). As Cyrus Patell writes, "This is a patriarch's view of women's freedom" (183). The dissent about the meaning of the communal oven and the need for change in the 1970s is perceived as a threat to the men's vision of home, and a group of scapegoats is blamed. Indeed, such zealous safeguarding of the town eventually leads to an aggressive attack on defenceless women, the very figures the founders had wanted to prevent from falling prey to white men. The patriarchs' laws to preserve their paradise also involve the rejection of persons with any racial variation. Infiltration, even by fellow blacks with some legacy of white blood, is perceived as detracting from the absolutist notion of community that they cherish.

The townsmen first demonise their neighbours: with their "streetwalkers' clothes and whores' appetites," members of the Convent household are said to form a "new obscene breed of female" that blasphemes against the Morgan twins' sacred ideal of womanhood (*Paradise* 297). The outsiders are depicted as agents of contamination, polluting an otherwise wholesome community. In particular, the women are condemned for their independent and ungodly way of life: "These here sluts out there by themselves never step foot in a church[....] They don't need men and they don't need God" (276). Their racially composite home also goes against all of the elders' sensibilities about segregation, the perceived threat being that such "mess" will penetrate and disease the town (276). Revealing the true nature of their Christianity, "When the men spoke of the ruination that was upon them—how Ruby was changing in intolerable ways—they did not think to fix it by extending a hand in fellowship[. . . .] They mapped defence instead and honed evidence for its need" (275). The patriarchs' hate campaign culminates in a shocking offensive during which "warm with perspiration and the nocturnal odor of righteousness [. . .] God at their side, [they] take aim. For Ruby" (18).[6] This disturbing aggression announces the final stage of the corruption and betrayal of the dream of Haven and reveals the attackers' practice of their faith to be oppressive, sanctimonious and ultimately destructive.

Reverend Misner's own faith offers an alternative to the Morgans' self-serving and judgemental Christianity. Indeed, he conceives of a Christ whose agents are the activists of contemporary America, envisaging his crucifixion as the "official murder" of a "woolly-head[ed]" man with "midnight skin," so repudiating the iconography of the white Christian church (*Paradise* 146). Misner also asserts a celebratory vision of an original "true home" that mythologises Africa (213).[7] This conception of belonging, of "roots," exposes the hegemonic displacements of colonisation and slavery (209). It poses a worldly paradise rather than a deferred heaven and echoes the Christian creation story, possibly making reference to Africa as the point of genesis for humankind (see 213). Misner's lyrical evocation, however, idealises Africa and perhaps also betrays a wishful impulse towards return. Indeed, Patricia Best responds by asking, "[I]s it just some kind of past with no slavery in it you're looking for? [...] Slavery *is* our past. Nothing can change that, certainly not

Africa" (210).[8] Although Misner is presented as a largely sympathetic character, the inclusion of such criticism within the narrative works to puncture the romanticism of his dream. Whilst the preacher's militancy and pan-Africanism appear empowering in comparison to the isolationist and reactionary stance of Ruby, the reader is prompted to question the seduction of Africa, and Morrison, I propose, goes on to put forward a different model of response to the dislocations of the black diaspora.

*Paradise* also problematises the Catholic Church, by illustrating the links between it and colonisation through the "Sisters Devoted to Indian and Colored People" working in Brazil and the establishment of a school to assimilate Native Americans in Oklahoma (223). Indeed, "CHRIST THE KING SCHOOL FOR NATIVE GIRLS," otherwise known as the Convent, provides an alternative example of institutional religion to the churches of Ruby (224). Just as the Morgans' Protestantism is allied with greed and repression, however, so Catholicism is shown to be complicit in other modes of imperialism. When founded, the Convent was envisaged as a pioneer outpost battling savagery, intended "to bring God and language to natives who were assumed to have neither; to alter their diets, their clothes, their minds; to help them despise everything that had once made their lives worthwhile and to offer them instead the privilege of knowing the one and only God and a chance, thereby, for redemption" (227). The creation of an establishment to re-educate Native Oklahomans during the 1920s thus illustrates the missionary project of organised religion. Christ the King attempted to assimilate its wards to European American ways of life and Christian worship. Morrison's narrative implicitly condemns this ambition, commenting satirically on "the privilege" of knowing a monotheistic God and the assumption that Natives are primitive, lacking cosmologies and civilisations of their own. This point is furthered by the story of Connie, an orphan rescued from Brazilian "street garbage" and converted by Mary Magna (223). The presence of Catholic "Sisters Devoted to Indian and Colored People" in South America recalls the connection between religion and European colonisation of the New World as well as introducing a wider sense of diaspora to the text (223).

Like Ruby, the Convent is also delineated as a space of patriarchal oppression. When the Sisters start their school in an old "embezzler's folly," they try to eradicate the decorative erotica that betrays the building's former function: "The embezzler's joy that could be demolished was" (*Paradise* 4). The licentious ornamentation, as representative of sensuality, not spiritual love, requires repression. Here Catholicism's emphasis on maintaining moral propriety, training women to chaste lives, divorcing religion from corporeality and enforcing censorship, is explored. Yet although "[t]he Sisters of the Sacred Cross chipped away all the nymphs [...], curves of their marble hair still strangle grape leaves and tease the fruit" around niches housing "Christ and his mother" (4).[9] In addition, despite their prudishness about the house built for pleasure, Morrison reveals the nuns are accompanied by Christian imagery not so very different from the condemned erotica. Whilst the mansion's "alabaster vagina" ashtrays may be lurid, equally so is the religious picture of "Saint Catherine of Siena" (72–74). This etching of a "woman. On her knees. A knocked-down look, cast-up begging eyes [...] pudding tits exposed on a plate," is illustrative of the damaging gender ideology implicit in Catholic teachings (74). It exposes how, although the nuns achieve a degree of independence from patriarchy in their remote all-female household, tied up with their religion is the figure of woman as abject supplicant, an obsession with self-sacrifice and a disturbing iconography of mutilated bodies.[10]

The story of Mary Magna's adoptee Connie explores both the process of cultural assimilation and the misogyny underlying the tenets of institutional Christianity. As a child at the Convent, Connie is taught "the gorgeous language made especially for talking to heaven" and the virtue of patience (*Paradise* 224).[11] This "lesson held [her] in good stead, and she hardly noticed the things she was losing. The first to go were the rudiments of her first language" (242). Thus the orphan's conversion was accompanied by the erosion of her native tongue of Portuguese and presumably her memories of home as well. Later when Mary Magna dies, Connie is left with "no identification, no insurance, no family, no work" (247). After thirty years of "offer[ing] her body and her soul to God's Son and His Mother as completely as if she had taken the veil herself," Consolata's deracination and personal sense of loss lead her to question her faith and the rewards promised by the Catholic Church for her labour and devotion (225).[12] This crisis engenders a turn towards alternative forms of worship, enabling Morrison to explore "uninstitutional religion" (Morrison quoted by Smith). Indeed, Connie synthesises different beliefs to forge her own faith, in particular rejecting Catholicism's elevation of the spiritual and corresponding denial of the fleshly.

When she exchanged chastity for a passionate affair with Deacon Morgan, letting "the feathers [...] come unstuck from the walls of a stone-cold womb," Consolata had recognised the Church's repression of the body and of female desire (*Paradise* 229). Yet in the end she found her relationship with the townsman to be as problematic as her former piety, "a simple mindless transfer.

From Christ, to whom one gave total surrender and then swallowed the idea of His flesh, to a living man" (240). Indeed, she equated her hunger for Deacon with devotion to Jesus and the consumption of a transubstantiated body in Holy Communion. Catholicism's fear of sensuality is echoed by the Protestant patriarch's reaction when, in a manifestation of her longing, Connie bites his lip and is promptly renounced for her act of dangerous carnality.[13] Only when she rejects the binary opposition of corporeality and spirituality can her dissatisfaction and such definitions be overcome.

Consolata's attraction to Deacon, however, is also linked to the issue of her cultural orphanhood or dislocation. Indeed, what she recognised in and sought to reclaim through him was something of the home that she was taken from by the church: she prays "Dear Lord, I didn't want to eat him. I just wanted to go home" (240). This longing for a different cultural connection indicates her deracination. The moment when Connie was first reminded of Brazil by the festivities of Ruby reveals the sensuality, physicality and "reckless joy" that she associates with her home and, by extension, other African Americans:

> [S]he heard a faint but insistent Sha sha sha. Sha sha sha. Then a memory of just
> such skin and just such men, dancing with women in the streets to music beating like
> an infuriated heart, torsos still, hips making small circles above legs moving so rapid-
> ly it was fruitless to decipher how such ease was possible [...] although they were liv-
> ing here in a hamlet, not in a loud city full of glittering black people, Consolata knew
> she knew them. (226)

Identifying with the townspeople and the pleasure they take in their holiday, their bodily ease and exuberance, Connie had embarked on an affair in part related to her homesickness for a city of "glittering black people." Unable to explain this longing to Mary Magna—"Sha sha sha. Sha sha sha, she wanted to say, meaning, he and I are the same"—she recognised a common bond, perhaps one shared by those displaced throughout the black diaspora (241).[14] "Sha sha sha" signals the kind of gratification or physical celebration missing from her life at the Convent, something found only when she reinvents her religion to encompass beliefs and practices from outside of the Judeo-Christian tradition.

Although Ruby's churches are, on the whole, associated with conservatism and orthodoxy, festivities like those at the founding of the town described above reveal the influence of an alternative cosmology. Indeed, within the community, the character of Lone DuPres possesses an unconventional reli-

gious faith that combines knowledge gained as a midwife and healer with institutional Protestantism. Occupying a liminal social position because of her
ability to "read minds" (viewed as ungodly) and her vocation ("[m]en scared
of us"), Lone nevertheless informs Consolata's development of a new kind of
worship (*Paradise* 272). She espouses a theology that rejects the division of the
earthly from the spiritual, cautioning her apprentice, "You need what we all
need: earth, air, water. Don't separate God from His elements. He created it
all" (244). Conceiving of "His works" holistically, Lone reads and draws on the
natural world and fosters Connie's own healing powers, telling her, "Let your
mind grow long and use what God gives you" (246). Although to begin with,
the Convent woman's "religious habits [are] entrenched," she does "practice,"
saving the life of Soane and Deacon's son and for a while keeping Mary
Magna alive, performing what she fears is "devilment" (244–246). Wary of
damning herself, Connie circumvents the Church's prohibitions about
"magic" by bending the rules (244). By naming her gift "in sight," she is able
to redefine her healing as not an act of intrusive entry or possession, but one
of vision and perception (247). This manipulation of language allows her to
negotiate doctrine whilst utilising her abilities, a step indicative of the reinven-
tions to come.[15]

Religious life is truly re-envisioned, however, when Connie leads the
women who have sought refuge at the former school on a journey of discov-
ery and transformation. Indeed, the South American orphan synthesises different beliefs to forge her own form of worship. Connie's mission is inspired
by an unusual visitation that introduces the suggestion of an alternative theology. Approached in the Convent garden by a stranger, she finds his mysterious
behaviour and conversation, if not his clothes and sunglasses, to indicate that
he is a divine messenger (see 252). Morrison's narrative leaves the status of this
figure ambiguous: he could be a revelation of God in the person of Jesus for—
intimating that his hostess should know him—his words recall those of the
newly resurrected Christ, or, alternatively, he could be a different deity altogether, a divine trickster/mediator calling on Connie to reinvent herself. The
latter possibility is reinforced by his attitude: he is playful, "flirtatious, full of
secret fun," rather than pious or commanding (252). His tea-coloured hair and
eyes "as round and green as new apples," in addition, offer a mirror image of
Connie herself (252). All this makes him a somewhat intriguing envoy, evocative of Eshu Elegbara, one of the orisha gods of Candomblé that Henry Louis
Gates Jr. discusses in *The Signifying Monkey*.[16]

The distinctive pattern of the visitor's speech is significant, too, as it does not follow that of standard American English. Indeed, his constructions, "I'm far country. Got a thing to drink? [...] I don't want see your girls. I want see you," echo Connie's own whilst she was losing her Portuguese: "Every now and then she found herself speaking and thinking in that in-between place, the valley between the regulations of the first language and the vocabulary of the second" (*Paradise* 252, 242). Connie recognises the messenger's phraseology and is drawn to it "like honey oozing from a comb" (252). She soon starts to reply in the same manner, "Look you in the house," her new mode of speech revealing a mixture of cultural influences (252).[17] The suggestion of South American survivals here anticipates the emergence of a religion informed by her Brazilian heritage.

After her visitation, Connie is transformed into "a new and revised Reverend Mother," growing "straight-backed and handsome," naming herself Consolata Sosa and assuming a role that can be likened to that of a *mãe-de-santo* or "mother-of-saints" in a *terreiro* or "temple" of Candomblé (265–266) (see Bouson 239).[18] Although concerned with redeeming the directionless lives of the "broken girls" who now occupy the Convent, her mission is very different from that of the nuns who adopted her (*Paradise* 222). Consolata sets forth her theology in a speech rejecting the separation of the material and the spiritual: "Hear me, listen. Never break them in two. Never put one over the other. Eve is Mary's mother. Mary is the daughter of Eve" (263).[19] She proposes that physical interactions and pleasures should not be divorced from spirituality, thus repudiating the Church's repression of sensuality. Her refusal of a hierarchical dichotomy that elevates the soul also revises gender ideology. Indeed, framing her teachings using the archetypal figures of Mary and Eve, Consolata rejects the polarisation enacted by patriarchal Christianity that situates Eve as the corrupter of Adam, responsible for his expulsion from Eden, and Mary as the immaculate vessel who facilitated the salvation of mankind, revered for her perfect love. Descended from Eve and cursed with childbirth, women are traditionally allied with the material, Mary alone being associated with the spiritual and so providing a paragon to be emulated.[20] By asserting that "Eve is Mary's mother. Mary is the daughter of Eve," Consolata presents an alternative and matrilineal holy family, her message being that one figure should not take precedence over the other. This new belief system, I would suggest, is informed by both her training in Catholicism and her memory of cultures evolved by slaves in South America.

This issue also has significance in terms of the history of African American oppression. For, by separating the material and spiritual spheres, slave owners could promise heavenly fulfilment after death for those slaves who uncomplainingly endured hardship and suffering in the present. Indeed, African American theologies are thought to have evolved in resistance to such divisions.[21] Consolata's religious imagination thus challenges the gender ideology, the denial of the bodily *and* the promises of deferred reward in heaven of the established church, allowing Morrison to engage critically with Christianity and its part in repressive diasporic encounters.

The starting point for Consolata's ministry is not the word of God, but rather a representation of the body: "*In the beginning* the most important thing was the template" (*Paradise* 263, emphasis added). On the cellar floor she has the Convent women create self-portraits that work as personal histories, connecting this image making with the exchange of their stories in a "loud dreaming" (264).[22] As the templates develop, signs of healing become evident. For example, instead of self-harming, Seneca starts to mark her cellar "silhouette" (263). This process of self-inscription, in addition, awakens the participants to their own physicality: "They had to be reminded of the moving bodies they wore, so seductive were the alive ones below" (254). Eventually, "unlike some people in Ruby, [they] are no longer haunted" (266). Connie's household hence rejects the patient acceptance and the repression of the flesh taught by Mary Magna. It also declines the self-serving religious sanctimony of the Morgans. Instead, the women celebrate their "moving bodies" and reconciled souls, becoming "bodacious black [and white] Eves unredeemed by Mary" (18).

The syncretic nature of the practices of Consolata and her followers is revealed, however, when they dance in a fall of much "longed for rain":

[T]hey entered it and let it pour like balm on their shaved heads and upturned faces[....] In places where rain is light the thrill is almost erotic. But those sensations bow to the rapture of holy women dancing in hot sweet rain. They would have laughed, had enchantment not been so deep[....] Seneca embraced and finally let go of a dark morning in State housing. Grace witnessed the successful cleansing of a white shirt that never should have been stained. Mavis moved in the shudder of rose of Sharon petals tickling her skin. Pallas, delivered of a delicate son, held him close while the rain rinsed away [...] all fear of black water. Consolata, fully housed by the god who sought her out in the garden, was the more furious dancer, Mavis the most elegant [....] Pallas, smoothing raindrops from her baby's head, swayed like a frond. (283)

This lyrical passage depicts the women, now described as "holy," participating in a sensual ritual that exorcises what troubles them from their traumatic pasts. Indeed, their shaved heads suggest renewal and rebirth, the balm of rain, an anointing. The reference to Consolata's visitor as a god, in addition, corroborates my identification of him as a deity from an alternative pantheon, an orisha of Candomblé. African-influenced forms of worship are suggested by the ecstatic dance itself, a celebration both physical and spiritual.[23] The Convent women's enchantment specifically recalls the initiation rites of Candomblé, during which initiates' heads are shaved; they learn the songs and movements of their particular orishas, and, when prepared to receive their god, they dance to induce a trancelike state of possession (see Bouson 240). Similarities between the activities at the Convent and the practices of Candomblé hence indicate that Morrison's narrative draws on African Brazilian religious culture to further its depiction of religion and to locate itself as part of a wider black diaspora.[24]

Consolata's distinctive vision of paradise also perhaps alludes to a remembered Brazilian landscape:

> She told [the women] of a place where white sidewalks met the sea and fish the color of plums swam alongside children. She spoke of fruit that tasted the way sapphires look [...] Of scented cathedrals made of gold where gods and goddesses sat in the pews with the congregation. Of carnations tall as trees. Dwarfs with diamonds for teeth. Snakes aroused by poetry and bells. Then she told them of a woman named Piedade, who sang but never said a word. (*Paradise* 263–264)

Connie evokes a fantastical and sensual heaven, the wonder and beauty of which captivate her audience. It is also, however, reminiscent of her home continent, because of both its fabulous nature, which echoes South American magic realist writing, and its coastal topography inhabited by a figure called "Piedade," a name that means "piety" or "compassion" in Portuguese. Consolata's dazzling vision thus signifies a symbolic return to or reconnection with Brazil. Hers is no sober or stately paradise, but rather a playful realm of jewels and fish, dwarfs and snakes, expression through poetry and song. Even religious worship appears to have been re-imagined, as in this land, the "gods and goddesses" sit amongst their followers. This implies poly- rather than monotheism and a form of divine authority different from that of Christianity. The deities' integration with the congregation evokes, in addition, the orishas of Candomblé, who join believers during rituals. The mysterious figure of Piedade, whose songs "could still a wave, make it pause in its curl listening to language it had not heard since the sea opened," is associated with ancient knowledge and uses a mesmerising musical mode of communication that, because she never *says* a word, subverts the Word of the patriarchal God of the Bible (285).

Significantly, Piedade is the focus of the final passage of Morrison's novel. Here, like Misner's black Christ, her image revises traditional Christian iconography:

> In ocean hush a woman black as firewood is singing. Next to her is a younger woman whose head rests on the singing woman's lap. Ruined fingers troll the tea brown hair. All the colors of seashells—wheat, roses, pearl—fuse in the younger woman's face. Her emerald eyes adore the black face framed in cerulean blue. Around them on the beach, sea trash gleams. Discarded bottle caps sparkle near a broken sandal. A small dead radio plays the quiet surf. There is nothing to beat solace which is what Piedade's song is about. (318)

Instead of an orthodox representation of Mary cradling her son's crucified body, the text offers a re-envisioned pietà, describing Piedade supporting Consolata on her lap. This is not a depiction of death, of mourning over a corpse, but one celebrating intimacy and life. The adored face "framed in cerulean blue" recalls Connie's relationship to her Mother Superior, whose "beautiful framed face" looked over her as a child, but also recalls the Virgin Mary (224). Yet, perhaps contrary to expectations of such images, Piedade is pictured as "black as firewood." *Paradise* thus invokes Catholic iconography while transforming, even appropriating it. Certainly Consolata's vision of a black Madonna constitutes a counternarrative to the institutional and assimilationist religion that "rescued" her.[25]

The image of heaven offered at the end of the novel, in addition, includes "sea trash," which grounds it in a worldly, rather than a celestial realm. Litter such as bottle tops and a broken radio, the detritus of modern technology and mass manufacture, signals materiality as well as the forces of consumption. The waste washed up on the shoreline resists the situation of paradise in a spiritual sphere, once more illustrating theological revision, but also perhaps evoking Brazil. Indeed, the items on the beach are reminiscent of some of the rites of mourning and burial performed in South America. Raboteau notes of African Brazilian funeral practices that "occasionally the cult objects formerly used by a member who has died are taken to the coast and placed in the sea to be received by his or her spirit" (30).[26] The fact that the trash "gleams" and "sparkle[s]" might even recall the rich decoration of religious icons.

This concluding pietà furthers my argument about the importance of Candomblé to the text. Brazilian religious practice often combines Catholicism, introduced by the European colonisers, with other beliefs derived from African and/or native cosmology. Morrison, I propose, draws on this mixed New World heritage in her depiction of Consolata's mission and vision of paradise. For example, by associating her Madonna with the sea, the author echoes the oceanic affinity of Yemanjá, another orisha god of Candomblé. Indeed, several of Yemanjá's characteristics can also be identified in Piedade. The novel hence alludes to the fusing of Christian figures with gods from other pantheons within diasporic American cultures. As Voeks notes, "One of the striking processes that occurred in Candomblé, as well as throughout the New World African religious landscape, was the intellectual integration of the Yoruba orixás ... with the deified saints of the Catholic Church" (59).[27] Here Consolata's formulation of a new religion synthesises cultural legacies from Brazil with the American Catholicism into which she was adopted. The Convent's revised belief system not only provides an alternative to institutional religion, but also enacts a positive model of creolisation.

My reading of the trajectory of *Paradise*, the devastating effects of Ruby's exclusivity and conformism and the evolution of an oppositional community at the Convent, can be furthered by reference to Edouard Glissant's ideas of *creolité* and *antillanité*. Although concerned with the specific history and culture of Martinique, in *Caribbean Discourse* Glissant also envisions a wider American configuration. Engendered by the displacements of slavery and colonisation in the New World, this nexus is one of disruption and alienation which nevertheless has "potential ... for the process of creolization" (Glissant 14). Glissant's paradigm of cross-cultural relations in the diaspora thus anticipates the work of Paul Gilroy in *The Black Atlantic*. Here Gilroy proposes a "transcultural, international formation" based upon exchanges and circulations of various kinds across the Atlantic Ocean, attempting to rethink modernity and mapping a dynamic space of enabling "routes" as well as a history of oppression (Gilroy 4, 9). Finding black diaspora peoples to be distinguished by the dislocations of their pasts, Glissant writes, "There is a difference between the transplanting (by exile or dispersion) of a people who continue to survive elsewhere and the transfer (by the slave trade) of a population to another place where they change into something different, into a new set of possibilities" (14). Yet he does not conceive processes of creolisation to be limited to such groups and refuses definitions of cultural exchange and mutation as corruptive, bastardising: "To assert peoples are creolized, that creolization has value, is to deconstruct in this way the category of 'creolized' that is considered as halfway between two 'pure' extremes" (Glissant 140).[28] Glissant also identifies the responses to colonisation of cultural diversion: "the mimetic impulse" and reversion, "the obsession with a single origin," in which "one must not alter the absolute state of being. To revert is to consecrate permanence, to negate contact" (16–18). Neither of these strategies alone is found to facilitate liberation: "Diversion is not a useful ploy unless it is nourished by reversion: not a return to the longing for origins, to some immutable state of Being, but a return to the point of entanglement, from which we were forcefully turned away; that is where we must ultimately put to work the forces of creolization, or perish" (Glissant 26). Glissant hence envisions a way forward from the effects of colonisation, going on to consider both instances of a failure to productively put to work the forces of creolisation and engagements that are more successful in turning towards the point of entanglement, renegotiating the experience of what he terms "nonhistory" (see Glissant 16–20).[29] This paradigm of cross-cultural relations and resistance can be usefully related to my discussion of the various communities in *Paradise* and in particular to Morrison's exploration of constructive and destructive religious practices.

In Consolata's reinvention of life at the Convent, Morrison evokes the syncretism of African Brazilian modes of worship. Connie subverts the European-originating Christian theology into which she had been assimilated and devises her own alternative, drawing on South American slave heritages. Hence *Paradise* incorporates an empowering use of creolisation, the reference to Brazilian culture apparently enabling Morrison to play out a process not evident within the American black community that she depicts. Whilst the churches of Ruby undoubtedly exemplify African American forms of Christianity, appropriating the Exodus story and, in the case of Misner, envisioning a black Christ, they can also be associated with the unproductive response of reversion. Both the Morgans' separatist and essentialist notion of community, and Misner's ideal of the originary time and space of an African home "consecrate permanence" and "negate contact." Consolata's mission, however, illustrates a turn towards the point of "entanglement" and implies a wider diasporic context.

The invocation of Brazil is significant both for its site outside of the United States—and therefore indicative of transnational black Atlantic relations—and for its particular history of slavery. Slavery persisted in Brazil until 1888, and slaves were transported there in far greater numbers than to North America, where after trading was prohibited, plantation owners depended on internal slave population growth.[30] The prolonged direct African influence of newly shipped slaves is thought to have contributed to the distinctiveness of African Brazilian culture. The Bahia region in particular received slaves traded from the coast of the Gulf of Guinea, including many Yorubas, whose African belief systems helped to shape Candomblé (Ramos 12, 82; see also Raboteau 40). This history undoubtedly informed the specific processes of creolisation at work in Brazil and perhaps Morrison's own creation of Consolata as a new and revised Reverend Mother. Yet whilst *Paradise* affirms Candomblé's African legacy for the empowering syncretism and connection it enables, it firmly rejects ethnic absolutism.[31] The Convent constitutes an inclusive, rather than exclusive cultural space: the dance is shared by all, black and white, North and South American.[32]

*Paradise*'s unusual epilogue concludes Morrison's exploration of religion by depicting the Convent women living an ambiguous afterlife. The narrative returns to the fatal attack that opened the novel, revealing that afterwards "[n]o bodies" could be found, "[e]ven the Cadillac was gone" (292). The fate of Consolata's followers is hence unclear, and the final section of the text, appearing to describe a space or dimension different to all those encountered so far, portrays them in turn participating in scenes of familial reconciliation (or at least assured indifference).[33] These suggest that the women have overcome their troubled pasts and moved on, yet remain physically embodied, experiencing both pain and sensory pleasure (see 310–317).[34]

The epilogue also presents the pietà featuring a black Virgin Mary and a second, mixed-race woman that I discussed earlier. In a fantastical land by the ocean, Consolata and Piedade sing of "the unambivalent bliss of going home to be at home" (318). "Another ship" approaches their shore, "but different, heading to port," carrying "lost and saved" (318). This mysterious vessel recalls those that once transported Africans across the Middle Passage yet, unlike the slave ships, it is "heading to port." The novel's closing scene hence evokes the dislocatory journeys of the black Atlantic as well as some form of homecoming. After this voyage, "crew and passengers" alike will share the fate of "shouldering the endless work they were created to do down here in paradise" (318). The phrase "down here" inverts the traditional ascent of the chosen to a celestial realm *and* hints at a South- (American?) bound geographical route. In addition, the labour awaiting the new arrivals appears to be egalitarian but also eternal—indicating, perhaps, a revision of both heaven and purgatory? Morrison thus concludes her trilogy in an unconventional but hopeful way, re-conceiving paradise itself as not "defined [...] by the absence of the unsaved, the unworthy and the strange" (306).[35]

The gratifying and redemptive nature of the image with which *Paradise* ends contrasts starkly with the spectacular failure of the utopian dream of Ruby.[36] Unlike her vision of the all-black town, Morrison's depiction of the Convent's holy community is celebratory. I propose that she here attempts to revise patriarchal Christianity, exposing damaging gender ideologies and the polarisation of the spiritual and the material, but also to investigate the complex evolution of New World cultures, drawing on the practices of Brazilian Candomblé. Thus Consolata's "unorganised magic" enacts an affirmative model of creolisation. *Paradise*'s symbolic evocation of South America foregrounds African cultural survivals but implies neither a nostalgic impulse to return to Misner's idealised African home nor the absolutism of the Morgans, thus avoiding the response of reversion. Ultimately, it would appear, the dislocations of the black diaspora necessitate new strategies of resistance.

## Notes

[1] The religion of Candomblé evolved in South America in part from "a set of beliefs, practices, and cosmology introduced by Yoruba slaves and freedmen" (Voeks 51). A syncretic faith, it also draws heavily upon Catholicism. Morrison's discussion of the original inspiration for *Paradise* corroborates my proposition that she makes reference to African Brazilian religion: "On a trip to Brazil in the 1980s, Ms. Morrison heard about a convent of black nuns who took in abandoned children and practised candomble.... The local populace considered them an outrage, and they were murdered by a posse of men. 'I've since learned it never happened.... But for me it was irrelevant. And it said much about institutional religion and uninstitutional religion, how close they are'" (Smith, *New York Times*).

[2] The author characterises Oklahoma, the novel's setting, thus: "You know you have liquor stores in Washington and banks in New York.... Well in Oklahoma there are churches.... It's a great place for religion.... There are churches everywhere ... two or three in a block, or just a large parking lot in the middle of no where and a nice church that people will go long distances to attend. In the little town of the novel there are three churches: a Methodist, a Baptist, and a Pentecostal" ("Blacks, Modernism and the American South" 14).

[3] The ministers' sermons during the 1960s and 1970s when "anger smallpoxed other places," illustrate their differences: "Evil Times, said Reverend Pulliam [...] Last Days, said Pastor Cary [...] the new preacher [...] said Good News: 'I will vanquish thine enemies before thine eyes', saith the Lord, Lord, Lord" (*Paradise* 102).

[4] Morrison has described Pulliam's as "the Old Testament 'Christ as Judge' very fundamentalist, puritan posture. The whole business of being a citizen in God's community as a test ... very stern." But "the progressive minister, who has had experience in the Civil Rights Movement, dislikes that intensely, and thinks of his religion, and the religion he wants to preach,

as kinder, more open, more individualistic, less punishing ... so he's in direct confrontation with the kinds of ministers who had flourished in Ruby" ("A Conversation with Toni Morrison").

⁵ Morrison comments that "religious fervor and devotion is in the main, a solace, a guide, a kind of protection against sin and evil, but it can freeze and become arrogant and prideful and ungenerous, and ... all religions and all people are vulnerable to that" ("A Conversation with Toni Morrison").

⁶ On invading the Convent, the Protestants view the aesthetics and practices of Catholicism with suspicion and misunderstanding: "graven idols were worshipped here. Tiny men and women in white dresses and capes of blue and gold stand on little shelves cut into niches in the wall. Holding a baby or gesturing, their blank faces fake innocence. Candles had obviously burned at their feet and [...] food had probably been offered as well" (*Paradise* 9). They condemn the women for a lack of piety: "in a place that once housed Christians—well, Catholics anyway—not a cross of Jesus anywhere" (7). In fact, as part of their spiritual reinvention, inhabitants have removed the symbols of orthodox religion: "Clean as new paint is the space where there used to be a Jesus" (12). In the cellar where the women have inscribed their self-portraits, the intruders "observe defilement and violence and perversions beyond imagination. Lovingly drawn filth carpets the stone floor [....] None dares step on it" (287). Such interpretations illustrate the townsmen's closed minds, but also their fears about female powers and perhaps of a woman-centred religion.

⁷ He asks, "Can't you even imagine what it must feel like to have a true home? I don't mean heaven. I mean a real earthly home [....] Not some place you went to and invaded and slaughtered people to get [....] Not some place you stole from the people living there, but your own home, where if you go back past your great-great-grandparents, past theirs, and theirs, past the whole of Western history, past the beginning of organized knowledge [...] on back to when rain was new, before plants forgot they could sing and birds thought they were fish, back when God said Good! Good!—there, right there where you know your own people were born and lived and died [....] That place. Who was God talking to if not to my people living in my home?" (*Paradise* 213).

⁸ She continues, "I just don't believe some stupid devotion to a foreign country—and Africa is a foreign country, in fact it's fifty foreign countries—is a solution for these kids [....] You want some foreign Negroes to identify with, why not South America? Or Germany, for that matter. They have some brown babies over there you could have a good time connecting with" (*Paradise* 210).

⁹ Elsewhere the narrative identifies other "traces of the sisters' failed industry. The female-torso candleholders in the candelabra hanging from the hall ceiling [...] The nursing cherubim emerging from layers of paint in the foyer. The nipple-tipped doorknobs" (*Paradise* 72).

¹⁰ The reference to St. Catherine of Siena, a figure who practiced extreme austerities and endured great physical hardships, is an interesting one as she also assumed an active role pleading many cases in the papal and political matters of fourteenth-century Italy. She, in addition, authored a significant body of correspondence and theological writing.

¹¹ "After arranging for her confirmation, [Mary Magna] had taken the young Consolata aside and together they would watch coffee brew or sit in silence at the edge of the garden" (*Paradise* 242).

[12] She asks of Mary Magna and her God, "Where is the rest of days, the aisle of thyme, the scent of veronica you promised? The cream and honey you said I had earned? [... T]he serenity duty grants us, the blessings of good works?" (*Paradise* 251).

[13] Deacon recoils from the "woman bent on eating him like a meal," seeing her as a "Salomé from whom he had escaped just in time" (*Paradise* 239, 280).

[14] As Matus points out, "The South American Consolata shares with African Americans a heritage from the era of slavery—a heritage that one day makes itself conscious when she sees some of the men of Ruby." This common heritage works to "shatter the narrow and exclusive notions of blackness to which the citizens of Ruby subscribe" (Matus 158).

[15] "Troubling as it was, yoking the sin of pride to witchcraft, she came to terms with it in a way she persuaded herself would not offend Him or place her soul in peril. It was a question of language. Lone called it 'stepping in.' Consolata said it was 'seeing in.' Thus the gift was 'in sight.' Something God made free to anyone who wanted to develop it" (*Paradise* 247). Her employment of the term "in sight" is particularly interesting, suggesting notions of truth and seeing connected to Enlightenment thought. Connie hence names her powers in a way that makes them acceptable in terms of orthodox theology, distancing herself from the associations with paganism that might accompany "stepping in." Her gift of vision, however, is accompanied by a gradual loss of real sight: "her eyes drained of what eyes were made for" until "she saw nothing clearly except what took place in the minds of others" (248). She believes this to be God's will: "a sunshot seared her right eye, announcing the beginning of her bat vision [...] Consolata had been spoken to" (241). This act of God is reminiscent of the biblical sun shot that struck Paul at the moment of his conversion.

[16] Raboteau writes, "Prominent among the African orisha and vodun of candomblé [is] Eshu (Legba), messenger of the gods [and] divine trickster" (19). "Of the music, myths, and forms of performance that the African brought to the Western Hemisphere," Gates chooses "one specific trickster figure that recurs with startling frequency in black mythology in Africa, the Caribbean, and South America" to unify his investigation of black literary tradition, vernacular and the double-voiced. This is the divine trickster figure of Yoruba mythology, Esu-Elegbara, associated with mediation, ambiguity, sexuality, humour and double-voicedness (Gates 4–5). In Morrison's allusion, the trickster reflects Connie's own mixed race appearance and surely reminds her of her South American cultural heritage.

[17] This shift is also evident in her speech to the Convent women: for example, "My child body, hurt and soil," "I agreed her," "so I wondering" (*Paradise* 263).

[18] This figure "represents the principal line of communication between the material world of mortals and the spiritual world of the deities" (Voeks 63). Connie's reinvention begins with a ceremonial meal at which she announces to the women "I call myself Consolata Sosa. If you want to be here you do what I say. Eat how I say. Sleep when I say. And I will teach you what you are hungry for [....] Someone could want to meet you" (*Paradise* 262). Even her preparation of the food, charted in lyrical detail and meant to stimulate the senses and satisfy bodily needs, hints at a new form of worship (see 252–262).

[19] Her oration problematises the Catholic exaltation of the eternal soul for its concomitant denial of the mortal body that made her "flesh [...] so hungry for itself it ate [Deacon]." From her experiences Connie concludes that too often "bones" or materialities are divided from spirituality (*Paradise* 263).

20 In her seminal examination of the cult of the Virgin Mary, *Alone of All Her Sex*, Marina Warner writes that for the patriarchal Church, "woman is the cause of the Fall, the wicked temptress, the accomplice of Satan, and the destroyer of mankind" (Warner 58). As Lucy Sargisson outlines, within the contexts of Western philosophical and theological traditions, "Woman, as represented by Eve, is commonly seen to be the embodiment of the privation or absence of spirit. Woman is pure (or rather impure) matter" (134). This association engenders degradation, but also demonisation of the kind illustrated by the men of Ruby.

21 Noel Erskine writes, "Black and Decolonising theologies contend that Black religion ... refused to ape European norms in dividing the world into the material and spiritual spheres. This division was one way in which the master sought to control Black people, by using missionary theology to instill in them the notion that the economic order was preparatory for the spiritual world which one could access only through death.... [Black Christians] claimed that the world in which slaves were brutalized and sought to make sense of their suffering ... was the world in which they experienced the presence of the divine through the working of the spirit" (Erskine xvi). Baby Suggs's preaching in *Beloved* asserts that "the prize," God's grace, is found through self-love and the affirmation of black flesh (*Beloved* 89).

22 "[T]hey step easily into the dreamer's tale," accompanying Mavis shopping whilst her twin babies suffocate in the car, feeling the terror of Pallas swimming to escape rapists and a treacherous mother, negotiating the tear gas and violence of a Detroit street protest along with Gigi, and enduring abandonment and prostitution with Seneca (*Paradise* 264). The "dreaming" is perhaps meant to be evocative of the Australian aboriginal *alcheringa* or sacred dreamtime. "The templates drew them like magnets [....] They understood and began to begin. First with natural features: breasts and pudenda, toes, ears and head hair. Seneca duplicated in robin's egg blue one of her more elegant scars [...] Gigi drew a heart locket around her body's throat [...] said it was a gift from her father which she had thrown in the Gulf of Mexico [...] Pallas had put a baby in her template's stomach. When asked who the father was, she said nothing but drew next to the baby a woman's face with [...] a crooked fluffy mouth[.... D]ays passed uncut from night as careful etchings of body parts and memorabilia occupied them" (*Paradise* 265).

23 In West Africa, Raboteau notes, "Dancing, drumming, and singing play a constant and integral part in the worship of gods and the ancestors.... So essential are music and dance to ... religious expression that it is no exaggeration to call them 'danced religions'" (15).

24 Morrison's posing of an alternative form of worship has not always been received kindly or identified as such. According to Geoffrey Bent, Consolata's "healing goes beyond mixing potions and medicinal teas; the woman literally raises the dead by 'going inside' people. During the climactic downpour, Consolata has her damaged flock paint things like fetuses and scars in the outlines she traces around their bodies on the floor. Then, after a rambling speech full of incantatory gibberish ('My flesh is so hungry for itself it ate him'), she has them shave their heads and dance naked in the rain, which miraculously washes away their traumas. One emerges from the bathos of a scene like this with the realization that magic, in such a context, has more to do with the sentimental than the supernatural" (Bent 148).

25 It is hinted earlier that Piedade is of African origin: "At night she took the stars out of her hair and wrapped [Consolata] in its wool" (*Paradise* 285). She has significance in terms of the representations of the Virgin Mary as black that are found within churches and shrines around the world. Ean Begg's study of this phenomenon offers a comprehensive analysis.

Discussing the Black Virgin's reputed powers, he writes, "She has always helped her supplicants to circumvent the rigidities of patriarchal legislation and is traditionally on the side of physical processes—healing the sick, easing the pangs of childbirth, making the milk flow. She knows how to break rigid masculine rules, bringing dead babies back to life long enough to receive baptism and escape from limbo to paradise, looking with tolerance on the sins of the flesh as when she acts as midwife to a pregnant abbess or stands in for a truant nun tasting for a time the illicit pleasures of sin" (Begg 28). Begg even catalogues a Black Virgin of considerable reputation in Brazil: "Aparecida de Norte Sâo Paulo ... Nossa Senhora de Aparecida, formerly do Conceiçâo. Brazil's most venerated religious image; terra cotta; 39 cm; standing on crescent moon in prayer; no child.... Many miracles; living cult. The Brazilian goddess of the seas and mother of the earth, Jemanja, is represented as black" (Begg 163). It has been suggested that the Black Madonna may have Gnostic Christian origins, a possibility that might relate to Morrison's choice of an epigraph from the *Nag Hammadi* for *Paradise*.

26 This refers to religious observances followed in West Africa: "The graves of the deceased of some West African peoples are elaborately decorated with the personal effects of the individuals buried there" (Raboteau 13). And within slave communities and the black diaspora, "cups, saucers, bottles, pipes, and other effects were left for the spirit of the deceased; frequently these items were broken or cracked in order to free their spirits and thereby enable them to follow the deceased" (Raboteau 83–85).

27 "Thus Oxalá is syncretized to Jesus; Iansã to Saint Barbara; Yemanjá to the Virgin Mary" (Voeks 61). Raboteau writes, "The most immediately apparent innovation that *Santeria*, *Shango* and *Candomblé* have brought to African theological perspectives is the identification of African gods with Catholic saints. Initially the veneration of saints must have provided the slaves with a convenient disguise for secret worship of African gods.... Furthermore, Catholic popular piety has long been open to syncretism with 'pagan' belief and practice" (Raboteau 22–23).

28 According to Michael Dash, in his "definition of the Caribbean in terms of openness, of *errance* and of an intricate, unceasing branching of cultures, Glissant is careful not to claim an exclusive right to this experience by Caribbean peoples. In deconstructing the notions of pure and impure, he sees the world in terms of ceaseless cultural transformation and subverts the old temptation to essentialist and exclusivist strategies" (Dash in Glissant 147).

29 His notion of nonhistory indicates not a lack of history, but a lack of a coherent or sedimented sense of the past for displaced populations.

30 Arthur Ramos cites the Brazilian historian Calogeras as claiming that over four centuries, eighteen million slaves were imported to Brazil (6).

31 This in itself reflects the nature of New World encounters: "The vestiges of these native African systems in the Americas are uniquely American: not distant outposts of ancient cultures, but amalgams of African, European, Amerindian, and other traditions" (Voeks 4).

32 Although Morrison's creation of the Convent as a female space has been interpreted as absolutist along lines of sex, in fact the women from the start have taken in male refugees as well as female (namely the alcoholic Vietnam veteran Menus Jury) and in the climactic scene of their rain dance, Pallas' newly born son forms a part of this vision of fulfilment.

33 This other dimension is hinted at when Anna Flood and Reverend Misner visit the Convent and become aware of some kind of portal or entrance. In the garden, near Connie's chair, "they saw it. Or sensed it, rather, for there was nothing to see. A door, she said later. 'No,

a window,' he said, laughing [...] focusing on the sign rather than the event [....] Anything to avoid reliving the shiver or saying out loud what they were wondering. Whether through a door needing to be opened or a beckoning window already raised, what would happen if you entered? What would be on the other side? What on earth would it be? What on earth?" (*Paradise* 305). Later, at a child's funeral, looking "at the coffin lid [Misner again] saw the window in the garden, felt it beckon toward another place—neither life nor death—but there, just yonder, shaping thoughts he did not know he had" (307). This signals the space of possibility written into the discourse that follows. Bouson calls it "a magical scene of escape and resurrection," whereas Matus refers to "the miracle of life transferred to a new realm or mode" (Bouson 213; Matus 164).

34 Possibly Morrison here alludes to African notions of the living dead. John Mbiti writes, "The living-dead are still 'people,' and have not yet become 'things,' 'spirits' or 'its'. They return to their human families from time to time, and share meals with them, however symbolically" (82).

35 As Justine Tally observes, "Far from a utopia built on exclusion and isolation, Morrison conceptualizes 'paradise' (with a small 'p') as an earthly endeavor constructed of a common bond and including all people, not just an exclusive few, 'crew and passengers' alike" (93). However, the epilogue has not always been favourably received: "Morrison wraps up the whole enormous tale with a rather self-conscious magical-realist conclusion, in which the shot women are snatched off into a mystical afterlife" (Walter 13); "the novel's one surreal set-piece feels like a hasty afterthought, clumsily grafted on to try to kick start the story to another level" (Kakutani).

36 Indeed, Tally writes, "The reader cannot help but relate the sterility of the isolationist, class-conscious, 'all-black' community of Ruby to the fecund, anarchic but vibrant inclusiveness of the 'raceless' Convent" (31).

## Works Cited

Bammer, Angelika. *Partial Visions: Feminism and Utopianism in the 1970s*. London: Routledge, 1991.

Begg, Ean. *The Cult of the Black Virgin*. London: Arkana, 1996.

Bent, Geoffrey. "Less Than Divine: Toni Morrison's *Paradise*." *The Southern Review* 35.1 (1999): 145–149.

Borger, Julian. "Paradise Lost." *Guardian*, October 6,1998.

Bouson, Brooks J. *Quiet As It's Kept: Shame, Trauma, and Race in the Novels of Toni Morrison*. Albany: State University of New York Press, 2000.

Cliff, Michelle. "Great Migrations." *The Village Voice*, January 27, 1998.

Conner, Marc C., ed. *The Aesthetics of Toni Morrison: Speaking the Unspeakable*. Jackson: University Press of Mississippi, 2000.

Denard, Carolyn. "Paradise." *Ms*, 8.5 ( ): 80.

Duvall, John N. *The Identifying Fictions of Toni Morrison: Modernist Authenticity and Postmodern Blackness*. New York: Palgrave, 2000.

Erskine, Noel Leo. *Decolonizing Theology: A Caribbean Perspective*. Trenton, NJ: Africa World Press, 1998.

Gates, David. "Trouble in Paradise." *Newsweek*, January 12, 1998.

Gates, Henry Louis Jr. *The Signifying Monkey: A Theory of African-American Literary Criticism*. New York: Oxford University Press, 1988.

Gilroy, Paul. *The Black Atlantic: Modernity and Double Consciousness*. London: Verso, 1993.

Glissant, Edouard. *Caribbean Discourse: Selected Essays*. Translated by J. Michael Dash. Charlottesville: University Press of Virginia, 1989.

Gray, Paul. "Paradise Found." *Time*, January 19, 1998.

Ireland, Rowan. *Kingdoms Come: Religion and Politics in Brazil*. Pittsburgh: University of Pittsburgh Press, 1991.

Kakutani, Michiko. "Worthy Women, Unredeemable Men." *New York Times*, January 6, 1998.

Klinghoffer, David. "Black Madonna." *National Review*, February 9, 1998.

Leonard, John. "Shooting Women." *Nation*, January 26, 1998.

Lubiano, Wahneema, ed. *The House that Race Built*. New York: Vintage Books, 1998.

Mantel, Hilary. "No Disco, No TV, No Diner, No Adultery." *Literary Review* April (1998): 26–27.

Matus, Jill. *Toni Morrison*. Manchester: Manchester University Press, 1998.

Mbiti, John S. *African Religions and Philosophy*. Oxford: Heinemann, 1989.

Morrison, Toni. 1987. *Beloved*. London: Picador, 1988.

———. "Blacks, Modernism and the American South: An Interview with Toni Morrison." With Carolyn Denard. *Studies in the Literary Imagination* 31.2 (1998): 1–16.

———. "Black Pearls." With Katharine Viner. *Guardian*, March 24, 1998.

———. "A Conversation with Toni Morrison." April 21, 2001. http://www.borders.com/features/ab99013.html

———. "Interview with Angels Carabi." *Belles Lettres* 10.2 (1995): 40–43.

———. "Morrison's Slice of Paradise." With Deirdre Donahue. *US Today*, April 21, 2001. http://www.usatoday.com/life/enter/books/b128.htm

———. *Paradise*. London: Chatto & Windus, 1998.

———. "Paradise Found: A Talk with Toni Morrison." With A. J. Verdelle. *Essence*, February 1998, 78–80.

———. "The Roots of Paradise." *Economist*, September 10, 1999. http://www.economist.com/archive/view.cgi

———. *Song of Solomon*. 1977. London: Vintage, 1998.

———. "This Side of Paradise." With Anna Mulrine. *US News*, April 21, 2001. http://www.usnews.com/usnews/issue/980119/19new.htm

Murphy, Joseph M. *Working the Spirit: Ceremonies of the African Diaspora*. Boston: Beacon Press, 1994.

Patell, Cyrus R. K. *Negative Liberties: Morrison, Pynchon, and the Problem of Liberal Ideology*. Durham, NC: Duke University Press, 2001.

Raboteau, Albert J. *Slave Religion: The "Invisible Institution" in the Antebellum South*. New York: Oxford University Press, 1978.

Sargisson, Lucy. *Contemporary Feminist Utopianism*. London: Routledge, 1996.

Schwarz, Roberto. *Misplaced Ideas: Essays on Brazilian Culture*. London: Verso, 1992.

Shockley, Evelyn E. "Paradise." *African American Review* 33.4 (1999): 718–719.

Smith, Dinitia. "Toni Morrison's Mix of Tragedy, Domesticity and Folklore." *New York Times*, 8 January 1998.

Tally, Justine. *Paradise Reconsidered: Toni Morrison's (Hi)stories and Truths*. FORECAAST 2. Hamburg: Lit Verlag, 1999.

Voeks, Robert A. *Sacred Leaves of Candomblé: African Magic, Medicine and Religion in Brazil*. Austin: University of Texas Press, 1997.

Wafer, Jim. *The Taste of Blood: Spirit Possession in Brazilian Candomble*. Philadelphia: University of Pennsylvania Press, 1991.

Walter, Natasha. "How Paradise Was Lost." *Guardian*, March 26, 1998.

Warner, Marina. *Alone of All Her Sex: The Myth and the Cult of the Virgin Mary*. London: Weidenfeld & Nicolson, 1976.

Wood, James. "The Color Purple." *New Republic*, March 2, 1998.

# 10

# THE MASTER'S TOOLS:
## MORRISON'S *PARADISE* AND THE PROBLEM
## OF CHRISTIANITY

*Shirley A. Stave*

That Toni Morrison has repeatedly, throughout the body of her work, invoked Christian imagery, symbolism, and language has become common knowledge to anyone even casually familiar with her works. From such obvious gestures as titling one of her novels *Song of Solomon* to the more subtle use of biblical myth, as for instance, in *Beloved*,[1] Morrison has required her readers to engage with the significance of the Christian church and its often contradictory teachings. To dismiss the centrality of Christianity in her work as simply an articulation of the significance of the church to the lives of African Americans—in other words, to view it as part and parcel of the setting—is, I would argue, naïve. However, to assume that Morrison's use of biblical themes and Christian theology is straightforward or that she endorses Christian teaching is, I believe, equally oversimplistic. Rather, we are better served by questioning how Morrison may be "signifying," to use Henry Louis Gates's often cited term,[2] on her biblical referents, using her narratives strategically to destabilize Christian theology and to contest its vision. Nowhere is her positioning more clearly articulated than her novel *Paradise*, in which, through her use of the techniques of magic realism, Morrison challenges Christianity—not to mention Western cultural epistemology—through a revitalizing exploration of true spirituality.

In presenting working versions of this essay at various conferences, I have encountered two forms of resistance to my argument. Scholars well-read in Gnostic studies argue that the radical ending of *Paradise*, with its very earth-centered paradise and its mother goddess Piedade, is entirely consistent with Gnostic views of life, death, and divinity. Therefore, the argument goes, Morrison's text should not be read as oppositional to, but rather, consistent with, Christianity. While I am well aware that the novel's epigraph comes from one of the Gnostic texts found at Nag Hammadi, I do not believe that requires one to read the entire text through Gnostic theology, especially given that internal evidence, as opposed to what we might call the extra-diegetic apparatus of the epigraph, includes nods in the direction of decidedly un-Christian theologies (more on this later). Additionally, while my study of theology from positions both within the church in the past, and outside of it now, have made me realize that many of those professing various Christian doctrines often have very little knowledge of the actual stand their own denominations take on a variety of theological issues,[3] my understanding of Gnosticism leads me to claim that much of it is inconsistent with most, if not all, of the contemporary American forms of Christianity, most specifically the ones Morrison represents within *Paradise*, i.e., Methodist, Baptist, and Pentecostal.[4] Finally, however, we must consider Morrison's own claim that in *Paradise* she has explored "organized religion and unorganized magic as two systems" (Boursin 209). On that basis alone, I find the attempts to read Connie's theology as in some fashion Christian to be untenable.

The second form of resistance I have encountered centers on my use of the term "magic realism," which I use as a descriptive term for a genre of fiction that specifically challenges Western cultural epistemology and in many cases insists on the primacy of the spiritual world, which can and does manifest itself routinely in the material world. Some listeners apparently feel the term "magic" is derogatory, suggesting charlatanism, perhaps even a mockery of the beliefs of spiritual people. However, in an excellent collection of essays on magic realism, Wendy B. Faris presents ample support for using that term to discuss books from a position of respect. She argues that "realism has been a European, or first world, export, in conjunction with its mimetic program, its claim to fashioning an accurate portrait of the world" (180). She goes on to point out that magic realism becomes a way for non-first world people to reclaim and re-fashion their own worlds. I would add simply this: for most of the world, throughout most of history, what some would choose to label "magic" was called "knowledge." Even now, far more people believe in the power of prayer, the workings of *gris-gris*, the existence of ghosts, the effectiveness of healing through energy, the possibility of miracle, the efficacy of spells, and the power of visualization, than do not. And Richard Dawkins's rants about superstitions notwithstanding,[5] these people base their beliefs on first-hand experience. "Science" may not be able to validate their knowledge through experiment, but for many people, that fact does not change what they know to be true. Morrison herself states that while she considers African Americans to be a "very practical people," "within that practicality we also accept what I suppose could be called superstition and magic. Which is another way of knowing things" (cited in Foreman 298). Furthermore, in her work on magic realism, Kristy Rose Leech argues that a vital component of the genre of magic realism is its valuing of "[t]he inexpressible, the transcendent, that which is beyond empiricism and language" (17). One concept that falls fully and completely within that area is religion, the spiritual, which falls outside the parameters of scientific knowledge. Leech goes on to speak of the genre's "resistance to closure and singular interpretations" (38) and claims that the authors of magic-realist texts "revitalize the act of reading through their open endings and invitation to multiple interpretations" (41). Throughout *Paradise*, Morrison repeatedly disables closure and refuses explanation, leaving scenes and characters open to readerly analysis. However, through her paralleling of the town of Ruby, associated with the Law of the Father, patriarchal religion, and racial and sexual oppression, with the Convent, a house under constant transformation, inhabited by cast-off women who undergo spiritual renewal, Morrison enables the reader's rejection of Ruby's ossified sense of the religious in favor of the mystery and the miracle of the Convent's true spirituality.

*Paradise* situates Christianity prominently within its narrative diegesis, which immediately enables the possibility of "magic" and the other-worldly, since much of what traditional Christians believe (transubstantiation, the assumption of the Virgin, the resurrection of Jesus, the Second Coming, not to mention the countless miracles performed by Moses and Jesus, among others) challenges what scientific-minded individuals would consider possible. Morrison very consciously parallels the biblical exodus of the Israelites with the post-slavery wilderness wandering of a group of "eight-rock" families seeking to establish an all-Black community removed from sites of oppression. Specifically, the text mirrors the divine intervention central to the original exodus, in which Jahweh's chosen people are led by a cloud by day and a pillar of fire by night; here, the founding families are led to Haven by a mysterious small man visible only to the group's leader, his son, and an occasional child. Summoned by Big Papa through a night of prayer that recalls Christ's experience in Gethsemene, the mysterious figure arrives to the sound of thundering, earth-shaking footsteps, heard by all and never, I would argue, narratively questioned—footsteps that reverberate again once the wanderers have arrived at their destination and the man vanishes. The parallel accounts of other-worldly intervention in human affairs impart a spiritual base for the founding of Haven; additionally, they insist on the possibility of miracle, not as existing only in mythic time, but as capable of happening in history, in the present. However, although the story takes on sacred status among the residents of Haven, as the older generation who experienced the mystical encounter passes, the nature of the belief in the story shifts. Sixty years later, when the town is dying, Steward and Deacon Morgan, fueled by the narrative of their grandfathers' heroism, persuade fifteen families to leave Haven to begin again elsewhere. However, they no longer seek or even desire divine intervention. In response to the belief of their parents that God would take care of them, the twins believe, "He did, safe to say, until He stopped" (16). For the twins, the possibility of miracle in their actual lives is not credible. Self-reliant to a point far beyond arrogance, they put their faith in their own leadership and leave God to His own devices. Ruby, unlike Haven, has no spiritual grounding, in spite of the three churches that grow up in the town. Rather, the bank owned by Deacon Morgan is the center for the town's vision of itself.

It becomes apparent that Deacon and Steward Morgan wish to halt the march of time, petrifying Ruby forever at the moment of their glory, with no outside (or inside) influences effecting change. Although as young men, the two brothers created a means by which they could replicate the heroism of their fathers and grandfathers, now as older men, they refuse the younger generation their turn to do the same. The crisis in Ruby revolves around the partially legible inscription on the Oven, originally built in Haven as a use-object and moved to Ruby, where it has taken on the weight of a dead signifier. However, Morrison's descriptions of the careful construction of the Oven when the original wanderers arrived in Haven and of its disassembling when "the ex-soldiers broke [it] up, […]and loaded it into two trucks even before they took apart their own beds" (16)—"[packing] it in straw like it was a mewing lamb" (86)—links the Oven with the Ark of the Covenant that featured significantly in the biblical Israelites' sense of identity as God's chosen people. Not surprisingly, then, when intergenerational tension springs up in Ruby, the Oven, so tied to these wanderers' sense of identity, becomes a site of contestation. At a town meeting called to discuss the situation, one of the young men says of the Oven, "It's our history too, sir. Not just yours" (86), effectively arguing for inclusion into the community, for recognition as equally chosen. Deek's reply—"That Oven already has a history. It doesn't need you to fix it"—forecloses the next generation's desire for entrance into narrative, into history, which, like spirituality, is grounded in the past, is finished. Only those sanctified by actually having been in the presence of the Old Fathers are permitted to "touch" the Oven with their interpretations, their meaning, just as the biblical Ark was off-limits to those not of the priesthood. In each case, transgression is treated very seriously. Whereas the biblical Uzzah is struck down by Jahweh when he touches the Ark to keep it from toppling over (I Chronicles 13: 9–10), in Ruby, Steward once again appropriates Jahweh's authority and claims, "If you, any one of you, ignore, change, take away, or add to the words in the mouth of that Oven, I will blow your head off just like you was a hood-eye snake" (87).

The differences between the earlier Haven and its later incarnation as Ruby become apparent also through the process of the naming of each town. Whereas the name Haven indicates the site is a sanctuary, a refuge for all the pilgrims, an earthly h(e)aven, Ruby is named for the woman who died upon arriving there. Significantly, she is the sister of the Morgan twins and the mother of K. D., hence both linking her with the patriarchal authority grounded in the past even as she is removed from the power structure upon which the town is founded. Reading the founding of Ruby through Lacanian theory, we can see how this "civilization" is predicated upon the death of the mother and exists as a representation of the Symbolic Order. In Judith Butler's summary of Lacan,

> the paternal law structures all linguistic signification, termed "the Symbolic," and so becomes a universal organizing principle of culture itself. This law creates the possibility of meaningful language and, hence, meaningful experience, through the repression of primary libidinal drives, including the radical dependency of the child on the maternal body. Hence, the Symbolic becomes possible by repudiating the primary relationship to the maternal body. The "subject" who emerges as a consequence of this repression becomes a bearer or proponent of this repressive law. The libidinal chaos characteristic of that early dependency is now fully constrained by a unitary agent whose language is structured by that law. This language, in turn, structures the world by suppressing multiple meanings (which always recall the libidinal multiplicity which characterized the primary relation to the maternal body) and instating univocal and discrete meanings in their place. (314)

Symbolically, the death of Ruby forecloses the possibility of the extension of the child's connection with the maternal body even as it allows the men of Ruby to enter the Symbolic Order, the world of law and language in which they quite literally act as enforcers of the repression of libidinal multiplicity in their assault on the Convent. Not surprisingly, the Convent is specifically seen as destructive in that one might argue it exists outside the Symbolic Order, but that, in embodying the Kristevian semiotique, it ruptures that Order. In the convent, libidinal chaos is not restrained and fixed meaning is not imposed; the binaries upon which the Symbolic Order is predicated do not exist there. The exclusively female community of the Convent does not define itself in opposition to men, nor does racial duality function there; since we never learn who the "white girl" is, obviously her color is irrelevant to the other women there. Finally, through the relationships of Mary Magna with Connie, Connie with the lost women, and Mavis with her dead children, the "child" here has continual access to the maternal body.

While the attempt of the Ruby men to resist what they perceive as the lawless sexuality of the Convent women is obvious, equally significant is their relationship to the Word, to language. The biblical signifying that Morrison employs allows us to identify their often reiterated narration of the original Disallowing of their forebears and their own founding of Ruby with sacred text, the language that itself partakes of the act and becomes consecrated, untouchable, unchangeable. Each retelling of the original story exactly replicates all the previous tellings (although the numbers are changing as fewer families are deemed worthy to be "holy"). The narrative has ossified, resisting any variations and with it, any possibility of the teller or the hearer entering the narration with any agency of his/her own. The stasis at the heart of the town's spiritual life is reflected in the biological stasis of the narrative's central players: Dovey has had a series of miscarriages, Soane's children have all died, Arnette's baby was born prematurely and died, and Sweetie's children are all severely physically and mentally handicapped.

What becomes apparent in the Haven/Ruby narrative is that, in spite of the obvious multiple allusions to the Hebrew Bible and the New Testament, no redemptive figure in the form of a Christ appears anywhere. From the perspective of the Ruby residents, the biblical parallels with their own story end with the nativity, with the proud and defiant Marys and Josephs, whom they see not as the original holy family, but rather as their own grandparents, turned away from town after town for their dark "eight-rock" skin. In their yearly re-enactment of the original Disallowing, the place of the baby Jesus is filled by a doll—empty, lifeless, incapable of agency. Convinced of their own righteousness, having projected "sin" or fragmentation elsewhere, the citizens of Ruby embrace neither a suffering nor a resurrected Jesus. However, Morrison audaciously does posit a Christ figure within the novel, albeit one very subversive of the Christian tradition: Connie, the presiding figure at the Convent.

Saved from a life of poverty and abuse early in life by a nun who later becomes Mother Superior of the Convent, Connie has lived almost the entirety of her life in a community of clerical women, although she herself has never taken holy orders. Her formal name, Consolata, would appear to align her with the Holy Mother, herself always depicted as a source of consolation and understanding, but Morrison sets Connie on a far different path from that traveled by the Blessed Virgin. Connie's devotion, we come to realize, is specific to the Mother Superior herself, rather than to any divine being, although for years Connie does live a nun's life with its cycle of prayer, service, and obedience. However, during those years, she also has a brief, intense love affair with Deacon Morgan, which ends as a result of his terror at her sexual voraciousness. Also, during those years, Connie, as a result of her interactions with Lone, the ancient mystical healer who was adopted by the eight-rock wanderers on the way to Haven, learns that she possesses psychic gifts, although Lone insists such gifts are available "to anyone who wanted to develop [them]" (247). Lone requires Connie's abilities first when Scout Morgan, the son of Connie's former lover, dies in an automobile accident. Lone pressures Connie, "Go inside him. Wake him up" (245), which Connie does. However, raising her own Lazarus from the dead creates anxieties for Connie not faced by her biblical predecessor: she fears she has dabbled in the black arts. Her terror at being abandoned once again, this time as a result of the imminent death of the Mother Superior, overrides her guilt, and she continues working magic: "So she had practiced, and although it was for the benefit of the woman she loved, she knew it was anathema, that Mary Magna would have recoiled in disgust and fury knowing her life was prolonged by evil" (247).

Once Connie does grant the Mother Superior's wish for death, she undergoes a long mourning, a dark night of the soul, during which she withdraws from life, remaining in a drunken stupor in the basement of the Convent while the assorted outcast women who have taken up residence there provide for her basic needs. Carol Christ claims, "For the mystic, the dark night of the soul is a period of purgation in which all ties with the conventional world are broken in anticipation of revelation and union with a higher source of being and value. The 'dark night' is a metaphor for the sense of emptiness felt by those who have broken their ties with conventional sources of values, but have not yet discovered their grounding in new sources" (10). Such is the case for Connie. Through her intense pain, loneliness, and despair, Connie comes to understand that the Catholic faith she has practiced is inadequate for her needs. At the same time, she re-evaluates her spiritual abilities and challenges the departed Mother Superior, both to make good on her promises to her young charge and to understand the significance of human love: "Where is the rest of days, the aisle of thyme, the scent of veronica you promised?[…] Was what I did for love of you so terrible?" (251) At the same time, she takes her leave of Christ, telling him, "I'll miss you […] I really will" (251). That phase of her life complete, Connie is immediately visited by a mysterious man, who causes her to begin speaking in the cadences of her childhood tongue, and who, more significantly, looks like a male version of her, with his long tea-colored hair and his eyes "round and green as new apples" (252). Although Morrison provides little other information about the man and most emphatically does not tie him to a fixed meaning, I would argue that he is Connie's animus, the god-self to her goddess-self, the only male divinity she need worship, since he is, in essence, a part of herself. J. Brooks Bouson, in a similar yet differently articulated interpretation of the mysterious male, refers to him as "the beloved: the authentic and divine part of the self hidden behind the socially constructed layers of the personality" (209). From this point on, Connie takes seriously her mission as a savior to the lost women of the Convent, but the redemption she offers differs radically from that of her New Testament counterpart.

Intriguingly, Dovey Morgan, wife of Steward, also is visited—on repeated occasions—by a mysterious man who is also never explained. However, if we read the two scenes involving visitations by mysterious men against one another, we can arrive at some understanding of how Dovey's visitor might function in the narrative. Although he is not identified as looking like her—we are told that he is at least twenty years younger than she is—he, like, Connie's visitor, moves mysteriously and speaks without moving his lips. His entrance into the narrative is marked by a flurry of persimmon colored butterflies that looks as if "a mighty hand dug deep into a giant sack and threw fistfuls of petals into the air" (90). The vivid color of the insects, along with their association with the flower gardens of the women of Ruby, allow us to read this man who speaks without language as antithetical to the Symbolic Order instituted by the Ruby patriarchs. We learn early on that the Morgan twins' obsession with creating their orderly town is fueled by a childhood memory of "nineteen Negro ladies [who] wore summer dresses the lightness, the delicacy of which neither of them had ever seen. Most of the dresses were white, but two were lemon yellow and one a salmon color" (109). Both of the men entangle the pastel dresses of these women with their sense of the feminine, their understanding of virtue in women. From their disgust with the colorful, unconventional dress of the Convent women to their dismay over "the disappointingly small harvest of radishes, or the too short rows of collards, beets" (89) that results from the women of Ruby using their free time to produce lush, lavish-colored flower gardens, the men of Ruby attempt to impose a rigid gender code on their wives and daughters. Dovey's visitor, who appears only at the small house in town that has effectively become Dovey's sanctuary away from her husband, falls outside the perimeter of what can be contained within the Symbolic Order, of what can be controlled by the Morgan twins.

Intriguingly, Dovey never asks her visitor his name, understanding that if she does, "he would never come again" (92). Connie, by then blind, does ask, to which her stranger replies, "Come on, girl. You know me" (252). His answer suggests that Dovey's hesitation stems from her denial of what the stranger represents. However, Morrison's narrative reveals that "she found reasons to remain on St. Matthew Street" (92) where he appears, rather than to spend time at her larger, more luxurious ranch home. On the night of the town meeting to discuss the Oven, the night Dovey is most critical of her husband, she hears a scratching at the window pane that she refuses to acknowledge. She decides, "He wasn't there. He never came at night. Deliberately she drove her mind onto everyday things" (81). Having moved herself to a site of rebellion against her husband, Dovey suddenly grows fearful of what another encounter, a nightly encounter, with her mysterious "other" would involve. Rejecting the possibility of growth and wholeness, Dovey chooses the mundane, the world of "everyday things," over the spiritual. In doing so, she is locked into all that Ruby represents, the Law of the Father, and thereby, her own oppression.

Connie, on the other hand, as a result of her mysterious visitation and the events that follow, undergoes what Tally identifies as a "final conversion," a "return to a more pantheistic faith" (70) and what John N. Duvall refers to as a "syncretic belief [that] encompasses, on the one hand, her love for the Reverend Mother (and by extension for the tropes and rituals of the Catholic Church [as well as] a power that precedes the logic of the Christian Word" (145). That return begins with Connie's cooking a delicious and nourishing meal for the women, which Tally reads as tied to the erotic and claims "reinforce[s] the idea of sensuousness and the wholeness of the female experience and sensuality" (78). Connie makes clear, to the reader if not necessarily to the women listening to her speech, her conviction that flesh and spirit must exist in harmony, not in the hierarchic duality fostered by Judeo-Christian thought. Again, while I am aware that many Christian theologians would concur with Connie, the fact remains that Christianity as a whole, in the tradition of both Aquinas and Augustine, privileges spirit over flesh and is particularly squeamish about dealing with sexuality as a manifestation of spirit, even in marriage, not to mention outside of it, as is the case with the Convent women. Significantly, Connie's speech disrupts accepted rules of grammar and syntax, once again pointing to the disruption of the Symbolic Order and gesturing in the direction of the Kristevian semiotique. Julie Rivkin and Michael Ryan point out how in *Revolution in Poetic Language,* Kristeva claims that such disrupted speech and writing "tap[s] into a well of as yet unordered language processes and unarticulated sounds to generate new possibilities for thought and for society, greater freedom to signify and greater liberation from the capitalist regime of utility, functionality, and work" (343). We see such possibilities at work in Connie's speech:

> My child body, hurt and soil, leaps into the arms of a woman who teach me my body is nothing my spirit everything. I agreed her until I met another. My flesh is so hungry for itself it ate him. When he fell away
> the woman rescue me from my body again. [...] After she is dead I can not get past that. My bones on hers the only good thing. Not spirit. Bones. No different from the man. My bones on his the only true thing.
> So I wondering where is the spirit lost in this? It is true, like bones. It is good, like bones. One sweet, one bitter. Where is it lost? Hear me, listen. Never break them in two. Never put one over the other. Eve is Mary's mother. Mary is the daughter of Eve.
> (263)

Like Jesus, Connie exhorts those around her, "follow me," but she leads them on a different path to a radically different paradise. Tally speaks of the meal that initiates their healing, which occurs shortly before the massacre, as a Last Supper (79), but I would argue that it is rather a first supper, a beginning of a life in the body that for these women does not end with the massacre.

The absence of stasis distinguishes the life-giving spirituality that occurs at the Convent with what passes for spirituality in Ruby. Like the Morgan twins, Connie delves into her own past as she leads the ritual and encourages the women, one by one, to tell and re-tell their own stories. Whereas the telling in Ruby has, as I have argued, become ossified—so that each telling is a reiteration of the form, so that no alterations in language may change one word of the narrative, so that nothing current in the lives of the speakers can allow for a reinterpretation of the past—with Connie, the narrative itself is vital. As she speaks it, she calls it into being. One might argue that Connie's memories of the home she left as a child are exaggerated, that no place on earth exists where "fish the color of plums swam alongside children," where "boys us[ed]

rubies for dice," "where gods and goddesses sat in the pews with the congregation" in "scented cathedrals made of gold," where "carnations [grew] as tall
as trees" and where a "woman named Piedade [...] sang but never said a
word" (264). The novel's conclusion, however, when Piedade herself enters the
diegesis, offers narrative validation for Connie's "memories." In a living spirituality, creation continues to occur and the words of each speaker are holy,
change is vital and ongoing, and the stories of the broken and the despairing
form a new sacred mythology.

It is not merely Connie's narrative that creates and heals. Unlike the
teenagers of Ruby, who are expected to be content with a history, a spirituality, and a collective memory that excludes them, the women of the Convent
fuse their stories, their "half-tales and the never-dreamed"; "it was never
important to know who said the dream or whether it had meaning" (264).
Each woman's narrative, each woman's pain, is equally validated and shared
by all as the specific boundaries of the individual selves are dissolved to create
a collective communal one; all have been crucified and all will be reborn.
Rather than merely identify with the sacred stories and re-script their own lives
as a parallel to them, the women create their sacred stories in the telling and
render themselves holy as a result.

Regardless of how much Morrison celebrates the creative power of
speech, the text reveals that language in itself is not enough. The self, made up
of intellect *and* intuition, body *and* mind, requires ritual, symbolic acts that
work as a catalyst on the unconscious as well. Mircea Eliade argues, "Rituals
are symbols in acted reality; they function to make concrete and experiential
the mythic values of a society, and they can therefore provide clues to the
mythic values themselves. Hence rituals *act*, they perform, modulate, transform" (164). Soane Morgan's reminiscences of the baptisms that took place
during the community's early days in Ruby address such a dynamic understanding of ritual:

> [T]he pastor held the girls in his arms, lowering them one by one into the newly hal-
> lowed water, never letting go. [...] Breathless, the girls rose, each in her turn. Their
> wet, white robes billow in the sunlit water. Hair and face streaming they looked to
> heaven before bowing their heads for the command: "Go now." Then the reassur-
> ance: "Daughter, thou art saved." [...] Slowly, then, hand in hand, heads on support-
> ing shoulder, the blessed and saved waded to the banks and made their way to the
> Oven. (103)

Her reverie concludes when she considers, "Now Calvary had an inside pool; New Zion and Holy Redeemer had special vessels for dribbling a little water on an upright head" (103). Soane's sorrow at the despoiled ritual points to the significance of action as well as language in a living ritual. The templates of the bodies of the aching women that Connie constructs on the floor of the Convent basement enable the women to heal through their visual significance. Since body and spirit, as Connie insists, cannot be divided, both must be tended if either is to heal. It is not enough to offer healing to a spirit while the body exists in pain, a point Morrison has insisted upon throughout the body of her work. On the other hand, the contemporary American Christian church has not only refused the kinds of political actions that would enable bodies to heal, it has often supported conservative political agendas that are predicated upon an absence of justice.[6] While radical forms of Christianity do exist that focus primarily on alleviating human suffering,[7] one can safely assume that the more typical American Christian response to the Mavises, Gigis, Senecas, and Divines they encounter would be strikingly similar to what those characters face in Ruby. Connie, through the templates, enables the women to look at their bodies from something of a distance; they use the psychological mechanism of projection to their advantage, rather than to shield themselves from self-knowledge. Those women like Seneca, who inflict pain on their bodies, now inscribe the templates instead, publicly acknowledging their self-destructiveness; those haunted by loss like Gigi, refashion the lost objects on the templates, allowing for healing and wholeness. Their spiritual purification is reflected in their bodily practices; they begin to subsist on "bloodless food and water alone" (263). After several months, Soane, noticing the new maturity evident in the women, thinks, "unlike some people in Ruby, the Convent women were no longer haunted" (266). Unlike some people in Ruby, these women have learned to shed those memories of the past that served to distort or cripple them.

The night before the massacre, the women essentially undergo the ritual of baptism, although not in any conventional sense of the term. The text allows us to grasp how thoroughly the women have been cleansed of what has haunted and maimed them when it speaks of "the rapture of holy women dancing in hot sweet rain" and calls attention to Consolata's being "fully housed by the god who sought her out in the garden" (283), that god being her green-eyed, tea-colored-haired male self. How thoroughly they have integrated body and spirit, how successfully they dissolve the boundaries between life and death, becomes apparent by the novel's stunning ending. Although critics and readers disagree about what happens to the women in the novel's final pages, I believe Morrison's text makes clear that the women do die. We are narratively present at Connie's death, and it is inconceivable that a woman shot at close range and that three other women gunned down with high-powered rifles could survive such attacks. The fact that none of the bodies are ever found signifies, of course, on the Resurrection of Jesus, as does the reappearance of four of the five slain women after their deaths. Tally identifies these sightings as revenants, spirits, in African legend, of those "who have been violently killed ... and [return] to visit the living" (46). Morrison, however, reaches beyond both Christianity and African religions in her treatment of Connie's death and the subsequent narrative involving her. After Steward shoots her in the head, Deek carries his former lover to a table where his wife and Lone attempt, unsuccessfully, to save her. When she dies, they "close the two pale eyes but can do nothing about the third one, wet and lidless, in between" (291). In referring to the bullet hole as Connie's third eye, Morrison reaches east, theologically, and indicates that Connie has achieved enlightenment,[8] that she sees fully, spiritually, no longer trapped by maya, the world of space and time, the world of becoming.

Richard and Anna grasp some of the mystery of what has happened when they return to the Convent after the massacre. Both experience a revelation that enables their acceptance of spirituality as yet unknown to them:

> It was when he returned, as they stood near the chair, her hands balancing brown eggs and white cloth, his fingers looking doubled with long pepper pods—green, red, and plum black—that they saw it. Or sensed it, rather, for there was nothing to see. A door, she said later. "No, a window," he said[....] They knew it was there. Knew it so well they were transfixed for a long moment before they backed away and ran to the car. [...] Anything to avoid reliving the shiver or saying out loud what they were wondering. Whether through a door needing to be opened or a beckoning window already raised, what would happen if you entered? What would be on the other side? What on earth would it be? What on earth? (305)

In attempting to make sense both of the massacre and of his subsequent vision, Richard arrives at a spiritual place not sanctioned by mainstream Christian theology. Although his understanding of Jesus is far more profound than that of the other ministers in town, it is doubtful whether his sense that the window he saw "beckon[ed] toward another place—neither life nor death—but there, just yonder" (307) can be reconciled with his previous beliefs.

The reader is provided with still more information that requires processing and reconciliation when four of the dead women confront, in one way or
another, family members with whom they need to settle scores in some way. In
one instance, pointedly shunning the mother who betrayed her, Pallas, now
carrying a sword, returns to her mother's home to retrieve a pair of shoes.
Mission accomplished, she returns to the car in which she arrived and "drove
off into a violet so ultra" (312) it broke her mother's heart. Morrison's play
with the concept of "ultraviolet" light indicates one way of reading the location of the missing "bodies." The women continue to exist, but they do so in
a plane not accessible by ordinary sight, just as we cannot see ultraviolet light
with the unaided eye. Billie Delia alone understands. She "was perhaps the
only one in town who was not puzzled by where the women were or concerned
about how they disappeared. She had another question: When will they
return? When will they reappear, with blazing eyes, war paint and huge hands
to rip up and stomp down this prison calling itself a town?" (308). Given that
after death Gigi carries a gun and Pallas a sword, Billie Delia's sense of how
the dead women are occupying their time may be accurate.

Finally, in the novel's stunning conclusion, we encounter Connie once
again, resting her head on the lap of the Mother Goddess Piedade, who sings
to her. Significantly, Piedade never speaks; she is that which precedes the
Symbolic Order, language, the Law of the Father. She is not a dead mother
but the eternal living Mother Goddess, accessible not through language but
through song, ritual, and memory. However, Piedade has taken on the "ruined
fingers" of Save-Marie, the first of the disabled Fleetwood children to die.
That this experience occurs on Earth rather than in some celestial otherworld
is evident from the "sea trash," the "[d]iscarded bottle caps," the "broken sandal," the "small dead radio" (318). As they watch, a ship arrives, bearing, not
"the blessed and the saved" (103) whom Soane remembers wading up from
the river after the baptism rituals, but the "lost and saved," who will rest in the
presence of Piedade (compassion) and Consolata (consolation) "before shouldering the endless work they were created to do down here in paradise" (318).
The beach scene is a far cry from the celestial Jerusalem envisioned by the
writer of Revelation. Not only does the beach debris challenge any concept of
otherworldly perfection, but more significantly, those who arrive are both the
lost and the saved. Unlike the Christian understanding of the afterlife, in
which these two groups arrive at different destinations, and unlike Ruby, which
Richard Misner understand to be a "hard-won heaven defined only by the
absence of the unsaved, the unworthy and the strange" (306), here all arrive,

not for the stasis of an otherworldly paradise, but to rest before they continue the "endless work" of life, which must be accomplished on Earth—the only possible paradise, in this text. Connie, now having achieved enlightenment, is no longer caught up in *samsara*, the cycle of birth, death, and rebirth. Save-Marie, who has known only love and compassion in her brief life, also fuses with the Mother Goddess for all time; as Misner says at her funeral, "[T]here never was a time when you were not saved" (307). Eventually, the text suggests, the others will also learn their own holiness and goodness, to the point where they will not need to leave the island, where their "endless work" will be reviving the spirits of still others, lost and saved, all on a journey that begins and ends down here in paradise.

## Notes

[1] See "Toni Morrison's *Beloved* and the Vindication of Lilith" by Shirley A. Stave in *South Atlantic Review*, January 1993, 49–66.

[2] The original literary source of the term is Henry Louis Gates, Jr.'s *The Signifying Monkey* (New York: Oxford University Press, 1988), in which he defines the term as an African American rhetorical practice that operates through "repetition and difference" as a writer revises an original source to "[realign] ... the signifier," (64) hence disrupting, complicating, and sometimes unraveling both the original meaning of a text and the intentions of its author.

[3] Several examples I often encounter will serve here. Although I teach in a state whose Catholic population is large, when I have brought up the matter of transubstantiation in class, my Catholic students will often claim that, although they attend mass and consider themselves Catholics in good standing, they simply cannot believe that the bread and wine literally transform into the body and blood of Christ, even though that is perhaps one of the very most basic tenets of Roman Catholic doctrine. Similarly, I have had Protestant students argue vehemently that the concept of the Trinity is biblical, when in fact it was created by decree, and no biblical sources can be found to support it.

[4] It is my understanding that these forms of Christianity believe in a heavenly afterlife for the "saved," as well as a literal and eternal hell for those who are not. While some forms of Protestantism do claim (at least their theologians do) that the kingdom of God either exists for an individual at this very moment or it will never exist at all, and do not believe in a literal return of Jesus in a "second coming," the three forms of Christianity Morrison cites in her text do not share those more radical doctrinal tenets.

[5] Richard Dawkins is a well-known biologist who readily admits to having a vendetta against Christianity or any other belief system and is not reticent about his views. One example, from his well-known book *The Selfish Gene* (Oxford: Oxford University Press, 1989), will suffice:

Faith is such a successful brainwasher in its own favour, especially a brainwasher of children, that it is hard to break its hold. But what, after all, is faith? It is a state of mind that leads people to believe something—it doesn't matter what—in the total absence of supporting evidence…. Faith cannot move mountains (though generations of children are solemnly told the contrary and believe it). But it is capable of driving people to such dangerous folly that faith seems to me to qualify as a kind of mental illness. (330)

6 I am thinking of the claims of "moral values" that led to George W. Bush's reelection to the White House in November, 2004, in which denying rights to gays and lesbians, attempting to block women's rights to reproductive freedom, refusing to develop a national health plan, approving the exploitation of the people and resources of peripheral countries in the name of capitalist greed, supporting religious intolerance and endorsing unprovoked attacks on countries are, in the most blatant case of Orwellian doublespeak, referred to as "moral" acts instead of what they actually are, outright acts of injustice.

7 I am thinking not only of liberation theology, which has effectively been rendered defunct as a result of the current conservative leadership of the Catholic Church, but also of the work of such theologians as Matthew Fox (who, admittedly, has been defrocked by the Church), Rosemary Radford Reuther, and Sallie McFague.

8 In Eastern religions, many believe that a soul continues to reincarnate back to physical life on earth, a cycle referred to as *samsara*, until such time as all moral lessons have been learned and the soul is able to transcend to *nirvana*, eternal life outside of time in a full understanding of the oneness of all. To arrive at nirvana, one must achieve enlightenment, which allows one to see with one's third eye, located between and above one's other two eyes; the third eye sees fully, the spiritual reality as opposed to the illusion of *maya*, worldly, physical reality.

## Works Cited

Boursin, J. Brooks. *Quiet As It's Kept: Shame, Trauma, and Race in the Novels of Toni Morrison*. Albany: State University of New York Press, 2000.

Butler, Judith. "Subversive Bodily Acts." In *Modern Critical Thought*, edited by Drew Milne. Malden, MA: Blackwell, 2003. 314–326.

Christ, Carol. *Diving Deep and Surfacing: Women Writers on Spiritual Quest*. Boston: Beacon Press, 1980.

Dawkins, Richard. *The Selfish Gene*. Oxford: Oxford University Press, 1989.

Duvall, John N. *The Identifying Fictions of Toni Morrison: Modernist Authenticity and Postmodern Blackness*. New York: Palgrave, 2000.

Eliade, Mircea. *Myths, Rites Symbols: A Mircea Eliade Reader*. Edited by Wendell C. Beane and William G. Doty. New York: Harper & Row, 1975.

Faris, Wendy B. "Scheherazade's Children: Magical Realism and Postmodern Fiction." In *Magic Realism: Theory, History, Community*, edited by Lois Parkinson Zamora and Wendy B. Faris. Durham, NC: Duke University Press, 1995. 162–190.

Foreman, P. Gabrielle. "Past-On Stories: History and the Magically Real, Morrison and Allende on Call." In *Magic Realism: Theory, History, Community*, edited by Lois Parkinson Zamora and Wendy B. Faris. Durham, NC: Duke University Press, 1995. 285–303.

Gates, Henry Louis, Jr. *The Signifying Monkey*. New York: Oxford University Press, 1988.

Leech, Kristy Rose. "Laughter and Lightning: Unearthing Magic Realism in the Fiction of Jeannette Winterson, Angela Carter, Gloria Naylor, and Toni Morrison." Senior Honors Thesis. Louisiana Scholars' College, 2001.

Morrison, Toni. *Paradise*. New York: Alfred A. Knopf, 1998.

Rivkin, Julie, and Michael Ryan. "The Class of 1968—Post Structuralism *par lui-meme*." In *Literary Theory: An Anthology*, edited by Julie Rivkin and Michael Ryan. Malden, MA: Blackwell, 1998. 333–357.

Stave, Shirley A. "Toni Morrison's *Beloved* and the Vindication of Lilith." *South Atlantic Review*. January (1993): 49–66.

Tally, Justine. *Paradise Reconsidered: Toni Morrison's (Hi)stories and Truths*. FORECAST 2. Hamburg: Lit Verlag, 1999.

# 11

# RITUAL AND "OTHER" RELIGIONS IN *THE BLUEST EYE*

## REBECCA DEGLER

Throughout her fiction Toni Morrison employs ritual to establish and sustain community (e.g., National Suicide Day in *Sula*, the Clearing meetings in *Beloved*, cooking at the Oven in *Paradise*). This lingering preoccupation begins with her first novel, *The Bluest Eye*, in which the enactment of ritual sacrifice brings into relief a community's collective identity and the classificatory system of belief, or religion, informing it. In *The Elementary Forms of Religious Life*, Emile Durkheim proposes that ritual action is a reflection and expression of social organization, as it is in and through ritual that a society creates and recreates aspects of itself. A community projects a conceptualization of itself by dictating whom it does and does not allow to participate in its rituals—in other words, by defining who does and does not belong. In the microcosm of society presented in *The Bluest Eye*, the community ostracizes and destroys Pecola Breedlove to signify who does not belong. Those who participate in excluding her—her teacher, classmates, Geraldine, even her mother—all do so to communicate how they think about themselves.[1] They "padded [their] characters" (205) and aggrandized their descriptions of themselves by abusing her character and labeling her everything they did not want or like. When Geraldine, the house-proud woman who despises "funkiness," finds Pecola standing small and upset in her home, she throws her out with anger unfitting to the potential threat any eleven-year-old child could pose: "'Get out,' she said, her voice quiet. 'You nasty little black bitch. Get out of my house'" (92). By throwing out Pecola, Geraldine symbolically throws out all the "nastiness" of being black. In a more elaborate, though equally dramatic and acute demonstration, the community as a whole effectively rids itself of Pecola, their appointed figurehead for what they deem nasty or undesirable, in an effort to rid themselves of that undesirability. It is, as Trudier Harris writes in *Fiction and Folklore*, a "scapegoating ritual as old as society" (42–43).

Perhaps these two go hand in hand because ritual in part determines society. Ritual is symbolically meaningful in its re-creation or reflection of social values and beliefs, but the act of creation in Durkheim's thesis suggests a functional role as well. In *Throughout Your Generations Forever*, Nancy Jay draws upon this suggestion when she notes, with reference to specific observed rituals, that ritual both signifies as well as *causes* membership in society. The very act of participating in ritual activities effectuates one's belonging; ritual activities are performative. For example, under the practice of totemism (the association between a community and an elected animal), sacrificing the totem animal not only signifies one's belonging to that particular totem group, but also makes one a member of that group.[2] The sacrifice is both the creation as well as recreation of a subjectivity. As we see, then, rituals such as sacrifice are a means of communicating ways of *thinking*, but they are also active, a matter of *doing* something, of creating something. What this means with regard to Pecola is that she is scorned as ugly and dirty not only so her community can project a comparative image of themselves as beautiful, good and clean, but also so they could *be* those things.

After all is said and done, the novel's main narrator, Claudia, sadly notes the way her community confiscated Pecola's identity in order to give themselves one: "all of our beauty [...] was hers first and [...] she gave [it] to us" (205). She gave them beauty not by seeing beauty in them and thus defining them as beautiful, but unwillingly, as their object; she was nothing more to them than a role that needed fulfilling. In her final interpretation of the narrative, Claudia unquestionably declares that Pecola's role shapes the community and its members:

> All of our waste which we dumped on her and which she absorbed [....] All of us—all who knew her—felt so wholesome after we cleaned ourselves on her [....] Her [...] guilt sanctified us, her pain made us glow with health [....] Even her waking dreams we used—to silence our own nightmares [....]
>
> We courted death in order to call ourselves brave, and hid like thieves from life. We substituted good grammar for intellect; we switched habits to simulate maturity; we rearranged lies and called it truth, seeing in the new pattern of an old idea the Revelation and the Word. (205–206)

Reminiscing about the way her community treated Pecola, Claudia announces that they "courted death." That death was Pecola's—at least symbolically[3]—and a reference to the ceremonial effect of sanctification indicates the sacrificial nature of that death. Blood does not need to be shed for the term "sacrifice" to apply; sacrifice essentially refers to the destruction of the proffered object (Hubert and Mauss, 12). Both Pecola's social experience and individual identity are destroyed through ostracization and insanity, respectively. What makes her destruction ritual sacrifice is the meaning ascribed to the event. Ritual theory identifies an action/thought dichotomy within ritual, in which behavior and belief are separate but equal components. Claudia acknowledges the meaning her community ascribes to their treatment of Pecola when she notes their resulting belief that Pecola "cleaned" and "sanctified" her whole community. When Pecola is raped by her father, causing her ostracization and sparking her demise into insanity, she is washing dishes, literally engaged in a daily cleansing ritual; what her destruction *does* is cleanse.

Claudia compares this larger cleansing purpose to the biblical sacrificial lamb of all humanity: "truth," "Revelation" and "the Word" are all designations for Jesus Christ. This comparison, despite or maybe because of certain similarities in the effects related to ritual sacrifice, problematizes our interpretation of Pecola's character and her community's conception of itself. This particular New Testament sacrifice presents a wholly pure sacrificial subject and suggests, by comparison, that we should read Pecola as pure, too. Apart from this reference, however, nothing in the novel supports such a reading. What we see instead is a community that selects an individual to represent its corruption. Perhaps Harris expresses it best when she argues that Pecola is "more than representative; she becomes a particular intensified reflection of the type. Pecola's society has taught her not merely to want to be beautiful but to be the most beautiful of all" (42). She wants not only to have blue eyes, but to have the bluest eyes. Her purity is one of type, not quality; she is an extreme example of a quality the community wishes to discourage because it reminds them of the degree to which the dominant culture infiltrates their community, as well as their shame in colluding with that culture. They choose to redefine themselves through "substitution." A similar principle guides ritual sacrifice, in which the sacrificial victim substitutes for the sins of the beneficiaries—the people performing the ritual. Destroying the victim metaphorically exterminates the sins he/she represents; what once was soiled is now clean. As Bloch argues, the most basic initiating reason for sacrifice is "when someone, or a group of people, feels penetrated by an outside force, which is believed either to cause or actually *to be* the disease" (31). We can more fully understand the manifestation of this belief and its implications for the community's and characters' identities by looking at the novel's invocation of other religious beliefs and practices, such as agrarian sacrificial rites.

The vegetation cycle literally structures *The Bluest Eye*. Broken down into four narrative sections named for each of the seasons, the story of Pecola Breedlove is told through one year of her life and one full vegetation cycle. That this is more than a coincidental relationship is apparent from Claudia's claim: "the seasons of a Midwestern town become the *Moirai* of our small lives" (189). In Greek mythology, the *Moirai* are the three personified sisters of fate: one who spins the thread at the beginning of one's life, a second who weaves the thread into the fabric of one's actions, and a third who snips the thread at the conclusion of one's life. Claudia's equation suggests that the events of their lives are dictated by the seasons of nature. In his anthropological study *The Golden Bough: A Study in Magic and Religion*, James George Frazer notes that a commingling of the natural and supernatural, such as Claudia suggests between the seasons of a Midwestern town and the anthropomorphized sisters of fate, is hardly uncommon. The conception that the natural world is "to a great extent worked by supernatural agents, that is, by personal beings acting on impulses and motives like [our] own, liable like [us] to be moved by appeals to their pity, their hopes, and their fears" has led to a kind of agrarian religion in which "prayers, promises, or threats may secure … fine weather and an abundant crop from the gods" (Frazer 10). Such prayers and other appeals to vegetation gods become ritual performances, or concrete expressions of beliefs. Like the Greek concept of Fate—which attempts to organize the random events of one's life into a coherent narrative, creating personal gods in order to explain random atmospheric conditions—agrarian rituals convert chaotic geological facts into an organized ideology.

Observing agrarian rituals around the world, Frazer argues that the logic behind them is based on the understanding of an immaterial connection or impulse between the practice and the result. In short, a sympathetic bind transmits intentions or desires (as expressed in the practice) into reality (the result). He refers to this category of thought and behavior as sympathetic magic, the principles of which are familiar to us as superstition. Examples of sympathetic magic abound in *The Bluest Eye*. From the women who believe that burying a sick woman's "slop jar and everything in it" will help heal her (137) to Soaphead Church's suggestion that Pecola's wish for blue eyes might be granted if she were to make "'some offering, that is, some contact with nature'" (175), the novel depicts how superstitious beliefs and the accompanying magic influence the behavior of the characters. In the prologue, Claudia explicitly refers to her and Frieda's actions to save Pecola's baby as "magic":

*[S]o deeply concerned were we with the health and safe delivery of Pecola's baby we could think of nothing but our own magic: if we planted the seeds, and said the right words over them, they would blossom, and everything would be all right [....] We had dropped our seeds in our own little plot of black dirt just as Pecola's father had dropped his seeds in his own plot of black dirt.* (5, emphasis original)

Claudia's symbolic link between their marigold seeds and Pecola's father's seed in his daughter reveals their use of what Frazer terms the homeopathic branch of sympathetic magic: to produce an effect by imitating it. These superstitions of homeopathic magic are based on the simple maxim that "like produces like." In order to achieve the desired results, one must perform a similar action, and the sympathetic connection between the designed and real outcomes will yield what one desires. On the basis of this principal element of homeopathy, Claudia and Frieda believe that the successful cultivation of their marigolds will produce the same healthy success for Pecola's pregnancy. Some interpret this deceptively clear logic as signaling a childlike perspective; Gureen Grewal argues that "only nine-year-olds may be excused for thinking 'that it was because Pecola was having her father's baby that the marigolds did not grow'" (119). Such an immediately dismissive conclusion blinds us to the evidence to the contrary, however, for not only nine-year-olds think this way.

This dismissive attitude is evident even in Frazer's anthropological terminology. While these homeopathic practices are rooted in a religious framework, Frazer's study and our critical and everyday usage refer to them as superstition and myth because we no longer ascribe to the belief systems they posit. Like myth, magic is commonly used as a pejorative word for religion. Although Frazer goes to great pains to define what he means by "magic"—a definition that absorbs validation from the volumes of empirical anthropological observations surrounding it—his definition ultimately denotes a belief system of a lesser or more primitive religion than the hegemonic ones we recognize. Inherent in this usage is a privileged opposition or hierarchy between civilized and uncivilized, rational and irrational, right and wrong. Religion is what we call *our* beliefs; magic and myth are what we call *others'* beliefs. Grewal's dismissal of Claudia's invocation of magic betrays both her interpretation of Claudia's belief system as primitive and also her own positivistic belief that all ills, including the failed growth of both the marigolds and Pecola's baby, are the result of irrationality and can therefore be "corrected" by reason. In this case, "reason" is simply a different belief system, one that does not support homeopathic connections between marigolds and babies. Her reading imposes a hierarchy of belief by disregarding the tone with which

Claudia invokes her magic. The girls could "think of nothing but their own magic"; they believe in it and think of it positively and passionately. Claudia does not use the word in a pejorative sense, but as a way of expressing her deeply held convictions and beliefs.[4]

While we might be tempted to treat with amused condescension the young girls' innocent belief that their failure to cultivate marigolds and Pecola's miscarriage were related, Claudia laments both with equal seriousness. She substantiates her abiding belief in the connection between the two by assessing their own invocation of magic in comparison to Cholly's violation of the incest taboo:

> *Our innocence and faith were no more productive than [Pecola's father's] lust or despair. What is clear now is that of all that hope, fear, lust, love, and grief, nothing remains but Pecola and the unyielding earth. Cholly Breedlove is dead; our innocence too. The seeds shriveled and died; her baby too.* (6, emphasis orginial)

Claudia despairs that their faith was not "productive," which hints at the cause-and-effect rationale behind homeopathic magic. As a taboo, incest follows the same homeopathic logic of "like produces like," but with one difference in that equation. A taboo is the negation of both sides, of both the cause and effect: we see what we should *not* do to avoid those results we do *not* desire. The girls' magic and Cholly's incest fuse; our horror and repulsion of one infuse the other. There is nothing trivial about this connection, especially if we consider its location in the narrative, immediately following the tripled primer section.[5] The defamiliarization created by the unsettling dissolution of the primer text carries over into the prologue and cautions us to not laugh off anything just yet. Even the narrator, the adult Claudia, has not completely dismissed her earlier notion. Despite her declaration that innocence led her to believe in this cause and effect, the construction of her sentence—"the seeds shriveled and died; her baby too"— indicates that she still links the two directly. The semicolon punctuation, which now stands out after the defamiliarizing removal of all punctuation and standardized formatting in the preceding primer text, suggests that the two halves of the sentence, both about death, are related not simply by the symmetry of meaning, but perhaps by some sympathetic ethereal connection as well. In fact, such principles of homeopathic magic do hold true in this instance, but in the opposite manner to what the girls hoped.[6] That Pecola's baby and the marigolds both "shriveled and died" is not lost on the adult Claudia.

Concurrent with Claudia's and Frieda's attempt to magically influence the health of Pecola's baby is their concept of sacrifice, as portrayed by Morrison. Along with the seeds they had planned to sell in order to buy a bicycle, they bury all the money they have made thus far and decide to give up the bicycle for the baby's sake. In their offering, the young Claudia decides that she will do the "singing this time'" and tells Frieda to "say the magic words" (192). With this division of roles, their practice assumes a ceremonial tenor, as if they must adhere to a prescribed form in order to achieve the effect they desire. As discussed above, this invocation of sympathetic magic relates to agrarian religions; they pray to God, who is the god of marigold growth as well as the god of human life, to accept their offering of seeds and money so that the seeds and Pecola's baby will be linked sympathetically. Moved by their grand gesture to sacrifice everything they have and even what they do not yet have, they hope, He will influence the healthy growth of Pecola's baby and reveal His approval of their act by also making the marigold soil fertile. This notion of sacrifice is noticeably different from the community's ritualized scapegoating of Pecola. The girls' sacrifice involves giving up something that is particularly valuable to them; their sacrificial subject is prized rather than scorned.

These two seemingly contradictory characterizations of sacrificial subjects are illuminated in part by the text's connections with a particular agrarian religious practice. We are told that when the girls receive the "magic package" of seeds, the "summer was already thick" (188). They then spend the rest of the summer selling the seeds and perform their ritual at the end of summer, beginning of autumn. This time of year is significant in vegetation cycles as it is when the fields are gleaned of the remnants of the past year's harvest; the old must be removed so the new can be introduced. Considering how much is at stake, this time carries with it intense spiritual connotations. The most zealous hope is that a vibrant or revived god will watch over and govern the new crops, but the personification of agricultural gods, mentioned above, means that they are subject to the same concerns that plague man—namely, the weakening effects of age. Death is necessary, then, to prevent a god weakened from a year of life-giving fruition from once again assuming those awesome responsibilities without a revitalizing break. Only once death has occurred can the divine spirit resurrect in full vigor. As Frazer argues, "The very value attached to the life of the man-god necessitates his violent death as the only means of preserving it from the inevitable decay of age" (296). He notes that a ceremony is often performed to symbolize this killing, or carrying out, of the old spirit of vegetation. Simply referred to as "Carrying out Death," the ritual involves carrying an effigy of Death through the whole town or village and then expelling it.[7]

What is curious about the Carrying-out-Death ceremony, and the dualistic portrayals of scorned and prized sacrifice in *The Bluest Eye*, is an apparent conflict in its tenor: "on the one hand, sorrow for the death, and affection and respect for the dead; on the other hand, fear and hatred of the dead, and rejoicings at his death" (Frazer 319). Lamentation is to be expected due to the loss of a positive, life-giving spirit, but fear, hatred and rejoicing seem noticeably out of place, raising questions about the nature or characterization of the death figure. Why is a beneficial spirit treated with such venomous joy after every harvest, regardless of what had occurred during the year leading up to that moment? This can only make sense, as Frazer argues, if that effigy had come to symbolize more than the spirit of vegetation. While the community was purging themselves of one weakened god who might not be able to protect their lifeblood, their vegetation, from the evils that might arise to attack it, it would make sense to purge other evils as well. Therefore, once a year the community loaded all of the evils that plagued or had the potential to plague the society onto one figure, the effigy of Death, which they destroyed in the hopes of destroying all that was negative. The ceremony of Carrying out Death consequently built up to the actual expulsion of the evil spirit, sacrificed at the end for the good of the community. The ritualized festivities included carrying the effigy from home to home so it would absorb whatever infected each person and structure in the community. Then, with varying ceremonies—some involve simply throwing the effigy outside of the boundaries of the community, while others require the drowning of the effigy—the figure symbolically containing all threatening evils is expelled (Frazer 307-311).

*The Bluest Eye* contains a number of parallels to this ritual. The doll that Claudia tears apart to "see of what it was made" (20), for example, resembles an effigy in that it literally embodies the values of the community and has the blue eyes Pecola so desperately wants and eventually sees herself as having. Pecola's peripatetic lifestyle also retraces the journey of the effigy before its expulsion; just as the effigy of Death is passed around from house to house to pick up the evils in each place, so Pecola is passed around from her family's storefront house to the homes of the MacTeers, Geraldine, the prostitutes and the rich white family. Finally, like the effigy imbued with all of the community's evils, she is removed from the community, placed in a "little brown house [...] on the edge of town" (205). This ceremony literally enacts the purification process discussed earlier. She is destroyed and ostracized, and, as Claudia notes, that process cleanses the rest of the community.

The time of year that this ceremony is performed also establishes links with the text's key literary influence. Northrop Frye argues that all literature is based on myths, particularly those related to the agricultural year, and that different genres of literature correlate to the different seasons: tragedy, he suggests, is associated with autumn. This association illuminates many aspects of *The Bluest Eye* and its portrayal of a sacrificial or scapegoating ritual. It would be easy to read the novel and immediately classify it as tragic, citing the blood (Pecola's first menstruation early in the narrative enables conception when her father rapes her), death (Pecola's baby dies after a premature birth; Cholly dies in a workhouse incident) and destruction (Pecola's mental stability deteriorates and she finally collapses into insanity) that permeates, and to a large degree carries, the narrative. To be sure, the story of an eleven-year-old black girl abused by her community, betrayed by her family and raped by her father, is necessarily and incontrovertibly tragic, but is it, in the classical sense, tragedy? By this contentious term,[8] I refer primarily to the ancient Greek, or more precisely, Attic, tragedy of the fifth century BCE. I use this conception of tragedy as the basis of my discussion not only because it is the form Morrison herself is trained in,[9] but also because of the noticeable Greek presence in the setting of the novel. The opening sentence of the first seasonal narrative states: "Nuns go by as quiet as lust, and drunken men and sober eyes sing in the lobby of the Greek hotel" (9). The Greek hotel suggests that the town's settlers include a propertied Greek constituency. This suggestion is later confirmed with the assignation of the Breedloves' home to a Greek landlord (34). The singing eyes have a twofold reference: to a musical or lyrical quality so much a part of the poetry of the Greek tragedies, and to facial imagery. Eyes that can sing emphasize the novel's consistent engagement with the expressiveness of eyes, but they also remind us, through the voice emanating from the implacable "sober" or serious eyes, of traditional face masks worn during dramatic presentations. Altogether, these suggestions culminate in an almost dream-image of silent, gliding religious figures (recalling the omnipresent gods of Greek tragedy), drunken revelry (recalling Nietzsche's intoxicated Dionysian[10]), and serious lyricism (the origination and form of all Attic tragedy), set against a specifically Greek architectural background. These oblique references to tragedy are reinforced throughout the narrative with explicit references, such as to the "omnipresence of the deity, strophe and antistrophe of the chorus" (143), as well as with analogous formal structures. The cadence of a tragic cho-

rus can be heard in the all-for-one and one-for-all "exchanges" in the narrator's soliloquies.[11] The events of the narrative build and fall in accordance
with tragic techniques to illustrate the elevation and fall of the protagonist,
including events that resemble what Aristotle terms "revelation" and "reversal
of fortune." In other words, this looks and sounds like Attic tragedy.

Although structural comparisons between performance drama and the
novel should not be overstated, the formal conventions of the elevation and fall
of tragic protagonists correspond to the Carrying-out-Death ritual. We know
a variant of this ceremony was common in ancient Greece. Plutarch witnessed
the annual ceremony in Chaeronea in which a human scapegoat was used,
and the practice was documented in Athens as well (see Frazer, Parker). The
typical custom in that region in the sixth century BCE (relatively close to the
heyday of Greek tragedy) was as follows:

> An ugly or deformed person was chosen to take upon himself all the evils which
> afflicted the community. He was brought to a suitable place, where dried figs, a bar-
> ley loaf, and cheese were put into his hand. These he ate. Then he was beaten seven
> times upon his genital organs with squills and branches of the wild fig and other wild
> trees, while the flutes played a particular tune. Afterwards he was burned on a pyre
> built of the wood of forest trees; and his ashes were cast into the sea. (Frazer 579)

The similarities between this described practice and the treatment of Pecola
are evident; she, too, is ugly and violated sexually before being sacrificed.
Immediately of concern as well is the beating upon the scapegoat's genitalia.
Since squills were seen to possess the "magical power of averting evil influences" (Frazer 580), this practice was perhaps not a form of punishment, but
rather a means of purifying him and encouraging the release of any generative powers. This reading concurs with the agrarian religious belief that it is
necessary to kill the vegetation spirit in fall in order for the spirit to return the
next year as new and refreshed. Beating the genital organs of the leaving spirit, then, would release whatever remained of his generative powers to transfer
them to the incoming spirit. The figs, barley loaf and cheese mentioned here
could be a further reference to the specific agricultural crops of the community, or they could also reflect a related practice of elevation. Because the scapegoat represents divinity but is in actuality "ugly or deformed," a short period
of elevation prior to the ceremony is required in order to assimilate this chosen scapegoat with the god or spirit he is to represent. So he/she was fed on
the choicest food, perhaps the best of their common crops such as figs, and
given free rein throughout the town or city until, of course, the day of sacri-

fice. It is this contrived elevation and the subsequent fall that leads me to draw extended parallels between Greek tragedy and Pecola Breedlove, whose budding self-consciousness early in the narrative—signified by her relation *to* an Other—sets her up for her complete collapse into insanity, signified by her conversations with herself *as* Other.

Pecola's precarious position on the cusp of maturity is significant in her role as a tragic protagonist as well as for its implications to sacrifice; initiation rites have long been associated with sacrifice (see Bloch, 24–45). We frequently refer to maturity or initiation in society as a "rite of passage" because it is a time, usually marked by a ceremony or ritual expressive of the society's collective identity, when an individual internalizes the belief systems or ideologies to which his/her society subscribes. The consciousness as the site of inculcation is therefore important.[12] Sartre argues in *Being and Nothingness* that when it comes to the location of consciousness or being, everything really is relative. Our experience of the world is not dictated by our physical being alone, but rather the dialogue between the two—that is, the dialogue between the body-for-itself, existing and operating as an independent organism, and the external world, existing and operating independent of our interaction with it. He writes that these two constructs are not "closed entities for which we must subsequently seek some explanation as to how they communicate," but rather, that "relation makes the world" (Sartre 306–307).

In the first flushes of an emerging consciousness, Pecola demonstrates a budding awareness of such a relation, of her self and the outside world and where those two meet. Lying in bed one morning after her mother and father have just had what we are given to understand as yet another one of their violent disputes, Pecola squeezes her eyes shut, prays to God to "'Please make me disappear'" (45) and slowly, ever so slowly, tries to imagine her way into nothingness. She manages to make all but her eyes fade away and struggles with them for a while, but "try as she might, she could never get her eyes to disappear" (45). Confronted with the inescapable reality of her physical being, she finally gives up in frustration, as her eyes "were everything. Everything was there, in them" (45). Though filtered through Pecola's childlike understanding, the conclusion she comes to, central to her character and to the action of the novel, immediately recalls Sartre's questions about the relational nature of consciousness and identity. Pecola is struggling to understand who she is by trying to pinpoint where she, the essence of her self, is located. Because it is her eyes that prevent her from achieving invisibility or non-being, she concludes that they must hold within them that which defines her being.

Rehearsing the logic that led her to this conclusion, she at first considers the location literally: "It had occurred to Pecola some time ago that if her eyes, those eyes that held the pictures, and knew the sights—if those eyes of hers were different, that is to say, beautiful, she herself would be different" (46). Equating different eyes with a different self suggests that the two are one and the same to her. As far as she is concerned her identity *is* her physical being, an understanding that carries disastrous consequences later.

She persists, though, and tries to discover what it is about that body that makes her ugly, in looks as well as in spirit: "Long hours she sat looking in the mirror, trying to discover the secret of the ugliness, the ugliness that made her ignored or despised at school, by teachers and classmates alike" (45–46). Here, Pecola's thought processes almost directly correspond to what Lacan terms the mirror stage. Lacan locates the development of consciousness at the time when a child starts seeing herself as a unified being, as in a mirror image, that is separate from the rest of the world (Sarup 8). When a child looks at herself in the mirror, she becomes at once both the subject viewing and the object viewed and therefore comprehends a distinction between the two. Pecola appreciates this coherent physical self in the mirror and differentiates between herself, reflected as an image that is "ignored" and "despised," and others, those who ignore and despise her. Failing to discern the ugliness in any tangible part of her, Pecola concludes that her own subjectivity, confirmed and constituted by her eyes interpreting her reflection, labels her as ugly. Her eyes register others' reactions to her, which she understands as a measure of who she is: "if she looked different, beautiful, maybe Cholly would be different, and Mrs. Breedlove too. Maybe they'd say, 'Why, look at pretty-eyed Pecola. We mustn't do bad things in front of those pretty eyes'" (46). In her understanding, Cholly and Mrs. Breedlove modify their behavior according to how they appear as Others. Their behavior, doing "bad things" in front of her, therefore reflects her insignificance or ugliness as a person. If she were a person of note, say a beautiful person, then they would be forced to acknowledge her eyes viewing them and potentially alter their behavior.[13] This recognition that an Other's thinking processes lead to definitive behavior signifies Pecola's attempt to understand the relationship between her own and the Other's self-consciousness. She attributes others with the knowledge not only of themselves as active beings, but also of their own Otherness.

Eventually grasping that it is a relationship, rather than a tangible presence or fact that defines both the subject viewing and the object viewed, Pecola transcends her dependence on physicality and realizes that the world is revealed only through the recognition of her self in it: she

> moves down an avenue gently buffeted by the familiar and therefore loved images. The dandelions at the base of the telephone pole. Why, she wonders, do people call them weeds? She thought they were pretty. But grown-ups say, "Miss Dunion keeps her yard so nice. Not a dandelion anywhere." Hunkie women in black babushkas go into the fields with baskets to pull them up. But they do not want the yellow heads— only the jagged leaves. They make dandelion soup. Dandelion wine. Nobody loves the head of a dandelion. Maybe because they are so many, strong, and soon. [...]
> These and other inanimate things she saw and experienced. They were the codes and touchstones of the world, capable of translation and possession. She owned the crack that made her stumble; she owned the clumps of dandelions whose white heads, last fall, she had blown away; whose yellow heads, this fall, she peered into. And owning them made her part of the world, and the world a part of her. (47–48)

Pecola seeks confirmation of her self-consciousness in two ways: by confirming that she is both separate from (physically) and part of (metaphorically) the world that surrounds her. Pecola's conception of dandelions as *not* weeds, though dependent on received definitions of beauty to react against, confirms her self-consciousness. It is not just her opposing stance, but also her ability to see herself as Other that truly defines her as such. She considers the dandelions in terms of their yellow heads and jagged leaves, and, broken down in this way, she acknowledges that one part is perceived negatively and the other positively, although the resulting overall definition as a "weed" remains negative.[14] She challenges this definition, declares them "pretty" and establishes her difference, her Otherness. The familiarity of the dandelions further contributes to their meaning to Pecola as it situates them in her consciousness. She sees herself in the process that changed them from the white heads of last fall to the yellow heads this fall. Partly a reflection of her growth as well as of vegetation cycles, the dandelions represent an ongoing exchange of meaning. They, as well as she, are part of a narrative. In "Storytelling and Moral Agency," Lynne Tirrell takes the timelessness out of Sartre's understanding of relation and argues that personhood is not derived from the facticity of our existence, but from our ability to conceive of ourselves as part of a story or narrative of that existence: "This consciousness of oneself and one's world crucially involves not just a 'consciousness of stimuli relevant to what in fact is self-maintenance in that world' but also a sense of oneself as a being in time, with a past, present, and future, with forebears and perhaps heirs" (Tirrell quoting Annette Baier 6). Pecola is able to conceive of a metaphorical narrative because she possesses the things around her as symbols, or "codes," rather than mere inanimate objects.[15] As an integrated part of that cycle, she, too, becomes "familiar and therefore loved" to and by herself. Drunk with experience, her walk down the avenue, "gently buffeted" by the images that ensconce her, positively affirms and transforms her being. It is this moment that represents Pecola's elevated position on the cusp of maturity.

However, like all tragic protagonists, she is doomed to fall.[16] At the conclusion of her walk of consciousness down Garden Avenue, she enters the general store of the white immigrant, Mr. Yacobowski. Here she tries to apply the same principles of reciprocity with an Other, but unlike her experiences communing with the natural world, her experiences in the social world deny rather than affirm her being. When Pecola meets the gaze of Mr. Yacobowski, the narrative that defined her before is abruptly truncated by the Look:[17]

> The gray head of Mr. Yacobowski looms up over the counter. He urges his eyes out of his thoughts to encounter her. Blue eyes. Blear-dropped. Slowly, like Indian summer moving imperceptibly toward fall, he looks toward her. Somewhere between retina and object, between vision and view, his eyes draw back, hesitate, and hover [....] [H]e senses that he need not waste the effort of a glance. He does not see her, because for him there is nothing to see [....]
>
> She looks up at him and sees the vacuum where curiosity ought to lodge. And something more. The total absence of human recognition—the glazed separateness[....] Yet this vacuum is not new to her. It has an edge; somewhere in the bottom lid is the distaste. She has seen it lurking in the eyes of all white people. So. The distaste must be for her, her blackness. All things in her are flux and anticipation. But her blackness is static and dread. (48)

Rudely sobered by Mr. Yacobowski's look, Pecola falls into a subjugated position. Mr. Yacobowski's contemptuous look reminds her, we are told, of her color and the "static" nature of that quality. One half of her consciousness is aware of the formless enthusiasm in her that is all "flux and anticipation," and the other half of her consciousness struggles with the facticity of her being, the realities of her image and specific bodily form. The moment of transition between these two states also constitutes a reversal, or *peripeteia*, a key structural element to tragedy. Aristotle defines a reversal as causing or achieving the opposite effect of one's stated intentions or expectations (*Poetics* 52a). The promise of nine Mary Janes, with their "resistant sweetness that breaks open at last to deliver peanut butter—the oil and salt which complement the sweet pull of caramel"—at the end of Pecola's journey causes a "peal of anticipation [to unsettle] her stomach" (48). Rather than living up to this promise, though, the Mary Janes ultimately represent the subsumption of her being into an Other. Immediately before she had been enjoying an enveloping relationship with the objects she encountered, but the returned gaze of an Other redefines this exchange. Confronted by the "total absence of human recognition" in his gaze, Pecola loses the ability to speak and can only mutely point her finger at the Mary Janes.

Almost as soon as she has discovered her freedom to participate in the world, that freedom is taken from her as she is dependent on an Other to recognize her and is therefore subjugated to him. Inherent in Sartre's understanding of social relations is just such a divestment of control or authority over one's own being. He writes:

> Such qualities as "evil," "jealous," "sympathetic" or "antipathetic" and the like are not empty imaginings; when I use them to qualify the Other, I am well aware that I want to touch him in his being. Yet I can not live them as my own realities. If the other confers them on me, they are admitted by what I am for-myself, when the Other describes my character, I do not "recognize" myself and yet I know that "it is me." (Sartre 274)

Even if we want to be evil or sympathetic or beautiful, we cannot be so strictly in our own selves. We must rely on an Other to define us as such; hence our ability to define who we are is confiscated by that Other. If the struggle for the controlling position of subject rather than object is stymied by a lack of recognition, as Pecola experiences, then the only way to "transcend" to the subject position is to absorb the Look that objectifies one.

Up until now this discussion has addressed only the unilateral recognition between one individual and another. However, in the scene at the general store, the fact of racial difference reinforces Mr. Yacobowski's Look with the prestige and power associated with the dominant culture. In "Self, Society and Myth in Toni Morrison's Fiction," Cynthia A. Davis, who similarly invokes Sartre's conception of the Look, argues that the process of absorbing the Other in order to transcend him becomes more complicated when that Other represents the dominant culture. Unable because of social divisions of power to return the Look as gazers, marginalized people are perpetually relegated to the object role of absorption. What happens then is a collective process of conformity, born out of a necessary alliance with other marginalized people and characterized primarily by fear—not just fear of the dominant culture, but fear of deserters or traitors to their own community who might take it upon themselves to act independently and potentially expose a vulnerability.

Davis ascribes the adherence of the characters to each other as a "retreat" from the gaze of the dominant culture and any assertive expression of individual character as "terrifying" in its threat to what little order and stability they have (31). Pecola is "profoundly frightening" and therefore, Davis implies, a threat to the group because her race, gender, class and age combine to establish her position so far at the bottom as to be "outside" the system of hierarchies the group has internalized from the dominant culture (33).

Whereas Davis argues that such weakness promotes solidarity, the novel actually depicts a more nefarious outcome.[18] The collective does not sympathetically embrace Pecola, but instead preys upon her vulnerability and answers her fear with cruelty and anger. When the children at the schoolyard taunt and torture Pecola, Claudia is furious at her fearful retreat: "She seemed to fold into herself, like a pleated wing. Her pain antagonized me. I wanted to open her up, crisp her edges, ram a stick down that hunched and curving spine, force her to stand erect and spit the misery out on the streets. But she held it in where it could lap up into her eyes" (73–74). Just as Claudia does not merely pity Pecola—she gets angry at her, frustrated by her and determined not to become like her—so, too, should the reader. In an afterword to *The Bluest Eye*, Morrison states that she does not want the reader to simply pity Pecola, because doing so would be to become "complicit … in the demonization process Pecola was subjected to" (211). Pity is a comfort enjoyed by those who retreat into apathy rather than being led "into an interrogation of [him/herself] for the smashing" (211). If we only pity, then we can hide behind empathy and say, "Isn't that a shame?' rather than ask, "What does this say about me?" The key to this response in the text is the mutual literary manifestations of ritual in both tragedy and the novel. Our understanding of tragedy should therefore inform our reading of Morrison's narrative. However, the traditional critical response to Pecola's character fails to reflect such an understanding. All too often readings such as Davis's, of the tragic heroine in *The Bluest Eye*, focus entirely on one level and involve only pity. In his *Poetics*, Aristotle declares that the essence of tragedy is to evoke pity and fear (49b). When an entirely "decent" person, he argues, undergoes a "change from good fortune to bad fortune … [it] does not evoke fear or pity, but disgust" (52b). We need to like the character just enough for his/her fall to be unsettling (and the oppression of Pecola and her community by the dominant culture *is* extremely unsettling), but not too much, or else the fall would be disgusting. Both this empathetic bonding and repulsive separation are achieved through protagonists who, though otherwise esteemed, have made one error or have one flaw (*hamartia*) that leads to their particular downfall. We do not claim, for example, that Oedipus (another character who had sex—albeit willingly and unknowingly—with a parent) is innocent: he, after all, did kill his father. Whether or not there are moral implications in the concept of *hamartia* is frequently questioned, but in *Miasma: Pollution and Purification in Early Greek Religion*, Robert Parker settles the issue when he points out that "etiologically … the *pharmakos* [the scapegoat in the real sacrificial rites upon which the dramas were modeled] is not merely a wretch but also a villain" (258). In *The Bluest Eye*, this villainy is suggested by the novel's questioning of not only the damaging aesthetics of a dominant ideology, but also the participation of the subjugated in accepting and collaborating with those aesthetics.

Davis's reading ignores the implications of *hamartia* in favor of straightforward pity, as she reduces all the characters to their fears, effectively seeing all as victims. Though she recognizes that Pecola falls into what Sartre terms "bad faith"—"a vacillation between transcendence and facticity which refuses to recognize either one for what it really is or to synthesize them" (Sartre 547)—she fails to recognize that Sartre consistently labels the object position in social relations as one of shame and *guilt*, because each individual participates and colludes in his/her subjugation by deliberately conforming to the values that alienate him/her. In spite of this, the overall implication of Davis's summation is that Pecola is entirely *happened upon*, that there is no collusion on her part in the forces that destroy her. To argue this is to argue, as many have, that Pecola shares no real responsibility (see, for example, Guerrero, Harris, Pérez-Torres and Tirrell; for exceptions see Gibson and Grewal).

Ultimately, Davis's argument, based as it is on "the unnatural position of blacks in a racist society" (30), presents racism as a mitigating factor for the individual and collective responsibility Morrison calls for. So it is that Geraldine—the proud homebody whose refinement according to the dominant culture's values taught her "how to get rid of the funkiness. The dreadful funkiness of passion, the funkiness of nature, the funkiness of the wide range of human emotions" (83)—is to be criticized for giving up whatever life she may have enjoyed, but not too much, because social politics prevent her from ever being fully free to pursue such "funkiness." Geraldine, Pauline (Mrs. Breedlove), and Pecola, along with their social cohorts, are forgiven by Davis (along with her critical cohorts) for internalizing the very values that alienate and marginalize them because they are victims of racism. What is arguably the central paradox of the racialized aesthetics that the novel brings into relief degenerates into unlimited pity, which the structure of the narrative does not support and the tone condemns. In a community fearful of any sign of independence, each individual is reduced to a trembling mass of indecision and hopeful anonymity. As Davis concedes, the immobilizing power of the dominant culture's Look "not only freezes the black individual but also classifies all blacks as alike, freezing the group" (31). Therefore, to wallow in victimization is to collude in the stripping away of individuality and the denial of subjectivity, which is perhaps why Davis fails to see a "recognizable public self" (31) for the community and its members.

But regardless of how much society, school, media, family, government or any other "authority" imposes the subjugating Look, the individual is culpable. Consider the case of Bigger Thomas in Richard Wright's *Native Son*. In the face of extraordinary circumstances and atrocious actions, we do not and cannot see Bigger entirely as a victim. He openly rejects Max's defense of him as such and all but pleads with us not to see him that way:

> Bigger felt a wild and outlandish conviction surge in him: *They ought to be glad!* It was a strange but strong feeling, springing from the very depths of his life. Had he not taken fully upon himself the crime of being black? Had he not done the thing which they dreaded above all others? Then they ought not stand here and pity him, cry over him; but look at him and go home, contented, feeling that their shame was washed away. (296)

> "For a little while I was free. I was doing something. It was wrong, but I was feeling all right. Maybe God'll get me for it. If He do, all right. But I ain't worried. I killed 'em 'cause I was scared and mad. But I been scared and mad all my life and after I killed that first woman, I wasn't scared no more for a little while." (354)

A sensational surge of repulsion, of a "strange but strong feeling," courses through Bigger as the others' pity and tears acknowledge his color and his circumstances but deny who *he* is. The empowered feeling is a "strange" feeling, which indicates that objectification and victimization are his norm. Bigger feels strange because he senses the deception in such a situation, for the concurrent victimization of racism, which is often treated as a sensitive and sympathetic response to subjugation (e.g., Davis's mitigated understanding), can be just as damaging as the initiating call. It encourages marginalized peoples to accept, if not the notion that they are flawed for being black, then the notion that their race is inherently bad in that it is what deprives them of equality. The demonization of blackness depends on the belief that it is somehow evil or marked, and we have been inculcated to avoid that which is stigmatized in this way. While the others wallow and collude in this criminalization of blackness, Bigger rejects that negative definition and enthusiastically embraces not that which is defined as bad, but the very concept of badness. He accepts his crime of color, which is not about the color itself, but the role he fulfills for others by being black, because to do so is to lay claim to his agency. One can only transgress if one has agency to act, to make the choice between conforming and transgressing. He uses life-affirming and active verbs to accept responsibility and therefore agency. He transgresses, he does that which the others all fear to do, and he never feels more alive or free. As he acknowledges, the anger and awkwardness gurgling up "from the very depths of his life" define that life. Pecola echoes Bigger's reflections on the creative worth of anger: as with him, a "sense of being" surges in her when she refuses to accept the "crime of being black":

> Dandelions. A dart of affection leaps out from her to them. But they do not look at her and do not send love back. She thinks, "They *are* ugly. They *are* weeds." Preoccupied with that revelation, she trips on the sidewalk crack. Anger stirs and wakes in her; it opens its mouth, and like a hotmouthed puppy, laps up the dredges of her shame.
> Anger is better. There is a sense of being in anger. A reality and presence. An awareness of worth. It is a lovely surging. Her thoughts fall back to Mr. Yacobowski's eyes, his phlegmy voice. The anger will not hold; the puppy is too easily surfeited. Its thirst too quickly quenched, it sleeps. The shame wells up again, its muddy rivulets seeping into her eyes. (50)

Before, the dandelions had been a symbol of her place in narrative; now they are part of a system that excludes her and that angers Pecola.[19] Unlike Bigger, though, she is unable to sustain that anger and therefore her claim to a "sense of being." Bigger's anger is anchored in action, which in turn defines him, but Pecola's rests on a fluctuating definition of relation. Her position is so tenuous and accidental that her mental and emotional upheaval manifests literally in a stumble over a sidewalk crack. The reference to a puppy reminds us that she is still in an early stage of physical, emotional and mental formation; she is just a child. However, her youth does not entirely acquit Pecola. The omniscient narrator's language reveals chastisement. We are told that her anger is "surfeited" or immoderately indulged, "too easily' and "too quickly." She is not only weak in giving in to her anger, but she is weak in giving herself over to it and indulging in it.

The third narrative voice of the text, the aforementioned tragic chorus, reinforces this criticism. At the beginning of the penultimate section of the novel, a nameless narrator intones the following: "And so it was. / A little black girl yearns for the blue eyes of a little white girl, and the horror at the heart of her yearning is exceeded only by the evil of fulfillment" (204). Is this the adult Claudia speaking, the moralistic gossipmongers she could not help but overhear as a child, an outside observer, a sociologist or critic, or the author? The lack of clarity is reminiscent of the common debate as to whether or not the chorus in Attic tragedy is a singular or plural voice, a biased or objective observer, a moral center or Devil's advocate (see note 11). The voice, potentially all of the above, warns us of both the "evil" of what happened to Pecola and the "horror" of what was in her heart. She is both pitied as a victim and grossly responsible; this is her flaw, her *hamartia*.

Immediately after this Claudia closes the narrative with her previously discussed invocation of biblical sacrifice and purification. Juxtaposed as it is with the tragic and agrarian beliefs, this parting reference becomes problematic. Not only does it imply that these other structural and thematic influences are just that—"Others"—it also suggests a direct comparison with a figure whose literary tradition dictates purity of character. Claudia's reference to an absolute monotheism often overshadows the overwhelming presence of other religious frameworks or belief systems in the narrative and encourages a strict absolute interpretation of Pecola's character and the text as a whole. As George Steiner argues in *The Death of Tragedy*, the New Testament completion of the biblical cycle, in its solution of the opening Fall with the sacrifice of the Lamb, resulting in resurrection and redemption for all of humanity, leaves no room for multiple interpretations or various endings. What this hugely influential rhetorical and narrative strategy has left us with is a single "Judaic vision" in which our understanding of narrative is grounded in an expectation of a clearly defined beginning, middle and end (see also Aristotle's definition of tragic plot completeness in *Poetics* 50b). The end will not only finish the story, but it will prove to be just; bad will be punished and good will be rewarded. Our modern grasp of tragedy is skewed because of this vision and hope. We see tragedy in the punishment of good; hence the traditional critical response to Pecola as purely innocent and good. Such an interpretation is compounded by Claudia's reference to a figure whose purity is literally unquestioned (in context). He is *the* Word, *the* Truth, *the* Revelation. It is only in "other" belief systems that a dualistic interpretation of the purifying sacrificial victim as both wretch and villain is possible. But those representations are couched in polytheism. So it is easy to dismiss the former when we dismiss the latter—to throw the baby out with the bath water, so to speak. The critical attempt to do so is its own brand of cleansing; it employs the validation of "religion" over "myth" and "magic" and purges anything that does not conform to authorized belief systems.

## Notes

[1] The only exceptions we witness are the acceptance of Pecola by the prostitutes, who were social outcasts themselves, and Claudia and Frieda MacTeer, friends by circumstance who play with her and protect her more, it seems, out of proving something about themselves than about her.

[2] An example Jay offers from our current wealth of social contractual practices is marriage. Wedding vows are not just an expression of a state of affairs, but the act of saying "I do" actually calls into being a union (6).

[3] As I will discuss later, the two key models for the sacrifice clearly suggested by this narrative—the sacrificial subject in agrarian religious practices and the scapegoat in Greek tragedy—were also symbolic figures. In *Miasma: Pollution and Purification in Early Greek Religion*, Parker writes that the best evidence we have now indicates that the figure in the real and dramatized rituals was, in fact, not killed (258).

[4] In *Fiction and Folklore*, Trudier Harris briefly refers to the power of belief in *The Bluest Eye*. She argues: "Pecola's belief in the possible transformation ties her to all believers in sympathetic magic. Her conviction that the blue eyes have been granted may be viewed as insanity, but it simultaneously fits the logic that has led to that final reward.... Belief is the single most important element in both outcomes" (18). Harris's argument is notable for being unique in labeling Pecola's belief logical irrespective of her age.

[5] Prefacing the novel and interspersed throughout are short excerpts from a fictional Dick and Jane primer modeled after the standard texts used to teach reading skills. The first section begins with a fourteen-line excerpt printed in standard font type and size with double spacing. Immediately after this the same excerpt is reprinted with only one-and a half spacing and without any punctuation. The same excerpt is then repeated a third and final time in single spacing still without any punctuation and now even without spaces between words. The gradual defamiliarization effect problematizes what we normally take for granted about standard texts. Instead of approaching the narrative as rote or routine, an aspect of the Dick and Jane stories that helps develop reading skills, this extract, through manipulation of its format, forces readers to concentrate on how meaning is formulated and comprehended. For an engaging reading of the primer texts in themselves and in their relation to the events of the narrative, see Grewal's "'Laundering the Head of Whitewash': Mimicry and Resistance in *The Bluest Eye*."

[6] This is not the only reference in the narrative to successful homeopathic practices. As Harris notes in *Fiction and Folklore*, there is a similar link between belief and result in Pecola's attempt to buy blue eyes from Soaphead Church. She wants blue eyes, seeks someone who can provide them, does what he asks, goes insane, and in that frame of mind, gets her blue eyes. The logic abides by the laws of sympathetic magic, but just goes horribly awry in terms of the unexpected price.

7 For Frazer's accounts of this or similar ceremonies, see his chapter on "The Killing of the Tree Spirit."

8 Terry Eagleton's recently published *Sweet Violence: The Idea of the Tragic* calls into question nearly every conclusive definition of tragedy, as well as the very concept of nominalism with regard to tragedy. While acknowledging the impressive extent of his survey and the (partial) validity of his argument, I identify such a category because the characteristics that largely and clearly define the dramatic productions of a certain age derivate from ritual relevant to this discussion.

9 Morrison was a classics minor at Howard University.

10 In *The Birth of Tragedy*, Nietzsche argues that tragedy stems from the conflict between and the harmonization of two impulses in the Greek character. One he terms the Apollonian, which he associates with dreaming and imagery. The other he terms the Dionysian, which he associates with intoxication and lyricism. Both are appropriately mixed here, where "lust" and "nuns," usually seen as at odds, are "quietly" harmonized.

11 I borrowed Hugo's *Three Musketeers* mantra of "all for one and one for all" because two of the most common conceptions of the chorus are that it represents either a) *a single* ideal spectator, or b) the fictional community *as a whole*. The ease with which the Attic tragedians slipped between the two suggests both an exchange and a soliloquy in a technique not unlike the inner life of an omniscient narrator.

12 Davis and Rigney have particularly considered this aspect in their discussions of female subjectivity in Morrison's work.

13 In her reading of this scene in "Rape, Madness, and Silence in the Novel," Miner inverts this cause and effect to argue that "if Pecola were to *see* things differently, she might *be seen* differently" (18–19). This relates to Sartre's conception of identity formation as a function of relation to the world, but it partially skews the order in which Pecola understands that relationship. In thinking that a difference in appearance would effect a difference in treatment, Pecola is thinking the inverse of Miner's statement—to *be seen* differently would be to *see* things differently.

14 Pecola's understanding of the "weed" that confirms her Otherness is analogous to her own role in her community. She, too, is perceived both negatively and positively with an overall negative definition.

15 This linguistic possession also suggests Lacan's symbolic or linguistic realm of ownership, which signifies the early development of one's consciousness.

16 Claudia's narrative frame supplants the Greek notion of fate, in which Pecola's fall is inevitable. In the prologue, Claudia announces the end event—that there were no marigolds in the fall of 1941 and that Pecola was pregnant with her father's baby. This early exposition retains fate's inevitability as well as its nonconformity to logic, as Claudia then explains that her story is only about "how," rather than "why," because the latter is too "difficult to handle" (6).

17 In "Tracking 'The Look' in the Novels of Toni Morrison," Ed Guerrero also reads this scene as a "psychological turning point" (33) in Pecola's maturity and identity formation. As I will discuss later, he, like Davis, concludes that "the nucleus of the problem lies in [Pecola's] blackness" (32), which entirely reduces her to a victim of racism in this pivotal moment.

18 It is clear from Davis's analysis that her conception of community in Morrison's work is an overwhelmingly positive force. She cites the social exclusion of the prostitutes Marie,

China and Poland—despite their apparent freedom from social constraints—as deprivation rather than fulfillment, for "freedom defined as total transcendence lacks the intention and significance that can come from commitment" (34). Valuing such commitment above all, Davis idealizes the community as a vehicle of security, soulful connection and nurturing. However, I share Marc Conner's view that the predatory nature of Morrison's portrayed communities is often overlooked, and therefore find criticism that relies on such automatic positive assumptions to be flawed.

19 Sartre argues that concurrent with the alienation of self that happens as a result of the Look is the alienation of the outside world. If the world is as it is only through our organization or experience of it, then when the processing self becomes fragmented by a Look, so, too, does the world it organizes (263).

## Works Cited

Aristotle. *Poetics*. Translated by Malcolm Heath. London: Penguin Books, 1996.

Bloch, Maurice. *Prey into Hunter: The Politics of Religious Experience*. Part of the Lewis Henry Morgan Lectures 1984. Cambridge: Cambridge University Press, 1992.

Bloom, Harold, ed. *Toni Morrison*. Major Novelists series. Broomall, PA: Chelsea House Publishers, 2000.

Conner, Marc C. "From the Sublime to the Beautiful: The Aesthetic Progression of Toni Morrison." In *The Aesthetics of Toni Morrison: Speaking the Unspeakable*, edited by Marc C. Conner. Jackson: University Press of Mississippi, 2000. 49–76.

Davis, Cynthia A. "Self, Society and Myth in Toni Morrison's Fiction." In Peach, *Toni Morrison*, 27–42.

Durkheim, Emile. *The Elementary Forms of the Religious Life*. 1915. Translated by Joseph Ward Swain. London: George Allen and Unwin Ltd, 1964.

Eagleton, Terry. *Sweet Violence: The Idea of the Tragic*. Oxford: Blackwell, 2003.

Frazer, James George. *The Golden Bough: A Study in Magic and Religion*, abridged edition, 1922. Wordsworth Reference Series. Hertfordshire: Wordsworth Editions Ltd, 1993.

Gibson, Donald B. "Text and Countertext in the Novel." In Bloom, *Toni Morrison*, 23–26.

Grewal, Gurleen. "'Laundering the Head of Whitewash': Mimicry and Resistance in *The Bluest Eye*." In McKay and Earle, *Approaches to Teaching*, 118–126.

Guerrero, Ed. "Tracking 'The Look' in the Novels of Toni Morrison." In Middleton, *Toni Morrison's Fiction*, 27–41.

Harris, Trudier. *Fictions and Folklore: The Novels of Toni Morrison*. Knoxville: The University of Tennessee Press, 1991.

Hubert, Henri and Marcel Mauss. *Sacrifice: Its Nature and Function*. 1898. Translated by W. D. Halls. London: Cohen and West, 1964.

Jay, Nancy. *Throughout Your Generations Forever: Sacrifice, Religion, and Paternity*. London: University of Chicago Press, 1992.

McKay, Nellie Y., and Kathryn Earle, eds. *Approaches to Teaching the Novels of Toni Morrison*. Approaches to Teaching World Literature Series. New York: MLA, 1997.

Middleton, David L., ed. *Toni Morrison's Fiction: Contemporary Criticism*. Critical Studies in Black Life and Culture Series. London: Garland Publishing, 1997.

Miner, Madonne. "Rape, Madness, and Silence in the Novel." In Bloom, *Toni Morrison*, 18–21.

Morrison, Toni. *The Bluest Eye*. 1970. Reprinted New York: Penguin, 1994.

Nietzsche, Friedrich. *The Birth of Tragedy*. 1872. Translated by Douglas Smith. Oxford: Oxford University Press, 2000.

Parker, Robert. *Miasma: Pollution and Purification in Early Greek Religion*. Oxford: Clarendon Press, 1983.

Peach, Linden, ed. *Toni Morrison: Contemporary Critical Essays.*. New Casebooks Series. London: Macmillan, 1998.

Perez-Torres, Rafael. "Tracing and Erasing: Race and Pedagogy in *The Bluest Eye*." In McKay and Earle, *Approaches to Teaching*, 23–25.

Rigney, Barbara. "Hagar's Mirror: Self and Identity in Morrison's Fiction." In Peach, *Toni Morrison*, 52–69.

Sartre, Jean-Paul. *Being and Nothingness: An Essay on Phenomenological Ontology*. Translated by Hazel E. Barnes. London: Methuen, 1957.

Sarup, Madan. *An Introductory Guide to Post-Structuralism and Postmodernism*. 2nd ed. London: Harvester Wheatsheaf, 1993.

Steiner, George. "The Death of Tragedy." *The Death of Tragedy*. New York: Alfred A. Knopf, 1968. Reprinted in *Tragedy*, edited by John Drakakis and Naomi Conn Liebler. London: Longman, 1998. 143–146.

Tirrell, Lynne. "Storytelling and Moral Agency." In Middleton, *Toni Morrison's Fiction: Contemporary Criticism*, 3–25.

Wright, Richard. *Native Son*. 1940. Restored text. New York: HarperPerennial, 1998.

# CONTRIBUTORS

Nancy Berkowitz Bate received her M.A. degree in English from Butler University and is currently working on her doctorate degree at Indiana University—Purdue University in Indianapolis. She has published articles on Edgar Allen Poe and on Isaac Bashevis Singer, and is currently working on an article concerning the Islamic subtext in Toni Morrison's *Song of Solomon*.

Beth Hawkins Benedix is an assistant professor of Religious Studies and Literature at DePauw University. She received her Ph.D. in Comparative Literature from the University of Illinois, Urbana-Champagne. She is the author of *Reluctant Theologians: Kafka, Celan, Jabes* and has contributed articles and reviews to journals such as *Shofar, Journal of Jewish Thought and Philosophy, Jewish Quarterly Review and Journal of the Kafka Society of America*.

Benjamin J. Burr is currently finishing is M.A. degree in English at Brigham Young University. He is in the process of completing his M.A. thesis on inter-textuality in the fiction of Cormac McCarthy. He is also interested in African American music and literature, Jewish American literature, and magic realism.

Rebecca Degler is a postgraduate student at the University of Essex. She is working on a thesis exploring language and the narrative construction of self and community in Toni Morrison's fiction.

Beverley Foulks received her M.Div from Harvard Divinity School and is currently pursuing a Ph.D. in the East Asian Languages and Civilizations Department at Harvard University. Her research interests include Chinese Buddhism, repentance, theodicy and comparative religious ethics.

Sharon Jessee is an Associate Professor of English and Women's, Gender and Sexuality Studies at the University of Wisconsin-LaCrosse, where she teaches a variety of courses in American literature, including African American women's literature. She has published articles on Ishmael Reed and Toni Morrison and is currently finishing a book on *Beloved, Jazz*, and *Paradise* as a postcolonial project which experiments with polyrhythm in fictional narrative.

Shirley A. Stave is an Associate Professor of English at the Louisiana Scholar's College. She is the author *of The Decline of the Goddess: Nature, Culture and Women in Thomas Hardy's Fiction*, the co-author a book on contemporary Wicca, and the editor of a collection of essays on Gloria Naylor. She has published articles on Wilkie Collins, Toni Morrison, and contemporary film.

Agnes Suranyi is an Assistant Professor in the Department of English Literatures and Cultures at the University of Hungary. She is in the process of completing her doctoral dissertation, which is on Toni Morrison. She has published articles on Angela Carter, Christina Stead, Virginia Woolf, Toni Morrison, Gloria Naylor, and Kurt Vonnegut.

Jennifer Terry is a Lecturer in English Studies at the University of Durham, UK. Her doctoral thesis, completed at the University of Warwick, examines the novels of Toni Morrison and her currents projects include a comparative exploration of African American and Caribbean fiction.

Anissa Janine Wardi, Associate Professor of English at Chatham College, is a past contributor to *African American Review* and *MELUS*. The author of *Death and the Arc of Mourning in African American Literature* and the co-editor of *African American Literature*, a Penguin anthology, she is currently working on a book entitled *Bodies of Water, Memory, and the African American South*.

David Z. Wehner received his M.A. degree in English literature from the University of Colorado and his doctorate in English literature from the University of Minnesota. His desseration examines the status of the conversion narrative in modern culture and studies the works of Kate Chopin, Flannery O'Connor, and Toni Morrison. He currently works as a post-doctoral associate at the University of Minnesota.

# AFRICAN AMERICAN LITERATURE AND CULTURE

## EXPANDING AND EXPLODING THE BOUNDARIES

*General Editor*
Carlyle V. Thompson

The purpose of this series is to present innovative, in-depth, and provocatively critical literary and cultural investigations of critical issues in African American literature and life. We welcome critiques of fiction, poetry, drama, film, sports, and popular culture. Of particular interest are literary and cultural analyses that involve contemporary psychoanalytical criticism, new historicism, deconstructionism, critical race theory, critical legal theory, and critical gender theory.

For additional information about this series or for the submission of manuscripts, please contact:

Peter Lang Publishing, Inc.
Acquisitions Department
275 Seventh Avenue, 28th floor
New York, New York 10001

To order other books in this series, please contact our Customer Service Department:

(800) 770-LANG (within the U.S.)
(212) 647-7706 (outside the U.S.)
(212) 647-7707 FAX

Or browse online by series:

www.peterlangusa.com